The Bloomsbury Companion
Philosophy of Language

The *Bloomsbury Companions* series is a major series of single volume companions to key research fields in the humanities aimed at postgraduate students, scholars and libraries. Each companion offers a comprehensive reference resource giving an overview of key topics, research areas, new directions and a manageable guide to beginning or developing research in the field. A distinctive feature of the series is that each companion provides practical guidance on advanced study and research in the field, including research methods and subject-specific resources.

The Bloomsbury Companion to the Philosophy of Language

Edited by
Manuel García-Carpintero and Max Kölbel

Bloomsbury Academic
An imprint of Bloomsbury Publishing Plc

B L O O M S B U R Y

LONDON • NEW DELHI • NEW YORK • SYDNEY

Bloomsbury Academic
An imprint of Bloomsbury Publishing Plc

50 Bedford Square	1385 Broadway
London	New York
WC1B 3DP	NY 10018
UK	USA

www.bloomsbury.com

BLOOMSBURY and the Diana logo are trademarks of Bloomsbury Publishing Plc

First published as The Continuum Companion to the Philosophy of Language 2012
First published in paperback 2014
Reprinted by Bloomsbury Academic 2015

British Library Cataloguing-in-Publication Data
A catalogue record for this book is available from the British Library.

ISBN: PB: 978-1-4725-7823-5
ePDF: 978-1-4725-7821-1
ePUB: 978-1-4725-7822-8

Library of Congress Cataloging-in-Publication Data
A catalog record for this book is avaliable from the Library of Congress.

Series: Bloomsbury Companions

Typeset by Fakenham Prepress Solutions, Fakenham, Norfolk NR21 8NN
Printed and bound in Great Britain

Contents

Contributors

Kent Bach is Professor of Philosophy at San Francisco State University.

Albert Casullo is Professor of Philosophy at the University of Nebraska-Lincoln.

Josh Dever is Associate Professor of Philosophy at the University of Texas at Austin.

Manuel García-Carpintero is profesor catedrátic in the Department of Logic, History and Philosophy of Science at the Universitat de Barcelona.

Kathrin Glüer is Professor of Theoretical Philosophy at Stockholm University.

James Higginbotham is Distinguished Professor of Philosophy and Linguistics and Linda MacDonald Hilf Chair in Philosophy at the University of Southern California.

Max Kölbel is ICREA Research Professor in the Department of Logic, History and Philosophy of Science at the Universitat de Barcelona.

Genoveva Martí is ICREA Research Professor in the Department of Logic, History and Philosophy of Science at the Universitat de Barcelona.

Michael Nelson is Assistant Professor of Philosophy at the University of California at Riverside.

François Recanati is Research Fellow at the Centre National de la Recherche Scientifique and at the Institut Jean Nicod, Paris.

José Zalabardo is Reader at the University College London Philosophy Department.

Preface

This book aims to provide a comprehensive guide for those who want to embark upon research in the philosophy of language. We have selected nine central areas of the philosophy of language, and were able to enlist the help of nine leading experts to write accessible, yet high-level and up-to-date introductions to each of these areas. Their contributions make up the main body of this book. We complemented this with an introduction recounting the history of the field, an essay on new directions of research, an A–Z of key terms and a bibliography containing suggested further readings in each of the areas. The result will, we hope, be a useful tool for advanced undergraduates, beginning researchers and anyone wishing to gain an overview about where the philosophy of language, or some of its sub-disciplines, stands today.

*The Continuum Companion to the Philosophy of Language** has been a long time in the making, and we are very grateful for all those who have helped bring it together. First and foremost, we thank the contributors, some of whom have been patient in waiting for their contribution to appear and some of whom have managed to find time to write their contribution when many more urgent demands were eating up their time. We would equally like to thank the editors at Continuum for their support and patience, in particular Sarah Campbell and Tom Crick. Finally, we would like to thank John Horden for preparing the index and helping with the proofreading.

Manuel García-Carpintero
Max Kölbel

---

* The original hardback edition published in 2012 as *The Continuum Companion to the Philosophy of Language*

1 Editorial Introduction: History of the Philosophy of Language[1]

Manuel García-Carpintero[2]

The Philosophy of Language has a history almost as long as the history of Philosophy itself. Plato's *Cratylus* and *Sophist*, and Aristotle's *De Interpretatione* and *Prior Analytics*, contain important reflections on topics such as the conventionality of language, the subject–predicate structure, valid inference and its relations with the structure of language and thought, truth, or the ontological implications of linguistic categories. Medieval philosophers carried out studies of reference ("suppositio") and generalization as sophisticated as any. The *Port-Royal* logicians, Hobbes and Locke took those discussions forward, and, in the latter case, anticipated current concerns about the way natural kind terms work. In the following few pages, however, I will limit myself to drawing a very rough (and rather idiosyncratic) map of the terrain of the contemporary scene, as it was set out in the work of Frege, Russell and the early Wittgenstein – the presupposed common background, taught to beginners in the discipline, for the themes to be further explored from a present-day perspective in the ensuing chapters. In the first part of the chapter, I will outline some core issues as they are presented in what in my view is the insightful systematic articulation of Frege's and Russell's themes in Wittgenstein's *Tractatus Logico-Philosophicus*. In the second part, I will sum up the main issues, describe some contributions to them in Frege, Russell, Wittgenstein and other historical landmarks, and indicate how they are approached today, as presented in the ensuing chapters. The introduction concludes with a brief discussion of research methods and problems in the field.

Meaning and Modality in the *Tractatus*

The core issues in the philosophy of language are first put forth with compelling self-conscious depth in Wittgenstein's *Tractatus Logico-Philosophicus*, his appraisal of the presuppositions of Frege's and Russell's Logicist Program

– even if the book would not have been possible without Frege's and Russell's ground-breaking research. It is true that, in contrast with Frege's and Russell's works, the *Tractatus* is an opaque piece, whose claims (and even more, the reasons, arguments or at least motivations for them) are difficult to make out, in this respect a reflection of the rather dogmatic methodological attitude of its author. It is also true that such dogmatism appears to have precluded Wittgenstein from seeing the, in some cases glaringly manifest, difficulties for the views he had put forward, and the extent to which the alternative views of his two predecessors, which he had haughtily dismissed, were much more sensible. However, in my view it was in the *Tractatus* that the proper dimensions and interconnections of the main problems confronted afterwards in the discipline are clearly envisaged for the first time. Neither Frege nor Russell appears to have paid much thought to what has become, since the *Tractatus*, a core issue in the philosophy of language – the link between grasping the representational contents of thoughts and sentences, and knowledge of modality; or so I will try to suggest in the next few paragraphs. For the most part they aim not mainly to establish this perhaps idiosyncratic historical point, but to sketch out these core problems, so that later we can trace the relations with how they are approached today, as presented in the chapters to follow.

Those core problems in the philosophy of language only perspicuously adumbrated in the early history of analytic philosophy in the *Tractatus* concern the relations between meaning, modality and our knowledge of them. Frege's project, which he pursued relentlessly for most of his intellectual life and whose (from his perspective) tragic failure Russell spotted, was the *Logicist Program*, aimed at proving that arithmetic reduces to pure logic. Frege's work was hardly a fully-fledged failure: he had come very close to at least reducing arithmetic to logic and set theory, along the lines used later in Russell's and Whitehead's *Principia* or in the independently pursued Cantorian program. In the process, he came up with outstandingly significant conceptual innovations, from modern logic and semantics to an original and influential view in the philosophy of mathematics that many still think fundamentally correct. However, a full appraisal of the epistemological and ontological yields of the project required an examination of the epistemological and ontological status of logic and logical validity themselves; and that in its turn leads to a thorough examination of the nature of the representational devices through which we carry out logically valid inferences: natural language and the thoughts it conveys (what we may call a *theory of intentionality*). Frege and Russell somehow saw this, and in fact made suggestions about the matter (outlined below) at times more sensible than those in the *Tractatus*, at times simply incorporated into it. But it is only in that work, I think, that the nature of the problems and their interconnections is systematically realized, through the realization that representation in natural languages and in thought is inextricably tied up with discrimination between possibilities.

Notoriously, the *Tractatus* contains a flawed theory of intentionality, the so-called "picture theory"; but, more than its failures, what is interesting for our present purposes is to appreciate what it set out to achieve – especially how Wittgenstein hoped that it would deliver what in his view Frege and Russell had failed to provide: a philosophically adequate account of logical validity and hence of the foundations of their *logicist* project.[3] To put it in the metaphor he later used in the *Investigations*, criticising his earlier views, Wittgenstein's objection in the *Tractatus* to the view on the nature of logical validity that Frege and Russell had defended is that it does not account for the "sublimity" of logic: they did not account for the characteristic modal properties of logical truths and validities, and our knowledge thereof, as resulting from essential properties of the representational means in which they are cashed out. It is such an account, according to him, that the picture theory provides.

According to Frege and Russell, logically valid propositions, and inferential transitions among them, are distinguished by their *maximal generality*; for instance: given that *a* equals *b*, and *b* equals *c*, we can infer that *a* equals *c*, no matter what *a*, *b* and *c* are. According to the *Tractatus*, however, this is wrong (*Tractatus* 6.1231). On the one hand, some logical truths are not literally speaking general (*if Hesperus is Phosphorus, and Phosphorus is Venus, then Hesperus is Venus* is *itself* a logical truth); on the other, a general truth may well be only accidentally true (we can express in purely general terms the claim that there are infinitely many things, which according to Wittgenstein is not a logical truth). Logical validities are *necessary*; and they are *a priori*.[4] Frege's and Russell's proposals do not account for this crucial fact: why should *maximal generality* entail *necessity* and *apriority*? It was the fact that, in his view, the picture theory accounted for it that mainly recommended it in his eyes. The picture theory is relevant to solve the problem because for Wittgenstein logical validities are expressed in natural languages (*Tractatus* 5.5563) – or the thoughts they convey – whose essential representational properties the picture theory characterizes. Artificial languages, far from being "ideal languages" worth studying in their own right as more adequate to carrying out valid inferences – as Frege and Russell thought – are mere "frictionless planes"; they are useful fictions whose study is a convenient means to exhibit in a simpler way the logical properties of our ordinary assertions and thoughts.

Aside from its motivation as a way of accounting for the modal properties of logical truth and validity, Wittgenstein supported his picture theory of intentionality arguing that only such a theory accounts for two fundamental facts about representation in language and thought. First, we understand linguistic representations and grasp thoughts (at least in paradigm cases, let us say, so as not to prejudice any relevant issue) without knowing whether or not they are correct, whether or not the represented reality is in fact as represented; I will summarize this henceforth with the slogan "representations may fail". Second ("representations may be new"), we can understand or grasp immediately, without further explanation, representations that we have not encountered before.[5] How is the picture theory supposed to deal effectively with these explanatory issues? (There will be no point in considering the further issue of whether it really is the only theory that accounts for them.) The picture theory, as I understand it, ascribes to any intentional system, i.e., any system exhibiting the two properties to be explained, two crucial semantic features, which we may describe as an *external* and an *internal* one. The external ingredient comprises a lexicon and the correlations of the items in it with independent objects, correlations which Wittgenstein thought of as consisting of implicit ostensive definitions. The internal ingredient is an abstract syntax applying to the items in the lexicon which signifies, by way of what Goodman (1976, 52) calls *exemplification*,[6] identical relations between the items correlated with them by the external ingredient. It is the latter feature that makes sentences and thoughts into *pictures*: the distinguishing feature of pictures is that they represent properties that they themselves exemplify; they represent thanks to the fact that there is a range of properties they literally *share* with the represented situations.

Let us see how this is supposed to solve the first problem, that representations may fail. The syntax determines a class of well-formed elementary sentences; not just any concatenation of items in the lexicon is acceptable, only some are permitted. Each of them is in that respect a *possibility*: it is possible to say it, as opposed to abstaining from saying it, independently of the others. *Saying* is here the lowest common factor of different speech acts – asserting, ordering, conjecturing, requesting, and so on – whose distinguishing differences Wittgenstein thought irrelevant for his concerns. The syntax thus determines a class of maximal "discourses" – allowed combinations of the two designated possibilities for each elementary sentence. Correspondingly, given that the syntax is *shared* by the lexicon and correlated items, it determines the possibility that the combination of items corresponding to the names in any given elementary sentence (a state of affairs) obtains, and the possibility that it does not obtain. It determines thereby a corresponding logical space of maximal combinations of these two possibilities for each state of affairs; only one of them can be actualized, constituting the actual world. What is required to understand a sentence is to know the interpreted lexicon from which it is built, and its logical syntax; what is thereby known is a possible state of affairs, the class of maximal combinations constituting the logical space compatible with its obtaining, what Wittgenstein calls (following Frege) the sentence's *truth-condition*; it is not required to know whether or not this class includes the actual world.[7]

According to this, all (and only) truth-conditions are (contents of) possible sayings, not only those expressed by elementary sentences. Some appropriate set of expressions (the "logical constants", on the Tractarian account) is needed, to gain the additional expressive potential needed to express all truth-conditions. But the claim made about the explanatory virtue of the picture theory for the case of elementary sentences is intended to apply also to complex sentences including these expressions. Understanding them requires, according to the picture theory, knowing the interpreted lexicon, their logical syntax and the identical "syntax" in the world signified by exemplification, plus the set of logical constants needed in order to express every possible truth-condition thereby determined. This assigns to any non-defective (neither tautologous nor contradictory) sentence a truth-condition, without thereby establishing whether or not it actually obtains. Wittgenstein (*Tractatus*, 2.1511; cf. *Investigations*, §§ 95, 194) particularly liked the fact that this little theory accounts for the first problem of intentionality, that representations may fail, while preserving an essential connection between linguistic representations and the world – and thus representations are of real items, not some intermediate ghosts, as in representationalist accounts of perceptual experience. This is achieved in that the represented possible states of affairs are made of real objects, constituting the actual world (all possible worlds, given that all lexical items are on the Tractarian view Kripkean "rigid designators", designating the same entity with respect to all possible worlds) and of equally real, possibility-determining, "syntactical" relations between them.

Accounting for the second explanatory issue (that representations may be new), assuming the picture theory as presented, is straightforward. Knowing the lexicon, the logical syntax that as we have seen signifies by exemplification, and the relevant set of logical constants suffices for understanding sentences beyond those that one has in fact encountered; in contrast, the meaning of any new lexical item must be explained to us.

Finally, this is how the picture theory is supposed to account for the "sublimity" of logic, the fact that we know *a priori* necessary truths and relations of necessary truth preservation, to conclude this sketchy outline: "It is the peculiar mark of logical propositions that one can recognize that they are true from the symbol alone, and this fact contains in itself the whole philosophy of logic" (*Tractatus*, 6.113). If the relations that determine which states of affairs are possible are reflected by identical relations determining which combinations of lexical items are logico-syntactically well formed, we have at the very least the impressionistic beginnings of an explanation. Knowing the facts that determine which possibilities there are, which ones correspond to a given saying, and which ones, expressed by a given saying, are included in the ones expressed by others is already a presupposition of understanding those (or any) sayings. Logical truth is just truth with respect to all possibilities, and logical validity the containment of all the possibilities for the premises in the possibilities for the conclusion. All these matters are determined by the logico-syntactical relations determining well-formedness, signified by exemplification (what I called the "internal" semantic relations). No particular set of "external" semantic relations (no specific lexicon, set of correlations with external objects) must be known for that, although some must; in that respect, the knowledge might be considered *a priori*.

I have summarily sketched the picture theory of representation that appears to be propounded in the *Tractatus*, the evidence allegedly supporting it, and how it is supposed to deal with what appears to be its main motivation, providing an account of the modal properties of logical truths and validities and our *a priori* knowledge thereof. But there are good reasons to remain sceptical about this account, to say the least. For starters, when one leaves behind the toy examples that Wittgenstein considered early on (such as three-dimensional models of car accidents) and moves to the paradigm cases to which the theory is supposed to apply – linguistic representations in natural languages and the thoughts they express – it seems unbelievable that there are any properties shared by the representation and the objects they are about. How could identical relational properties, no matter how abstract, relate lexical items to determine logico-syntactical well-formedness, on the one hand, and the items they stand for to determine possible situations, on the other? Agreed, this is not obviously wrong. Wittgenstein mentions, to justify his view, the case of transitive relations and the sentences representing them (*Tractatus*, 3.1432). At first sight, the syntactic resources that "accusative" languages and "ergative" languages use to represent transitive eventualities are indeed very different. However, some grammarians argue that, at a sufficiently abstract level, all languages use the same syntactical relations (Baker, 1997). Granting this, however, does not yet take us to the claim that *the very same* abstract syntactic relations are instantiated in the represented transitive eventualities.

Aside from this, the theory appears to be plainly false, and therefore actually unable to provide the explanations predicated of it. If the picture theory were true, at most elementary logical validities would be necessary, and known *a priori*. But modal intuitions as strong as those establishing the necessity and apriority of elementary logical validities credit the same modal status to *red is a colour* or *nothing can be entirely red and entirely green*, and the suggestions by Wittgenstein to deal with these cases on behalf of his theory lead nowhere; not to mention his suggestions of how to deal with mathematical truths, or alleged philosophical truths, like the picture theory itself. And there also are Kripkean examples such as the necessity, given its truth, that *water contains oxygen*, also established by compelling modally relevant intuitions (more on them below). None the less, even though the picture theory stands as refuted as any philosophical view might be, one can see how it is supposed to account for some philosophically relevant data; and, in so doing, it draws attention to the data: there must be a philosophical account of logical validity, which should explain, or at least explain away, the "sublimity" of logic – our *a priori* acquaintance with modal reality manifest in this case; such an account should rely on a philosophical account of intentionality; a philosophical account of intentionality should explain our capacity to understand new thoughts, and our capacity to understand false thoughts.

Some psychologists are prouder of discovering "effects" (unexpected data for any theory to account for) than of the theories they put forward to account for them: the theories will probably be superseded, while the effects will probably remain. A similar attitude might well prevail in philosophy. The picture theory highlights what in my view makes the *Tractatus* important, which is the conglomerate of philosophical "effects" just mentioned. In the second section, I will indicate how they (and related suggestions by Wittgenstein's predecessors) have been developed in the current literature, as discussed in the ensuing contributions. I will refer the reader to the chapters in which further elaboration can be found, expanding only on a few issues not taken up by our contributors.

Contemporary Themes from Frege, Russell and the *Tractatus*

(i) *Reference*. Genoveva Martí's chapter, "Reference", presents the debates that have occupied centre stage in contemporary philosophy of language between the descriptivist accounts rooted in the work of Frege and Russell and the New Theory of Reference put forward since the 1970s by philosophers such as Burge, Donnellan, Kaplan, Kripke, Perry and Putnam. Here I will present some differences between Frege's and Russell's forms of descriptivism – in the *Tractatus*, Wittgenstein hails Russell's Theory of Descriptions as a philosophical turning point, adopting the Russellian view.

The core claim of the Theory of Descriptions (cf. Neale's (1990) excellent discussion) is that, in at least one of their semantic functions, definite descriptions such as "the King of Spain" or "my father" make contributions to the contents expressed by sentences in which they occur analogous to those of quantifiers such as "every" or "some", and contrasting with those of genuinely referential expressions, such as some proper names and indexicals. Russell himself made the point by contending that descriptions are "incomplete symbols" which, having merely "contextual definitions", lack a meaning of their own, and disappear on analysis; but this was just a product of the theoretical tools – the formal system – by means of which he presented the view. Thus, consider a sentence such as (1):

(1)   The King of Spain is tall.

The way Russell put it, the main claim of the theory is that, in at least one of its semantic interpretations, this sentence expresses a content equivalent to the one expressed by (2) – a more or less strained natural language equivalent of (3), (1)'s formalization in the sort of formal system Russell was using, assuming the obvious translation key.

(2)   Someone is such that he is King of Spain, there is no King of Spain other than him, and he is tall.

(3) $\exists x\ (Kx \wedge \neg\exists y\ (Ky \wedge y \neq x) \wedge Tx)$

Indeed, in (2) the definite description has vanished as a specific constituent, distributed into quantifiers, negation, and the identity relation. However, as Neale explains, this aspect of Russell's view can be shown to be idiosyncratic by presenting the core of Russell's theory by means of a different formal system.

In contemporary semantics, quantifiers are analysed in the framework of the theory of Generalized Quantifiers. I refer the reader again to Neale (1990) for additional details and references; Josh Dever's chapter in this book, "Formal Semantics", has a useful introduction to the use of formal frameworks in semantic theorizing, and, in Section 7, further information about the Generalized Quantifiers framework. In an intuitive version of this framework, quantifiers such as "every" and "some" contribute to express quantity relations between the classes of objects to which two predicates apply. For instance, "some writer smokes" expresses the claim that the class of writers and the class of smokers share at least one object; and "every writer smokes", the claim that the difference between the class of writers and the class of smokers has no members. One advantage of this framework, relative to the one Russell was using, is that it allows us to account for other similar expressions, such as "few", "most", "many", etc.

In this framework, what I take to be the core of Russell's theory can be put like this: in at least one of its semantic functions, "the" is an expression in the general category of determiners, including also "every", "some", "most", "few", "many" etc; when it occurs in sentences of the form *the P Q*, it helps to make the claim that the class to which *P* applies has just one member, and it is fully included in the class to which *Q* applies. Put in this way, descriptions do not disappear after analysis: in the semantic analysis, "the P" is as much a specific constituent as "every P" in "every P Q". What remains is what I take to be the core claim of a Russellian Theory of Descriptions; to repeat: in at least one of its semantic functions, definite descriptions contribute to making general, quantificational claims, exactly like quantificational expressions such as "every child" do, in contrast with the singular claims made with the help of genuine referential expressions such as some proper names and indexicals.

Before moving on to explain what this contrast might be between making singular and general claims, I need to elaborate on a few issues I have passed by quickly in the previous paragraphs. In the first place, I have been speaking of *at least one* of the semantic functions of definite descriptions because, as we are about to see once we have said more about the difference between singular and general terms, the Russellian should allow for the possibility that definite descriptions also have a referential function. Russell himself, and many Russellians, reject that view; but the core Russellian claim, I take it, is only that descriptions behave like quantifiers in at least one of their semantic uses. The second warning I need to make at this point is that I have been ignoring issues of context-dependence. Thus, "tall" in (1) is a context-dependent expression: what counts as being tall in a context differs from what counts as such in other context. Also, for the predicate "King of Spain" with which "the" forms the definite description in (1) to apply to just one object, some hidden context-dependence must be presumed; it might be that the predicate is somehow "*present* King of Spain", or that quantificational expressions somehow presuppose a contextually given "domain of discourse". The other example of definite description I mentioned, "my father", is more obviously context-dependent. Kent Bach's chapter, "Context Dependence", discusses this issue in general, and Dever's chapter, "Formal Semantics", describes ways for formal theories to encompass the phenomenon.

Let us go back now to the contrast between general and singular claims. Following Kripke (1980, 14), by relying on the Tractarian view that a crucial component (if not the whole) of the contents of sentences and thoughts that we grasp are their *truth-conditions* (the way they discriminate between possibilities, those relative to which the relevant content would obtain from those relative to which it would not) we get the following characterization. When we consider different possibilities for a general claim such as "every writer smokes" to be true, the smoking writers in some of them might well differ from those in others; all that matters is that all writers in each possible state of affairs smoke. The same applies to definite descriptions such as "the first Spaniard to win the Tour de France", in the sense that Russell's Theory of Descriptions captures. The false sentence "the first Spaniard to win the Tour de France was born in Cuenca" is easily intuitively understood in such a way that it selects possible worlds where F. M. Bahamontes, the actual first Spaniard to win the Tour de France, was born in Cuenca rather than being born in Toledo as in fact he was, but it also selects possible worlds where the actual second Spaniard in winning the Tour, L. Ocaña, who was actually born in Cuenca, is in fact the first Spaniard to win the Tour. In other words, the person satisfying the description might differ from possibility to possibility, among those where the content obtains.

However, only worlds of the first kind are selected by "F. M. Bahamontes was born in Cuenca". In this sense, definite descriptions are not "rigid designators": they pick out different individuals with respect to different worlds; but proper names such as "F. M. Bahamontes" (and indexicals such as "this man", uttered pointing to the same person) are.[8] These "intuitions of rigidity", the fact that when we consider possible states of affairs compatible with the truth of a given utterance we keep fixed the denotation, if any, of the referential expression in the actual state of affairs, is the most important mark distinguishing singular from general claims. Kripke pointed out that, as we just confirmed, "we have a direct intuition of the rigidity of names, exhibited in our understanding of the truth conditions of particular sentences" (Kripke 1980, 14; cf. 6, 62).

Russell might have been sensitive to this intuition. In the famous chapter "Knowledge by Acquaintance and Knowledge by Description" in *The Problems of Philosophy* (p. 30), after asking us to consider the use that Bismarck himself makes of "Bismarck" to refer to himself, he says: "Here the proper name has the direct use which it always wishes to have, as simply standing for a certain object, and not for a description of the object." Russell is contrasting here a "direct" use that names "wish" to have, in cases in which we understand them by being "acquainted" with their contents (as Bismarck is with himself), with the descriptive one they most of the time have, according to him, for reasons we are about to see; this "direct use" might well be that rigid use that our intuitions about the truth conditions of particular sentences reveal, according to Kripke. In Russell's direct use, the name simply stands for the bearer; the bearer is the name's content: no wonder that, when we consider possible situations relative to which sentences including the name are true, all that we have to examine is how things stand with the bearer in each situation.

Most of the time, however, proper names such as "Bismarck" (for instance, when they are used by people other than Bismarck himself) express according to Russell the contents of definite descriptions; understanding them involves that descriptive knowledge, and not an acquaintance with their referents that, for Russell, would be impossible to have in that case.[9] Why is this? A main epistemological consideration for Russell and Wittgenstein – let us refer to it as *potential wreck* – is that, unlike when used by Bismarck himself, a use of "Bismarck" cannot guarantee the existence of a referent. In the "direct" use, however, the referent is the meaning; without referent there would be no meaning, for the name or for the sentences including it. Intuitively, however, even if Bismarck were a massive hoax and in fact there was no Bismarck, "Bismarck was Prussian" is meaningful in our mouths. Another epistemological consideration (*aspectual bias*) is that names with the same referent, such as "Hesperus" and "Phosphorus" (or a single name, for different users), might be associated with different purportedly identifying aspects of the intended referent, so that replacing one with the other in a sentence might intuitively alter its significance. *Aspectual bias* suggests that in the relevant cases the referent cannot be all that there is to the meaning of a referential expression; *potential wreck*, that the referent is not even a constitutive part of it.

The reader will find in Genoveva Martí's chapter considerations speaking in favour of Russell's form of descriptivism (fundamentally, the way it accounts for *aspectual bias* and *potential wreck*), and also the almost decisive reasons offered by Kripke and others against it. It is worth noticing at this point that Russell's (and Wittgenstein's) descriptivism was not exposed to the problem presented in Michael Nelson's chapter, "Intensional Contexts", Strawson's reduplication argument – that, intuitively, reference would be unacceptably indeterminate given descriptivism, for we cannot exclude that there are qualitative duplicates of our intended referents. For, as we have seen, both Russell and Wittgenstein accepted the thesis of direct reference (that the referent exhausts the term's meaning-contribution; see also Martí's and Nelson's chapters for further clarification) for some expressions, which they thought were not subject to the two concerns of aspectual bias and potential wreck. Entities in this category that Russell mentions as objects of acquaintance and direct reference include the self (until Wittgenstein talked him out of it), sense data, and their universal qualities.[10] Wittgenstein himself is cagier, speaking merely of *simples* without giving any example; but, on the basis of some of the latter remarks in the *Tractatus*, his critical discussion of his previous views on the early sections of the *Philosophical Investigations*, and other indirect material, I think it is clear that he also had in mind sense data and their attributes. In any case, if the descriptions of entities such as Bismarck are allowed to include directly referential expressions to a self, or to the particular sense data a self is aware of, reduplication will not pose a problem; reference would be determinate, for it would not be solely based on qualitative identification. The Kripkean arguments that Martí presents, however, still show how implausible this Russellian–Wittgensteinian descriptivist conception of reference is.

Structurally, the alternative views proposed by partisans of New Theories of Reference do not differ much from the one we have just described; it is mostly the epistemology that changes. Some expressions (most proper names, including "Bismarck" in all of its uses, indexicals) refer directly; their referents are their contents, and for speakers to understand them they must be acquainted with their contents – but acquaintance is now conceived on the basis of a more lenient epistemology, allowing for acquaintance with the spatiotemporally remote. Not all proper names are like that, however; on most of those views, "descriptive" names (such as Gareth Evans's "Julius", which by definition refers to whoever invented the zip fastener, if anybody uniquely did) can be understood without any acquaintance with their referents, and are therefore excluded from the picture, even if partisans of these views are unclear about what their semantics is. The reader is referred to Martí's and Nelson's chapters to find out how *aspectual bias* and *potential wreck* are supposed to be handled by New Theorists.

Although Frege's picture is also motivated by these two problems, and can be naturally classified as descriptivist, it in fact differs importantly from Russell's. The difference originates, I think, in the fact that Frege focused on the other use of definite descriptions I had in mind when, in presenting above the Theory of Descriptions, I spoke of "at least one of the uses" of descriptions. Suppose that, in telling an episode in the biography of F. M. Bahamontes, I say "and so, the first Spaniard to win the Tour de France might have been born in Cuenca". It is clear in the context that I am using "the first Spaniard to win the Tour de France" as a merely rhetorical alternative to "F. M. Bahamontes" or "he", to avoid boring repetitions of that name, presupposing that my audience is fully aware of the fact that Bahamontes was in fact the first Spaniard to win the Tour de France. This is a case of what Donnellan (1966) calls "referential use" of descriptions. There has been a debate confronting strict Russellians, for which these uses are merely "pragmatic", perhaps to be accounted for in the model of Gricean conversational implicatures (cf. Kripke 1977), those for whom definite descriptions are just semantically ambiguous between the referential and quantificational uses, and "contextualists" who reject the dichotomy as both parties in the debate understand it. François Recanati's chapter, "Pragmatics", introduces the reader to these debates. For our purposes, however, we only need to keep in mind both that the quantificational uses that Russell's theory accounts for undoubtedly exist, and that referential uses also exist, be they "semantic" or "pragmatic".

Now, the reader might check his or her intuitions to establish that in the referential case the expression works "rigidly": all the possibilities with respect to which my claim would be true concern F. M. Bahamontes, and not anybody else who happens to be according to those possibilities the first Spaniard to win the Tour de France. Frege had a semantic category of proper names ("Eigenname") in his system, including ordinary proper names, descriptions and indexicals; it seems clear to me that he was thinking of referential uses of descriptions as the paradigm case. This leads to a view rather different from the Russellian division between expressions understood by acquaintance with their contents, and expressions understood by definitional synonymy with general expressions, even if it is similarly descriptivist, and motivated by the same problems of aspectual bias and potential wreck.[11]

The main difference lies in that, instead of a dichotomy of types of referring expressions, the Fregean proposal has a dichotomy of semantic features for referential expressions (in fact for all expressions). The problem of *aspectual bias* is dealt with by ascribing to referential expressions a descriptive sense, in addition to the referent ("Bedeutung" in the original German). The problem of *potential wreck* is dealt with by classifying cases of reference failure as somehow derivative from cases of reference success. The most straightforward version of this proposal, due to Evans (1982) and McDowell (1977), would be a "disjunctivist" account, on which both cases are essentially different, the referent being an essential component of the meaning of a successful referential expression; but there are other, less radical variants (cf. Sainsbury 2005). Proposals along these lines may still be subject to Kripkean criticisms, this time not of views on which referential expressions are synonymous with descriptions, but rather of views on which descriptions are supposed to "fix their referents". The "two-dimensional" semantics mentioned in the next epigraph provides another framework for alternative neo-descriptivist, neo-Fregean contemporary perspectives on reference. I refer the reader again to Martí's and Nelson's chapters for a fuller appraisal than can be undertaken here.

(ii) *Meaning and modality*. As we have seen, in the *Tractatus* Wittgenstein was centrally concerned with accounting for the modal properties of logical truths: how it is that they are necessary, and how it is that, consistently with our potentially knowing their modal status, we can come to know them. According to his own remarks later, the picture theory is intended to provide the required explanations in a way that allows for the objectivity of the modal status of necessary truths, i.e., it avoids characterizing them as "mind-dependent" in any way. In spite of the failure of the picture theory, he was successful in convincing philosophers of the importance of the topic; and his logical positivist followers, such as Carnap or Ayer, were influenced by his suggestion that the way to approach the issue was through a theory of intentionality. They gave it an anti-realist, conventionalist twist, however. The view now was, in a nutshell, that the semantic rules of a given language, which have a conventional status, determine the space of possibilities and with it the necessary truths, which can be known by knowing those rules and are to that extent knowable *a priori* and analytic. Albert Casullo's chapter, "Analyticity, Apriority, Modality", carefully explains these concepts, providing important distinctions and clarifications. He presents Ayer's and Carnap's view, the main challenges to it in the work of Quine and Kripke, and critically evaluates these challenges.

To a large extent, recent debates about these matters have focused on the scepticism about our modal knowledge that Kripke's views in particular might engender, and to developments of the "two-dimensional" suggestions that Kripke's own work already intimates, which Casullo's chapter also helpfully introduces. As we have seen, Kripke (1980) argued that referential expressions such as indexicals and demonstratives, proper names and natural kind terms are *de jure* rigid designators – expressions that designate the same thing with respect to every possible world. This feature distinguishes them from other singular terms such as definite descriptions, which (putting aside referential uses) might also behave *de facto* as rigid designators, but *de jure* are not so.

Kripke was well aware that his proposals created a philosophical puzzle. His view about referential expressions and alethic modalities entails the existence of *modal illusions*: truths that are in fact necessary appear to be contingent. Paradigm cases are instances of the schema *if n exists, n is F*, with a rigid designator in the place of "n" and a predicate signifying a hidden essential property of its referent in the place of "F". For the sake of illustration, let us replace "F" in the schema with "is-identical-to-Hesperus" and "n" with "Phosphorus":

(1)   If Phosphorus exists, Phosphorus is-identical-to-Hesperus

The existence of those modal illusions elicited by Kripke's views about referential expressions and alethic modalities is puzzling in the light of another compelling view about the epistemology of modality: that we have a reasonably reliable access to possible worlds. Kripke suggests this (to me, at least) when he states the intuition that a possible world "isn't a distant country that we are … viewing through a telescope … 'Possible worlds' are *stipulated*, not *discovered* by powerful telescopes" (Kripke 1980, 44); "things aren't 'found out' about a counterfactual situation, they are stipulated" (*op. cit.*, 49). Of course, according to Kripke himself we are not free to stipulate any possible world we want into existence; otherwise, it would make little sense to speak of modal illusions, such as those previously described. What the dichotomy of stipulation vs. discovery rather suggests is that we have a *prima facie* reliable access to modal reality – that, *prima facie*, what we conceive as possible *is* possible.

   This puzzle is not an outright paradox constituted by contradictory claims; that one has in general reliable access to the modal realm allows for mistaken modal impressions. However, Kripke's views suggest that modal illusions do not arise only in a few, systematically unrelated cases; on the contrary, a systematic and far-reaching pattern is predicted. To sustain modal reliabilism requires thus a philosophical account of the illusions consistent with it. Kripke is sensitive to this, and, in his characteristically nuanced, cautionary mood, he provides one: "Any necessary truth, whether *a priori* or *a posteriori*, could not have turned out otherwise. In the case of some necessary *a posteriori* truths, however, we can say that under appropriate qualitatively identical evidential situations, an appropriate corresponding qualitative statement might have been false" (Kripke 1980, 142). In cases such as (1), something more specific can be said:

   In the case of identities, using two rigid designators, such as the Hesperus-Phosphorus case above, there is a simpler paradigm which is often usable to at least approximately the same effect. Let "R_1" and "R_2" be the two rigid designators which flank the identity sign. Then "$R_1 = R_2$" is necessary if true. The references of "R_1" and "R_2", respectively, may well be fixed by nonrigid designators "D_1" and "D_2", in the Hesperus-Phosphorus case these have the form "the heavenly body in such-and-such position in the sky in the evening (morning)". Then although "$R_1 = R_2$" is necessary, "$D_1 = D_2$" may well be contingent, and this is often what leads to the erroneous view that "$R_1 = R_2$" might have turned out otherwise. (Kripke 1980, 143–4)

What Kripke proposes here, cautiously, only as a possible model applying in some cases, is the blueprint for two-dimensional accounts; the central idea is that "an appropriate corresponding qualitative statement", different from the original, necessary one, which, unlike this "might have been false", is somehow mixed up with it, thus engendering the illusion of its contingency. Kripke refrains from making general claims about the applicability of this model. Nevertheless, his influential arguments against mind–body identity later in the *Naming and Necessity* lectures depend essentially on the premise that the model is the only available one that properly explains the facts at stake.

This core two-dimensionalist idea can also be invoked to deal with the other puzzling Kripkean category of the contingent *a priori*, although Kripke's indications about this application are less clear. As he also famously noted, if one stipulates that a designator N is to be used to refer to an object introduced by a description D that thus fixes its reference, one can be said to know thereby *a priori* "in some sense" (*op. cit.*, 63) the truth of the corresponding statement "N is D if N exists"; (2) provides an example, corresponding to (1):

(2)   Phosphorus is whatever appears as shining brightly in the east just before sunrise, if it exists.

To apply the model here we should have that, although what (2) says is a contingent proposition, there is "an appropriate corresponding qualitative statement" which expresses a necessary one. This would provide for the partial rescue that Kripke (1980, 63 fn.) envisages for the traditional view that everything *a priori* is necessary.

Kaplan (1989) had suggested related ideas, for specific examples of the contingent *a priori* involving indexicals, like "I am here now" or "I am the utterer"; Kent Bach's chapter, "Context-Dependence", discusses them. Kaplan invoked his distinction of two different semantic features of context-dependent expressions, indexicals such as "I", "here" and "now" in particular, a *character* that captures the standing meaning of the expression, and a *content* that consists of their truth-conditional contribution in particular contexts. Given a particular context, sentences such as "I am here now" express a contingent content; however, they are "character-valid" in that expressions in them have characters such that they will always express truths when uttered in any context.

Finally, Kripke suggested that the availability of (what I am presenting as his blueprint for) the core two-dimensionalist explanation of the necessary *a posteriori* and the contingent *a priori* supplies an important role for conceptual analysis, compatible with the Aristotelian-essentialist view that there are *de re* necessities which can only be known through empirical research:

> Certain statements – and the identity statement is a paradigm of such a statement on my view – if true at all must be necessarily true. One does know *a priori*, by philosophical analysis, that *if* such an identity statement is true it is necessarily true ... All the cases of the necessary *a posteriori* advocated in the text have the special character attributed to mathematical statements: philosophical analysis tells us that they cannot be contingently true, so any empirical knowledge of their truth is automatically empirical knowledge that they are necessary. This characterization applies, in particular, to the cases of identity statements and of essence. It *may* give a clue to a general characterization of *a posteriori* knowledge of necessary truths. (Kripke 1980, 159)

Kripke's and Kaplan's suggestions were taken up and developed in technically systematic ways in the two most influential articles originating the two-dimensional tradition after Kripke's inaugurating considerations, Stalnaker's (1978) "Assertion" and Davies and Humberstone's (1980) "Two Notions of Necessity". Other writers, including Chalmers (1996), Jackson (1998, chs 1–3) and Peacocke (1999, ch. 4) in particular, have subsequently elaborated on the idea.

(iii) *Compositionality and Semantic Theorizing.* As we saw, following suggestions in Frege and Russell as well as his own insight, Wittgenstein highlighted two pieces of data that any philosophical account of representational systems such as natural language should capture: the fact that we can understand sentences we have never encountered before, and the fact that in understanding declarative sentences (those susceptible of evaluation as true or otherwise) we typically grasp possibilities that need not be actual (truth-*conditions*). Both issues inform two of arguably the most successful and influential programs for understanding natural languages, initially propounded in the 1960s and leading to work that is still flourishing today. One is the Chomskian program in linguistics; the other is the tradition of formal truth-conditional semantics started in slightly different directions by researchers such as Richard Montague and Donald Davidson. Recent manuals introducing the very substantial explanatory achievements of the Montagovian and Davidsonian traditions such as, respectively, Heim and Kratzer (1998) and Larson and Segal (1996) show the extent to which the Chomskian program in linguistics and truth-conditional semantics in each of those versions are converging nowadays into a fruitful research program. James Higginbotham's chapter, "The Nature of Language", together with the ones already mentioned by Josh Dever, "Formal Semantics", and Kathrin Glüer, "Theories of Meaning and Truth Conditions", will provide the reader with further elaboration and references on these matters.

(iv) *Semantics and Pragmatics.* As already mentioned, Wittgenstein concentrated in the *Tractatus* on the representational properties of what he called *sayings*, whose core he took to be truth-conditions. Material from his lectures and conversations in the late 1920s and early 1930s shows that he was well aware that, as part of our mastery of language, we do not merely deploy declarative sentences susceptible of truth and falsity, but also, say, interrogative or imperative sentences not subject to truth-evaluation; we do not merely *assert* by means of language, or perform other similarly truth-evaluable speech acts, but we also *ask, request, promise*, and so on and so forth. The early Wittgenstein might have dismissed this point with a move made explicit much later by speech act theorists such as John Austin or John Searle – work presented in François Recanati's chapter, "Pragmatics". Those other acts may also be evaluated in terms of, say, their fulfilment or satisfaction or otherwise, if not truth or falsity. Their contents, which we grasp as competent speakers, then encode these *fulfilment* conditions, which might be entirely coincident with the truth-conditions of assertions, and which pose the same two problems that Wittgenstein highlighted: we can understand the fulfilment conditions of orders we consider for the first time, and we grasp them independently of whether or not they are actually fulfilled. The semantic undertaking may thus be characterized as purporting to systematically characterize these fulfilment conditions, using "truth" instead of "fulfilment" in an extended way. Contents in this generic sense appear to be what Wittgenstein meant by *sayings*, something very close to what Austin later called *locutionary acts*. Characterizing the nature of what, in addition to the potentially common contents or fulfilment conditions, distinguishes the different speech acts (what Austin called *illocutionary acts*) is one of the tasks left to pragmatics; the early Wittgenstein, in this way, did not overlook this task but simply dismissed it as unimportant for what he took to be his main concern – accounting for truth-conditions.

Something similar might be said about another task usually left to pragmatics, context-dependence in general and the working of indexicals in particular – but the reader should examine both Recanati's and Bach's chapters for developments and important reservations about the purely pragmatic nature of the meaning of context-dependent expressions. Frege had occupied himself with the topic, and, of course, the author of the *Tractatus* was greatly concerned at the very least with the way "I" functions.[12]

Notoriously, in his later writings Wittgenstein rejected his earlier dismissive attitude towards such "pragmatic" matters. In a much discussed program-matic paper, discussed again here in both Glüer's "Theories of Meaning and Truth Conditions" and Recanati's "Pragmatics", Strawson spoke of a "Homeric struggle" confronting, according to him, the truth-conditional formal semanti-cists with an opponent emphasizing instead the constitutive character in the philosophical account of meaning of notions such as intentional action, norms or conventions. The linchpin, according to Strawson, concerns the possibility of a sufficiently substantive explanation of the nature of *truth* and the *truth*-conditions that the "formal semanticist" appeals to. According to Strawson, such an account can only come from the role the notion has in the appraisal of speech acts such as assertion, which according to him gives the victory to the opponent. In recent discussions, Kripke's (1982) related reconstruction of the later Wittgenstein's remarks on the normativity of meaning has been very influential; many researchers have focused in particular on the bleak consequences for projects such as Chomskian linguistics or truth-conditional semantics that appear to follow from Kripke's account. José Zalabardo's chapter, "Semantic Normativity and Naturalism", takes up these matters. On a related note, different writers – some influenced by the later Wittgenstein and other philosophers in the "Meaning–intention–action" Strawsonian camp, such as Austin or Grice, others simply as a result of their paying close heed to the implications of the many forms of context-dependence present in our use of natural languages (as discussed in Kent Bach's chapter on the topic) – have emphasized that the contribution to what sentences signify from a systematic, compositional semantic component appears to be very abstract and remote from ordinary intuitions (if there is any such contribution at all, which some of these "contextualist" writers such as Charles Travis doubt). Recanati's and Bach's chapters will further present these matters to the reader.

Research Methods in the Philosophy of Language

In this summary of themes and topics from the early history of analytic philosophy of language, I have at several points made appeal to *intuitions*. For instance, we saw that Kripke claims that our intuitive understanding of the distinctive truth-conditions of sentences including proper names gives us a direct intuition of their rigidity; and I mentioned that we have similar intui-tions about the rigidity of definite descriptions in referential uses. Similarly, in one of his most celebrated arguments against descriptivist theories – discussed in Martí's chapter – Kripke famously elicits our intuitions about a thought-experiment concerning a fictitious situation, in which the person usually addressed by the name "Kurt Gödel", whose passport registered that name, etc., in fact did not prove the incompleteness of arithmetic, but stole the proof from someone called "Schmidt". Under the (probably true) assumption that all the descriptive information we associate with the name "Gödel" is *the discoverer of the incompleteness of arithmetic*, if the imagined circumstances were real, by "Gödel" we would be referring to Schmidt. However, intuitively this does not seem so, Kripke contends.

Intuitions are generally supposed to play an important evidential role in contemporary analytic philosophy; particularly intuitions concerning circumstances imagined in thought experiments such as the one just mentioned, which act as "crucial experiments" with respect to contrasting theories about the nature of some concepts in which philosophy is interested (such as the descriptivist and direct theories of reference). Thus, Gettier's (1963) three-page article famously refuted the claim that knowledge is justified true belief by means of one such thought experiment, describing a situation in which (we would intuitively concur) someone has justified true belief without having knowledge. Similarly, intuitions also play a fundamental evidential role in contemporary linguistics: intuitions about the acceptability or otherwise of sentences play such a role in syntax, and the sort of intuition about the truth-conditions of specific sentences we saw Kripke appealing to above, to establish the rigidity of proper names, similarly play a fundamental evidential role in semantics.

What are intuitions? To secure for them a central evidential role in philosophy, Bealer (1998) takes intuitions to be "intellectual seemings" – specific mental states such as perceptual experiences are usually thought to be, playing in philosophy a similar role to the one played by experiences in empirical knowledge: like perceptual experiences, they are "given", they cannot be justified or unjustified; none the less they have justificatory power, making beliefs based on them immediately justified (justified not by other beliefs), even if they can be illusory (keeping their "pull" or attraction while we resist it, as in the Müller-Lyer illusion); they provide basic information about the intension of concepts – the conditions under which they apply in possible circumstances – confirming or disconfirming *a priori* general theories about their nature (the way Kripke's thought experiment disconfirms the descriptivist theory of reference, and Gettier's the traditional theory of knowledge), and thereby establishing conceptual necessities, which is what philosophy is about. Others such as Sosa (2007, ch. 3) argue that there are important differences between experiences and intuitions; Sosa suggests understanding them instead as conscious entertainings of content which attract our assent; under that guise, he also gives them an equal epistemologically salient role in philosophy, understood as a fundamentally *a priori* discipline providing theories about the nature of fundamental concepts such as *knowledge* or *reference*.

Finally, others such as Williamson (2007, ch. 7) – sceptical of the traditional conception of the philosophical undertaking as conceptual analysis conducted *a priori* and seeing philosophy, in a Quinean light, as continuous with science and ordinary empirical belief – refuse to understand intuitions as anything other than conscious opinions or beliefs that we find appealing for some reason or other. Although Williamson disqualifies the main Quinean arguments for such scepticism – contending that notions such as synonymy, meaning, belief, necessity and possibility, are in a sufficiently good standing, even if we have to understand them in terms of each other – he ends up propounding a similar view. Meaning-determining factors are, according to him, facts about our linguistic practices and dispositions, at most empirically accessible (2007, 121–30); and thought-experiments should be understood as a form of reasoning about counterfactual circumstances, essentially dependent on premises only known *a posteriori*. "Intuitions" (i.e., just conscious judgments we find appealing) do constitute evidence, but the evidence consists of the contents we thus intuitively accept, not the psychological fact that we have those intuitions.

Here Williamson's view is close to Soames's (1984, 174) "Platonistic" view of what linguistics is about, and his corresponding view about the role of intuitions in that discipline: "even intuitions of grammaticality are not *data* for theories in linguistics; whereas facts about grammaticality are"; Soames is assuming here that "data" is "what theories make claims or predictions about." Intuitions of grammaticality, or semantic intuitions, are like mathematical or geometrical intuitions: indications, which we must take to be reliable if we are to have some starting point at all, of some of the facts – the only real *data* – about numbers or space that mathematicians aim then to collect under an encompassing system characterizing the structure of numbers or space. Number theory is about *two plus three being five* and related intuitive facts, not about *our intuition* that this is so; similarly, linguistics, on this view, is about abstract languages, say, languages that have "the cat is on the mat" as a grammatical sentence, and "some cat is on the mat" as logically following from it – not about our intuition that any of this is so: these intuitions merely provide the facts to be captured and systematized by the linguist.

In the case of linguistics, there is, I think, a decisive reason to reject Soames's view, and to take intuitions themselves, not just their contents, as evidence to be accounted for by linguistic theories. The reason is the guiding role that the Principle of Compositionality plays in linguistic theorizing, which we have already mentioned at several points above. The syntactic and semantic structure assigned by those theories to natural languages is taken to explain the facts that lead us to accept the Principle of Compositionality. But these are facts such as our capacity to understand new sentences, manifested by the intuitions expressing understanding of those "new" sentences, and their grammatical acceptability. (The reader will find useful Higginbotham's chapter on "The Nature of Language" in this regard.) In a nutshell: if the Principle of Compositionality is to have any theoretical bite, it is because only theories that accommodate it are capable of explaining our having specific syntactic and semantic intuitions.

In the case of philosophy, in order to confront Williamson's sceptical challenge, the friend of conceptual analysis and the conception of philosophy as a fundamentally *a priori* discipline providing knowledge of conceptual necessities should try to point out that the having of intuitions themselves, and not just their contents, provides crucial data for philosophical theories to account for. In this case, the idea to be articulated is that intuitions about cases (in particular, the interesting intuitions elicited by well-designed "crucial" thought-experiments, such as Kripke's or Gettier's) are just manifestations of the possession of the relevant concepts, and constitute access to their intensions. I refer the reader to Ichikawa and Jarvis (2009) for interesting recent suggestions along these lines; but it must be said that the difficulties of these attempts highlight the importance of Williamson's challenge.

A more radical challenge – in that, if compelling, it questions both the traditional conception of philosophy and Williamson's *a posteriori* methodological alternative – has been recently posed by some results of the so-called "experimental philosophy". This consists in the design of empirical experiments of the kind psychologists regularly conduct, addressed to examine whether or not ordinary people have the intuitions which are supposed to be elicited by philosophical thought-experiments such as Gettier's or Kripke's. Some of the researchers conducting them argue that, surprisingly, whether or not people share those intuitions appears to be influenced by factors such as culture, race or social class. These results would question the traditional approach to philosophy (as traditionally understood, the method would at most provide information about culturally idiosyncratic concepts) but also Williamson's, because they would suggest that the contents to which we have intuitive access are very doubtfully *facts*. The last section in Genoveva Martí's chapter discusses some of these experiments – those relating to the concept of *reference* and Kripke's thought-experiment – and provides further references.

Assuming we can have a convincing reply to the experimental philosophy challenge, and no matter whether we end up supporting a form of *a priori* methodology or rather think we must make sense of the methodology we employ in philosophy along the lines envisaged by Williamson, it seems plausible that we need to adopt a "wide reflective equilibrium" view of the kind described by Daniels (2011) thus: "working back and forth among our considered judgments (some say our 'intuitions') about particular instances or cases, the principles or rules that we believe govern them, and the theoretical considerations that we believe bear on accepting these considered judgments, principles, or rules, revising any of these elements wherever necessary in order to achieve an acceptable coherence among them." In particular, we need to make sure that philosophical theories are consistent with the results of empirical science (the way a philosophical account of persistence in time should be consistent with Special Relativity), and we should admit that philosophical theories are defeasible on the basis of empirical evidence; Jeshion (2000) provides good reasons why this should be so even on the most aprioristic conception of the discipline. Thus, in the case of the concept of *reference* we have been discussing, writers have appealed to facts about the understanding by autistic people or little babies of referential expressions, contending for instance that they are incompatible with descriptivist views (cf. García-Ramírez and Shatz (2011) for a recent example of that line of argument, and references therein). Reflective equilibrium, however – as Williamson (2007, 244–6) points out – is not what distinguishes philosophy. A similar methodology is employed in science; but what is characteristic of science is the way it depends on empirical evidence, and the criteria for selecting adequate empirical evidence. Likewise, in the case of philosophy the crucial issue is the role that intuitions play, whether it is distinctive and whether it underwrites an *a priori* knowledge of necessary truths. On that matter, as we have seen, the jury is still out.

Notes

1. I am grateful to Max Kölbel for comments on a previous version that led to improvements. Financial support for my work was provided by the DGI, Spanish Government, research project FFI2010-16049 and Consolider-Ingenio project CSD2009-00056; through the award *ICREA Academia* for excellence in research, 2008, funded by the Generalitat de Catalunya; and by the European Community's Seventh Framework Programme *FP7/2007–2013* under grant agreement no. 238128.
2. Departament de Lògica, Història i Filosofia de la Ciència, Universitat de Barcelona, email: m.garciacarpintero@ub.es
3. There are many indications of the centrality of this issue among the problems that Wittgenstein was concerned with at the time, beginning with the amount of discussion devoted to it in the *Tractatus* itself. The early letters and notebooks reflect how his focus on intentionality evolved from his primary interest in giving an account of logical validity improving on those put forward by Frege and Russell. Another piece of evidence comes from the *Investigations*. The early hundred-odd sections of that work read like a criticism of the Tractarian philosophy. While providing, to serve as a foil, some glimpses of his new views on the issues, Wittgenstein criticises there several aspects of the *Tractatus*, in an order that appears to retrace in reverse the intellectual path leading to them: the disregard for the differences between illocutionary forces (to which we will come back later) and its focusing only on what I will call *sayings*; the notion of a logical name, and the correlative notion of a simple (to which we will also

come back); the assumption of a unique analysis of all contents, and so on and so forth. After all this, in § 65 we are told that "the great question which lies behind all these considerations" is the problem of giving "the general form of propositions", for which the picture theory provided the intended answer. There follows a therapeutic bashing of the assumptions setting this as an issue, and finally we are told, in § 89, that the problem to which the preceding considerations lead is "In what sense is logic something sublime?"

4. For Wittgenstein, as for Kant before him, these properties are manifestly coextensive; Albert Casullo's chapter, "Analyticity, Apriority, Modality", discusses these notions.

5. The central element of the picture theory that Wittgenstein marshals to account for these features is the claim that the picture and its represented reality share a certain "form". Thus, regarding the first explanatory issue, 2.17 says that, in order for a picture to be able to depict reality correctly or incorrectly, it "must have in common" with reality its form; regarding the second, 4.02 says that we can see that a proposition is a picture of reality "from the fact that we understand the sense of a propositional sign without its having been explained to us". (I assume that the demonstrative "this" occurring in 4.02 refers to material in 4.01, the paragraph immediately preceding it in the "alphabetic" order indicated by their numbers.)

6. The way a sample signifies a set of properties by itself instantiating those very properties.

7. Kathrin Glüer's chapter, "Theories of Meaning and Truth-Conditions", develops the notion further.

8. In fact, they are *de jure* so, Kripke contends, unlike descriptions such as "the even number", which merely *de facto* pick out the same entity with respect to every possibility. Kripke never explains what he means with the *de jure – de facto* dichotomy; what it suggests is that proper names are rigid as a matter of the semantic *norms* or *rules* governing them.

9. See Sainsbury (1993/2002) for a nuanced examination of Russell's actual views, in contrast with what it is attributed to him in contemporary discussions.

10. We have been discussing singular terms so far, but our considerations apply to expressions in other categories. If we thought that common nouns such as "water" and "tiger", or predicates such as "electrically charged", "yellow" or "circular", signify objective kinds or properties, whose nature is to be discerned (to the extent that it is) only through scientific investigation, then we would have equivalents of the *aspectual bias* and *potential wreck* problems; according to descriptivism, they would have similar solutions.

11. For Russell's actual views, the reader should consult Sainsbury (1993/2002).

12. The proposal in the *Tractatus*, as explained later by the author in lectures and conversations in the late 1920s and early 1930s, appears to be close to David Lewis's (1979) account of so-called *de se* contents – the contents whose "irreducibly indexical" character is pointed out by Perry (1979) with forceful examples. Lewis's proposal is to take away the subject from the content itself, and thinking of truth-conditions not as functions from worlds to truth-values (i.e., not as discriminating among possible worlds), but rather as functions from subjects, worlds and times to truth-values (i.e., as discriminating among possible subjects, as they are at a particular time in their lives at a given possible world).

References

Baker, Mark (1997), "Thematic Roles and Syntactic Structure", in L. Haegeman ed. *Elements of Grammar*, Dordrecht: Kluwer, 73–137.

Bealer, George (1998), "Intuition and the Autonomy of Philosophy", in M. R. DePaul and W. Ramsey (eds), *Rethinking Intuition*, Oxford: Rowman and Littlefield, 201–39.

Chalmers, David (1996), *The Conscious Mind*, Oxford: Oxford University Press.

Daniels, Norman (2011), "Reflective Equilibrium", *The Stanford Encyclopedia of Philosophy* (Spring 2011 Edition), Edward N. Zalta ed. forthcoming. Available online at http://plato.stanford.edu/archives/spr2011/entries/reflective-equilibrium/ (accessed 12 September 2011).

Davies, Martin and Humberstone, Lloyd (1980), "Two Notions of Necessity", *Philosophical Studies* 38, 1–30.

Donnellan, Keith (1966), "Reference and Definite Descriptions", *Philosophical Review* 75, 281–304.

Evans, Gareth (1982), *The Varieties of Reference*, Oxford: Clarendon Press.

García-Ramírez, E. and Shatz, M. (2011), "On Problems with Descriptivism: Psychological Assumptions and Empirical Evidence", *Mind and Language* 26, 53–77.

Gettier, E. (1963), "Is justified true belief knowledge?" *Analysis* 23, 121–3.

Goodman, Nelson (1976), *Languages of Art*, Indianapolis: Hackett.

Heim, I. and Kratzer, A. (1998), *Semantics in Generative Grammar*, Oxford: Blackwell.

Ichikawa, J. and Jarvis, B. (2009), "Though-Experiments and Truth in Fiction", *Philosophical Studies* 142, 221–46.

Jackson, Frank (1998), *From Metaphysics to Ethics*. Oxford: Oxford University Press.

Jeshion, Robin (2000), "On the Obvious", *Philosophy and Phenomenological Research* 60, 333–55.

Kaplan, David (1989), "Demonstratives", in J. Almog, J. Perry and H. Wettstein (eds), *Themes from Kaplan*, Oxford: Oxford University Press, 481–563.

Kripke, Saul (1977), "Speaker's Reference and Semantic Reference", in French, P., Uehling, T. and Wettstein, H., *Contemporary Perspectives in the Philosophy of Language*, Minneapolis: University of Minnesota Press, 255–76.

—(1980), *Naming and Necessity*, Cambridge, Mass.: Harvard University Press.

—(1982), *Wittgenstein on Rules and Private Languages*, Cambridge, Mass.: Harvard University Press.

Larson, Richard and Segal, Gabriel (1996), *Knowledge of meaning: Semantic value and Logical Form*, Cambridge, Mass.: MIT Press.

Lewis, David (1979), "Attitudes *De Dicto* and *De Se*", *Philosophical Review* 88, 513–43.

McDowell, John (1977), "On the Sense and Reference of a Proper Name," *Mind* LXXXVI, 159–85.

Neale, Stephen (1990), *Descriptions*, Cambridge, Mass.: MIT Press.

Peacocke, Christopher (1999), *Being Known*, Oxford: Oxford University Press.

Perry, John (1979), "The Problem of the Essential Indexical", *Noûs* 13, 3–21.

Russell, Bertrand (1912/1980), *The Problems of Philosophy*. Oxford: Oxford University Press.

Sainsbury, Mark (1993/2002), "Russell on Meaning and Communication", in *Departing from Frege*, London: Routledge, 85–101.

—(2005), *Reference without Referents*, Oxford: Clarendon Press.

Soames, Scott (1984), "Linguistics and Psychology", *Linguistics and Philosophy* 7, 155–79.

Sosa, Ernest (2007), *A Virtue Epistemology*, Oxford: Clarendon Press.

Stalnaker, Robert (1978), "Assertion", in P. Cole ed. *Syntax and Semantics* 9, New York: Academic Press, 315–32.

Strawson, Peter (1969), *Meaning and Truth. An Inaugural Lecture delivered before the University of Oxford on 5 November 1969*, Oxford: Clarendon Press.

Williamson, Timothy (2007), *The Philosophy of Philosophy*, Oxford: Blackwell.

2 On the Nature of Language: A Basic Exposition

James Higginbotham

Introduction

Language, like other natural phenomena, can be studied from different points of view. In this chapter we aim to convey at least part of the source of interest in two of these, namely: (i) the abstract character of language, or the features of linguistic systems that have been an object of reflective study since ancient times, following especially Greek, Indian, and Oriental scholars; and (ii) the issues that arise when we take up the fact that these systems are exemplified in human cognition; i.e., that they *belong* to us in some sense, even apart from any reflective or scholarly understanding on our part.

The latter issues, if not the former, are above all associated with the work of Noam Chomsky, and have been carried forward by many, with the variety of disagreements over matters of principle as well as detail that may be expected in such an enterprise. There are several excellent, and popularly written, introductions to the subject, including Pinker (2007), Guéron and Haegeman (1998), and others. But we will begin further back, with some observations about English that should exemplify some of the attainments, and some of the tensions, in the subject. My exposition will be elementary, but I hope that this simplicity will if anything highlight the moral of the story.

We take it as evident that words fall into different categories, or "parts of speech", as many of us were taught in school (in fact the distinctions we were taught to make amongst categories of words emerged as the result of scholarly study and reflection over many centuries). We also assume meaningful elements that can only occur as parts of words, such as the "-ed" of the regular English past tense, or the "-er" that converts "view" into "viewer", "walk" into "walker", and so forth. Distinguishing as we do amongst the major categories of Noun, Verb, Adjective, and Preposition, and allowing the rough-and-ready notions of subject and object, a point that marks a distinction between inventories of words and the inflections such as "-ed" and "-er" that go with them, on the one hand, and the understanding of the construction of whole sentences on the other, is the realization that complexes of words themselves belong to categories, and that expressions of these categories can occur as constituents of others. Thus a complete nominal, such as "the red house", can occur as part of a sentence; but sentential elements, such as the relative clause in "the house which/that I saw", can occur inside nominals. The process can of course be iterated, yielding a nested infinity of syntactic complexes. The study of the structures that go with the combinatorial devices of language is the study of *syntax*, as opposed to the study of *morphology*, the makeup of words, or *lexicography*, the enumeration and description of primitive words, or the primitive parts of words.

Within recent history an important step was taken by Harris (1951), who proposed descriptive systems for syntax. As an illustration, we consider his treatment of the nominal system of English (roughly, those expressions that can constitute the subject of a complete sentence). We have at a minimum the following inventory:

(i) Pronouns (e.g. "I", "he", "she", or "they", standing alone);
(ii) Demonstratives that must stand alone (e.g., "now" or "then");
(iii) Demonstratives that can be followed by (possibly modified) Nouns (e.g., "these (old) books", or "those books (on the shelf)");
(iv) Articles and expressions of generality that must be followed by Nouns (e.g., "the", "every").

Modification raises interesting questions, in part because the order of adjectives is restricted (so it is far more natural in English to say "the old red house" than "the red old house"). Further, in English, relative clause modifiers follow the Noun, as in "the book that I read". Abstracting from many details, we may have the following picture: the English Nominal is a Noun Phrase (hereafter: NP); the elements in (i) and (ii) above are NP by themselves; those illustrated in (iii) and (iv) consist of Nouns, possibly accompanied by modifiers in certain positions, and preceded by a demonstrative or expression of generality (which in simple plurals such as "big houses" need not be explicitly realized). Modifiers can be iterated; but there is a unique licensing (or *head*) Noun (so in nominal compounds the final Noun will be the head, as "the soap bar" refers to a bar of soap, whereas "the bar soap" refers to any quantity of soap in a bar shape); moreover, the insertion of an article or expression such as "every" *closes off* the construction, so we cannot have *"the every book", where the asterisk "*" indicates (the author's judgment) that the element in question is syntactically deviant, in whatever language is in question.

Now, Harris observed that the above simple description can be systematized in the following way: we have three levels of Nominal: the simple Noun N (a word, generally, though perhaps a complex such as "Soviet Union"); the clutch of modifiers, which can be augmented without limit, constituting an N^1, say, and a final part of speech, the *Determiner*, which closes it off as, say N^2.

The superscripts thus indicate the nominal level, and the system is abstractly described through the following two syntactic rules:

(Ri) If X is an N or N^1, and Y is a suitable modifier, then $X^{\wedge}Y$ (or $Y^{\wedge}X$, depending) is an N^1;

(Rii) If X is an N or N^2, and Y is a determiner, then $Y^{\wedge}X$ is an N^2.

where the arch "$\wedge$" linking X and Y just indicates the result of writing X followed by Y (perhaps with a space between; we suppress this mark in what follows).

Harris's method can be extended to Verbal complexes, and others, as well. From the general point of view taken here, what is critical about the system is that it envisages the layout of syntax in terms of an *explicit inductive definition* of membership of expressions in categories. Of course this step had long been taken in the study of formal languages, going back to Gottlob Frege (1879), and was common coin in mathematical logic. What was novel in Harris's approach, and taken up in much greater explicit detail in Chomsky (1957; itself expounding his earlier work) was the application of the method to human first languages (conceiving of these, as it were, as formal languages for which the formalization was being sought). The system of rules, together with lexical stipulations (e.g., that "book" is a Noun) could together constitute a *grammar* (or the syntactic part thereof) of a language in use.

A general mathematical picture of languages admitting grammars of the sort illustrated in (Ri) and (Rii) above is straightforwardly given: a grammar consists of a set of *categories*, and rules that allow the replacement of a category C by a sequence XY ... Z of elements each of which is a category or primitive expression; and a sequence of replacements that results in a final sequence s of primitive expressions is a *derivation* of s from C, or a proof that $s \varepsilon C$. We indicate the replacement by the arrow "→". So, for one of the Nominal examples above, we might have, where $C=N^2$:

$N^2 {\rightarrow} D\ N^1$

$N^1 {\rightarrow} A\ N^1$

$N^1 {\rightarrow} N$

$N {\rightarrow} house; A {\rightarrow} big, A {\rightarrow} red; D {\rightarrow} the$

deploying these so as to derive "the big red house" (where the rule "$N^1 {\rightarrow} DN^1$" must be used twice, once for each modifier). The full sequence will be:

N^2

$D N^1$

DAN^1

$DAAN^1$

$DAAN$

and finally, after appropriate lexical replacement:

the big red house

Equivalently, we can represent the derivation by a tree as in (1)

(1)

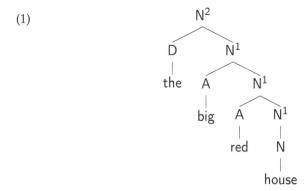

which itself reflects the conversion of the rules followed in the above derivation by the clauses of an inductive definition along the lines of (Ri) and (Rii), together with the stipulation that certain words are given as belonging to certain categories.

There is no doubt that a system such as that illustrated, technically a *context-free phrase structure grammar*, is adequate not only for formal languages (and most computer languages, though some deviate in various respects) but also for large tracts of English and other first human languages. Even the elementary differences are interesting, as showing that the hierarchical dimension of language is critical for linguistic description: thus for instance the Nominal in Cambodian is very nearly the reverse of English, so that the natural phrase for "the big red house" comes out as "house red big the", which is what you would get if you flipped (1) around on the page as if it were a mobile. We turn now, however, to two of the questions taken up by Chomsky (1957, 1965 and later work), namely:

(I)   Are grammars assigning phrase structures to sentences and other categories in the manner discussed above in principle adequate to human languages; and

(II) What can be said about the relations of an adequate grammar for a speaker and the linguistic powers of the speaker whose grammar it is?

For (I): Chomsky and others argued at length that, in addition to rules generating phrase structures, there were relations between such abstract structures that were not in any reasonable way expressed in terms of relations between whole sentences. An early example, discussed extensively in Chomsky (1957), is the verbal auxiliary of simple tensed sentences of English. English simple sentences must carry Tense, which figures as an affix on the Verb, either Present or Past (as in "is" versus "was"). Besides Tense, there are optional elements, namely: the Modals ("will", "can", "may", "must", etc.), the Perfective "have", and the Progressive "be". All are present in (2):

(2)   The child may have been reading the book.

The order of these elements is fixed, namely Tense–Modal–Perfective–Progressive (though all but the first can be omitted). We note now that the Perfective conditions the suffix on the Progressive, so if the former is omitted we have, not *"the child may been reading the book" (the asterisk "*" indicating that the following is not a properly formed or grammatical expression, in this case of the category Sentence) but rather (2):

(2)   The child may be reading the book.

Similarly, if the Progressive is omitted, then the suffix "-ing" does not appear with the Verb. We have (3):

(3)   The child may have read the book.

And finally, if the Tensed Modal "may" is omitted, then the Tense must appear on whatever follows, as in (4) and (5):

(4)   The child has read the book.

(5)   The child is reading the book.

These observations (and others like them in the Germanic and Romance languages) suggest a rule of the following sort:

(6)   The fundamental sequence is Tense-Modal-"have"+"-en"-"be"+"-

ing"-Verb, where each of the affixes (Tense, "-en", "-ing") moves in the course of the derivation to the element that follows it.

A rule such as (6), which must apply in the course of a derivation, is obviously not a phrase structure rule: Chomsky (1957) used the term *transformation* to describe the operation of (6) and similar rules. However, it expresses a simple generalization that reduces the space that would otherwise be taken up in giving the forms of the auxiliary. The example of (6) (a statement of "affix-hopping", to use the name sometimes given to it) is typical of principles that suggest the need for descriptive power that goes beyond phrase structure.

Besides the verbal auxiliary, there are other examples that suggest the need for transformations; see Guéron and Haegeman (1998), or other texts, for examples. The point of this rehearsal of a central argument that phrase structure can be only part of the story about grammars for human languages is that it puts us, even with only this much, in a position to raise question (II) above. Obviously, native speakers of English "follow" (6), in the sense that they produce, and perceive as normal, potential sentences that are in accord with it, and do not produce, and perceive as strange, sentences that are not. What, beyond this, can be said about the relation of the rule to the native speaker of English?

The answer to (II) suggested by Chomsky (1965) is that speakers stand in an epistemic relation to the rules of grammar, which he dubbed their *competence*. The term is perhaps unfortunate, since it suggests that competence is a property possessed by the competent; what is intended, however, is that the speaker's competence is just what the speaker knows, a system of rules and/or principles from which the consequences for the data of grammatical theory are deductive consequences. The reference to knowledge is more than a metaphor, because it involves understanding the grasp of a first language as an intellectual accomplishment, arrived at on the basis of linguistic and perceptual experience, thus giving rise to the subject of Developmental Psycholinguistics.[1] Seen in this light, and bearing in mind that there is considerable variety in human languages, there is a tension between the posited formal properties of grammar and the known course of linguistic maturation: the relevant properties of grammar must be inferable from principles on the basis of the ambient evidence; but those principles cannot be so strong as to rule out possible human languages.[2]

To adopt Chomsky's terminology, we posit a *language faculty* (perhaps a specialization of more general mental faculties) that, through principles we hope to discover, quickly zeroes in (by the age of 6, say) on the critical properties of the ambient language, on the basis of such evidence as human children actually receive. The question of the "Nature of Language", from this point of view, is first of all concerned with the nature of that faculty.

We have concentrated above on the matter of syntax, or the order and arrangement of words, parts of words, and whole phrases and sentences. But exactly similar considerations apply to phonology, the theory of the sounds of speech, and to semantics, or that part of a general account of meaning that is conveyed through linguistic form.

It was remarked above that there is a simple mapping between phrase structures and the clauses of an inductive definition (the latter being the operation "Merge" of Chomsky (1995, and later work by him) and others). In standard formalized languages, such as the language of first-order logic, the clauses that build formulae come each with its characteristic semantics. The result is a grammar and semantics (an account of reference and truth, either in a model or absolutely) that run in parallel, and are equally unambiguous, representable by trees in the sense used above (the need for explicit mention of the trees is secured by means of parentheses, which distinguish, e.g., "A & (B v C)" from "(A & B) v C", where the trees

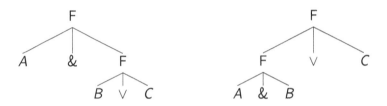

vividly and faithfully reflect the scope distinction). A quick survey shows that human languages are not so neatly organized, at least on the surface: there is an ambiguity of quantification, for instance, in (7) (did one man go into every store, or was every store visited by some man or another?), and (8) can mean either that John was reluctant to be instructed, or that Mary was reluctant to instruct him:

(7)   A man went into every store.

(8)   John was reluctantly instructed by Mary.

(Crucially, a person asserting (7) or (8) must intend one of their two interpretations: for that reason, we know that we have genuine ambiguity and not mere vagueness.) Both of these are cases of *structural* ambiguity, in the sense that they are ambiguous even though no word they contain is ambiguous. The question therefore arises whether there is a level of analysis – hence, by hypothesis, a level of linguistic knowledge – where these and similar ambiguities are sorted out, either through syntactic representation or perhaps through the operation of semantic rules that are not strictly determined by linguistic structure.[3]

Similar questions arise for the interaction of linguistic form with features of context that go into interpretation.[4] If Mary says after the party, "Everyone had a good time", of course she means, and intends to be understood as meaning, that everyone who came to the party had a good time; but she does not actually say that. In the next section, we consider some elements of syntactic variation, turning afterwards to the articulation of a framework for semantic theory.

Cross-Linguistic Features

A general feature of human languages is *displacement*; i.e., the occurrence of a linguistic element in a syntactic position other than the position where it would be licensed in basic phrase structure. One canonical example is the displacement (in English and elsewhere, as discussed below) of the question-words and longer phrases "who", "which game", "how many cats", and so forth in questions, as in (9) and (10):

(9)   Who did you see?

(10)   John learned how many cats they kept in the cages.

(the question in (9) is said to be *direct*; that in (10), which figures as the object of "learn", *indirect*). Clearly, the "who" of (9) is understood as questioning the object of the Verb "see", and "how many cats" in (10) is the object of "kept". This fact suggests a transformation, called *WH-movement*, which displaces the object to the front of its clause. (For its general features in English, see Guéron and Haegeman (1998).) Such a transformation is found in many languages, but hardly in all: in Chinese, for example, the question words are found in exactly the position to which the displaced element is related, as in (11), translating (9):

(11)   Ni   kan-jian   shei?

       You   see   who?

and no displacement is possible. Moreover, there are a number of intermediate cases attested in other languages.

In English, the WH-expressions double as introducing relative clauses, as in (12):

(12)   book [which I saw]

and the WH-expression may be replaced by "that", or (in English in particular, though not, e.g., in German) omitted entirely, as in (13):

(13)   book [that/∅ I saw]

The relative clause is of course a modifier constructed out of a clause; and it occurs following the Noun modified; and it has its linguistic markers, the WH-expression or the word "that". There is a straightforward contrast here with Chinese, where, although the determiner precedes the Noun, as in English, (a) the WH-expressions only have a use in questions; (b) there is no word comparable to "that"; and (c) the clause precedes rather than follows the Noun with which it is in construction. This difference may illustrate in a simple fashion how much may be gained by abstracting from linear order to consider instead the hierarchical arrangement of phrases. Thus the Chinese for (12) or (13) is (14):

(14)   Wo kan-guo-de shu[5]

     I   saw   book

     "book that I saw"

The difference of order does not affect the hierarchical structure, which is the same in both languages; and the full structure, with linear order, is just the mirror image of the English, as indicated, with details omitted, in (15), the result of "flipping" the English so as to match the Chinese word order:

(15)

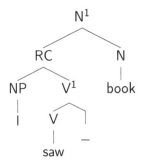

Evidently, this material raises the question what, if anything, to say about the position of the missing object, marked above by the blank "__". Although it would take us too far afield to go deeply into this matter here, I note that it has been widely assumed that the position is in fact occupied by an "empty" element *t* (for "trace")[6], syntactically present but not pronounced. To clarify somewhat in terms of customary logical notation: obviously in (12)–(14) what (so to speak) glues the elements together, the Noun "book" and the relative modifier "I saw" or Chinese equivalents, is the sharing of a variable, so that in "the book I saw" some single thing is said to be a book and seen by me, or notationally as in (16):

(16) book(x) & I saw x

We considered, above, the case of displacement of question (in English, WH-) expressions. There are a number of other examples that have been argued to fall under something like the syntactic conditions that apply to these expressions, as *topicalization*, illustrated by (17), and *negative inversion*, illustrated by (18):

(17) John I thought no one would pay attention to *t*.

(18) Not one book did the teacher ask us to read *t*.

where in each case the position to which the displaced element is in relation is marked by the trace *t*. Besides these cases, where the displaced element moves outside the core clause altogether, there are others in which displacement moves from one clausal position to another. We illustrate with two of these.

The *Passive* is marked by the alteration of the Verb to its perfective form (e.g., "see" to "seen", "fly" to "flown", etc.) and construction with "be" as in (19):

(19) The plane was flown to Paris.

Here the displacement is from the object position of "fly" to the subject position in the sentence. The process can *iterate*, so we have for instance (20):

(20) The plane was thought to have been flown to Paris.

This suggests a double displacement, starting from a structure as in (21), and ending with doubly-marked traces, as in (22):

(21) __ was thought [__ to have been flown the plane to Paris]

(22) The plane was thought [*t* to have been flown *t* to Paris]

In a similar vein, the operation usually called *raising* displaces a subject to the subject position of a higher clause. Thus the tensed complement in (23) contrasts with the untensed (infinitival) complement in (24):

(23)   It seems [(that) John is a nice fellow]

(24)   John seems [to be a nice fellow]

In (23) the subject position is taken by pleonastic "it"; but in (24) it is filled by the subject of the complement of the Verb. So the latter is a case of displacement; and if we follow the thesis that displacement leaves a trace of the vacated position the subject of the infinitive is *t*, appropriately related to the surface subject "John". Moreover, displacement in a complement as in (23) is impossible, and that in the infinitival (24) obligatory, as shown by the ungrammaticalities (25)–(26):

(25)   *John seems (that) is a nice fellow.

(26)   *It seems John to be a nice fellow.

Again, displacement may iterate, as in (27):

(27)   Mary seems [*t* to be certain [*t* to be elected *t*]]

where "Mary", the object of "elected", has moved first to the Passive subject position, then (because the Passive is also an infinitive) to the subject position of "certain", and finally to the subject position in construction with the tensed Verb "seems".

An account of these latter displacement phenomena, suggested originally by Jean-Roger Vergnaud, is that they reflect an abstract condition, that every Nominal construction must bear a Case, either nominative or some other. In English, Case is visible only on pronouns, such as "I" Nominative (i.e., together with Tense, in the subject position) versus "me" for everything else, for example. If, however, we suppose that Case is given in the syntax even if not overtly in speech, and it is assumed that neither the Passive form of a Verb nor the infinitive allow Case on the following Nominal, it follows that the Nominal must be displaced to a position where Case is possible. That rules out (26), and forces the iterated movement in (22) (on the assumption that displacement must pass through the intermediate position), but allows (24) and (27). If we add further that once Case is made available then displacement is not possible, we rule out (15) as well.

Knowledge of Meaning

We have been considering some features of English syntax, with sidelong looks at cross-linguistic data. Meaning has not been neglected: on the contrary, we have appealed regularly to sameness and difference in meaning in judging various examples. But that is not to give an explicit account of meaning, to which question we now turn.

The target of semantics, like that of syntax, will be taken to be the (native) speaker's competence: she can interpret any of an unbounded range of sentences (and expressions of other categories) in such a way as to act appropriately given her understanding. Thus what mediates between the use of language and the action then undertaken will comprise the conception of meaning that we aim to capture. At dinner I ask the person on my left if she could please pass the broccoli; that is, I say, "Could you pass the broccoli?" No problem: a certain physical object containing broccoli gets moved towards me. Her understanding of my words, and the point of my remark, led her to effect a physical change in the world. How did that happen? A satisfactory account of meaning must provide a conception of understanding that fits appropriately with a general account of interactions between intentional agents.

We do not require anything as elaborate as a developed human language to illustrate meaning. It has long been known that a variety of animals have more or less elaborate signals that have meaning at least in the sense of being emitted on particular stimulus occasions, and effecting reactions on the part of the recipients of those signals. Some simple interjections of English – "ouch!" – say, may have this property as well. But our interest must turn to more elaborate matters, where so far as we know only humans have the systems that we take for granted even in small children. Whether, in light of the more developed view we take of human language, we should regard the elements of the primitive systems as truly meaningful would appear to be at best a terminological question.

When I spoke to the neighbour on my left and asked if she could pass the broccoli, I used a syntax whose final Noun admitted any number of possibilities: "Could you pass the ____." The individual Nouns will have meanings, which will combine freely with the meanings of the other items to generate the meaning of the whole. It is customary, and correct as far as is known, to distinguish sharply between *lexical* meaning, or the meaning of words in isolation, and the *combinatorics* of meaning, or the principles that determine the meanings of whole sentences and other complex phrases from the meanings of their parts. For an elementary but canonical example, consider (28):

(28)   Fido barks.

The syntax is unproblematic, and may be given as in (29):

(29)

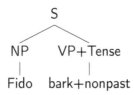

Suppose that "Fido" answers to (or, as we shall say shortly, *refers to*) a certain dog, and "barks" signifies being prone to make barking noises (however these are described). We now have the syntax and (the relevant fragment of) a dictionary. But what we want as a conclusion is something to the effect that someone who, say, makes an assertion using (28) asserts *that Fido barks*; and this we are as yet in no position to derive.

The above point may not be obvious, just because a language that we use is so transparent to us. An observation that may underscore the point is the difference between (30) and (31):

(30)   I saw John happy.

(31)   I saw happy John.

The lexical items are exactly the same in (30) and (31). But their modes of composition are different. (30) means that I saw John at a time when he appeared evidently happy to me (generally relaxed and smiling, for instance); but (31) only means that I saw some person who is known by the nickname "happy John". What is the source of the distinction here?

On reflection it is clear that in (30) the word "happy" is actually *predicated* of John, as in my informal description of the meaning, whereas in (31) it is a modifier, and there is no predication (I could see happy John sad, for instance).[7] It happens that in English the semantic distinction is correlated with constituent order.

As semantics, the study of meaning in language, is customarily practised, the central notions that are wanted for combinatorics are those of *reference* and *truth-value* (perhaps relative to various contextual parameters, as noted below). In keeping with this conception, reference will come in distinct but related forms, depending upon category of expression; but also reference will be, to put it simply but appropriately, to the publicly available things we talk about (see Chapter 7 on Context-Dependence). Thus: the reference of "John" (in an appropriate context) will be to a certain person (even if there are lots of people named "John"); the reference of a predicate will be to the things to which it properly or truly applies – "happy" applies to the things that are happy, "barks" to the things that are (at the time of speaking) prone to bark. And, finally, we conclude that the reference of (28) is truth if indeed the thing Fido is amongst the things to which "barks" truly applies, and falsehood otherwise.

Here, then, is how we fill in the gap between the syntax (29) for (28) and the referential understanding of its NP and VP+nonpast so as to derive the conclusion that we want: consider (32):

(32) For all trees Σ with root S and branches NP and VP+nonpast, and t any time, and for all x, if NP refers to x, and for any ϕ, VP+nonpast applies to an object y at t just in case ϕ applies truly to y at t, then: Σ is true just in case ϕ applies truly to x at t.

Such is the wanted combinatorial statement, which ties the dictionary entries for the ingredients of the sentence to its syntax so as to produce something that can be the content of an assertion.

The statement (32) is of course perfectly general: it says nothing about any particular items in the language. So long as NP is complete, whether a name such as "Fido" or an elaborate subject such as "the man I told you about yesterday", and so long as VP+nonpast, whether VP consists of a simple Verb or includes modifiers and complex objects, as in "falsely believes that the Yankees will win the pennant", it cranks out what happens to Σ with root S, provided only that we know how to fill in the relevant values x for NP and condition ϕ for VP+nonpast. The project of combinatorial semantics, on this view, is to elucidate the general rules, as in (32), for the interpretation of whole syntactic structures. For any *particular* example to which (32) applies, a statement of what is to be known of its truth conditions will follow once the parameters of time, NP-reference, and condition ϕ on the predicate are filled in: thus once we have said that the NP "Fido" refers to (the dog) Fido, that the time t is 1 April 2011, and that the condition on the VP+nonpast "barks" is that it applies truly to just the things that are prone to bark, we would deductively obtain (33):

(33) The (potential) utterance u of (29) on 1 April 2011 is true just in case Fido is prone to bark.

Conditions on reference and truth are bound to be sensitive to non-linguistic parameters: obviously, the reference of demonstratives such as "this" or "that", or longer phrases containing them, such as "this book", are not determined by linguistic form; similarly for many uses of the personal pronouns, and for the first person in particular. Linguistic form does contribute to reference: thus

"I" and "me" refer to their own speakers; "this" is in opposition to "that" as referring to the more proximate of two objects; and if you refer to a thing as "that ashtray" you will retract upon learning that it is a candy dish; and anyway we have already relativized truth and falsehood to time of speech in giving the combinatorial rule (32). In general, the use of a language with such context-sensitive devices would not be possible without knowledge of the context, including the knowledge and assumptions that we make about others' purposes in speaking (again, see Chapter 7 on Context-Dependence). But semantics itself tracks the specifically linguistic contributions to our speech acts, generalizing over contextual domains, and therefore leaving specific values on an occasion to be determined jointly by language and context.

We have thus far emphasized what in philosophy are often called the *cognitive* aspects of meaning; i.e., those aspects that go to determining the objects spoken of, and what properties they are said to have. Lacking such information, one is said not to know, or not fully to know, the meaning of an expression. Simple examples abound: I (and many of us) know that fuel pumps and gaskets are found in automobiles, but we don't (or didn't always) know what they are, and either now or then could not tell one from another. Still, the words were in our lexicons, and we could even use them in indirect discourse, as when we explained that the mechanic has told us that there's a leak in the gasket. Likewise, honest mistakes are possible, where we regard ourselves as corrected when the meaning is explained to us. In this regard, it is worth emphasizing that ignorance of meaning is not only lexical, but may be combinatorial as well; and that the information required for knowledge of meaning is by no means equivalent to any philosophical distinction between "truth by virtue of meaning" (analytic truth, if there is such) and "truth by virtue of the way the world is" (synthetic truth), or between necessary truth and contingent truth (see also Chapter 10, Analyticity, Apriority, Modality).

To illustrate the first point: Bowerman (1982) documents the use by children of resultative complements that overgeneralize the patterns available to adults. A resultative that is acceptable for both adult and child is (34), where the direct object of the verb is the subject of the adjectival complement:

(34)   I wiped the table clean.

The meaning of (34) is that I wiped the table, with the result that it became clean. It is easy to imagine circumstances in which I could wipe the table, with the result that it became dirty. However, the resultative complement in (35) is deviant:

(35)   I wiped the table dirty.

The sentence (35), although interpretable as a resultative, is somehow "strange". Children learning English, according to Bowerman's research, are not so inhibited as we are. She collected examples such as (36):

(36) I pulled it unstapled.

(37) I'm patting her wet.[8]

(In the latter case, one child was patting another with a wet hand.) Evidently, pulling can cause a document to become unstapled, and patting with a wet instrument can cause the pattee to be wet; so the causal nexus in (37), said to hold between action and result, is fine. What has gone wrong?

An obvious suggestion is that the resultative construction imposes a closer link between action and result than mere causation: it must be that the *purpose* of some family of actions as given by the Verb, the reason that such actions are intentionally undertaken, is to bring about the results indicated. Wiping is undertaken so as to clean things, not so as to make them dirty; patting to get them dry, not wet; and pulling may be to get them (in a literal or metaphorical sense) down, up, closed, or over, but not to bring about the unstapled state of a document. In sum, there is a teleology built into the construction that the children (aged 3–6) fail to appreciate, or so it would appear.[9]

For the second point, that the distinction to be drawn in semantic theory, viewed as articulating normal human linguistic competence, does not line up neatly with any proposed distinction between analytic and synthetic, or necessary and contingent, truth, it is sufficient, it would seem, to draw attention to the information that a competent speaker would give to someone who didn't know a word or other expression. Often, that information is perceptually imparted, and thus gives a handle on meaning through means of recognition, which may or may not be necessary. Further, local, contingent information is intuitively critical. One would not be said to know the meaning of the word "dog" who did not know that dogs are kept as pets; or so I would say.[10]

There are other elements of meaning besides reference, including but not limited to the expression of attitudes toward the objects of reference, and collateral information that is wanted to interpret figures of speech. For the first, we have epithets such as "Chink" (Chinese person), and euphemisms like "pass away" (die). The reference of the epithet or euphemism is just the reference of the expression for which it is an epithet or euphemism; but the former convey derogation, and the latter avoidance of unpleasantness. For the second, consider, "He's a regular Napoleon" (a disciplinarian), "The night is like a nun" (comforting), and many others.[11] Evidently, speakers expect others to know the point of using these expressions (even if they do not use them themselves). At an extreme end, some terms are taboo – so strong that they are not to be used or mentioned under any circumstances – but even their taboo status is, so to speak, earned through being fully understood. There is no reason for semantics to sweep aside these elements of meaning in favour of reference; note also that their understanding cannot replace reference, but actually depends upon it, as with the referential equivalence of "pass away" and "die".

Semantic Computation

We have seen that the lexicon and grammar conspire together to generate the interpretations of complex phrases, of the sentential or other categories. The fundamental objects that *have* meanings are syntactic trees, or utterances corresponding to them, decorated as it were with linguistic information: identity of lexical elements, category or word or phrase, linguistic relations of various sorts, and so on. Interest therefore attaches to the question of the nature of the principles through which interpretations of complex structures are generated from their parts. In this respect, a working assumption has been that interpretation proceeds by *local composition*, as follows.

Let Σ be a syntactic structure, and let X be a point in Σ. Σ itself, being a linguistic tree, will have a root; and any point in Σ may be viewed as the root of the syntactic structure consisting of the points dominated by X. That substructure of Σ will have X immediately dominating a sequence of (simple or complex) elements $Y_1, ..., Yn$, and they in turn may be the roots of further complex substructures. For simplicity, taking $n=2$, we might have:

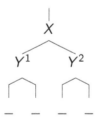

with material both above X and below Y_1 and Y_2, as indicated by the slashes. Now, these points will come with certain formal information (often taken to be given in the form of binary features), and it is evident from the simplest examples that the interpretation of X will depend upon the interpretations of Y_1 and Y_2, as "Fido barks" does upon the interpretations of "Fido" and "barks". A natural conjecture is then that X depends *only* on the interpretations of Y_1 and Y_2, and nothing else in the structure; nothing, that is, above or to the side of X, and nothing below Y_1 and Y_2 themselves. We may call this principle *local compositionality*.[12]

It is easy to devise languages for which local compositionality fails; where, for example, information not only about the meanings of Y_1 and Y_2, but also about how they were arrived at, is crucial to determining the meaning X is to have, or where the computation of the meaning of X must look up the tree to see what it is embedded within. At the same time, the standard formal languages of mathematics, e.g., the languages of Peano Arithmetic or first-order logic, are locally compositional.[13]

The assumption of local compositionality has led to a number of interesting questions about semantic computation, particularly as regards structural ambiguity: should we suppose that examples like (7) or (8), repeated below, are disambiguated at some level of structure, or that the disambiguation is effected by having multiple possibilities for semantic computation (that is, a semantics that is nondeterministic in the formal sense)?

(7)   A man went into every store.

(8)   John was reluctantly instructed by Mary.

We do not take a position on this question here. But it should be noted that, however the matter is pursued, the hypothesis of local compositionality is not only advanced as formally narrowing the abstract space of possible human languages, but also may provide a window into the acquisition of language. The learner must grasp many words only through the context of whole sentences in which they are used, and is in this sense presented with a problem in many unknowns, a set of simultaneous equations as it were. Then, just as semantic information about words may be critical for determining the meanings of sentences, so conversely information, even partial information, about sentence meaning may provide evidence for the meanings of individual words.[14]

Conclusion

In the above brief remarks I have tried to give the reader new to the subject some orientation towards, and some of the issues in, contemporary generative grammar conceived as the study of linguistic competence. Of course, I have considered only a fractional crumb of what has become over time a considerable enterprise, involving many hundreds of researchers gathering and analysing often new material. In subsequent chapters in this volume you will find far more detailed discussion than I have been able to present here. At the same time, I hope to have imparted one sense in which "figuring out how language works" is a complex undertaking, and for many an exciting journey aimed at mapping one feature of the anatomy of the human mind.

Notes

1. For a recent basic text, see Guasti (2004).
2. Chomsky has repeatedly emphasized this tension; for a recent statement see Chomsky (1995).
3. Higginbotham (1985) surveys some of the possibilities here.
4. See Merchant (2001) for a recent discussion of ellipsis and similar phenomena.
5. In this example, "guo" is (roughly) a marker of the past, and "de" a particle separating modifier from Noun. Tone marks here and elsewhere are omitted.
6. Alternatively, by a copy of the missing element, but one that has no vocal realization. We abstract from this detail in what follows.
7. The modifier is, in classical grammatical terms, *appositive*, in that the interpretation of the name is fixed independently, and the Adjective supplies a further determination. Many Nominals are ambiguous as between the appositive and the *descriptive* interpretations. Thus "the unfortunate conclusion" can be understood descriptively (the conclusion that is the unfortunate one), but perhaps occurs more frequently in apposition (the conclusion is so-and-so, and that so-and-so is unfortunate). Before names, the appositive interpretation is obligatory, as in the only natural interpretation of "the misguided Independence Party" and the like. Of course, the combinatorics of the appositive–descriptive distinction must be a target of semantic inquiry as well.
8. Bowerman (1982), 113.
9. There are other indications of teleological conceptions being "built into" complex causative constructions. It would take us too far afield to examine any of these in any detail, but I note that languages (Chinese, for example) having so-called Serial Verb constructions of the form V-V^NP, as in (to paraphrase) "cook-eat the chicken", or "bring-sell carrots", the compounding amounts to more than conjunction: the examples do not mean merely that the subject cooked the chicken and ate it, or brought the carrots and sold them, but implicate also that the chicken was cooked *in order* that it be eaten, the carrots were brought *with the intention of* selling them, and the like. Something of the same order is observed in English by omitting the Determiner in "take the cow to (the) market", "go to (the) College", and many others: one may take the cow to the market for any purpose, but to take the cow to market is to take it in order to sell it; similarly, to go to College (not "the College") is only to attend it as a student. Still another case from English is found in one class of *denominal* Verbs as "saddle (the horse)", "shelve (the book)", etc., where the purpose of the objects referred to by the Noun from which the Verb is derived, here "saddle" and "shelf", is fulfilled by the action: saddles are made for horses and other animals to be ridden, shelves for books and other things to be stored, and so forth. Hence the meaning of the Verb "saddle", for instance, is not to be paraphrased by anything so simple as "put a saddle on" – I can put a saddle on an armchair, but I can't saddle an armchair. See Higginbotham (2009) and references cited there for further discussion.
10. Hilary Putnam (1978) and elsewhere speaks of the "stereotype" associated with the term; e.g., stripes with tigers. The view I sketch here is defended at some length in Dummett (1974).

11. Of course, there is debate over the exact characterization of figures of speech and the rest. But the point of Cohen and Margalit (1972) is well-taken: metaphor and simile, and the interpretation of epithets and euphemisms, are not achievements set on top of linguistic competence, but develop and are deployed in conjunction with it, and form part of it. For further discussion of metaphor see Stern (2000) among others.
12. For some elaboration upon this theme, see Higginbotham (2007).
13. And even when they are two-dimensional, they are explained in terms of locally compositional language, as for instance

$$\int_a^b f(x)\mathrm{d}x$$

is explained as referring to $(g(x) \text{ for } x=b) - (g(x) \text{ for } x=a)$, where g is the antiderivative of f.
14. In this regard, see Gleitman (1990) and others on "syntactic bootstrapping".

References

Bowerman, Melissa (1982), "Starting to Talk Worse". In S. Strauss ed. *U-Shaped Behavioral Growth*. New York: Academic Press, 101–45.

Chomsky, Noam (1957), *Syntactic Structures*. The Hague: Mouton.

—(1965), *Aspects of the Theory of Syntax*. Cambridge, MA: The MIT Press.

—(1995), *The Minimalist Program*. Cambridge, MA: The MIT Press.

Cohen, L. Jonathan and Margalit, Avishai (1972), "The Role of Inductive Reasoning in the Interpretation of Metaphor." In D. Davidson and G. Harman (eds), *Semantics of Natural Language*. Dordrecht: Reidel, 721–62.

Dummett, Michael (1974), "What is a Theory of Meaning?" In S. Guttenplan ed. *Mind and Language*. Oxford: Oxford University Press, 97–138.

Gleitman, Lila (1990), "The Structural Sources of Verb Meanings". *Language Acquisition* 1(1), 3–55.

Guasti, Maria Teresa (2004), *Language Acquisition: The Growth of Grammar*. Cambridge, MA: The MIT Press.

Guéron, Jacqueline and Haegeman, Liliane (1998), *English Grammar: A Generative Perspective*. Oxford: Blackwell.

Harris, Zellig (1951), *Methods in Structural Linguistics*. Chicago: The University of Chicago Press.

Higginbotham, James (1985), "On Semantics". *Linguistic Inquiry* 16(4), 547–93.

—(2007), "Remarks on Compositionality". In G. Ramchand and C. Reiss (eds), *The Oxford Handbook of Linguistic Interfaces*. Oxford: Oxford University Press, 425–44.

—(2009), *Tense, Aspect, and Indexicality*. Oxford: Oxford University Press.

Merchant, Jason (2001), *The Syntax of Silence: Sluicing, Islands, and the Theory of Ellipsis*. Oxford: Oxford University Press.

Pinker, Steven (2007), *The Language Instinct: How the Mind Creates Language*. New York: HarperCollins.

Putnam, Hilary (1978), "Meaning, Reference and Stereotypes". In F. Guenthner and M. Guenthner-Reutter (eds), *Meaning and Translation: Philosophical and Linguistic Approaches*, New York: New York University Press, 61–81.

Stern, Josef (2000), *Metaphor in Context*. Cambridge, MA: The MIT Press.

3 Formal Semantics

Josh Dever

Human languages are sophisticated tools for transferring mental states from one person to another. Consider an example: Jones believes that Smith would be bored at the party tonight, because boolean algebras will be the dominant topic of conversation. She assembles a collection of words, with appropriate meanings appropriately related, into an organized structure. On the basis of that structure, she produces certain sounds by moving her mouth, throat, and diaphragm in particular ways. Smith hears those sounds and reconstructs both words and structure from them, receiving the sentence "Everyone will be talking about boolean algebras." He works out the meaning of that sentence by combining knowledge about the meanings of words and their combinations with contextual information suggesting that "everyone" here picks out those at the party. Inferring that Jones would only give him this information about the party as a warning, and taking her to be sincere and well-informed, he comes to share Jones's belief that he would be bored at the party.

An exchange of this sort can seem simple and pedestrian, because we are so adept at the skills deployed in carrying it out. But skilfulness can often mask enormous complexity in the underlying task. An analogous case: walking across a street may *seem* a simple task, but decades of work in reproducing this task in robotics has shown that bipedal walking requires a computationally and conceptually demanding integration of visual data about the environment, proprioceptive data about the bodily positioning of the walking agent, and information about a dynamic centre of gravity and proper production and distribution of forces.

The use to which Jones and Smith put language in the above exchange is complicated, and we are far from having a full theory of how this and other similar exchanges occur. It is common, however, to think that the following four stages are involved in language use:

1. **Syntax:** A theory of syntax determines rules according to which lexical items enter into valid structural arrangements, such as phrases, clauses, and complete sentences.
2. **Phonetics and Phonology:** Theories of phonetics and phonology determine the relation between a structured sequence of lexical items

and a sequence of sounds (phonology) and the physical production and auditory reception of those sound sequences (phonetics).

3. **Semantics:** A theory of semantics assigns a meaning to each structure provided by the syntactic theory (or, a meaning to each contextualized use of each structure).

4. **Pragmatics:** A theory of pragmatics determines how speakers ought to react (update their beliefs and plans of action) upon linguistic reception of a particular piece of information.

Very roughly: Jones wants Smith to know that he would be bored at the party. Jones knows that Smith is uninterested in boolean algebras, and that Smith is aware that the party is the current topic of conversation, and that what she, Jones, says will be relevant to that topic. Jones is thus, via her grasp of a theory of pragmatics, able to work out that Smith, upon receiving the information that all of some unspecified group will be talking about boolean algebras, will (a) conclude that for the claim to be relevant, the unspecified group must be the group of party-goers, and (b) realize that, given his interests, he would be bored at the party. Jones thus decides that a speech act whose semantic content is *that all of some unspecified group will be talking about boolean algebras* will meet her communicative goals. By combining her grasp of a theory of syntax and a theory of semantics, Jones is able to determine that the words "everyone", "will", "be", "talking", "about", "boolean", and "algebras" can be combined (in a particular structural arrangement) to form a sentence whose semantic content is then the desired *that all of some unspecified group will be talking about boolean algebras*. Jones then uses her grasp of a theory of phonology to map that sentence to a particular sequence of sounds, and her grasp of a theory of phonetics to determine how he should move his mouth to produce those sounds. (Of course, Jones's grasp of the theories will typically be in some sense tacit or implicit, as with her grasp of the theory of walking. She can do what needs to be done, but is not usually aware of *how* she does it.)

Smith then more or less goes through this process in reverse order. He uses a theory of phonetics to characterize his auditory perception as a sequence of sounds, and a theory of phonology to map those sounds to the sentence "Everyone will be talking about boolean algebras." With a theory of syntax, he assigns a structure to that sentence. That structure is then fed into a semantic theory, which outputs the semantic content *that all of some unspecified group will be talking about boolean algebras*. Using a pragmatic theory, Smith then determines first that the unspecified group must be the group of party-goers, and then determines that Jones wants him to know that he will be bored at the party. (As with Jones, Smith's grasp of the theories is tacit or implicit.)

The focus of this chapter will be on the semantic component of this multi-stage process. In particular, we will focus on the project of *formal semantics*.

There is no precise delineation of what counts as formal semantics. Roughly, though, formal semantics is the attempt to give precise accounts of the relation between syntactic structures and semantic values, typically while making use of tools from mathematics and logic. Many of the central ideas of formal semantics originated in giving truth definitions and model theory for formal, artificial languages, such as first-order logic or various programming languages. The model theory of a language of formal logic comes with a well-defined notion of what counts as a *meaning*, or *semantic value* – for example, predicate extensions (conceived as subsets of a model-theoretic domain) or sets of sequences (used as assignments to free variables), in the case of first-order logic. The semantic tools developed for these artificial languages have then been adapted, and extended, for natural languages as well. The goal is to produce theories that rigorously and systematically assign appropriate semantic values to natural-language constructions. The project is often coupled with the dual thoughts that (a) the attempt to produce such rigorous theories will uncover complexities in the function of natural language that might otherwise have been overlooked, and that (b) it will often then be possible to systematize those complexities under general theories of considerable elegance and explanatory power.

A Semantic Puzzle Case

Many different styles of formal semantic theories have been developed and presented. We will not attempt a systematic survey here, but will instead sample briefly from various styles in order to give a sense of the kinds of resources and methods that formal semantic theories can use. Our eventual goal in this discussion will be to see how formal semantics can aid our understanding of certain aspects of psychological attitude reports. Consider a belief report claim, such as:

(1)   John believes that the tallest spy is in Paraguay.

It is often thought that such claims are ambiguous.[1] Consider two scenarios:

1. **S1**: John's job at the CIA is to keep track of spy movements around the world. He has managed to have devices that combine GPS tracking with some basic biometric telemetry hidden on the bodies of spies around the world. Right now his tracking board shows one of the spies in Paraguay. He has no idea who the spy is, but he can tell, from the telemetry, that it is the tallest of all the spies.
2. **S2**: John's next-door neighbour Karl is 7′ 2″ tall. Unbeknownst to John,

Karl is in fact a spy. In fact, he is the world's tallest spy. Karl recently told John that he was headed off to Paraguay for vacation (in fact, he is going to Paraguay to assist with an "extraordinary rendition").

Both **S1** and **S2** look like scenarios in which John believes that the tallest spy is in Paraguay. But John believes this in different ways in the two scenarios – one indication of this is that in each scenario, while there is a sense in which John believes that the tallest spy is in Paraguay, there is also a sense in which John does *not* believe that the tallest spy is in Paraguay. In **S1**, John has a *de dicto* belief (or, John's belief is being reported in a *de dicto* manner – we will not concern ourselves here with the question of whether the relevant distinction is between kinds of beliefs or between kinds of belief reports). His belief characterizes the object of belief in a particular way (as *the tallest spy*), but he does not know who it is that is so characterized. (In at least some sense of *knowing who*.) (In fact, *de dicto* beliefs are compatible with there in fact being no object so characterized. There might, for example, be no spies – perhaps John is the victim of a massive scheme of international deception – and hence no tallest spy.) In **S2**, John has a *de re* belief. His belief is about a certain object, and in reporting on the belief we characterize that object in a certain way, but without requiring that John think of the object in that way, or realize that it can be so characterized. (The *de re* sense can be emphasized by the construction:

(2)   John believes of the tallest spy that he is in Paraguay.

but is available also in the construction (1).)

What is wanted, then, is a theory that can in a systematic way assign two distinct meanings to (1). Crafting such a theory involves both a conceptual component – working out what sort of things meanings are, and how they are related to data such as truth in a scenario – and an engineering component – working out how to assign meanings to linguistic expressions on the basis of their internal syntactic structure.

Possible Worlds Semantics

This is a tall task. We will begin with something much more humble: giving a very simple first-draft meaning theory for a fragment of the language. From that humble beginning, we will work up a step at a time towards the more ambitious goal. Here, then, is a starting thought. We want meanings to determine truth conditions for utterances. Suppose, then, that we have a notion of a *possible world*.[2] We associate each sentence in the language with a set of possible worlds – namely, the worlds at which that sentence is true. Such a set would provide at least a decent first approximation to truth conditions.

For this idea to be realized in a theory, we want a systematic method of making the required association. In particular, it is standard to assume that we want a finite set of basic principles from which we can, for any given sentence, calculate the associated set of possible worlds. The formal semantic theory is meant to be an articulation of something both (a) *known* (albeit tacitly) to competent speakers, and (b) *acquired* by speakers via contact with a finite sample of the language. Both of these features – and especially the second – seem to point toward a finite theory.[3] Since natural languages have an infinite number of sentences, this means, minimally, that our formal theory cannot simply consist of a list pairing sentences with sets of possible worlds. This is the first of a collection of ideas deriving from formal semantical considerations that we will set out as we proceed:

- **Idea #1**: Human linguistic understanding is an infinite capacity, but must be a capacity with a finite origin. Thus we want a semantic theory that, on the basis of a finite collection of basic principles, assigns semantic values to each of an infinite number of sentences in the language.

Suppose, then, that we have a language **L** that has a finite list $s_1, ..., s_n$ of simple (atomic) sentences. Let **L** contain the truth-functional connectives ¬, ∧, ∨, and →, and allow creation of complex sentences from these connectives using the following syntax:

1. (**R1**) Every simple sentence s_i is a sentence.
2. (**R2**) If A is a sentence, then ¬A is also a sentence.
3. (**R3**) If A and B are sentences, then $(A \land B)$, $(A \lor B)$, and $(A \to B)$ are also sentences.

This syntax produces infinitely many sentences from the initial stock of simple sentences. A possible world can then be taken to be an assignment of truth value to each simple sentence. We can write $w(i) = T$ to show that possible world w assigns truth to simple sentence s_i, and $w(i) = F$ to show that w assigns falsity to s_i. Let $[A]$ symbolize the set of possible worlds assigned by the theory to a given sentence A. Then the behavior of $[\cdot]$ is fully determined by the following basic principles:

1. (**P1**) For a simple sentence s_i, $[s_i] = \{w : w(i) = T\}$.
2. (**P2**) For any sentence A, $[\neg A] = W - [A]$. (Where W is the set of all possible worlds.)
3. (**P3**) For any sentences A and B, $[A \land B] = [A] \cap [B]$.

4. **(P4)** For any sentences A and B, $[A \vee B] = [A] \cup [B]$.
5. **(P5)** For any sentences A and B, $[A \rightarrow B] = (W - [A]) \cup [B]$.

This little theory is a bare-bones version of *possible worlds semantics*. It incorporates two ideas that each play an important role in some versions of formal semantics:

- **Idea #2**: The meaning of a complex expression is a systematic function of the meanings of its component parts. Thus, syntax and semantics go hand-in-hand: the syntactic structure of an expression is a roadmap for the calculation of the semantic value of that expression.
- **Idea #3**: Meanings can be constructed from truth conditions, conceived as functions from possible situations to truth values.

This little theory allows us to use some basic set theory to extract some simple semantic predictions. For example, we have:

$$[\neg A \vee \neg B] = [\neg A] \cup [\neg B]$$
$$= (W - [A]) \cup (W - [B])$$
$$= W - ([A] \cap [B])$$
$$= W - [A \wedge B]$$
$$= [\neg(A \wedge B)].$$

The semantic theory thus predicts the semantic equivalence of a negated conjunction with the disjunction of the negated conjuncts. In similar fashion, it can shown that any two logically equivalent sentences have the same semantic value. This prediction isn't without some problems. While logically equivalent sentences clearly have *something* in common, full synonymy may seem like too tight a connection. A robust literature on the so-called *problem of logical omniscience* has arisen in response.[4] But even with some problems, it's not bad for a first attempt.

Another prediction: define @, the *actual world*, to be the world that assigns truth to a sentence s_i just in case s_i is, in fact, true. Then we can define truth for sentences:

- A sentence A is true if and only if @ $\in [A]$.

Consider a sentential connective * – either a one-place connective, combining with a single sentence A to form a complex sentence *A, or a two-place connective, combining with two sentences A and B to form a complex sentence $(A * B)$. * is an *extensional* connective if, whenever A and C have the same truth value, *A and *C have the same truth value, and $(A * B)$ and $(C * B)$ have the

same truth value (and similarly when *B* and *C* have the same truth value). Extensional connectives, that is, allow substitution of materially equivalent sentences in their immediate scope *salva veritate*. Our toy theory has the easy consequence that ¬, ∧, ∨, and → are all extensional connectives.

Modals

The above formal semantic theory is a bare-bones version of *possible worlds semantics*.[5] From these humble beginnings, additional elements can be added to the theory. We can easily, for example, add modal operators to the language. The most straightforward way to do this adds a *might*, or *possibly*, sentential operator ◊, and a *must*, or *necessarily* sentential operator □, by adding the basic principles:

1. **(P6)** For any sentence *A*, $[\![\Diamond A]\!] = \{w : [\![A]\!] \cap W \neq \varnothing\}$.
2. **(P7)** For any sentence *A*, $[\![\Box A]\!] = \{w : W \subseteq [\![A]\!]\}$.

These simple principles have the consequence that a sentence of the form *Might A* is true if and only if *A* is true at some possible world, and a sentence of the form *Must A* is true if and only if *A* is true at every possible world.

However, attention to the behaviour of modal vocabulary in natural languages quickly shows that this semantic analysis is *too* simple. *Must* and *might* introduce modalities of a variety of flavours:[6]

1. **Deontic**: You must cross the street at the crosswalk.
2. **Circumstantial**: You must water your tomato plants for them to remain healthy.
3. **Epistemic**: There might be life on other planets.
4. **Metaphysical**: McCain might have been president.
5. **Preferential**: We might go see a Godard movie tonight.
6. **Dispositional**: If you must sneeze, please cover your mouth.

Since the same sentence will typically have different truth conditions when the modal is given (for example) an epistemic rather than a deontic reading, the simple principles **(P6)** and **(P7)** must not be the whole story. Even once a flavour of modality has been settled, truth conditions can still vary. The same epistemic-modal-containing sentence can be true when uttered by one speaker and false when uttered by another, if the evidence base of the two speakers differs. The same circumstantial-modal-containing sentence can be true in one context and false in another context, if standards of strictness change across contexts. (*Must* you water your tomato plants for them to remain healthy? The answer may depend, for example, on how salient the possibility of drought is.) Finally, *must* and *might* are far from the only modals in the language. Other modals such as *normally, can, ought,* or *probably* will require semantic analyses going beyond the simple principles (**P6**) and (**P7**).[7]

Here is a slightly (but only slightly) more sophisticated theory of modals. Take each modal to be associated with a *modal base*. Roughly, a modal base is a set of possible worlds: those worlds that are relevant to the particular flavour (and contextualized use) of the modal in question. More carefully, a modal base is a function from possible worlds to sets of possible worlds, giving in each possible situation those worlds that are, in that situation, relevant to the particular modal flavour in question.[8] Sentences can now be assigned sets of possible worlds *relative to a modal base*. Instead of the simple $[A]$ – the set of possible worlds assigned to sentence A – we have $[A]^g$ – the set of worlds assigned to sentence A relative to modal base g. For sentences without modals, the relativization to modal bases will have no effect. Thus our earlier principle (**P1**) is given an idling modification:

1. (**P1g**): For a simple sentence s_i, $[s_i]^g = \{w : w(i) = T\}$

Because g does not appear on the right-hand side of the identity, the choice of modal base makes no difference to the semantic value assigned to s^i. The situation is the same for (**P2**) – (**P5**). The principles for modals, however, make non-trivial use of the modal base:

1. (**P6g**) For any sentence A, $[\Diamond A]^g = \{w : g(w) \cap [A]^g \neq \varnothing\}$.
2. (**P7g**) For any sentence A, $[\Box A]^g = \{w : g(w) \subseteq [A]^g\}$.

For example, given a modal base that maps each world to the possible worlds that are moral exemplars for that world, $\Box A$ will have as its content all of those worlds in which A is true at all moral exemplars, and thus will express the deontic necessity of A.

A modal base determines a set of relevant worlds for a modal. Some modals may require, in addition to a set of relevant worlds, also an organization of worlds into *closer* and *farther*, or *more and less significant*. *Normally* and *probably*, for example, can be analysed using an ordering of worlds, with these modals placing constraints on the closer worlds. We will set aside issues arising from ordering sources in the remainder of this discussion.

The modal base semantics assigns semantic values relative to a modal base. How are we to understand this extra parameter? For example, how do we now define truth for sentences? The previous definition will now make truth, too, relative to a modal base:

- A sentence A is true relative to g if and only if $@ \in [A]^g$.

But surely we want a notion of truth *simpliciter* – in part so that our semantics can properly interact with our pragmatics, which may contain principles such as *assert only that which you know to be true*. One obvious suggestion is that we have here a specific instance of a very general phenomenon of *context sensitivity* in natural languages. The context sensitivity of modals is rather subtle; much context sensitivity in language is considerably more overt, such as that of indexical expressions such as "I", "you" and "here".[9] To model context sensitivity we will want a representation of context. Some context-sensitive aspects of language, such as overt indexicals, will demand a representation of context that springs primarily from the environmental situation of the utterance (facts about the producer of, the location of, and the time of the utterance, for example). Other context-sensitive devices in language will place different demands on the representation of context – modals, on the current approach, will impose the requirement that the context in which a sentence is used contain information sufficient to determine a modal base. The semantic content of a contextualized utterance of a sentence is then the semantic content of that sentence relative to the contextually-determined modal base, and the truth value of a contextualized utterance is the truth value of the uttered sentence relative to the contextually-determined modal base. Here we have another idea:

- **Idea #4**: Context-sensitivity of language can be modelled in a formal semantic theory by assigning semantic values relative to a context, or by assigning semantic values that are functions from contexts to more standard semantic values. A semantic theory of this sort will then engage with a theory of pragmatics that determines, for a particular speech situation, what the context is that fills the function's argument place.

Belief Contexts

The semantic techniques that are used for modals can be used for other expressions that are not obviously modal in nature. In particular, belief contexts can be treated as a kind of intensional context.[10] Given a person P, let W_p be a function from worlds to sets of worlds such that $W_p(w)$ is the set of worlds that are consistent with everything P believes in w – call these P's *belief worlds*. Then we can say:

1. **(P8)** $[P$ believes that $A] = \{w : W_p(w) \subseteq [A]\}$.

P believes that A is then true (in the sense that $@ \in [P$ believes that $A]$) just in case every one of P's belief worlds (in the actual world) is an A world – that is, just in case every world consistent with what P (actually) believes is a world that makes A true.

This semantic theory for belief context has some immediate consequences:

1. **Belief contexts are non-extensional**: Suppose A and B have the same truth value. Thus either $@ \in [A]$ and $@ \in [B]$, or $@ \notin [A]$ and $@ \notin [B]$. But suppose $[A] \neq [B]$, so A and B are not intensionally identical, or synonymous. In particular, suppose there is a world w such that $w \in [A]$, but $w \notin [B]$. If we have $W_P (@) = [A]$, then we will trivially have P *believes that A* true. But P *believes that B* will be false, because $W_P (@)$ is not a subset of $[B]$ (since w is in the first but not in the second), and hence $@ \notin [P$ believes that $B]$). Thus sameness of truth value does not guarantee intersubstitutability in a belief context. This is a good result – just because P believes one true sentence, it does not follow that he believes every true sentence.

2. **Belief contexts are sensitive to the believing agent**: Let P and Q be two persons. Since W^P and W^Q are just two independent functions from worlds to sets of worlds, it is straightforward, for a given sentence A, to set things up such that P *believes that A* is true and Q *believes that A* is false. We could, for example, let $W_P (@) = [A]$, and let $W_Q (@) = [\neg A]$. Again, this is a good result. Different people have different beliefs, and an adequate formal semantics should make it easy to vary the truth value of belief reports as the believing agent varies.

3. **Beliefs are closed under logical consequence**: If P believes A_1 and A_2, and A_1 and A_2 jointly entail some sentence B, then the semantic theory is committed to the claim that P also believes B. If A_1 and A_2 jointly entail B, then any world in which A_1 and A_2 are true is a world in which B is true. Thus $[A_1] \cap [A_2] \subseteq [B]$. Since P believes A_1, $W_P (@) \subseteq [A_1]$. Since P believes A_2, $W_P (@) \subseteq [A_2]$. Thus $W^P (@) \subseteq [A_1] \cap [A_2]$. It then follows that $W^P (@) \subseteq [B]$, and hence that P believes that B.

Is this a good result? It entails, for example, that anyone who believes a conjunction believes both conjuncts, and that anyone who believes both conjuncts of a conjunction also believes the conjunction. Those seem like good results. On the other hand, it entails that anyone who believes all of the axioms of set theory also believes all of the theorems of mathematics – a rather less impressive result. The question of the extent to which beliefs are closed under any form of logical entailment is a difficult one, and the current theory certainly gives a rather naive answer to that question.

We now have a basic theory of belief reports, but the theory won't yet help in explaining our guiding puzzle of John's belief about the tallest spy. With our current tools, all we can do is ask whether the semantic value assigned to

The tallest spy is in Paraguay has John's belief worlds as a subset. We have no method available for assigning *two distinct* readings to the belief report.

Type-Theoretic Semantics

To remedy this problem, we need to add techniques for dealing with *subsentential structure*. The formal semantic theories sketched so far take as their starting point a collection of atomic sentences, and then construct and analyse complex sentences built from those atoms. But a more thorough theory will take individual words as starting points, and then build up meanings of larger expressions, including the simplest sentences, from the meanings of their component words. What would such a theory look like? Let's begin with easy cases, such as the sentence:

(3)   Mary snores.

Here are two assumptions to guide the construction of a semantic theory intended to cover this sentence, and others like it:

1. The semantic value of whole sentences should (still) be sets of possible worlds.
2. The semantic value of a proper name, like "Mary", is the object/person to which the name refers.

Both of these assumptions are controversial, but they serve as plausible and helpful starting points. Importantly, together they tightly constrain the semantic value of the other sentential component, "snores". That semantic value must combine with the semantic value of "Mary" (the person Mary) to determine the semantic value of "Mary snores" (the set of possible worlds in which Mary snores). "Snore" could thus be assigned:

- A set of ordered pairs $< x, w >$ of objects and worlds, where $< x, w > \in \llbracket snores \rrbracket$ iff x snores in w.
- A function from objects to sets of worlds, where $w \in \llbracket snores \rrbracket(x)$ iff x snores in w.
- A function from objects to a function from worlds to truth values, where $\llbracket snores \rrbracket(x)(w) = T$ iff x snores in w.

There is, obviously, little to choose from among these formally interchangeable options. As a formal convenience, we will adopt the third.[11] This formulation has the advantage of beginning a systematic procedure of calculating semantic values of complex expressions via functional application of the semantic value of one component of the complex on the semantic value of another component. Thus:

- $[Mary\ snores] = [snores]([Mary])$

(This then requires that the semantic value of a sentence be a function from worlds to truth values, rather than a set of worlds. However, functions from worlds to truth values and sets of worlds are immediately interchangeable, by taking the function to be the characteristic function of the set.)

Generalizing, proper names have objects as semantic values, sentences have functions from worlds to truth values as semantic values, and intransitive verbs have functions from objects to functions from worlds to truth values as semantic values. But how do we proceed as sentences become more complex? Consider two slight increases in complexity:

(4)   Mary snores loudly.

(5)   Mary admires Susan.

How should we work out the semantic contribution of the adverb "loudly", or of the transitive verb "admires"? It would be nice to have a systematic way of determining at least the *type* of semantic value needed.

Here is a method. Begin with the two assumptions above. Proper names have objects as semantic value; sentences have functions from worlds to truth values. Combine these assumptions with the principle that semantic values of complexes are the result of functional application of one component's semantic value to another component's semantic value. Then work backwards through the syntactic structure of the sentence in question. Assume, for example, that "Mary admires Susan" has the syntactic structure:

- 1. [Mary [admires [Susan]]]

No very sophisticated syntactic theory is needed (or used!) here – all we need is that the immediate components of "Mary admires Susan" are "Mary" and "admires Susan", and that the components of "admires Susan" are "admires" and "Susan". Then we reason as follows:

1. $[Mary\ admires\ Susan]$ is a function from worlds to truth values. That semantic value must be either (a) the result of applying $[Mary]$ to $[admires\ Susan]$, or (b) the result of applying $[admires\ Susan]$ to $[Mary]$.

2. $\lceil$Mary$\rceil$ is an object, and hence not a function. It thus cannot be applied to anything, and option (a) is ruled out.
3. So we must have $\lceil$Mary admires Susan$\rceil$ = $\lceil$admires Susan$\rceil$($\lceil$Mary$\rceil$).
4. Since $\lceil$Mary$\rceil$ is an object and $\lceil$Mary admires Susan$\rceil$ is a function from worlds to truth values, $\lceil$admires Susan$\rceil$ must be a function from objects to functions from worlds to truth values.
5. The semantic value of "admires Susan" must be either (a) the result of applying $\lceil$Susan$\rceil$ to $\lceil$admires$\rceil$, or (b) the result of applying $\lceil$admires$\rceil$ to $\lceil$Susan$\rceil$.
6. $\lceil$Susan$\rceil$ is an object, and hence not a function. It thus cannot be applied to anything, and option (a) is ruled out.
7. So we must have $\lceil$admires Susan$\rceil$ = $\lceil$admires$\rceil$($\lceil$Susan$\rceil$).
8. Since $\lceil$Susan$\rceil$ is an object and $\lceil$admires Susan$\rceil$ is a function from objects to functions from worlds to truth values, $\lceil$admires$\rceil$ must be a function from objects to functions from objects to functions from worlds to truth values.

"A function from objects to functions from objects to functions from worlds to truth values" is a bit of a mouthful. Let's add some notation to make it easier to keep track of complicated semantic values such as these. Let e (for *entity*) be the set of objects (the referents of proper names). Let i (for *intension*) be the set of functions from worlds to truth values (the meanings of whole sentences). Any proper name then has a semantic value of type e; any sentence has a semantic value of type i. We can then construct other semantic values from the starting point of e and i. Let (e, i), for example, be the set of functions from items of type e to items of type i – that is, functions from objects to functions from worlds to truth values. Then any intransitive verb has a semantic value of type (e, i).

More generally, we have the following idea:

- **Idea #5**: The collection of all semantic values we need to analyse arbitrary lexical, complex subsentential, and sentential expressions can be systematically generated from the starting point of the two basic types e and i. Let α and β be any two types. Then (α, β) is an additional type: the type of functions from things of type α to things of type β. Functions from objects to functions from objects to functions from worlds to truth values are then items of type $(e, (e, i))$. Types of increasing elaborateness can then easily be constructed by iterating the parenthesis notation.[12]

Types and the Syntax–Semantics Interface

The type of the semantic value of the whole sentence must be i. Now consider any complex component expression E of the whole sentence (including the sentence itself). Suppose that complex expression is the syntactic result of combining two component expressions E_1 and E_2, and that the complex expression has a semantic value of type α, for any α. Since semantic values combine via functional application, E_1 and E_2 must have semantic values of type (β, α) and β, for some β. Working our way down the syntactic tree for the sentence, we can work out possible semantic value types for all of the parts of the sentence.

So consider "Mary snores loudly". Suppose the syntactic structure of that sentence is:

- 1. [Mary [snores [loudly]]]

The whole sentence is of type i, and "Mary" is of type e, so "snores loudly" is of type (e, i). Thus one of "snores" and "loudly" must be of type $(\beta, (e, i))$ and the other of type β, for some β. We don't yet know which is of which type, and what type β is, so the semantic typing isn't yet fully determined. But we have independent reason, from consideration of the sentence "Mary snores", to think that "snores" is of type (e, i). If this is right, then "snores" is not of type $(\beta, (e, i))$ for any β, so it must be the expression of type β, and the particular β in question must be (e, i). Thus "loudly" must be of type $((e, i), (e, i))$.

To know the types of the semantic values is not yet to know the specific semantic values within those types. $\lfloor Mary \rfloor$ is of type e, and hence is an object. But that is not yet to say which object it is. To assign specific semantic values, we must also consider the truth conditions of the sentence "Mary snores loudly". These truth conditions then lead to the following assignment:

- $\lfloor \text{Mary} \rfloor$ = Mary
- $\lfloor \text{snores} \rfloor$ = the function that maps each object x to a function that assigns to a world w the true if and only if x snores in w. Such a function is equivalent to a function that maps each object to the set of worlds in which that object snores. Roughly speaking, we can think of semantic values of type (e, i) as being *properties* – in this case, the property of snoring.
  – Some notation to make this kind of specification of functions easier: take an arbitrary sentence, such as "John owns a car ". Then take a name that appears in that sentence, such as "John", and replace it with a variable, such as x. Finally, prefix to the modified sentence a *lambda-extract operator* λx. The result is $\lambda x(x$ owns a car$)$. This expression represents a function that takes as input an object o, and produces as output the truth value of the sentence "x owns a car ", when x is taken to refer to o.
     The semantic value of of "snores" can then be given, using this λ-notation, as $\lambda x \lambda w(x$ snores in $w)$.[13]
- $\lfloor \text{loudly} \rfloor$ is the following rather complicated function f. f takes as input a

function g that maps an object to a set of worlds (i.e., to a function from worlds to truth values). f then produces as output a function h that takes each object o to those worlds w in which o has whatever feature caused f to map o to a set of worlds including w, and in addition has that feature loudly.

– It should be obvious that this specification of the semantic value of "loudly" is far from unproblematic. The appeal to a *feature causing a function to map an input to an output* is not, in the end, legitimate, since we have done nothing elsewhere in the semantics to ground such talk of features and causation. Furthermore, it is not at all obvious that, for example, snoring loudly is the same as having loudly the feature of snoring (or, indeed, that the latter makes sense at all). This leads to another idea:

- **Idea #6**: By pursuing a thorough and rigorous formal semantic theory, we can discover unexpected complications in the language. At a first glance, one might have thought that adjectives and adverbs would function semantically in much the same way. But when we attempt to describe both adjectives and adverbs in the type-theoretical framework, we discover that adverbs create complications that don't arise with adjectives, and are forced to better understand the language to deal with those complications. That better understanding can then have interesting further consequences. The most prominent formal semantic method for analyzing adverbs is to take verbs to introduce *events*, and then to take adverbs as, in effect, adjectives describing events.[14] "Mary snores loudly", on this approach, becomes equivalent to "There is a snoring event that is loud, and that has Mary as its agent". Careful attention to the formal semantic details, then, allows us to uncover a ubiquitous tacit ontology of events in natural languages.

- $[$snores loudly$]$ is then determined by functional application of $[$loudly$]$ on $[$snores$]$, and is thus the function that maps each object o to those worlds w in which o has the feature that caused $[$snores$]$ to map o to a set of worlds including w, and moreover has that feature loudly. Since (in a world w) the feature that causes $[$snores$]$ to map o to a set of worlds including w is the feature of snoring in w, this then simplifies to: the function that maps each object o to those worlds in which o snores, and does so loudly.

- $[$Mary snores loudly$]$ is, finally, determined by functional application of $[$snores loudly$]$ on $[$Mary$]$, and is thus the set of worlds in which Mary snores loudly.

Quantified Noun Phrases

How, in this type-theoretical setting, are we to understand *quantified noun phrases* such as "every philosopher " and "some linguist"? These noun phrases have the same syntactic distribution as proper names like "Mary":

(6)   Mary snores.

(7)   Every philosopher snores.

(8)   Some linguist snores.

One option, then, is to give them the same semantic type as "Mary" – type *e*. But if "some linguist" is of type *e*, then ⌈some linguist⌉ is an object. Which object could it be? No *particular* linguist will yield the right truth conditions, since, for each particular linguist, "Some linguist snores" can be true even if that linguist does not snore. So ⌈some linguist⌉ must be some strange new object – the *arbitrary linguist*, perhaps, distinct from every particular linguist. But this is a *very* strange object. Since "Some linguist snores" is true, the arbitrary linguist must snore. But since "Some linguist does not snore" is also true, the arbitrary linguist must not snore, and hence must have contradictory properties. Reasoning along the same lines, we will find that ⌈every philosopher⌉ is a different kind of strange object – one which for many properties P, has neither P nor not-P.[15]

The careful formal semantic analysis of language may uncover unexpected metaphysical commitments lurking in our linguistic practice, but it would be nice if the commitments were not quite this outrageous. Fortunately, there is another option. Our analysis of "Mary snores" commits us to ⌈snores⌉ being of type (e, i). ⌈Some linguist snores⌉ is of type i, and must be either (a) the result of functional application of ⌈snores⌉ to ⌈some linguist⌉, or (b) functional application of ⌈some linguist⌉ to ⌈snores⌉. The first option requires ⌈some linguist⌉ to be of type e, which then leads to the strange objects described above. But the second option requires ⌈some linguist⌉ to be of type $((e, i), i)$, and hence does not require "some linguist" to refer to an object.

Let's explore the possibility of giving quantified noun phrases semantic values of type $((e, i), i)$. Recall that a semantic value of type (e, i) is, roughly, a property (something that, given a world, determines a set of objects that have that property at that world). A semantic value of type $((e, i), i)$ can thus be thought of as a function from properties to functions from worlds to truth values, or a function from property-world pairs to truth values, or, roughly, a property of properties. But *which* properties of properties? Suppose, plausibly, that "Some linguist snores" is true. Then we need @ ∈ ⌈some linguist snores⌉, which means we need ⌊some linguist⌋ to be a property of properties such that the property ⌊snores⌋ (that is, the property of snoring) has, in the actual world, that (second-order) property. And the same holds for *any* property Q. If the sentence "'Some philosopher Q's" is true, then ⌊some philosopher⌋ must be a second-order property that is instantiated, in the actual world, by Q. Thus we have:

- ⌊some philosopher⌋ is the second-order property of *being a property that some philosopher has.*

Let's suppose that common nouns, such as "linguist", have semantic values of type (e, i) (they express properties, such as the property of *being a linguist*. Since "some linguist" is of type $((e, i), i)$, the determiner "some" must be of type $((e, i), ((e, i), i))$. "Some", that is, is a function that takes a property to a property of properties. We can specify the proper function for "some" as follows:

- ⌊some⌋ takes as input a property P and produces as output the second-order property of *being a property that has a non-empty intersection with P.*

A bit of thought shows that the proper semantic value for "every" is:

- ⌊every⌋ takes as input a property P and produces as output the second order property of *being a property that has P as a subset.*

There are many properties of properties, so we now have a robust space of possible semantic values for quantified noun phrases, and hence for determiners, to take.[16] We can have, for example:

1. ⌊most⌋ takes a property P to the second-order property of being a property whose overlap with P is larger than its overlap with not-P.
2. ⌊no⌋ takes a property P to the second-order property of being a property that has an empty intersection with P.
3. ⌊at most three⌋ takes a property P to the second-order property of being a property whose overlap with P contains at most three objects.
4. ⌊the⌋ takes a property P to the second-order property of being a property such that property P holds of exactly one object, and holding of that object.

The discovery of this space of possible quantified noun phrases points to another idea:

- **Idea #7**: A formal semantic theory can provide not only specific semantic values for specific lexical items, but also categories of semantic values.

Identifying these categories can then aid in identifying diverse constructions or lexical items as sharing a semantic structure, or in guiding
cross-linguistic investigation into appearances of other members of the
same category.

We can also characterize general features of quantified noun phrases. For
example, there is a class of *monotone increasing* quantified noun phrases:

- **Monotone increasing**: A quantified noun phrase QNP is monotone
  increasing if, given any property P that instantiates $[QNP]$ and any
  property Q such that every instance of P is an instance of Q, it follows that
  Q also instantiates $[QNP]$.[17]

"Some", "every" and "most" all produce monotone increasing quantified
noun phrases. Monotone increasing phrases support inferences of the general
form:

1. Some linguists own red cars. Therefore, some linguists own cars.
2. Every philosopher owns a red car. Therefore, every philosopher owns a
   car.
3. Most mathematicians own a red car. Therefore, most mathematicians own
   a car.

"No", "at most three" and "exactly two", on the other hand, are not monotone
increasing, and do not support this inference form:

1. No linguist owns a red car. But it does not follow that no linguist owns a
   car.
2. At most three philosophers own a red car. But it does not follows that at
   most three philosophers own a car.
3. Exactly two mathematicians own a red car. But it does not follow that
   exactly two mathematicians own a car.

The flip side of monotone increasing phrases are *monotone decreasing* phrases:

- A quantified noun phrase QNP is monotone decreasing if, given any
  property P that instantiates $[QNP]$ and any property Q such that every
  instance of Q is an instance of P, it follows that Q also instantiates $[QNP]$.

"No" and "at most three" both produce monotone decreasing phrases, and
such phrases support the opposite direction of the inferences supported by
monotone increasing phrases:

1. No linguist owns a car. Therefore, no linguist owns a red car.
2. At most three philosophers own a car. Therefore, at most three philosophers own a red car.

The categories of monotone decreasing and monotone increasing quantified noun phrases have a number of predictive applications. For example, many natural languages contain *negative polarity items*, which can be used only in a negative environment.[18] "Ever" is a negative polarity item in English. Compare the acceptable:

(9)   Albert does not ever read Hegel.

to the unacceptable:

(10)   *Albert does ever read Hegel.

But a precise characterization of "negative environments" is difficult. A helpful first step can be made by observing that monotone decreasing quantified noun phrases, but not monotone increasing and not non-monotonic phrases, license negative polarity items. So compare the acceptable:

(11)   At most three philosophers ever read Hegel.

with the unacceptable:

(12)   *At least three philosophers ever read Hegel.

and:

(13)   *Exactly three philosophers ever read Hegel.

The formal semantic framework thus predicts that a determiner newly introduced to English, or a determiner in a newly discovered language, will license negative polarity items if it produces monotone decreasing quantified noun phrases. Here we see:

- **Idea #8**: Careful formal semantic theorizing can bear fruit by bringing into engagement phenomena from distinct parts of the language. We start with two puzzles: how to provide semantic values for quantified noun phrases, and how to characterize the environments in which negative polarity items can appear. But these two puzzles interact, since the syntactic flexibility of the language allows the possibility of quantified noun phrases being one of the licensing environments. That interaction then allows formal tools from one phenomenon to inform theorizing about the other phenomenon, and provides indirect confirmation for theories of both areas, by showing that those two theories interact well.

Scope Ambiguities

Among the determiners set out above was the definite article "the". Given the central role of the definite description "the tallest spy" in our problematic belief report, this is a promising step toward a formal semantic analysis of the ambiguity. But it is only a first step, since our tools still assign a single semantic value to every sentence and thus fail to capture ambiguity. As a first step toward the desired ambiguity, we consider scope ambiguities arising from multiple quantified noun phrases. Consider the sentence:

(14)   Every philosopher admires some linguist.

This sentence has two readings. On what we will call the "$\forall\exists$" reading, it requires that each philosopher have a linguist he admires, but allows that different philosopher may admire different linguists. On the $\exists\forall$ reading, it requires that there be a single linguist who is admired by every philosopher. How can we use the type-theoretic formal semantics given above to capture these two readings? We begin by noting that there is a typing problem created by quantified noun phrases in direct object, rather than subject, position. Recall that we have typed quantified noun phrases $((e, i), i)$, and transitive verbs $(e, (e, i))$. The crude syntactic structure of (14) is [[Every philosopher] [admires [some linguist]]. Thus "admires" and "some linguist" must semantically combine. But the two types $((e, i), i)$ and $(e, (e, i))$ cannot combine in either order. The first requires an argument of type (e, i), and the second of type e. Thus the current framework simply fails to assign semantic values to expressions with quantified noun phrases in direct object position.

One approach (among many) to this problem begins with the syntax. The ambiguity between the $\forall\exists$ and $\exists\forall$ reading will for many people already be familiar as a *scope ambiguity* – roughly, an ambiguity resulting for two possible processing orders for the two quantifiers. In a formal system like first-order logic, the ambiguity is eliminated through a syntax in which quantifier sequencing is mandatorily determined by the linear ordering of the quantifiers in the sentence. $\forall x \exists y\, Rxy$ receives only the $\forall\exists$ reading, and $\exists y \forall x\, Rxy$ receives only the $\exists\forall$ reading. In English, the processing order of quantifiers need not match their linear ordering (hence the availability of a $\exists\forall$ reading of (14).

But we can reproduce in English the formal-system solution of matching linear ordering and processing ordering of quantifiers if we adopt a bolder syntactic theory. The *surface form* of (14) has the two quantifiers in a specific linear ordering (namely, universal followed by existential). But many syntactic theories posit hidden levels of syntactic representation, in which the components of a sentence may not appear in the same positions as they do in surface form. For example, a syntactic theory may incorporate a rule of *Quantifier Raising*, or **QR**:

- **QR**: There is a syntactic level of representation called *Logical Form*, or **LF**. **LF** is derived from surface form via the application of a rule **QR**. **QR** requires each quantified noun phrase to be *moved* from its position in surface form and *adjoined* to a **S**(entence) structure of which it is, in surface form, a part.[19]

Consider first a simple example. The sentence:

(15)   Albert sees many logicians.

contains a quantified noun phrase in direct object position. Suppose the surface form syntactic organization of (15) is:

- (15s) [$_S$ [$_{NP}$ Albert] [$_{VP}$ [$_{TV}$ sees] [$_{NP}$ many logicians]]]

"Many logicians" must then, at the level of **LF**, move out of its surface position and adjoin to the **S** node at the root of the syntactic tree. Adjoining an expression to an **S** node involves (a) creating a new **S** node, and (b) placing both the adjoined expression and the original **S** node immediately below then new **S** node. The result of applying **QR** to (15) is then:

- (15l) [$_S$ [$_{NP}$ many logicians*t*] [$_S$ [$_{NP}$ Albert] [$_{VP}$ [$_{TV}$ sees] [$_{NP}$ t]]]]

When "many logicians" moves from its surface position, it leaves behind a *trace* – an "invisible" lexical item without any phonological content.[20]

Why should we accept a quantifier raising story about syntax? Here are some basic considerations:

1. Consider the behaviour of wh-phrases in English, such as "which linguist" and "what philosopher". These phrases seem to undergo movement already at surface form. Thus in:

    (16) Which linguist does John admire?
    the phrase "which linguist" appears to be displaced from its natural location after "admires" (since it is the direct object of that verb) to an initial position adjoined to the main **S**. Similarly with imbedded questions, as in:

(17) John knows what philosopher Mary met.

in which "what philosopher " again appears displaced from its natural location after "met". This initial impression of movement can be bolstered by considering case assignment. Thus compare:

(18) John knows whom Mary met.

(19) *John knows who Mary met.

The mandatory accusative case on "whom" is explained if "whom" begins life as the direct object of "met", and then undergoes movement to the adjoined position. Another consideration: compare the pair:

(20) Which philosopher does John wanna invite to the party?

(21) *Which philosopher does John wanna invite Susan to the party?

In (20), but not in (21), the informal contraction of "want to" to "wanna" is acceptable. The difference in acceptability is explicable if we assume that, in both sentences, the wh-phrase "which philosopher " is displaced from an original position:

(22) John wants to invite which philosopher to the party?

(23) John wants which philosopher to invite Susan to the party?

If we assume, as above, that movement leaves a trace in the original position, then in (21), but not in (20), a trace intervenes invisibly between "want" and "to", blocking the "wanna" contraction.[21]

2. Wh-phrases share a syntactic category with quantified noun phrases. Both are the result of combining a determiner with a noun phrase. This is a *prima facie* reason to think that the same movement possibilities apply to both. But the *prima facie* case can be strengthened. Movement of wh-phrases is unavailable in some contexts. For example, wh-phrases cannot move out of coordinated conjunctions. We can have:

(24) John saw Chomsky and which philosopher?

but not:

(25) *Which philosopher did John see Chomsky and?

But we also discover that coordinated conjunctions make unavailable certain scope readings of sentences with quantified noun phrases. Thus in:

(26) Some linguist saw Chomsky and every philosopher.

there is no $\forall\exists$ reading, requiring that, for every philosopher, there is some linguist who saw both Chomsky and that philosopher. In general, inverted scope readings are unavailable in exactly the same contexts in which wh-phrases cannot be moved. If the application of **QR** can explain scope ambiguities, as suggested below, then this convergence is further evidence that quantified noun phrases share, albeit at logical form, the movement behaviour of wh-phrases.

These syntactic considerations bring out:

- **Idea #9**: Because a formal semantic theory seeks a close alignment between syntactic structure of expressions and the calculation of semantic values of those expressions, it becomes possible for evidence that bears directly on syntactic theories to bear indirectly on semantic theories, and improve methodological tools for confirming or disconfirming those theories.[22]

Now consider the application of **QR** to (14). We can, for example, move the quantified noun phrase "some linguist", to create the structure:

- (14)l$_1$ [$_S$ [$_{NP}$ some linguist$_t$] [$_S$ [$_{NP}$ every philosopher] [$_{VP}$ [$_{TV}$ admires] [$_{NP}$ t]]]]

QR must then be applied again to the quantified noun phrase "every philosopher". If we assume that a given **S** node can have only a single phrase adjoined to it, we are then forced to adjoin "every philosopher" to the new, higher, **S**:

- (14)l$_2$ [$_S$ [$_{NP}$ every philosopher$_u$] [$_S$ [$_{NP}$ some linguist$_t$] [$_S$ [$_{NP}$ u] [$_{VP}$ [$_{TV}$ admires] [$_{NP}$ t]]]]]

However, we could instead have made "every philosopher" the target of the first application of **QR**, creating:

- (14)l$_3$ [$_S$ [$_{NP}$ every philosopher$_u$] [$_S$ [$_{NP}$ u] [$_{VP}$ [$_{TV}$ admires] [$_{NP}$ some linguist]]]]

and then applied **QR** to "some linguist", to create the **LF**:

- (14)l$_4$ [$_S$ [$_{NP}$ some linguist$_t$] [$_S$ [$_{NP}$ every philosopher$_u$] [$_S$ [$_{NP}$ u] [$_{VP}$ [$_{TV}$ admires] [$_{NP}$ t]]]]]

We thus are able to derive two distinct logical forms for (14). In one, the quantifiers are linearly ordered in a $\forall\exists$ manner; in the other, the quantifiers are linearly ordered in an $\exists\forall$ manner. The existence of two logical forms for the same surface form is significant because of:

- **Idea #10**: A formal semantic theory can explain ambiguous expressions by combining with a syntactic theory that assigns two distinct syntactic forms to the ambiguous expression, and then calculating semantic values from those two forms. The relation between surface form and logical form is one-many, while the relation between logical form and semantic value is one-one.

The bracket notation used above can be replaced, for easier visualization, with tree notation. On the tree notation, the surface form of (14) is:

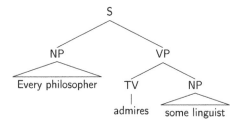

The two possible logical forms are:

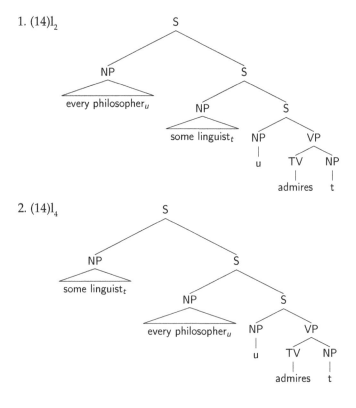

The more sophisticated syntax thus allows us to assign two distinct syntactic forms to (14), one with each of the desired quantifier scopings.

Recall the goal that prompted investigation of a syntax with a **QR** rule. We want to give a formal semantic explanation of the two truth-conditional readings of (14). With **QR** in hand, we now have two different logical forms for (14). This is a promising start, but the two logical forms will be helpful only if we can couple them with semantic rules that process them into the desired $\forall\exists$ and $\exists\forall$ readings. But here we quickly discover that our earlier typing problems persist. Consider first a simple quantified sentence such as (15). We have taken on the following commitments:

- The semantic type of "Albert" (a proper name) is e.
- The semantic type of "sees" (a transitive verb) is $(e, (e, i))$.
- The semantic type of "many logicians" (a quantified noun phrase) is $((e, i), i)$.
- The semantic type of any **S** node is i.

On the plausible assumption that a trace is of type e, the lower **S** node $[_S\ [_{NP}$ Albert] $[_{VP}\ [_{TV}$ sees] $[_{NP}\ t]\ ]\ ]$ works out to be of type i, as desired. But now we must combine an expression of type i with one of type $((e, i), i)$ to produce a terminal semantic type of i, and neither direction of combination works. Again the semantic processing crashes.

Given the **QR** syntax, quantified noun phrases will appear in **LF** as adjuncts to **S** nodes, and hence will reliably be items that combine with an item of type i to produce an item of type i. This then suggests that quantified noun phrases need, in this syntactic setting, to be of type (i, i), rather than of type $((e, i), i)$. But a semantic type of (i, i) is puzzling for quantified noun phrases. Recall that the type i consists of functions from worlds to truth values. Truth values alone are clearly insufficient for giving the semantics of quantified noun phrases. If quantified noun phrases are of type (t, t), where t is the type of truth values, then quantified noun phrases are serving semantically as monadic functions from truth values to truth values (just like negation). But this cannot yield the right results – there are only four such functions, and there are more than four logically distinct quantified noun phrases. And it is not all obvious how adding worlds and intensions will help, since quantified noun phrases appear to be extensional, and can be used in purely extensional contexts.

Complicating the Base

What has gone wrong here? One answer can be reached by considering the standard Tarskian semantics for quantified logic.[23] On this semantics, the fundamental semantic concepts are truth, reference and satisfaction (in a model) relative to an assignment function. Assignment functions directly determine the reference of variables and derivatively, via a recursive procedure, the reference of all terms. Sentences (both open and closed) then are satisfied or not by assignment functions, and the recursive satisfaction clauses define, for example, satisfaction of quantified sentences in terms of the satisfaction of their component parts, as in the familiar:

- $\exists x A$ is satisfied by assignment function σ iff there is an assignment function σ', differing from σ at most in its assignment to x, such that σ satisfies A.

We can introduce these Tarskian ideas into a type-theoretic semantics by replacing the basic types e and i with *relativized* types $e*$, $t*$, and $i*$. $e*$ is the type of *assignment-function-relative objects*, or functions from assignment functions to objects. $t*$ is the type of *assignment-function-relative truth values.*, or functions from assignment functions to truth values. $i*$, finally, is the type of mappings from worlds to items of type $t*$. Type t contained only two entities – the True and the False – and thus provided too few options for quantifiers. Type $t*$ is much larger – if assignment functions have infinite domains, then $t*$ is uncountable in size. These assignment-function-relative semantic values represent another significant idea:

- **Idea #11**: The technical flexibility of a theory can be substantially increased by making use of various forms of *indexed truth*. Truth relative to an assignment function is one example, as are truth relative to a world, a time, or a stance of assessment. Versions of indexed truth allow for a wide range for non-extensional operators that shift the value of indices in various manners. Indexed truth can be a *theory internal* semantic notion, appearing only in the internal calculation of semantic values of component parts of expressions, but giving way to truth *simpliciter* for entire sentences. Such an approach can be thought of as having two types of semantic value – *ingredient* semantic value, exploiting the indexed truth, and *assertoric* semantic value, using truth *simpliciter* and determining the way in which linguistic agents engage with utterances. Or indexed truth can persist throughout the theory, so that terminal semantic values are also given in terms of indexed truth – in this case, the pragmatic theory will need to be constructed to receive and engage with indexed truth, as in recent versions of truth-relativism.[24]

Proper names will receive as semantic values functions that are indifferent to the input assignment function, as in:

- $\lfloor\text{Albert}\rfloor$ is a function f such that for all σ, $f(\sigma) = \text{Albert}$.

Traces, on the other hand, will receive as semantic values functions that are sensitive to the input assignment function, as in:

- $\lfloor t \rfloor$ is a function f such that for all σ, $f(\sigma) = \sigma(t)$.

Many of the semantic details can be easily transposed from the previous framework. The intransitive verb "snores", for example, will be of semantic type $(e*, i*)$, and will take as its specific semantic value in this type the following:

- $\lfloor\text{snores}\rfloor$ is a function f that takes as input a function g from assignment functions to objects, and outputs a function that maps a given world w to a function h that maps an assignment function σ to the True just in case $g(\sigma)$ snores in w.

Quantified noun phrases now compositionally receive a natural and elegant treatment as expressions of semantic type $(i*, i*)$. For example, "some linguist" receives the following semantic value:

- $\lfloor\text{some linguist}_t\rfloor$ is a function f that takes as input a function that maps each world w to a function g from assignment functions to truth values, and outputs a function that maps w to a function that maps an assignment function σ to the True just in case there is an object o that is a linguist in w, and an assignment function σ^t that differs from σ at most in its assignment to t, and g maps σ^τ to the True.
  - (Alternatively, let $[\sigma_t]$ be the set of assignment functions that differ from σ at most in the t position. Then $\lfloor\text{some linguist}_t\rfloor$ takes as input a function that maps each world w to a set of assignment functions, and produces as output a function that maps w to those assignment functions σ such that σt has a non-empty intersection with the set of assignment functions whose t-value is a linguist in w.)

In order compositionally to achieve this semantic value for "some linguist", "some" must receive a semantic value in the type $((e*, i*), (i*, i*))$. In particular, it must receive a value in that type that takes as input a semantic value of the type $(e*, i*)$ (the type of common nouns), and produces as output a semantic value of the type $(i*, i*)$, where the relevant output $(i*, i*)$ item is of the sort described in the semantic value of "some linguist", but with the specification that o is a linguist in w weakened to the requirement that o be an object such that any function mapping every assignment function to it combine with the input ($e*$, $i*$) semantic value to produce a function that maps every assignment function truth in w.

When the appropriate semantic values are combined with the syntactic forms ($14l_2$) and ($14l_4$), the desired ∀∃ and ∃∀ truth conditions fall out.

A Semantic Puzzle Solved

We are now (finally!) in a position to offer a preliminary analysis of the problematic belief report sentence:

(1)   John believes that the tallest spy is in Paraguay.

We begin with a simple surface form syntactic analysis of (1):

(1)sf [$_S$ [$_{NP}$ John] [$_{VP}$ [$_{SV}$ believes [$_{CP}$ [$_C$ that] [$_S$ [$_{NP}$ the tallest spy] [$_{VP}$ is in Paraguay]]]]]]

Because there are two **S** nodes in (1sf), there are two landing spots for the quantified noun phrase "the tallest spy" when **QR** is applied. The two resulting logical forms are:

(1)l_1 [$_S$ [$_{NP}$ John] [$_{VP}$ [$_{SV}$ believes [$_{CP}$ [$_C$ that] [$_S$ [$_{NP}$ the tallest spy$_t$] [$_S$ [$_{NP}$ t] [$_{VP}$ is in Paraguay]]]]]]]

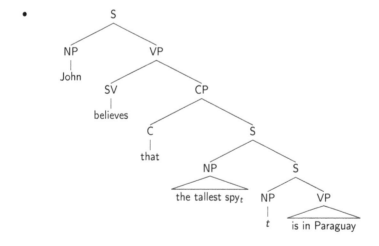

(1)l_2 [$_S$ [$_{NP}$ the tallest spy$t$] [$_S$ [$_{NP}$ John] [$_{VP}$ [$_{SV}$ believes [$_{CP}$ [$_C$ that] [$_S$ [$_{NP}$ t] [$_{VP}$ is in Paraguay]]]]]]]

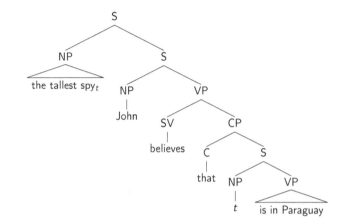

The semantic typing works out properly. Let the sentential verb "believes" be of type $(i*, (e*, i*))$, and the complementizer "that" be of type $(i*, i*)$. Then:

1. In (1)l_1, the type $e*$ trace t combines with the type $(e*, i*)$ verb phrase "is in Paraguay" to form an expression of type $i*$. This then combines with the type $(i*, i*)$ quantified noun phrase "the tallest spy" to form another expression of type $i*$. This combines with the type $(i*, i*)$ complementizer "that" to form yet another expression of type $i*$. This combines with the type $(i*, (e*, i*))$ "believes" to form an expression of type $(e*, i*)$. Finally, this combines with the type $e*$ "John" to form the final semantic type of $i*$.

2. In (1)l_2, the type $e*$ trace t combines with the type $(e*, i*)$ verb phrase "is in Paraguay" to form an expression of type $i*$. This then combines with the type $(i*, (e*, i*))$ "believes" to form an expression of type $(e*, i*)$. This combines with the type $e*$ "John" to form an expression of type $i*$. This then combines with the type $(i*, i*)$ quantified noun phrase "the tallest spy" to form the final semantic type $i*$.

"The tallest spy^t" will then take as its specific semantic value in the type $(i*, i*)$ a function f that takes as input a function that maps each world w to a function g from assignment functions to truth values, and outputs a function that maps w to a function that maps an assignment function σ to the True just in case there is a unique object o that is the tallest spy in w, and an assignment function σ' that differs from σ at most in its assigment to t, and g maps σ' to the True.

When the pieces are assembled, we get the following results:

1. $(1)l_1$ is true with respect to a world w just in case in every world u that is one of John's belief worlds in w, there is a unique object that is the tallest spy (in u), and that object is in Paraguay (in u).
2. $(1)l_2$ is true with respect to a world w just in case there is a unique object that is the tallest spy (in w), and in every world u that is one of John's belief-worlds in w, that object is in Paraguay (in u).

In the first reading, the quantified noun phrase is processed inside the belief context, and hence it selects for assignment functions whose t value is the tallest spy in the belief world, rather than in the actual world. This reading is thus compatible with there being no determinate object about which John thinks (because the satisfier of "tallest spy" varies from belief-world to belief-world) and also with there being no actual tallest spy. Its truth conditions thus match those of the *de dicto* reading of (1). In the second reading, the quantified noun phrase is processed *outside* the belief context, and hence it selects for assignment functions whose t value is the actual tallest spy. The question of whether that object is in Paraguay in each of John's belief worlds – but not the question of whether that object is the tallest spy in each of John's belief worlds – is then considered. This reading is thus compatible with John believing that no one in Paraguay is a spy. Its truth conditions thus match those of the *de re* reading of (1). We now have a formal semantic theory that in a systematic way assigns two distinct semantic values to (1), semantic values that fit naturally with the two readings we initially identified.

Two Predictions

The analysis of *de re* and *de dicto* readings of belief reports developed above correlates the *de re*/*de dicto* distinction with the distinction between a quantified noun phrase taking wide scope (outside the belief context) and taking narrow scope (inside the belief context). In this section, we extract two quick consequences of this mechanism for explaining *de re* and *de dicto* readings, and consider the ramifications for the formal semantic account of those two consequences.

Suppose a belief report contains two quantified noun phrases in the complement sentence to the verb "believes". Then for each noun phrase there is a question about whether it is to be interpreted in a *de re* or a *de dicto* manner. Thus consider:

(27)   John believes the tallest spy followed the shortest diplomat.

As before, we can read (27) such that there is in fact no tallest spy, or such that there is no determinate spy that John thinks about – producing a reading *de dicto* with respect to "the tallest spy". We can also read (27) such that John believes of an individual who, unbeknownst to John, is the tallest spy – a reading *de re* with respect to "the tallest spy". The same options are available for "the shortest diplomat". Perhaps there is no shortest diplomat, or perhaps there is no determinate diplomat that John thinks about (readings *de dicto* with respect to "the shortest diplomat"). Perhaps John has a belief about an individual who, unbeknownst to him, is the shortest diplomat (readings *de re* with respect to "the shortest diplomat").[25]

There are thus potentially four readings of (27):

1. *De dicto* with respect to both "the tallest spy" and "the shortest diplomat".
2. *De dicto* with respect to "the tallest spy"; *de re* with respect to "the shortest diplomat".
3. *De re* with respect to "the tallest spy"; *de dicto* with respect to "the shortest diplomat".
4. *De re* with respect to both "the tallest spy" and "the shortest diplomat".

And, conveniently, there are for each of these readings appropriate ways of scoping the two quantified noun phrases:

1. $[_S [_{NP}$ John $] [_{VP} [_{SV}$ believes $] [_{CP} [_C$ that $] [_S [_{NP}$ the tallest spy$_t] [_S [_{NP}$ the shortest diplomat$_u] [_S [_{NP} t] [_{VP} [_{TV}$ followed $] [_{NP} u]]]]]]]]]$
2. $[_S [_{NP}$ the shortest diplomat$_u] [_S [_{NP}$ John $] [_{VP} [_{SV}$ believes $] [_{CP} [_C$ that $] [_S [_{NP}$ the tallest spy$_t] [_S [_{NP} t] [_{VP} [_{TV}$ followed $] [_{NP} u]]]]]]]]]$
3. $[_S [_{NP}$ the tallest spy$_t] [_S [_{NP}$ John $] [_{VP} [_{SV}$ believes $] [_{CP} [_C$ that$] [_S [_{NP}$ the shortest diplomat$_u] [_S [_{NP} t] [_{VP} [_{TV}$ followed $] [_{NP} u]]]]]]]]]$
4. $[_S [_{NP}$ the tallest spy$_t] [_S [_{NP}$ the shortest diplomat$_u] [_S [_{NP}$ John $] [_{VP} [_{SV}$ believes $] [_{CP} [_C$ that $] [_S [_{NP} t] [_{VP} [_{TV}$ followed $] [_{NP} u]]]]]]]]]$

Note that for "the tallest spy" to be *de re* and "the shortest diplomat" to be *de dicto*, the first must take wide scope over the belief context and the second must take narrow scope inside the belief context. It then follows that the first takes scope over the second. In this particular example, this does not matter, because the relative scoping of the two definite descriptions does not affect the truth conditions. But with different determiners, it will matter.

Consider the sentence:

(28)   John believes that some linguist followed every philosopher.

In this sentence, there is both an ambiguity between $\forall\exists$ and $\exists\forall$ readings of the two quantified noun phrases, and also an ambiguity for each noun phrase between being read *de dicto* and read *de re*. There are thus in principle eight distinct readings of the sentence (pick a scoping and a *de dicto*/*de re* reading for each quantified noun phrase). However, the syntax only produces six possible scopings:

1. $[_S$ $[_{NP}$ John $]$ $[_{VP}$ $[_{SV}$ believes $]$ $[_{CP}$ $[_C$ that $]$ $[_S$ $[_{NP}$ some linguist$_t$ $]$ $[_S$ $[_{NP}$ every philosopher$_u$ $]$ $[_S$ $[_{NP}$ t $]$ $[_{VP}$ $[_{TV}$ followed $]$ $[_{NP}$ u $]$ $]$ $]$ $]$ $]$ $]$ $]$ $]$

   • $\exists\forall$, *de dicto*, *de dicto*

2. $[_S$ $[_{NP}$ John $]$ $[_{VP}$ $[_{SV}$ believes $]$ $[_{CP}$ $[_C$ that $]$ $[_S$ $[_{NP}$ every philosopher$_u$ $]$ $[_S$ $[_{NP}$ some linguist$_t$ $]$ $[_S$ $[_{NP}$ t $]$ $[_{VP}$ $[_{TV}$ followed $]$ $[_{NP}$ u $]$ $]$ $]$ $]$ $]$ $]$ $]$ $]$

   • $\forall\exists$, *de dicto*, *de dicto*

3. $[_S$ $[_{NP}$ every philosopher$_u$ $]$ $[_S$ $[_{NP}$ John $]$ $[_{VP}$ $[_{SV}$ believes $]$ $[_{CP}$ $[_C$ that $]$ $[_S$ $[_{NP}$ some linguist$_t$ $]$ $[_S$ $[_{NP}$ t $]$ $[_{VP}$ $[_{TV}$ followed $]$ $[_{NP}$ u $]$ $]$ $]$ $]$ $]$ $]$ $]$ $]$

   • $\forall\exists$, *de re*, *de dicto*

4. $[_S$ $[_{NP}$ some linguist$_t$ $]$ $[_S$ $[_{NP}$ John $]$ $[_{VP}$ $[_{SV}$ believes $]$ $[_{CP}$ $[_C$ that $]$ $[_S$ $[_{NP}$ every philosopher$_u$ $]$ $[_S$ $[_{NP}$ t $]$ $[_{VP}$ $[_{TV}$ followed $]$ $[_{NP}$ u $]$ $]$ $]$ $]$ $]$ $]$ $]$ $]$

   • $\exists\forall$, *de dicto*, *de re*

5. $[_S$ $[_{NP}$ some linguist$_t$ $]$ $[_S$ $[_{NP}$ every philosopher$_u$ $]$ $[_S$ $[_{NP}$ John $]$ $[_{VP}$ $[_{SV}$ believes $]$ $[_{CP}$ $[_C$ that $]$ $[_S$ $[_{NP}$ t $]$ $[_{VP}$ $[_{TV}$ followed $]$ $[_{NP}$ u $]$ $]$ $]$ $]$ $]$ $]$ $]$ $]$

   • $\exists\forall$, *de re*, *de re*

6. $[_S$ $[_{NP}$ every philosopher$_u$ $]$ $[_S$ $[_{NP}$ some linguist$_t$ $]$ $[_S$ $[_{NP}$ John $]$ $[_{VP}$ $[_{SV}$ believes $]$ $[_{CP}$ $[_C$ that $]$ $[_S$ $[_{NP}$ t $]$ $[_{VP}$ $[_{TV}$ followed $]$ $[_{NP}$ u $]$ $]$ $]$ $]$ $]$ $]$ $]$ $]$

   • $\forall\exists$, *de re*, *de re*

The missing combinations are:

• A reading with a $\exists\forall$ scoping, that is *de dicto* with respect to "some linguist" and *de re* with respect to "every philosopher ".
• A reading with a $\forall\exists$ scoping, that is *de dicto* with respect to "every philosopher " and *de re* with respect to "some linguist".

The current formal semantic theory thus *predicts* that these two potential readings cannot, in fact, be obtained from the English sentence (28). The crucial question, then, is whether this prediction is borne out. Consider the following scenario:

> **S3**: Susan, Albert, and Mary are linguists. John knows each of them, but is unaware that any are linguists. John is under the incorrect impression that there are exactly three philosophers (although he takes himself not to know who they are, and although in fact there are no philosophers). He thinks that Susan followed one of the philosophers, Albert followed another, and Mary followed a third.

Is this a scenario in which John is correctly described as believing that some linguist followed every philosopher (on any disambiguation of that belief report)? Judgments about such intricate cases are delicate and unreliable (and one of the points of interest of formal semantic theories is that they bring to light, by highlighting the significance of cases such as this, important methodological questions about the source and stability of data for linguistic theorizing). But it at least *appears* that the scenario cannot be so reported. If this is correct, it is a significant validation for the given formal semantic approach.

We now consider a second consequence of the scoping explanation of the *de dicto/de re* distinction. We noted earlier that the syntactic rule of **QR** cannot be applied to quantified noun phrases in certain contexts, such as in coordinated conjunctions. Consider belief reports containing quantified noun phrases in such coordinated positions, as in:

(29)   John believes that Albert and the tallest spy are in Paraguay.

(30)   John believes that Albert and every philosopher are in Paraguay.

If *de re* readings of quantified noun phrases are generated by the use of **QR** to lift the quantified noun phrase out of the belief context, and if the application of **QR** is blocked by the coordination construction, then the quantified noun phrases in (29) and (30) should have only *de dicto* readings. Is this correct? Consider the following two scenarios:

> **S4**: Susan is the tallest spy. Although John is acquainted with Susan, he is unaware that she is the tallest spy. John thinks that Albert and Susan are both in Paraguay.
> **S5**: Susan, Albert, and Mary are all the philosophers. John knows each of them, but is unaware that any are philosophers. He believes that the three of them, together with Albert, are all in Paraguay.

If (29) is true in **S4** and (30) is true in **S5**, then – contrary to the predictions of the theory we have developed – those two belief reports *do* have *de re* readings. In fact (although the data is again murky and delicate), it seems that (29) can be read as true in **S4**, but (30) cannot be read as true in **S5**. The theory is thus halfway verified – it produces one correct and one incorrect prediction. Halfway isn't good enough, of course, so something must be changed. Perhaps some new mechanism needs to be added; perhaps some quantified noun phrases, such as definite descriptions, need a different treatment from that developed here; perhaps the entire scope-based approach is fundamentally mistaken.[26]

But we have now followed this line as thought as far as possible in the current context.

Conclusion

In this chapter we have explored one part of one approach to developing a formal semantic analysis of one puzzling construction. There is more to say to finish developing this approach; there are other radically different approaches to the same puzzling construction; there are vastly many other interesting cases to theorize about. We have set out some of the important technical tools, some of the explanatory goals, and some of the methodological constraints of formal semantics. But much of the full strength of the approach of formal semantics lies in attempting to satisfy simultaneously constraints imposed by problematic constructions from all different parts of the language, and by the interactions among these constructions in more complex sentences. Constructing a theory that describes in a precise and rigorous manner the way in which the meanings of diverse parts of the language interact is an extraordinarily difficult task, but one which is both essential to a full understanding of human linguistic exchanges and which promises to reveal many unexpected features of our intricate linguistic tools.

Notes

1. The observation of the ambiguity is introduced into the contemporary philosophical discussion by Quine, 1956.
2. For detailed examination of the nature and philosophical applications of possible worlds, see Lewis, 1986, and Divers, 2002.
3. The finitude constraint as been emphasized by, e.g., Davidson, 1984.
4. See, for example, Parikh, 1987, Stalnaker, 1991, and chapter 9 of Fagin *et al.*, 1995.
5. Possible worlds semantics is endorsed as a semantic framework throughout Stalnaker's work, as in Stalnaker, 1979. The idea of possible worlds semantics reaches back at least as far as Kripke, 1959.

6. See Kratzer, 1977, for development of this observation.
7. See, for example, Kratzer, 1981, for a proposal for treating "probably" within this framework, Yalcin, 2010, for some criticisms of that proposal, and von Fintel and Iatridou, 2008, for some discussion of treating "ought" in this framework.
8. This is a slight simplification of the framework for modals given in Kratzer, 1981.
9. The canonical work on context sensitivity of this overt type is in Kaplan, 1989.
10. The use of a possible worlds semantics to model belief contexts, and other propositional attitude contexts, goes back to Hintikka, 1969.
11. In doing so, we follow the model of Montague, 2002.
12. For thorough development of this idea, see Montague, 2002, and Lewis, 1970. The underlying idea of a collection of types of this sort goes back to Ajdukiewicz, 1967.
13. The *lambda-calculus*, which provides a formal theory for this type of notation, was developed by Church, 1932.
14. The event semantics for adverbs is introduced in Davidson, 1967.
15. See Lewis, 1970, for this observation on the sort of objects needed to treat quantified noun phrases as of semantic type *e*.
16. See Barwise and Cooper, 1980, and Keenan and Westerstahl, 1997, for overviews of *generalized quantifier theory*. Russell's (1905) theory of definite descriptions is a crucial early point in the recognition that there is a common semantic framework for quantified noun phrases in natural language.
17. See Barwise and Cooper, 1980, for further discussion of *monotone increasing* and *monotone decreasing* as properties of quantifiers.
18. See Ladusaw, 1979, for a classic discussion of negative polarity items.
19. The rule of quantifier raising is introduced in May, 1977, and now features in many standard syntactic theories.
20. The idea of a trace is introduced in Chomsky, 1973.
21. The connection between traces and "wanna" contraction is made in Chomsky, 1976.
22. This connection between syntactic and semantic theories is a central thought behind the *principle of compositionality*. See Dever, 2006, for an overview of compositionality.
23. See Tarski, 1983, for the classic historical work, and standard textbooks on first-order logic, such as Enderton, 2001, for more concise presentation of the central ideas.
24. See, for example, Kölbel, 2002, MacFarlane, 2003 and 2005, Egan *et al.*, 2005, and Egan, 2007, for recent developments of truth-relativism.
25. Kripke, 1989, considers a similar case in which the scope theory of the *de dicto/ de re* distinction is tested using a construction in which a quantified noun phrase is embedded under two propositional attitude verbs.
26. See, for example, Kamp, 1981, and Jacobson, 2000, for theories that treat some quantified noun phrases quite differently from the treatment developed here, and provide tools for a different style of analysis of ambiguities in attitude contexts.

References

Ajdukiewicz, K. (1967), "Syntactic connexion". In S. McCall ed. *Polish Logic*. Oxford: Clarendon Press.

Barwise, J. and Cooper, R. (1980), "Generalized quantifiers and natural language". *Linguistics and Philosophy*, 4:159–219.

Chomsky, N. (1973), "Conditions on transformations". In S. Anderson and P. Kiparsky (eds), *A Festschrift for Morris Halle*. New York: Holt, Reinhart and Winston.

—(1976), "Conditions on rules of grammar". *Linguistic Analysis*, 2:303–51.

Church, A. (1932), "A set of postulates for the foundation of logic". *Annals of Mathematics*, 33:346–66.

Davidson, D. (1967), "The logical form of action sentences". In N. Rescher ed. *The Logic of Decision and Action*. Pittsburgh: University of Pittsburgh Press.

—(1984), "Theories of meaning and learnable languages". In *Inquiries Into Truth and Interpretation*. Oxford: Oxford University Press.

Dever, J. (2006), "Compositionality". In E. Lepore and B. Smith (eds), *The Oxford Handbook of Philosophy of Language*. Oxford: Oxford University Press.

Divers, J. (2002), *Possible Worlds*. London: Routledge.

Egan, A. (2007), "Epistemic modals, relativism, and assertion". *Philosophical Studies*, 133:1–22.

Egan, A., Hawthorne, J. and Weatherson, B. (2005), "Epistemic modals in context". In G. Preyer and G. Peter (eds), *Contextualism in Philosophy*. Oxford: Oxford University Press.

Enderton, H. (2001), *A Mathematical Introduction to Logic*. New York: Academic Press.

Fagin, R., Halpern, J., Moses, Y. and Vardi, M. (1995), *Reasoning about Knowledge*. Cambridge, MA: The MIT Press.

Hintikka, J. (1969), Semantics for propositional attitudes. In J. D. Davis *et. al.* (eds), *Philosophical Logic*. Dordrecht: Reidel.

Jacobson, P. (2000), "Paycheck pronouns, Bach-Peters sentences, and variable-free semantics". *Natural Language Semantics*, 8:77–155.

Kamp, H. (1981), "A theory of truth and semantic representation". In Groenendijk, J., Janssen, T. and Stokhof, M. (eds), *Truth, Interpretation, and Information: Selected Papers From the Third Amsterdam Colloquium*. Dordrecht: Foris.

Kaplan, D. (1989), "Demonstratives". In J. Almog, J. Perry and H. Wettstein (eds), *Themes From Kaplan*. Oxford: Oxford University Press.

Keenan, E. and Westerstahl, D. (1997), "Generalized quantifiers in linguistics and logic". In J. van Bentham and A. ter Meulen (eds), *Handbook of Logic and Language*. New York: Elsevier.

Kölbel, M. (2002), *Truth Without Objectivity*. London: Routledge.

Kratzer, A. (1977), "What 'must' and 'can' must and can mean". *Linguistics and Philosophy*, 1:337–55.

—(1981), "The notional category of modality". In P. Portner and B. Partee (eds), *Formal Semantics: The Essential Readings*. Oxford: Blackwell.

Kripke, S. (1959), "A completeness theorem in modal logic". *Journal of Symbolic Logic*, 24:1–14.

—(1989), "Speaker's reference and semantic reference". In P. French, Jr. *et al.* (eds), *Contemporary Perspectives in the Philosophy of Language*. Minneapolis: University of Minnesota Press.

Ladusaw, W. (1979), "Polarity Sensitivity as Inherent Scope Relations". PhD thesis, Austin, TX: University of Texas.

Lewis, D. (1970), "General semantics". *Synthese*, 22:18–67.

—(1986), *On the Plurality of Worlds*. Oxford: Blackwell.

MacFarlane, J. (2003), "Future contingents and relative truth". *The Philosophical Quarterly*, 53:321–36.

—(2005), "Making sense of relative truth". *Proceedings of the Aristotelian Society*, 105:321–39.

May, R. (1977), *The Grammar of Quantification*. New York: Garland Publishing.

Montague, R. (2002), "The proper treatment of quantification in ordinary English". In Portner, P. and Partee, B. (eds), *Formal Semantics: The Essential Readings*. Oxford: Blackwell.

Parikh, R. (1987), "Knowledge and the problem of logical omniscience". In Z. Ras and M. Zemankova (eds), *International Symposium on Methodology for Intelligent Systems 1987*. The Hague: Elsevier.

Quine, W. V. (1956), "Quantifiers and propositional attitudes". *The Journal of Philosophy*, 53(5), 177–87.

Russell, B. (1905), "On denoting". *Mind*, 14:479–93.

Stalnaker, R. (1979), "Assertion". In P. Cole ed. *Syntax and Semantics 9*. New York: Academic Press.

—(1991), "The problem of logical omniscience, I". *Synthese*, 89:425–40.

Tarski, A. (1983), "The concept of truth in formalized languages". In *Logic, Semantics, Metamathematics*. Indianapolis: Hackett.

von Fintel, K. and Iatridou, S. (2008), "How to say *Ought* in foreign: The composition of weak necessity modals". In J. Guéron and J. Lecarme (eds), *Time and Modality*. Dordrecht: Springer.

Yalcin, S. (2010), "Probability operators". *Philosophy Compass*, 5:916–37.

4 Theories of Meaning and Truth Conditions

Kathrin Glüer

Philosophical Meaning Theory

In the philosophical theory of linguistic meaning, a distinction can be drawn between theories aiming at correct semantic description of individual languages and theories the subject of which is linguistic meaning as such. Theories of the first kind can concern formal languages such as the language of first-order predicate logic, or (fragments of) natural languages such as English. They are usually formally worked out and, therefore, the discipline of developing them is called "formal semantics". While formal semantics is a subject belonging to logic and linguistics as much as to philosophy, philosophical meaning theory is a more "foundational" enterprise. Philosophical meaning theory aims at answering the most basic questions concerning linguistic meaning, questions about its very nature.[1]

The most general and basic such question is of course the following: What *is* meaning? Or, in Donald Davidson's much quoted words: "What is it for words to mean what they do?" (Davidson 1984, xiii). Davidson himself suggested approaching this matter by asking two different questions: What *form* should a formal semantics take? And: What is it that makes a semantic theory correct for a particular language, i.e. what *determines* meaning?[2]

The second question concerns the place of semantic facts in a wider metaphysical space: How do these facts relate to non-semantic facts? Can they be reduced to non-semantic facts, do they merely supervene on non-semantic facts, or are they something like metaphysical primitives? In the second half of the twentieth century, philosophers of language have been especially interested in the relation between semantic facts and facts that can be described in natural-istic terms, and different versions of reductive and non-reductive naturalism have been discussed. Another, though related, debate concerns the question whether the facts determining meaning (and thought content) are facts in some sense internal, or external, to the subject saying or thinking something.

Here, we shall focus on Davidson's first question, however: What form should a formal semantic theory take? To be at all relevant for the basic concerns of philosophical meaning theory, a formal semantics needs to be applicable to *natural language.* Not only would we not have understood the general nature of meaning if our theories concerned only artificial languages; the expressions of artificial languages would not have any meaning without the prior meaningful use of natural language. Linguistic meaning, thus, ultimately arises in natural language communication; if we want to understand its nature such communication is what we should look at. But linguists and philosophers doing formal semantics for natural language have developed a number of different frameworks. Davidson himself suggested that Tarski-style truth-theories ("T-theories") can be used as formal semantic theories for natural language. Other theories on the market include Possible-worlds and Proof-Theoretic Semantics, Situation Semantics, Game-Theoretic Semantics, and Discourse Representation Theory, to name but a few. This of course prompts the question, which framework, which form of semantic theory is the best or the right one. But why is this a question for the philosophical theory of meaning?

Take a particular formal semantic theory for (a fragment of) English. This theory describes English by means of a *central,* or *basic, semantic concept.* For Davidson, this concept is *truth.* A Davidsonian semantics for English ascribes *truth conditions* to the sentences of English. If Davidson is right about the form a semantic theory should take, the concept of truth can be used to ascribe meanings to linguistic expressions. By answering the form-question we thus learn something about the nature of meaning, about its essential relation to truth. Different semantic frameworks, however, work with different basic semantic concepts. The basic semantic concept of possible-worlds semantics, for instance, is that of *truth at a possible world,* and that of proof-theoretic semantics is that of *proof* or *rule of inference.* Consequently, if we know what form the semantic theory should take, we know what the basic semantic concept is, the concept by means of which we can characterize, explain or elucidate that of meaning.

There is, thus, a natural connection between formal semantics and philosophical meaning theory. This connection is, however, hostage to a number of conditions. For one, the basic semantic concept used by a semantic theory must be *sufficiently different* from that of meaning (and very closely related concepts such as reference). Otherwise, there would at least be some danger of theoretical circularity.[3] For another, natural language must actually be such that it can be adequately described by the formal methods originally developed for "artificial" languages such as the language of first-order predicate logic. For instance, natural language must be such that what can be expressed by means of it has a sufficiently large, and sufficiently stable, *"core" of literal, or semantic, meaning.* Without such a core, semantic theory would have no role to play in explaining communication by means of natural language.

Some philosophers and linguists, such as radical contextualists and others influenced by certain readings of the later Wittgenstein, have disputed the existence of a literal or semantic core in natural language.[4] This, however, is not a question to be decided on principle. How much of natural language, and natural language communication, can be accounted for by means of systematic semantic theory, or by means of systematic semantic theory complemented by systematic pragmatic theory, has to be found out by careful and creative theory construction and testing – much as for any other complex and *prima facie* disorderly empirical phenomenon.

What we shall concentrate on here, however, are questions concerning the fundamental concept(s) of philosophical meaning theory. More precisely, we shall use the suggestion that *truth* is the basic semantic concept, and some of the most serious problems for truth-conditional semantics, as the focus of our discussion.

Truth-Conditional Semantics and the Davidsonian Programme

A line of thought going back at least to Frege and the early Wittgenstein connects sentence meaning with truth conditions. For Wittgenstein, this connection essentially involves the idea that the meaning of a sentence is what a competent speaker of the language in question understands, or knows, when she understands the sentence, or an utterance of it. What such a speaker knows, Wittgenstein's idea is, is under what conditions the sentence is true: "Einen Satz verstehen, heisst, wissen was der Fall ist, wenn er wahr ist" (T 4.024).[5] In this way, meaning is essentially bound up not only with truth, but also with the activities and the psychology of competent speakers.

Linguistic competence, the ability to understand the sentences of a natural language, has a certain unbounded character: There is an enormous variety, a seemingly limitless supply of sentences with different meanings that natural language has on offer for its speakers. And competent speakers possess an astounding capacity to efficiently and speedily produce and understand these sentences, even if they have never heard them before. An account of meaning as an object of knowledge, the product of a competence possessed by ordinary speakers, has somehow to come to terms with the limitless character of this competence.

Sentences have a constituent structure; they are composed of "smaller" parts, and their meaning seems to depend, in a systematic manner, on the parts they are built of, and the way in which these parts are put together.[6] The idea that

(PC) the meaning of a sentence, or complex expression in general, is determined by, or a function of, the meanings of its constituent parts and mode of composition is well known since Frege (cf. Frege 1892): It is called the "principle of compositionality".[7] If natural language is in fact compositional, accounts of linguistic competence can systematically exploit this feature. Compositional accounts start with simple expressions, specify their meanings or semantic values, and then specify the meanings of complex expressions by means of recursive rules for "building them up" on the basis of those of the simple ones.

Davidson then suggested that the formal apparatus used by Tarski to define truth for certain formal languages could be used to put these two Fregean ideas – compositionality and truth conditions – together; he proposed to use Tarski-style truth definitions (T-theories) to ascribe truth conditions to natural language sentences in a compositional way. Tarski had shown how to define a predicate 'true-in-L' for a language L of a certain kind by means of a recursive definition of the notion of satisfaction for L. That is, he provided a formal machinery that allows for constructing a finitely axiomatized theory of truth for a language L on the basis of L's syntactic structure. From a T-theory for L, we can derive, for every sentence s of L, a theorem (a so-called "T-sentence") specifying s's truth conditions. The theory works, Davidson explains,

> by giving necessary and sufficient conditions for the truth of every sentence, and to give truth conditions is a way of giving the meaning of a sentence. To know the semantic concept of truth for a language is to know what it is for a sentence – any sentence – to be true, and this amounts, in one good sense we can give to the phrase, to understanding the language (Davidson 1967, 24).

The theorems of a T-theory have the following basic form:

(T)   's' is true iff p,

where 's' is replaced by a sentence of the language we are specifying truth conditions for, the "object-language", and 'p' by a sentence of the language the theory is formulated in, the "meta-language".

Tarski had shown that a truth-definition for a language L is "materially adequate", i.e. defines a predicate true-in-L that is co-extensional with the truth predicate as intuitively understood, if, and only if, for every sentence s of L it implies a T-sentence such that what replaces p is a *translation* of s (and object- and meta-language satisfy certain formal conditions). Translation, however, is identity of meaning across languages; Tarski thus connects his otherwise uninterpreted true-in-L predicates with truth *simpliciter* by means of the concept of meaning.

To understand truth in terms of meaning is, according to Davidson, philosophically misguided. Meaning is a much more obscure concept than truth, he maintains; moreover, "truth is one of the clearest and most basic concepts we have" (2005, 55). He therefore suggests to turn Tarski on his philosophical feet, and to use the formal machinery of Tarskian truth theories to understand meaning (cf. Davidson 1984, xiv).[8] If we can construct correct T-theories for natural language, the idea is, we can understand the meaning of sentences in terms of their truth conditions, and the meaning of sub-sentential linguistic expressions as the systematic contribution they make to the truth conditions of sentences. Since he is convinced that this can be done – at least for fragments of natural language large enough to vindicate the idea – Davidson also claims that the theory of meaning can do *without meanings*: There is no need to identify meanings with some kind of abstract object such as propositions. If we understand meaning in terms of systematic contributions to truth conditions, the association of such entities with expressions is simply redundant (cf. Davidson 1967, 20f).

Intriguing as this idea is, it is faced with a formidable range of problems. Less serious are observations such as that not all utterances of natural language are of whole sentences, or that even of those that are, many do not seem to express truth-evaluable contents. The observation that questions, requests or commands, for instance, do not seem to have truth conditions requires drawing a distinction between the *speech act* performed by means of uttering a sentence and the *propositional, or truth-conditional, content* of that speech act. It seems natural to think that the propositional content of the question "Is there butter in the fridge?" and the assertion "There is butter in the fridge" is the same. This content can be specified by a so-called "that-clause": that there is butter in the fridge. Ascribing truth conditions to its sentences thus can be seen as characterizing the semantic core of a language. Phenomena such as irony or metaphor show that the semantic theory is restricted to *literal* language use; it describes the literal core of a language.[9] One way of conceiving of the connection between this core and the actual use of expressions in complete speech acts would then be the following: What a semantics delivers is the content of literal assertion, i.e. for every sentence *s* it specifies what would be (literally) asserted were *s* to be uttered assertorically.[10] Standard accounts of indexicals, however, require further restriction of these claims. According to Kaplanian semantics for indexicals, for instance, the proposition asserted by means of an utterance of a sentence like 'I am here' is determined by its meaning (what Kaplan calls "character") together with the extra-linguistic context of the utterance. Recent debates around phenomena such as "modulation" – using, for instance, the sentence 'The ham sandwich left without paying' to claim that the person who ordered the ham sandwich left without paying – suggest that the (systematic) influence of context on the content asserted might be much more pervasive than traditionally expected.[11]

More serious is the question whether natural language indeed is such that it can, to a sufficiently large degree, be described by means of the formal apparatus of a T-theory, or any other version of truth-conditional semantics such as possible-worlds semantics. For a sentence *s* to be "fed into" the machinery of a T-theory, for instance, it has to be possible to assign *s* a "logical form" expressible in the language of first-order predicate logic. A lot can be handled that way, but not everything. Problems arise, for instance, for conditionals and for intensional contexts such as those created by propositional attitude operators such as 'believes that' or modal operators such as 'it is necessary that'. Problematic also are attributive adjectives ('good', as in 'good actress'), indexicals ('I', 'this'), mass terms ('snow', 'water'), tense operators, and many more (cf. Davidson 1967, 35f). In many of these areas, considerable progress has been made since the days when Davidson suggested that a formal semantics for a natural language should take the form of a T-theory. Some of these, notably the possible-worlds treatments of alethic modal operators such as 'it is necessary that' or 'it is possible that', however, require leaving "pure" truth-theoretic semantics behind and adopting something stronger, a version of possible-worlds semantics.

Even if sufficiently much of natural language could be "tamed" by truth-conditional semantic theory, however, more fundamental questions would remain. Most importantly in our context, we could still ask whether truth (or truth at a possible world) really is the fundamental concept of meaning theory. This has been challenged from several directions. Let's look at some of the most important objections in turn.

Strawson's Homeric Struggle

One early important challenge to truth-conditional semantics, issued by Strawson in the late 1960s, took the form of a general challenge to formal semantics – even though Strawson in effect was concerned only with truth-conditional semantics. Strawson argued that truth cannot be the fundamental concept of meaning theory because the attempt to understand meaning in terms of truth leads to theoretical circularity. Since truth itself needs to be spelled out in terms of "communication intention", Strawson contended against Davidson, the fundamental concepts of meaning theory ultimately are not those of formal semantics.

In his 1969 inaugural lecture in Oxford, Strawson famously described the "conflict between the theorists of communication-intention and the theorists of formal semantics" as a "Homeric struggle" (Strawson 1969, 5).[12] In our context this struggle is interesting precisely because Strawson sets it up as concerning "the fundamental concept in the theory of meaning" (Strawson 1969, 6).

On what we shall call an "intentional account" of meaning, the fundamental concept is that of "an utterer's *meaning something by* an audience-directed utterance on a particular occasion" (*ibid.*). Meaning, that is, is to be understood in terms of the communicative intentions with which speakers utter linguistic expressions. To get a basic idea of how this might work, let us take Grice's account as our model.[13] Grice works with a basic distinction between natural and non-natural meaning, where natural meaning is meaning in the sense in which smoke means fire or reddish spots mean measles. Linguistic meaning is a prime example of non-natural meaning, and Grice suggests the following analysis (cf. Grice 1957):

(M_{NN}) An utterer U means that p by an utterance x iff there is an audience A such that
   (i) U, by means of x, intends to induce A to form an attitude φ towards p (for instance, to believe that p), and
   (ii) U intends A to recognize U's intention (i), and
   (iii) U intends that this recognition be part of A's reason for forming φ towards p.

These rather complex, and in some sense self-referential, intentions involved in non-naturally meaning something are often called "M-intentions". Grice not only suggested analysing the utterer's meaning in terms of such M-intentions, but contended that the further notions of an expression's meaning something, either on particular occasions of utterance or in a timeless sense, can be defined on the basis of M-intentions.

In his rather programmatic 1969 paper, Strawson predicted that the intentional theorist would win the struggle against the truth-conditional semanticist. What he was concerned about was the very notion of a truth condition. Strawson's first question was simply: What, exactly, *is* a truth condition? Unless we say something informative about that, our whole foundational enterprise might be built on sand. And this is a bigger enterprise than it might *prima facie* seem, for to understand the notion of a truth condition we need to understand the notion of *truth*.

So far, the challenge is fair enough; clearly, the truth-conditional semanticist ought to be able to tell us something interesting about truth and truth conditions. Before we look into possible replies, however, we have to ask what this challenge might have to do with intentional accounts of meaning.

Strawson boldly surmised that any answer to the question of the nature of truth itself would have to make use of speech act theoretic concepts such as assertoric content. The notion of truth, he claims, can only be understood in application to intentional human acts such as the utterance of sentences in assertoric speech acts. Consequently, the truth of an assertion, and therewith the truth of the *content* of such a speech act, would be analytically prior to that of the sentence uttered. Strawson concluded that the notions of communicative intention were more fundamental in the theory of meaning than that of truth.

However, one of the most serious problems of the Gricean analysis of linguistic meaning is the following. Suppose *U* utters the sentence 'Sweden is in the North of Europe' with the M-intention to get her audience *A* to believe that Sweden is in the North of Europe. Suppose, moreover, that *U* succeeds. Even if we grant that Grice's conditions are satisfied in every such case of successful communication, we do not get an answer to the following question: What is it about *the uttered sentence* that makes it usable for inducing precisely the that belief? What connection is there between 'Sweden is in the North of Europe' and the belief that Sweden is in the North of Europe – as opposed to any other belief, for instance the belief that it is cold at the South Pole? Intuitively, it is the fact that the sentence *means that* Sweden is in the North of Europe that makes it possible to utter it with the intention to induce that belief. Intuitively, that is, meaning here seems to explain the content of the intention, rather than the other way around, thus reversing the explanatory relation.

What we need, but do not get from Grice – at least not immediately – is a systematic account of what it is that makes the sentences of a language such apt vehicles for conveying thoughts *with particular contents*. And again, what we need is an account able to cope with the enormous variety of sentences that natural language has on offer for its speakers. Intuitively, there does not seem any limit to the sentences thus standing ready conveying particular contents.

What emerges from these considerations is the need for supplementing the Gricean account with a systematic account of sentence meaning. More precisely, supplementing it with an account that can handle speakers' ability to quickly and efficiently produce and understand an enormous variety of natural language sentences, including sentences they have never heard before. Compositionality arguably is the best way of handling these features of natural language communication.[14] If so, the demand is that for a compositional account of sentence meaning.

But can such an account be incorporated into the Gricean framework? To make good on the claim that the fundamental concept of meaning theory is that of communicative or M-intention, the compositional account of sentence meaning itself would need to be formulated in Gricean terms. That is, we would need to be able to explain at least reference and predication in terms of M-intentions.[15] There is very good reason to doubt that this is feasible, however. Like any other compositional theory, such an account would have to contain axioms specifying reference for simple singular terms, and extensions for simple predicates. But the use of the very notions of communicative or M-intentions in these axioms will create intensional contexts.[16] Consequently, in such a theory, valid theorem derivation depends on prior relations of synonymy: Intensional axioms license substitutions only if they preserve meaning. Since it presupposes understanding of the very concept it is supposed to illuminate, it appears doubtful that such a theory can tell us very much about meaning.[17, 18]

There is thus reason to think that Strawson was wrong: It does not look as if intentional accounts could provide meaning-theoretical foundations.[19] Nevertheless, it remains of course true that the mere truth-conditional form of a semantic theory does not, by itself, tell us anything about how the truth predicate is to be interpreted. Moreover, it is not clear that truth ultimately can be understood in terms not involving meaning. And that brings us to the first part of the Strawsonian challenge: The challenge to say something interesting about truth without begging any meaning-theoretical questions.

Contemporary theories of truth can roughly be categorized by means of their answers to the following two questions: First, is truth a substantive property? And second, if yes, is it an epistemic or a non-epistemic property? Redundancy theorists and deflationists deny that truth is a substantive property. Epistemic theories hold that it is a substantive, but in principle epistemically accessible property. Epistemicism about truth is often also called "anti-realism". Realists about truth hold that truth is a substantive property independent of our beliefs and cognitive abilities.

Epistemic conceptions of truth have been thought of as motivated by meaning-theoretical concerns. Michael Dummett suggests to account for meaning in terms of *verification* instead of truth (see below, pp. 97ff), and argues that, on such an account, the notion of truth must be explained "in terms of our capacity to recognize statements as true" (Dummett 1976, 75). Inspired by the later Wittgenstein, philosophers such as Crispin Wright have argued that, on pain of the kind of Platonism attacked by Wittgenstein in the rule-following considerations (esp. *Philosophical Investigations* 138–242), meaning has to be understood in terms of an epistemic concept of truth (cf. Wright 1980). Anti-realism about truth strikes many as having very counterintuitive consequences, however; Dummett, for instance, argues that sentences about the past are made true not by past facts in themselves but by what is presently known or knowable. He is one of the few anti-realists who embrace this consequence; others, such as Wright, argue against this actually being a consequence of anti-realism (cf. Wright 1986).

Dummett also argued that redundancy theorists and disquotationalists cannot understand meaning in terms of truth conditions (cf. Dummett 1959, 7). Both hold that ''p' is true' means the same as 'p'; disquotationalists claim that there is nothing more to the truth predicate than its function as a device of disquotation[20] or "semantic ascent", a device of "replacing talk about the world with logically equivalent talk about words" (Williams 1999, 547).[21] Such a device adds expressive resources to a language since it allows speakers to endorse things they cannot directly assert.[22] Nevertheless, "the function of truth talk is *wholly* expressive, thus *never* explanatory" (*ibid.*). Most deflationists agree with Dummett and take this to imply that meaning cannot be explained in terms of truth (cf. for instance Horwich 1998, 71ff). More precisely, problems arise as soon as the deflationist tries to account for certain uses of the truth-predicate, uses exemplified by T-sentences: metalinguistic ascriptions of truth to sentences of an object language not identical with the metalanguage. Since the correct application of the truth predicate here depends on translation, the disquotationalist cannot use T-sentences simultaneously to explain what it is for object language sentences to have meaning and to explain how the (metalinguistic) truth predicate functions (cf. Patterson 2005).

Davidson originally thought that Tarski-theories in fact provided some sort of correspondence theories of truth (cf. Davidson 1969), but later argued that this was a mistake (cf. Davidson 2005, 38ff, esp. fn 4). He came to think that truth cannot be defined at all, not even in the "minimalist" way the deflationists favour, and that the only way to say something revealing about the concept of truth is by tracing its relations to concepts equally fundamental and beyond definition (cf. Davidson 1996, 20f).[23] He suggested that, even though often beyond recognition, truth is essentially related to the propositional attitudes: The truth predicate is interpreted only through the "pattern" truth makes amongst the attitudes, including speech and action, and their causes. It has empirical content precisely because T-theories can be *applied to* intentional creatures, can be correct or incorrect for a speaker, or group of speakers: "If we knew in general what makes a theory of truth correctly apply to a speaker or group of speakers, we could plausibly be said to understand the concept of truth" (Davidson 2005, 37).

Given our overall meaning-theoretical project, we cannot take meanings for granted in characterizing truth, however. We must, that is, find a way of relating truth to the very same *non-semantic data* about speakers' behaviour in observable circumstances that, according to Davidson, provide the determination base for meaning, or content in general: "I therefore see the problem of connecting truth with observable behaviour as inseparable from the problem of assigning contents to all the attitudes" (Davidson 1996, 37). Ultimately, then, belief and truth are part of a set of basic, irreducible and interdependent concepts capturing what is essential to intentional minds. Their empirical content derives from the metaphysics of content determination. According to Davidson, content is determined on the basis of *non-semantic facts*; more precisely, facts about observable behaviour in observable circumstances, by means of the "principle of charity". It requires "assigning truth conditions to alien sentences that make native speakers right when plausibly possible" (Davidson 1973, 137). As a principle of content determination in general, charity requires the beliefs of intentional creatures to be minimally coherent, rationally connected with desires and actions, and, in the most basic cases, "about" the objects which typically cause them (cf. Davidson 1991).[24] Because of its non-semantic determination base, content determination by charity thus allows us to say something revealing also about truth: "by relating it to concepts like belief, desire, cause and action" (Davidson 1996, 21). On a Davidsonian picture, Strawson was right in so far as truth cannot be characterized in complete independence from human intentionality. This does not mean, however, that it cannot be characterized without any meaning-theoretically question-begging use of the notion of (assertoric) content.[25]

Intensionality and Indeterminacy

Another important challenge to truth-conditional semantics questions the very idea that truth conditions ever can do the job of meanings. Meanings might determine truth conditions, but not the other way around; there are, the argument goes, simply not enough truth conditions around to do duty as meanings. A maybe slightly different worry can be put in terms of T-theories: All we can require of their theorems is that they be true. But what reason is there to expect true T-sentences to capture meanings?

As Davidson himself points out, a T-sentence such as

(G)   'Snow is white' is true iff grass is green,

while true, certainly does not specify the meaning of 'snow is white' in English (cf. Davidson 1967, 25). Let's call T-sentences that specify meanings "interpretive", and T-sentences that do not, "non-interpretive". T-theories implying non-interpretive T-sentences such as (G) can be excluded because a T-theory is correct for a language *L* only if it implies a true T-sentence for *every* sentence of *L*. A T-theory implying (G) will most probably have other consequences such as that 'that is white' is true iff the demonstrated object is green, or that 'that is snow' is true iff the demonstrated object is grass. Therefore, no reasonably simple theory implying (G) is such that it implies a true T-sentence for every sentence of the language, Davidson claims (Davidson 1967, 26, fn. 10).

The problem is more serious than that, however: Intuitively, there are numerous non-interpretive T-sentences the truth of which depends on nothing but the co-extensionality of non-synonymous predicates such as

(C)   'Pigs are renate' is true iff pigs are cordate.

In response, Davidson stressed the empirical nature of semantic theories. It is an empirical question whether a T-theory is correct for a particular natural language or not. That means, Davidson argues, that its theorems are *law-like statements*: They formulate natural laws, and therefore must not only be true, but also counterfactual supporting. Thus, for instance, (C) would have to be true even under counterfactual circumstances where it is not the case that creatures with a liver also possess kidneys. This, he argues, goes at least some way towards distinguishing between non-synonymous, but co-extensional expressions (Davidson 2005, 54). Still, it is far from clear that sufficiently fine-grained distinctions in meaning can be achieved this way; necessarily co-extensional but arguably non-synonymous predicates such as 'triangular' and 'trilateral', for instance, cannot be distinguished this way.[26]

Problematic also are all those non-interpretive true T-sentences that result if the right-hand side of an interpretive T-sentence is replaced by something necessarily equivalent with it, as illustrated by the following pair:

(S)   'Snow is white' is true iff snow is white.

(S′)   'Snow is white' is true iff snow is white and two plus two equals four.

For any such pair of T-sentences, both are implied by exactly the same T-theories. Here, Davidson invokes the idea of a canonical proof: Only T-sentences derived by means of a canonical proof are interpretive, he claims; i.e., only T-sentences that can be directly derived from the relevant axioms alone.[27]

Besides those of a formal nature, there are, according to Davidson, empirical constraints on acceptable T-theories. As we saw, these are empirical theories, and as such to be holistically confirmed by the available evidence; the correct T-theory is that which achieves the overall "best fit" with the data (Davidson 1973, 136). T-theories can thus be ranked by how well they fit the data, and the principle governing this ranking is, again, the principle of charity: The most charitable theory is also the best. Charity thus places massive empirical restrictions on acceptable T-theories.

Taken together, Davidson claims, the formal and empirical constraints on acceptable T-theories are strong enough to let only those pass that actually can be used to interpret the speakers of *L*.[28] Nevertheless, it is unlikely that they will narrow the number of acceptable T-theories down to one. There might well be more than one theory fitting the evidence to an equal degree. Davidson considers such theories as *empirically equivalent*, and he holds that any such theory can be considered as a correct meaning theory for *L*. From his Quine-inspired perspective on meaning determination, what cannot be determined about meaning from the evidence available in radical interpretation simply is *indeterminate*.[29] This indeterminacy, Davidson argues, is rather harmless, however; it is analogous to that between measuring temperature in degrees Fahrenheit or Celsius. Nothing significant is lost by switching between scales like that (cf. Davidson 1977, 225). Both the extent to which this analogy succeeds and the extent to which indeterminacy can ever be an acceptable consequence, rather than a *reductio ad absurdum,* of a meaning theory remain matters of dispute, however.[30]

Meaning and Understanding

Frege, Wittgenstein and Davidson all initially think of meaning in terms of truth conditions because of the link between *understanding*, or knowing, the meaning of a sentence and its truth condition. The philosopher of language who probably has made most of this link, however, is Michael Dummett. Like Davidson, he was convinced of the crucial meaning-theoretic significance of the form of our semantic theory, but he also was convinced that truth cannot be the fundamental semantic concept. Rather, this role has to be given to a notion such as *proof, warranted assertibility* or *falsifiability* (cf. Dummett 1976) – precisely because the ultimate goal of a theory of meaning is a theory of understanding:

> To grasp the meaning of an expression is to understand its role in the language: a complete theory of meaning for a language is, therefore, a complete theory of how the language functions as a language. [...] [A] theory of meaning is a theory of understanding; that is, what a theory of meaning has to give an account of is what it is that someone knows when he knows the language, that is, when he knows the meanings of the expressions and sentences of the language (Dummett 1974, 2f).

Dummett, that is, conceives of linguistic competence as a form of knowledge, and of the theory of meaning as the object of this knowledge.[31] Language use, he emphasizes, is an essentially *rational* activity. It is rationally motivated by our knowledge of meaning. Just like knowledge of any other subject matter, knowledge of meaning joins forces with our wants and desires to provide reasons for action, linguistic or otherwise. This essentially rational character of language use, Dummett claims, requires the theory of meaning to be a theory of understanding.

Moreover, only a "full-blooded" – as opposed to "modest" – theory of meaning can hope to be a theory of understanding (Dummett 1974, 4ff). A *full-blooded theory of meaning* must, "in explaining what one must know in order to know the meaning of each expression in the language, simultaneously explain what it is to have the concepts expressible by means of that language" (*ibid.,* 4). A modest theory, on the other hand, only gives "the interpretation of the language to someone who already has the concepts required" (*ibid.,* 5). The force behind the demand for full-bloodedness derives from the claim that there are any number of concepts that only language-users can have. Amongst the most important of these are concepts such as those of expressing a thought or asserting that *p*. In order to fully understand meaning and language use, then, we must, in our meaning theory, not make use of any such concepts. And that, in turn, means that we must explain what it is to meaningfully use linguistic expressions without presupposing the ideas of expressing thought contents and possessing concepts. As McDowell explains,

> [t]here is indeed a connection with the question how concepts might be imparted; but it is not that a subject ought to be able to acquire the concepts expressible in the language by being told what the theory states, but that, if the description of linguistic practice does what is required of it, a subject can acquire those concepts by achieving mastery of the practice that the theory describes (McDowell 1997, 109).

On the basis of these demands, Dummett presents the truth-conditional semanticist with a basic dilemma: If a T-theory is used to specify truth conditions, the account of meaning thereby given either remains modest, or it has to go holistic. Neither option is any good (cf. Dummett 1974, 20).

Taken *individually*, Dummett argues, the theorems of a T-theory for a language *L* do not tell us any more than a translation manual for *L* would; to understand *L* you either need to know the meta-language, or the language that *L* is translated into, in advance. Consequently, a T-theory does not provide more than a modest theory of meaning. But trying to escape this consequence by taking the theory *as a whole* to model linguistic competence is to jump from the frying pan into the fire, according to Dummett. "Going holistic" in effect amounts to giving up on a systematic account of linguistic competence altogether. "On such an account", Dummett argues,

> there can be no answer to the questions what constitutes a speaker's understanding of any one word or sentence: one can say only that the knowledge of the entire theory of truth issues in an ability to speak the language (*ibid.*, 16).

But this is precisely what we need to have a theory of understanding: For each particular word or sentence, we need to be able to say what constitutes understanding that very word or sentence. That holism cannot be an answer here becomes manifest in the consequences Dummett takes semantic holism to have for language learning. It basically makes language learning completely mysterious, if not impossible: "[O]n a holistic view, it is impossible fully to understand any sentence without knowing the entire language" (Dummett 1976, 44). A theory of understanding, Dummett argues, therefore can only be given if language is "molecular": If there is, for every sentence *s* of a language *L*, a limited fragment of *L* understanding of which suffices for understanding *s*. Only then is there any hope of providing a full-blooded theory of meaning.

But this way out is not open to the truth-conditional semanticist. For, even though the meaning of many sentences can be learned through verbal explanations, this cannot be the most basic form of language learning. Therefore, even though knowing the meaning of many sentences can be understood in terms of the ability to understand their verbal explanations, a speaker's

> understanding of the most primitive part of the language [...] cannot be explained this way: if that understanding consists in a knowledge of the truth conditions of sentences, such knowledge must be implicit knowledge, and the theory of meaning *must supply us with an account of how that knowledge is manifested* (ibid., 45, emph. mine).

It is this requirement, often called the "manifestation requirement", on which the truth-conditional account ultimately falters, according to Dummett. For "natural language is full of sentences which are not effectively decidable, ones for which there exists no effective procedure for determining whether or not their truth conditions are fulfilled" (*ibid.*, 46). Examples of such sentences are sentences quantifying over infinite or unsurveyable domains, subjunctive conditionals, or certain sentences about the future or the past. For such "verification transcendent" sentences, Dummett submits, "there is no content to an ascription of *implicit* knowledge of what [their truth condition] is, since there is no practical ability by means of which such knowledge can be manifested" (*ibid.*, 46).

Dummett therefore comes to the conclusion that the basic semantic notion cannot be truth.[32] He considers two alternatives: verificationism or falsificationism (cf. Dummett 1976, 62ff). According to verificationism, understanding consists in the ability to recognize the conditions under which a sentence is verified, and according to falsificationism it consists in the ability to recognize the conditions under which it is falsified. Dummett argues that the verificationist conception of the meaning of mathematical sentences that has been developed within the intuitionistic tradition provides us with a good model for a general verificationist semantics (cf. *ibid.*, 70f). The basic semantic notion thus becomes that of *proof*. Knowledge of the meaning of a sentence then consists in being able to tell for any given object *a*, whether the property *a is a proof of y* does, or does not, apply to it.

For a proof-theoretic semantics to apply to natural language in general, we need an understanding of what "proofs" of non-mathematical statements consist in. The basic idea would be to use related, more general notions such as that of *warranted assertibility*, and to think of meaning in terms of the conditions under which inferences from given premises are valid in a broader sense. Nevertheless, it remains far from clear that proof-theoretic semantics can be extended so as to cover sufficiently large fragments of natural language. A related, but no longer verificationist, idea would be to conceive of meaning entirely in terms of inferential connections, and to use *inferential role* as the basic semantic concept.[33]

Most importantly, however, Dummett's charge that truth-conditional semantics is doomed to remain modest can be disputed. McDowell, for instance, argues that modesty is a virtue, not a vice. According to him, the holistic nature of meaning and mind precludes anything but a modest theory of meaning. This, however, does not prevent us from gaining philosophical insights into understanding meaningful use of language; such understanding, he submits, needs to be conceived of as not requiring any kind of "interpretation", but as an acquired ability to literally hear another's meanings in their words (cf. McDowell 1987).

More substantively, the consequences Dummett charges semantic holism with can be disputed. According to Dummett, such holism makes language acquisition impossible, but this charge is justified only for certain versions of semantic holism. Davidsonian semantic holism, for instance, does not have this consequence: According to Davidson, meaning is determined by the principle of charity on the basis of non-semantic facts about sentences held true under observable circumstances. The principle of charity induces a many–one determination relation between these non-semantic facts and meanings, thus preventing the holism from implying that every new acquisition of a word changes the meaning of every other expression (cf. Pagin 1997; 2006a). Davidson himself and others have argued that meanings can be partially acquired (cf. Davidson 1965). The idea, then, that a truth-conditional formal semantic theory, be it of the T-theoretic or possible-worlds kind, can holistically model linguistic competence might after all turn out to be a viable answer to one of the foundational questions of philosophical meaning theory.[34]

Notes

1. This distinction between formal semantics and philosophical meaning theory resembles that drawn by Robert Stalnaker between "descriptive semantics" and "foundational semantics": "First, there are questions of what I will call 'descriptive semantics'. A descriptive semantic theory is a theory that says what the semantics for the language is, without saying what it is about the practice of using that language that explains why that semantics is the right one. [...] Second, there are questions, which I will call questions of 'foundational semantics', about what the fact are that give expressions their semantic values, or more generally, about what makes it the case that the language spoken by a particular individual or community has a particular descriptive semantics" (Stalnaker 1997, 535). But philosophical meaning theory is not restricted to the question of meaning determination; rather, it comprises any kind of

philosophical inquiry into the nature of linguistic meaning. One such question that has been crucially important during the second half of the twentieth century is precisely one concerning the philosophical significance of the choice of formal semantics: The question of what form such a semantics is to take.

2. Cf. Davidson 1973, 125; 1984, xiii. For Davidson, meaning is essentially public, that is, accessible to, or knowable by, the speakers of a natural language. According to him, this means that meaning is determined by observable behaviour in observable circumstances. Such behaviour at the same time provides the evidence for a semantic theory. For Davidson, the question of meaning determination therefore coincides with the question of what the evidence for a semantic theory is. It is sometimes objected that this amounts to "verificationism" (see, for instance, Williamson 2004, 137), but as long as the objection does not take on the specifics of the Davidsonian account of meaning determination, it is hard to see what is wrong with the claim that natural language meaning is, in principle, knowable by its speakers.

3. This is not the same thing as requiring that meaning must be *analysable in terms of*, or *reducible to*, something completely different. One might well hold – as for instance Davidson does – that no such analysis, or reduction, will be forthcoming, and yet insist on some minimal condition of informativeness.

4. Philosophical examples include Searle (1978) and Travis (1989). Less radical contextualists such as Recanati (2004) and Pagin and Pelletier (2007) argue that, even though pragmatic influences on understanding linguistic utterances usually start before a truth-evaluable content is output, this neither prevents semantic theories from being indispensable for explaining linguistic communication nor does it prevent an account of such understanding from being systematic. Semantic minimalists, such as Borg (2004) and Cappelen and Lepore (2004), hold that every utterance of a (non-indexical) sentence expresses one and the same semantic content, the "minimal proposition" (according to Cappelen and Lepore, many other propositions might be expressed at the same time, however).

5. The Ogden translation (1922; see Wittgenstein 1921) has: "To understand a proposition means to know what is the case if it is true."

6. That the way in which the parts of a sentence are put together, i.e. its syntactic mode of composition, plays a role here can be seen from examples such as 'Bob kicks Mary' and 'Mary kicks Bob'. These sentences are composed of the same parts, but differ in meaning. The difference depends on which syntactic role the parts play.

7. For more on compositionality, see Pagin and Westerståhl 2010a, 2010b.

8. This strategy consequently involves conceiving of the semantic concepts used "inside" the theory, such as the concepts of reference and satisfaction, as purely theoretical concepts. No pre-theoretic understanding of these concepts is presupposed; they are interpreted (to the extent that they are) by means of being part of an empirical theory that gets its empirical content exclusively through its theorems and their connection with the data, the evidence supporting it.

9. One traditional way of drawing the semantics–pragmatics distinction is precisely this: Semantics is whatever can be described by means of a systematic truth-conditional semantics for a language. Everything beyond this core belongs to pragmatics:

Speech act theory, the theory of indirect discourse including the theory of non-literal language use, etc. On this picture, pragmatic mechanisms are basically Gricean in the sense that they operate on complete propositions, i.e. truth-evaluable contents. Recently, this picture has come under considerable pressure; today, there seems to be some consensus that pragmatic processes such as saturation and modulation (the terms are Recanati's (2004)) already operate on simpler concepts.

10. This is true (for non-indexical sentences) on a truth-conditional, but not on a possible-worlds semantics. Possible-worlds propositions have truth values at possible worlds, but an assertion concerns only the actual world. Lepore (1982) argues that this is a defect of possible-worlds semantics precisely because it is the job of a semantic theory to deliver the contents of assertions. However, what accounts for the connection with the actual world might be the force of the utterance, not its content; cf. Recanati (2007, 37).

11. See note 9 above.

12. Amongst philosophers, he lists Frege and the early Wittgenstein. Regarding Frege, this is most probably historically misleading; he was not primarily interested in semantics, but in the reduction of mathematics to logic. However, Frege did develop the basic formal methods that allow the construction of a formal semantics for first-order quantified logic, and formulated a version of compositionality (more precisely, Frege formulated what is called the "substitution version" for what he called "Bedeutung" (reference)). What Strawson in effect almost exclusively discusses is Davidson's seminal article *Truth and Meaning* (1967). Somewhat comically, Strawson also lists Chomsky as a "theorist of formal semantics" (cf. Strawson 1969, 5). – On the opposite side, the side of the "theorists of communication-intention", Strawson names Grice, Austin and the later Wittgenstein (*ibid.*).

13. Cf. Grice 1957, 1968. For discussion and defence of a modified version of the Gricean account, see Schiffer 1972.

14. Cf. Pagin 2009.

15. Grice's own attempt, in terms of resultant procedures, simply uses the semantic concepts of reference and satisfaction; cf. Grice 1968. It can thus not form the sought meaning-theoretical completion of intentional meaning theory. Schiffer (1972) and Bennett (1976), both inspired by Lewis's account in terms of convention (1969, modified 1975), provide Gricean alternatives.

16. Cf. Taylor 1982. Taylor uses Schiffer's (1972) version of a Gricean account as his example account.

17. Even anti-reductivists about meaning (see note 3 above) should not be happy with so blatant, or "narrow", a theoretical circularity.

18. Davidson 1967, 22f, argues that the theorems delivered by a compositional meaning theory for precisely this reason cannot be of the form 'S means that p'. See also note 28 below.

19. It could be argued that there is some sort of mutual dependence between truth-conditional and intentional accounts of meaning: each is in need of supplementation – more precisely, in need of the kind of supplementation the other could provide. For an argument to this effect, see Rumfitt 1995.

20. "Disquotation" because the truth predicate works like this: predicated of a quoted sentence, the result has the same meaning as the "disquoted" sentence, i.e. the sentence without the quotation marks.

21. Cf. Patterson 2005, however, for a more careful characterization of the nature of the equivalence.
22. Thus, I might for instance use 'Fermat's last theorem is true' to assert that Fermat's last theorem is true even though I don't remember the theorem.
23. Some disquotationalists argue that Davidson is mistaken in taking himself to explain meaning in terms of truth (cf. Williams 1999; Kölbel 2001): In a Davidsonian framework, only considerations of radical interpretation, i.e. meaning determination on the basis of the ultimate evidence, go into this explanation, they claim. Radical interpretation, however, does not (Williams), or need not (Kölbel), involve (a substantive notion of) truth. This might be partly a terminological dispute concerning the use of the term "explanation". What seems right is that the method of radical interpretation, as used for constructing a T-theory, is neutral on the interpretation of the truth predicate. It would not be right, however, to conclude from this that the very choice of formal semantics does not have any meaning-theoretical significance. Radical interpretation, if possible at all, would look very different if what the radical interpreter had to construct was a proof-theoretic semantics. That truth is the basic semantic concept thus remains an important part of the Davidsonian "explanation" of meaning.
24. For more on the principle of charity as the general principle of content determination in Davidson, and its epistemic and modal status, cf. Glüer 2006, 2007; Pagin 2006b.
25. Thus, Davidson always insisted that "truth is one of the clearest and most basic concepts we have" (2005, 55) and that "meaning not only is a more obscure concept than that of truth; it clearly involves it: if you know what an utterance means, you know its truth conditions" (1996, 37). This goes together with the claim that truth is one of a set of interdependent concepts endowed with empirical content by content determination: The overall "theory" being interpreted by its relation to the non-semantic evidence uses the concepts of belief and truth, but not those of meaning and content. The relevant concept of belief, for instance, could be characterized as intentional, but not intensional – it is that of a propositional attitude individuated as an attitude in abstraction from any particular propositional content (cf. Davidson 2005, 67). And the same holds for the other elements of the basic "intentional set" – belief, desire, speech, and action.
26. Even if we conclude, however, that only semantic theories working with more fine-grained intensions will come sufficiently close to our intuitive synonymy judgments, this is not a problem such theories won't have. Possible worlds semantics, for instance, cannot by itself capture differences between necessarily equivalent predicates, either. Nor does it achieve the fineness of grain intuitively required by attitude ascriptions.
27. A classic source for these problems is Foster 1976. See also Davidson 1976, Soames 1992.
28. It has been observed that, once we have an interpretive T-theory, we can go one step further and from each of its T-sentences derive a sentence explicitly stating what object language sentences mean (see, for instance, Kölbel 2001). Kölbel argues that we could even incorporate this step into our formal semantic theory

(2001, 618ff). That is mistaken. Incorporating inference rules into the T-theory that would license the derivation of "meaning theorems" would be possible only if all the constraints on interpretive T-theories were purely formal. Davidson is very clear, however, that both formal and empirical constraints are required. The possibility of deriving "meaning theorems" from an interpretive T-theory does not imply that using it to illuminate the nature of meaning would be question-begging, or theoretically circular, either. Whether or not we derive "meaning theorems" from it, all the explanatory work is done by the inner workings of the T-theory together with the formal and empirical restrictions placed on it.

29. Cf. Quine 1960, chapter 2.
30. For further discussion, see Lepore and Ludwig 2005, II.15.
31. Most of this knowledge has to be construed as implicit knowledge. Dummett repeatedly struggles with the precise characterization of such knowledge – on the one hand, it cannot be propositional in character, but on the other it cannot be a merely practical ability such as the ability to ride a bicycle, either. Cf. esp. Dummett 1978.
32. It is sometimes assumed that Dummett's arguments only establish that the basic semantic concept cannot be "bivalent" truth, or truth as "realistically", or non-epistemically, understood. This is mistaken; even if we define being true as, for instance, having a proof, meaning could not consist in truth conditions: For, even though the property of being a proof is a decidable one, the property of having a proof is not. Cf. Pagin 1998.
33. For more on this, see Greenberg and Harman 2006, Peregrin 2008.
34. I would like to thank Peter Pagin and the editors of this volume for helpful comments. The latter also provided the basic outline of this chapter.

References

Bennett, J. (1976), *Linguistic Behaviour*. Cambridge: Cambridge University Press.

Borg, E. (2004), *Minimal Semantics*. Oxford: Oxford University Press.

Cappelen, H. and Lepore, E. (2004), *Insentitive Semantics. A Defense of Semantic Minimalism and Speech Act Pluralism*. Oxford: Blackwell.

Davidson, D. (1965/1984), "Theories of meaning and learnable languages", in *Inquiries into Truth and Interpretation*, Oxford: Clarendon, pp. 3–15.

—(1967/1984), "Truth and meaning", in *Inquiries into Truth and Interpretation*, Oxford: Clarendon, pp. 17–36.

—(1969/1984), "True to the facts", in *Inquiries into Truth and Interpretation*, Oxford: Clarendon, pp. 37–54.

—(1973/1984), "Radical interpretation", in *Inquiries into Truth and Interpretation*, Oxford: Clarendon, pp. 125–39.

—(1976/1984), "Reply to Foster", in *Inquiries into Truth and Interpretation*, Oxford: Clarendon, pp. 171–9.

—(1977/1984), "Reality without Reference", in *Inquiries into Truth and Interpretation*, Oxford: Clarendon, pp. 215–25.

—(1984), *Inquiries into Truth and Interpretation*. Oxford: Clarendon.

—(1991/2001), "Three Varieties of Knowledge", in *Subjective, Intersubjective, Objective*, Oxford: Clarendon Press, pp. 205–20.

—(1996/2005), "The folly of trying to define truth", in *Truth, Language, and History*, Oxford: Clarendon, pp. 19–37.

—(2005), *Truth and Predication*. Cambridge MA: The Belknap Press of Harvard University Press.

Dummett, M. (1959/1978), "Truth", in *Truth and other Enigmas*, Cambridge, MA: Harvard University Press, pp. 1–24.

—(1974/1993), "What is a theory of meaning (I)", in *The Seas of Language*, Oxford: Oxford University Press, pp. 1–33.

—(1976/1993), "What is a theory of meaning (II)", in *The Seas of Language*, Oxford: Oxford University Press, pp. 34–93.

—(1978/1993), "What do I know when I know a language?" in *The Seas of Language*, Oxford: Oxford University Press, pp. 94–105.

Foster, J. (1976), "Meaning and truth theory", in G. Evans and J. McDowell (eds), *Truth and Meaning*. Oxford: Oxford University Press.

Frege, G. (1892/1952), "Über Sinn und Bedeutung". English translation in P. Geach and M. Black (eds), *Translations from the Philosophical Writings of Gottlob Frege*, Oxford: Blackwell, 56–78.

Glüer, K. (2006), "The status of charity I: conceptual truth or aposteriori necessity?" *International Journal of Philosophical Studies* 14, 337–59

—(2007), "Critical notice: Donald Davidson's Collected Essays". *Dialectica* 61, 275–84.

Greenberg, M. and Harman, G. (2006), "Conceptual Role Semantics", in E. Lepore and B. Smith (eds), *Oxford Handbook of the Philosophy of Language*, Oxford: Oxford University Press, pp. 295–322.

Grice, P. (1957/1987), "Meaning", in *Studies in the Ways of Words*, Cambridge, MA: Harvard University Press, pp. 213–23.

—(1968/1987), "Utterer's Meaning, Sentence-Meaning, and Word-Meaning", in *Studies in the Ways of Words*, Cambridge, MA: Harvard University Press, pp. 117–37.

Horwich, P. (1998), *meaning*, Oxford: Clarendon Press.

Kölbel, M. (2001), "Two Dogmas of Davidsonian Semantics". *Journal of Philosophy* 98, 613–35.

Lepore, E. (1982), "What Model Theoretic Semantics Cannot Do". *Synthese* 54, 167–87.

Lepore, E. and Ludwig, K. (2005), *Donald Davidson. Meaning, Truth, Language, and Reality*. Oxford: Oxford University Press.

Lewis, D. (1969), *Convention: A Philosophical Study*. Cambridge, MA: Harvard University Press.

—(1975), "Languages and Language", in K. Gunderson ed. *Minnesota Studies in the Philosophy of Science*, Volume VII, Minneapolis: University of Minnesota Press, pp. 3–35.

McDowell, J. (1987), "A plea for modesty", in B. Taylor ed. *Michael Dummett. Contributions to Philosophy*. Dordrecht: Nijhoff, pp. 59–80.

—(1997), "Another plea for modesty", in R. G. Heck ed. *Language, Thought, and Logic*. Oxford: Oxford University Press, pp. 105–29.

Pagin, P. (1997), "Is compositionality compatible with holism?" *Mind & Language* 12, 11–33.

—(1998), "Bivalence: meaning theory vs. metaphysics". *Theoria* 64, 37–66.

—(2006a), "Meaning holism", in E. Lepore and B. Smith (eds), *Handbook of Philosophy of Language*. Oxford: Oxford University Press, pp. 213–32.

—(2006b), "The status of charity II. Charity, probability and simplicity". *International Journal of Philosophical Studies* 14, 361–83.

—(forthcoming), "Communication and the complexity of semantics", in W. Hinzen, E. Machery and M. Werning (eds), *Oxford Handbook of Compositionality*. Oxford: Oxford University Press.

Pagin, P. and Pelletier, J. (2007), "Content, context and composition", in G. Peter and G. Preyer (eds), *Content and Context. Essays on Semantics and Pragmatics*. Oxford: Oxford University Press, pp. 25–62.

Pagin, P. and Westerståhl, D. (2010a), "Compositionality I: Definitions and Variants". *Philosophy Compass* 5, 250–64.

—(2010b), "Compositionality II: Arguments and Problems". *Philosophy Compass* 5, 265–82.

Patterson, D. (2005), "Deflationism and the truth conditional theory of meaning". *Philosophical Studies* 124, 271–94.

Peregrin, J. (2008), "An inferentialist approach to semantics: time for a new kind of structuralism?" *Philosophy Compass* 3, 1208–23.

Quine, W. V. O. (1960), *Word and Object*. Cambridge, MA: MIT Press.

Recanati, F. (2004), *Literal Meaning*. Oxford: Oxford University Press.

—(2007), *Perspectival Thought*. Oxford: Oxford University Press.

Rumfitt, I. (1995), "Truth conditions and communication". *Mind* 104: 827–62.

Schiffer, S. (1972), *Meaning*. Oxford: Oxford University Press.

Searle, J. (1978), "Literal meaning". *Erkenntnis* 13, 207–24.

Soames, S. (1992), "Truth, meaning, and understaning". *Philosophical Studies* 65, 17–35.

Stalnaker, R. (1997), "Reference and necessity", in B. Hale and C. Wright (eds), *A Companion to the Philosophy of Language*. Oxford: Blackwell, pp. 534–54.

Strawson, P. F. (1970), *Meaning and Truth. An Inaugural Lecture delivered before the University of Oxford on 5 November 1969*. Oxford: Clarendon Press.

Taylor, B. (1982), "On the need for a meaning theory in a theory of meaning". *Mind* XCI, 183–200.

Travis, C. (1989), *The Uses of Sense*. Oxford: Oxford University Press.

Williams, M. (1999), "Meaning and Deflationary Truth". *Journal of Philosophy* 96, 545–64.

Williamson, T. (2004), "Philosophical 'Intuitions' and Scepticism about Judgement". *Dialectica* 58, 109–53.

Wittgenstein, L. (1921/1961), *Tractatus Logico-Philosophicus* (T). English translation C. K. Ogden, London: Routledge & Kegan Paul 1922; transl. D. F. Pears and B. F. McGuinness, New York: Humanities Press.

—(1953), *Philosophische Untersuchungen*. English translation: *Philosophical Investigations*, transl. G. E. M. Anscombe, Oxford: Blackwell.

Wright, C. (1980), *Wittgenstein on the Foundations of Mathematics*. London: Duckworth.

—(1986), *Realism, Meaning and Truth*. Oxford: Blackwell.

5 Reference

Genoveva Martí

Introduction

We talk about things. When we say "New York is a large city" or "Cicero was a Greek general" we say something about a town or about a man, something that is either true or false. What connects our words with the things they are about? What makes it possible for a word to represent an object, so that something, true or false, can be said about it?

This is a fundamental question for the theory of reference, perhaps *the* fundamental question, so it is no wonder that philosophers of language have devoted a lot of attention to singular terms, expressions that seem to be designed to allow us to talk about things: proper names – "New York", "Cicero" – definite descriptions – "the tutor of Alexander the Great", "the British Prime Minister during World War II" – and indexicals or demonstratives – terms such as "I" or "that man".

For a long time philosophers took definite descriptions to be the paradigm case of how reference occurs, and they would explain the link between names and their referents in descriptivist terms. "The inventor of bifocals" refers to Ben Franklin because he is the individual who uniquely satisfies the attributes expressed by the description – being the person who invented bifocal lenses. From a descriptivist perspective, a proper name functions roughly in the same way: a name is semantically tied to a definite description, and the referent of the name is the individual who fits the descriptive profile.

But starting in the 1970s we find an approach that sees fundamental differences between the way in which descriptions and proper names manage to refer. From this perspective, the connection between a name and its referent is not to be explained in terms of the referent's satisfaction of a profile semantically connected to the name. When it comes to basic semantic questions, such as "what determines the reference of a name?" and "what do names contribute to the truth conditions of sentences?", this approach holds that names are entirely devoid of descriptive content.

My purpose here is to present and discuss the change of perspective that led a substantial number of philosophers of language away from the traditional descriptivist approach, and to examine the new theory that emerges from that change of perspective as well as some of the challenges the new theory faces.

Descriptivism

Proper names look very different from definite descriptions. For one thing, they are simple, seemingly structureless expressions that do not have parts that are themselves meaningful expressions. "The inventor of bifocals" has a meaning that depends on the meanings of "the", "inventor", "of" and "bifocals". It is those meanings that contribute to the meaning of the whole description. If that complex meaning applies to an object, then that's the referent of "the inventor of bifocals".

"Franklin", on the other hand, is not made out of other meaningful expressions, say "frank" and "lin", so it is *prima facie* hard to see why one would be tempted to think that the two kinds of terms are semantically similar. As Bertrand Russell put it:

> A name is a simple symbol (i.e., a symbol which does not have any parts that are symbols), a simple symbol used to designate a certain particular [...]. "The author of *Waverley*", is not a name because it is a complex symbol. It contains parts which *are* symbols. It contains four words, and the meanings of those four words are already fixed and they have fixed the meaning of "The author of *Waverley*" [...] In that respect, it differs from "Scott".[1]

Nevertheless, descriptivism is an attractive position. Bertrand Russell himself, in spite of the remarks just quoted, held explicitly the view that ordinary proper names, proper names such as "Scott", "Cicero" and "Ben Franklin", are in fact abbreviations of definite descriptions.[2] And Gottlob Frege, arguably the father of the philosophy of language, can be interpreted as suggesting a similar view.[3] According to Frege, proper names and definite descriptions, like all meaningful terms, express a *sense* and that sense determines a *referent*. Followers of Frege traditionally equated the sense of a proper name to the sense of some associated definite description, or some family of descriptions.[4]

There are powerful motivations for descriptivism. For instance, think about how we learn names, how we incorporate them to our vocabulary. Often times we are introduced to the person named. In many other cases we are told something about the referent: when we first encounter the name "Aristotle" we are told that he wrote the *Nichomachean Ethics* or that he defended hylemorphism. In all these cases, either by perception or by testimony, we acquire some information about the referent, some piece of information that identifies the referent for us. It is very natural then to think that this information is stored as a description, and it is precisely because of the association with the description that the name becomes significant to us, that we feel capable of using the name to say something about the referent, the person that the information encapsulated in the description applies to. In other words, we do not just learn names in a vacuum; when we learn a name, we always attach descriptive information to it.

Certainly, when we think about the names of our friends or people in our family it might seem that our uses of their names are almost like acts of pointing. There is probably some evolutionary reason that explains why, if I point at a dress in a window and utter "beautiful, but too expensive!", my audience will know what I am talking about. There may be a similar explanation of why we have names. As John Perry has claimed, cave dwellers probably invented names only so that they could call their children to dinner.[5]

But we do not only refer to the people around us. We also can refer to people long gone, or very distant from us, people we've never had any contact with. How do we do that? Descriptivism provides a natural answer: the description we associate with the name does the work for us. As soon as the words "the inventor of bifocals" leave our lips they, all by themselves and because of what they mean, find their referent, so to speak. If names are semantically associated with descriptions they also, all by themselves and because of what they mean, find their referent. We talk about Ben Franklin when we use "Ben Franklin" because the associated description, "the inventor of bifocals" or some other description, applies to him. In other words, we refer to things we do not seem to have any connection to; the view that a name operates via an associated description gives us an explanation of how we manage to do that; it gives us an account of the mechanism of reference.

Descriptivism also allows us to explain the cognitive differences between different names of one and the same thing. In ancient times people saw a bright heavenly body in the evening sky and called it "Hesperus". They also saw a bright heavenly body, the last one to fade in the morning light, and they called it "Phosphorus", thinking they were naming two different things, when in fact it was just one thing, the planet Venus (as the Babylonians discovered). Now, the sentences "Phosphorus is bright" and "Hesperus is bright" are both true and for exactly the same reason: the ball of rock that is Venus is indeed bright. But competent speakers could accept one sentence as true and reject or be in doubt about the other; or, after having accepted one sentence as true, they could find the other sentence informative. That is a difference in *cognitive significance* between the two sentences that cannot be explained just by appeal to the references of the terms involved, for those are the same. But it can be naturally accounted for if names are associated with definite descriptions: the terms "Hesperus" and "Phosphorus", tied to different descriptions, present the referent in different ways. Accepting "Phosphorus is bright" is tantamount to accepting that the beautiful heavenly body seen in the morning sky is bright. Learning then that Hesperus is bright, i.e., that the heavenly body seen in the evening sky is bright, is obviously a new piece of information.

All these considerations provide strong reasons to favour the view that names are semantically guided by definite descriptions, and to endorse the claim that the behaviour of descriptions provides a uniform explanation of the referential link that connects words to things. In fact, descriptivism was for years the dominant view in the philosophy of language. And then came 1970.

Rigidity

The year 1970 was a bad year for descriptivism. Both Saul Kripke, in the seminal lectures *Naming and Necessity* delivered in January of that year, and Keith Donnellan, in his paper "Proper Names and Identifying Descriptions", came up independently with powerful arguments against the descriptivist stance.[6]

Semantic theory is supposed to provide, among other things, an account of the contribution that expressions make to the truth conditions of the sentences in which they occur. In *Naming and Necessity*, Kripke argues that names and definite descriptions do not operate semantically the same way, for their contribution to truth conditions is different, something that can be observed by reflecting on the *modal profile* (i.e., the variation of truth value across different counterfactual circumstances) of sentences containing names versus sentences containing definite descriptions. Suppose that Ben Franklin had never developed an interest in optical instruments, devoting all his energies to politics after drafting the Declaration of Independence, and that some small-town optician, entirely uninterested in politics, had come up with the idea of bifocals in the late eighteenth century. If the world had been that way, "Ben Franklin signed the Declaration of Independence" would still be true, but the sentence "the inventor of bifocals signed the Declaration of Independence" would be false. So, it is simply not the case that "Ben Franklin" and "the inventor of bifocals" – or any other of the descriptions that encapsulate the information we have about Ben Franklin – operate semantically the same way, for their contributions to the truth conditions of sentences are different. The truth or falsity of "Ben Franklin signed the Declaration of Independence" depends on whether that man, our beloved and respected Ben Franklin, put his signature on the document, and it does not depend in any way on whether he was an accomplished inventor. The truth or falsity of "the inventor of bifocals signed the Declaration of Independence" depends on whether or not some person did two things: invent bifocals and sign the Declaration. That's why the two sentences can differ in truth value when we consider them against the background of a counterfactual situation (or possible world) that is different from the way the world happens to be. Proper names, simply, do not behave like definite descriptions when it comes to determining what the world has to be like in order for a given sentence to be true. Proper names, Kripke argued, are *rigid designators*: the referent of a name is the individual relevant in the evaluation of sentences in all possible worlds – or, as Kripke put it, proper names designate the same individual with respect to all possible worlds. Definite descriptions such as "the inventor of bifocals", "the Roman orator that denounced Catiline's conspiracy", "the tutor of Alexander the Great" are not: they designate different individuals with respect to different ways the world might be, depending on which individual satisfies the descriptive profile expressed by the definite description.

Descriptivist Responses: Widescopism and Rigidification

According to some descriptivists, Kripke's arguments do not threaten descriptivism. Most famously, Michael Dummett argued soon after 1970 that all Kripke succeeded in showing is that the descriptions associated with proper names always take wide scope when combined with modal operators in sentences such as "it is possibly the case that Ben Franklin did not invent bifocals".[7] Consider the description "the inventor of bifocals" in the sentence "it is possible that the inventor of bifocals did not invent bifocals" Now, there are two ways of reading that sentence. On one of them, the description takes narrower scope and the modal operator takes wider scope; on that reading the sentence says that it is possible, or in other words, that the world could be such that the person who invented bifocals did not invent bifocals. Now obviously, this is false; the world cannot be such that someone who does F does not do F. There is another reading in which the description takes wider scope; on that reading the sentence says that the person who (in fact) invented bifocals could have not done so, i.e., that the world could be such that that man (the one who has in fact invented bifocals) did not do so. There is nothing puzzling about such an assertion; in fact, it is very likely true. Now, according to Dummett the sentence "it is possible that Ben Franklin did not invent bifocals" must be read always giving the description synonymous to "Ben Franklin" wider scope over the modal operator. Thus names, after all, are synonymous with definite descriptions; it's just that they always take wider scope in the presence of modal operators.

Saul Kripke responded to Dummett's argument in the Preface to the written version of *Naming and Necessity* that appeared in 1982. As Kripke pointed out, his original arguments were not based on the evaluation of sentences containing any modal operators. The point in Kripke's argument, and in the story about Ben Franklin discussed above, has nothing to do with sentences of the form "it is possibly the case that S" or "it is necessarily the case that S". The argument relies on the evaluation of simple sentences such as "Ben Franklin invented bifocals" or "Ben Franklin signed the Declaration of Independence", and it hinges on what makes those sentences true or false under different circumstances. If Kripke is right, the truth conditions of "Ben Franklin signed the Declaration of Independence" depend on the man, Ben Franklin, having or not having signed the Declaration of Independence, whereas the truth conditions of "the inventor of bifocals signed the Declaration of Independence" depend on there being a person who invented bifocals and on his or her signing or not signing the Declaration of Independence. Clearly the truth conditions of those simple sentences are different, and they can go different ways. The question of scope does not even come up.[8]

A different descriptivist reaction to Kripke's arguments relies on the observation that, although definite descriptions are typically non-rigid, some definite descriptions are rigid designators. For instance "the successor of eight" designates the number nine given the way the world is and in every other possible circumstance; although we could call the number nine by another name, it would still be a mathematical truth that the number nine (by whatever name) is the successor of eight. So, although Kripke's notion of rigidity draws a line between names and most definite descriptions, it does not just by itself draw a line separating the semantics of names from the semantics of definite descriptions. Some descriptivists, sensitive to the considerations put forward by Kripke, argued that names are semantically connected to *rigid* definite descriptions, for instance, that the description tied to "Ben Franklin" is rather something like "the *actual* inventor of bifocals", a description that, relative to any counterfactual situation, will refer to whoever is the inventor of bifocals in the actual world. In that way we obtain the same distribution of truth values relative to all circumstances of evaluation for "Ben Franklin signed the Declaration of Independence" and "the actual inventor of bifocals signed the Declaration of Independence", defusing Kripke's criticism.[9] The success and plausibility of such a move has been contested.[10] But, arguably, the appeal to rigidified descriptions misses the deeper lesson of Kripke's argument, a lesson that may not be obvious if we just focus on the conclusion that names are rigid designators. For, even if we get the same distribution of truth values across possible worlds with a name and with a rigidified definite description, if Kripke is right, the contribution to the determination of those truth values (i.e., the contribution to truth conditions) made by "Ben Franklin" and by "the actual inventor of bifocals" is different. The name contributes just the referent, the description contributes a condition: that there be a unique object that happened to *actually* invent bifocals.

Direct Reference: The New Theory of Reference

Declaring names to be rigid fails to clearly separate names from all descriptions. But focusing on how each contributes to the truth conditions of sentences does. Going beyond the claim of rigidity, semanticists moved by Kripke's arguments have stressed that names are *directly referential*, meaning that their contribution to the determination of truth conditions of sentences – or, as it is often put, their contribution to the propositions expressed by sentences – is just the referent.

Kripke and Donnellan offered other, and perhaps stronger, arguments against descriptivism. Often competent speakers are not in possession of sufficient information to uniquely individuate the referent of a name. Many people only know about Cicero that he was an orator. But so were Demostenes and Cato. The use that those speakers make of "Cicero" is not guided by a description that uniquely fits Cicero and can be the thread that connects the name to its referent; yet, when those speakers use "Cicero", they do refer to Cicero.[11]

Moreover, speakers often attach the wrong descriptive information to a name. Kripke reports that many people think that Einstein was the inventor of the atomic bomb. Yet, when they use "Einstein", they refer to Einstein, not to some physicist member of the Manhattan Project.[12]

Kripke's and Donnellan's conclusion is that competent speakers refer using names even if they are not in possession of uniquely identifying information, a *definite* description. And they manage to refer to what intuitively is the right referent, even though they attach an erroneous descriptive profile to a name. What a name refers to is not determined by an associated definite description.

So, names and descriptions not only make different contributions to truth conditions, something that would entail that a name is not *synonymous* to a definite description. The conclusion of the ignorance and error arguments is that, when a speaker uses a name, the reference of her use of the name is not *fixed* by a description (neither a non-rigid nor a rigidified one).

Neither Kripke nor Donnellan deny that speakers attach descriptive information to names. As we have pointed out, we very often learn names by being given information about the referent. And it would be hard to deny that the descriptive information we store – even if insufficient or incorrect, or both – plays an important role in our cognitive lives and in the explanation of the cognitive significance of sentences containing names. The point that Kripke and Donnellan press is that such descriptive information does not determine the referent of the name. The theory of reference that emerges from these considerations, *direct reference theory*, is fundamentally anti-descriptivist. Unlike descriptions, proper names are not and are not connected with profiles that do the work of searching and identifying the referent. Descriptions behave as search mechanisms; they are "prescriptions for finding an object", as Ruth Barcan Marcus put it. Names, on the other hand, are mere tags: "To count as a proper name an expression must refer without being tied to any particular characterization of the object."[13] This approach finds inspiration in some remarks on names by John Stuart Mill, and in particular in his example involving "Dartmouth".[14] Dartmouth is at the mouth of the river Dart, and this fact played a very important role in the decision to call the town "Dartmouth". But had the river changed course, it would not be incorrect to continue to apply "Dartmouth" to Dartmouth. In fact, were we to discover that Dartmouth never was near the river, the name would not fail to name the town. By contrast, if Ben Franklin didn't invent bifocal lenses, "the inventor of bifocals" does not apply to him and never did. What this way of thinking about reference stresses is that the properties the referent has or is supposed to have, the profiles that it satisfies or appears to satisfy, may play an important role in the *decision* to use a certain expression to name it; those properties and profiles are exploited as much as other background and contextual factors in the process of introducing a name and in using it subsequently, i.e., in establishing and in maintaining reference. But they are not what the expression *means*, they are not an attached semantic search mechanism that connects term and object.[15]

But if the referent of a name is not determined by associated descriptive information, then how do names connect to their bearers? Descriptivism had an answer for this fundamental question; it gave us an account of the mechanism of reference. How does a name refer, according to direct reference theory?

The Causal-Historical Chain of Communication

As we have mentioned, we use proper names to refer to very distant objects, distant in space and in time. I cannot point at Aristotle for the simple reason that he does not exist anymore, so the model of a use of a name as an act of pointing does not apply in this case.

According to the proponents of direct reference theory, the fact that we are embedded in a chain of communication that connects our use of a given name to previous uses, stretching all the way back to the moment of introduction of the name, explains how we manage to refer to such distant objects. I may have insufficient or even wrong information about Cicero, yet when I use the name "Cicero" my connection to other speakers in my community from which I have borrowed the name, and their connection to previous speakers from which they have borrowed the name, and so forth, leads all the way back to the referent of "Cicero", the person I am talking about when I use his name, independently of my capacity to single him out, descriptively or otherwise. Here is how Kripke presents the picture:

> Someone, let's say, a baby, is born; his parents call him by a certain name. They talk about him to their friends. Other people meet him. Through various sorts of talk the name is spread from link to link as if by a chain (*Naming and Necessity*, p. 91).

So, reference is initially fixed, often in some kind of dubbing ceremony in which the referent is present and perceived so that the name can be bestowed upon it. Afterwards those present in the original introduction use the name to refer to the object in question when they are talking to others not present in the dubbing ceremony. In that way the name gets passed from speaker to speaker and from generation to generation, perhaps suffering changes in its spelling and its pronunciation, especially when it is passed from speakers of one language to speakers of another language. Each new link in the chain uses the name with the intention of referring to whatever object the previous link referred to when she used the name.[16] Each new link in the chain may attach some, the same or different, descriptive information to the name. In fact speakers attach not only descriptive information to names; they also associate images, memories, smells and all sorts of connotations. All these associations undeniably play a very important role in cognition and they may explain the psychology of communication and understanding. What the proponent of the new theory of reference denies is that they determine what a user of a name is referring to when she uses a name. In using a name, with whatever associations, a speaker refers to the object that is at the end of the chain of communication leading to her present use. What explains reference is not something that the speaker has in her head (descriptive or otherwise); it is the non-mental, non-internal, very worldly fact that the speaker is part of a network.

It is important to stress what chains of communication are and what they are not. A chain of communication makes an expression preserve whatever linguistic function it has from one generation to the next. Chains are mechanisms of propagation of language and preservation of meaning, and as such the chain picture applies not specifically to names but to any expression in a language. There is a chain of communication that connects my use of "Aristotle" to previous uses. There is equally a chain of communication that connects my use of "table" to previous uses, and my use of "not".

Changes do occur: it may happen that a group of speakers systematically make a mistake; the mistake may catch on, and be passed to other speakers, until in the end what was a mistake becomes regular practice as if a new dubbing (or a new term introduction) had occurred. There is a story according to which the inhabitants of the East Coast of Africa called a portion of the mainland "Madagascar". Portuguese explorers got the name from the natives and mistakenly thought that it was the name of the island. The explorers surely intended to conform to the natives' practice, but by their repeated use of "Madagascar" in their dealings with the obvious intention to say something about the island (a use that must have left the natives in the mainland flummoxed if they ever interacted with the explorers at all) it was the island that became known to the world as "Madagascar" as if a new protracted dubbing had taken place. Nowadays, when we use "Madagascar" we are certainly referring to the island.[17]

Another point, which may be less apparent, is that the causal-historical explanation is not *per se* an alternative to descriptivism, in the sense of being a theory that contradicts descriptivism. The causal-historical approach holds that a chain of communication passes from link to link whatever accounts for the semantic behaviour of an expression. The descriptivist could take on board chains of communication: what is passed from a link alongside a name, he thinks, is precisely a description that determines the reference each time a speaker uses the name.

The disagreement between the descriptivist and the new theorist is not about the existence of chains. What contradicts descriptivism is the argument that reference is possible without the mediation of a description, i.e., that a speaker can manage to refer without having to acquire from the previous link, or in any way master, a description that uniquely identifies the referent. Different speakers may attach different, right or wrong, sufficient or insufficient descriptive information to a proper name (as well as images and other connotations). None of that, the anti-descriptivist thinks, determines what she is referring to with a use of a name. The reliance on the network by itself provides what is required to acquire a name and use it to refer to its bearer. [18]

Some descriptivists have argued that the chain of communication itself provides a description, implicitly or explicitly known by the speaker, that determines the referent of a name. On this kind of view, when a speaker uses "Ben Franklin", the reference of the name is determined by a description such as "the individual at the end of the chain that leads to this use of 'Ben Franklin'", or "the person that the members of my community from which I inherit my use of 'Ben Franklin' refer to", or something similar.[19] Since chains of communication are not a name-only phenomenon, the mechanism appears to be quite general: when a speaker uses "table" there is a description of the sort "the kind of thing that is at the end of the chain that leads to my use of 'table'", or some such description. It is not entirely clear that being in possession of such a description determines reference (or application) rather than just being the expression of a speaker's awareness that she relies on shared meanings and conforms to her community's practice, for names and for any other word.

Other Expressions

Descriptivism is not just an approach to the semantics of proper names. Other singular terms, such as indexicals ("I", "here", "now", "today" …) and demonstratives ("this", "that"), were also taken to fit the semantic mould of definite descriptions.[20] On a descriptivist approach, "I" means something like "the person who is speaking", "here" means something like "the place where the speaker is located", and "this" means "the object I am pointing at or somehow demonstrating".

Indexicals and demonstratives are context-sensitive expressions. My present utterance of "today" refers to October 10th but my utterance of "today" last week referred to October 3rd; you refer to yourself when you utter "I" and I refer to myself when I do the same. By saying "I am hungry" you and I are talking about different people; moreover, you may be saying something true while I, having just had breakfast, am saying something false. If a speaker says something true whereas another speaker says something false, they clearly are not saying the same thing, even if they are using the same words. If I say "I am hungry" and you want to report what I said, you will say "she is hungry" (probably pointing at me, or making sure that I am somehow salient so that it is clear you are talking about me). In this case two speakers say the same thing, even though they are using different words – in fact, they have to use different words: if you used "I am hungry" you would not be reporting what I said.

Following an argument reminiscent of the truth-conditional considerations about names and descriptions, David Kaplan argued in "Demonstratives"[21] against the descriptivist approach to names and indexicals. Suppose that "I" means "the person who is speaking", and that I say "I am a philosopher". We need to ask ourselves about the conditions under which what I said is true. I am a philosopher, so what I said is true. The way things are, it is true that I am a philosopher and it is also true that the person speaking is a philosopher.

But now suppose that instead of being a philosopher I had become a chef. If the world were like that, it seems quite clear that what I said would be false. Now, imagine that in that situation I am not speaking and someone else, who is a philosopher, is uttering out loud "I am a philosopher". In this case it is true that the person speaking is a philosopher, even if it is false that I am a philosopher.

In other words: when I utter "I am a philosopher" the truth and falsity of what I said is determined by whether or not I am a philosopher, not by whether or not I am speaking; an utterance of "I am a philosopher" and an utterance of "the person speaking is a philosopher" have different truth conditions. But, as in the case of names, the important point is not that the two sentences' truth values with respect to different circumstances do not coincide. The important point is that what determines truth value across different circumstances (i.e., what determines truth conditions) differs. When the indexical is used, the referent determines truth conditions. Indexicals and demonstratives, like names, are directly referential.[22]

However, unlike names, indexicals and demonstratives do have some descriptive content. For instance, "I" refers to the person who is speaking in the context of utterance. That descriptive content clearly plays a role in determining the referent of each utterance of "I": there is no way I can refer to "Hume" when I use "I", simply because I am the object that fits the descriptive profile expressed by "the person who is speaking in the context of the utterance". Moreover, mastery of the use of indexicals and demonstratives requires mastery of rules of use that are specific. The rule that governs the use of "I" (something like "in all contexts, an utterance of 'I' refers to the speaker in that context") is different from the rule of use that governs the use of "today" (something such as "in every context of use, an utterance of 'today' refers to the day in that context") and, even though speakers may not quite put the rules in those terms, it seems patent that they have to master those rules. In this regard, indexicals and demonstratives differ from names too, for it does not seem *prima facie* plausible to say that "Ben Franklin" and "Bill Clinton" are associated with different rules of use. They are names: learn to use one, you've learnt to use them all. As Russell said (in moments where he put aside his contention that proper names are abbreviations of definite descriptions), a name "is merely a noise or shape conventionally used to designate a certain person".[23]

Contextually sensitive expressions such as indexicals and demonstratives are governed by rules of use that can be expressed as descriptions that, in a given context of use, determine the reference of the use of one of those expressions. Yet, it is not those descriptions that constitute the contribution to the truth conditions of uses of sentences containing indexicals or demonstratives. So, indexicals and demonstratives are partly like names (they contribute referents to the determination of truth conditions) and partly like definite descriptions (descriptive information determines the referent in each occasion of use).

From the point of view of the new theory of reference, if the criterion of classification of terms is contribution to truth conditions, descriptions would be in one category, names, indexicals and demonstratives in another. But if the criterion is the mode of connection between the use of an expression and its referent, then indexicals and demonstratives fall in line with definite descriptions, whereas names stand alone as purely conventional stand-ins for their referents.

When Reference Fails

The function of a name, according to direct reference theory, is to make an object, the referent, the subject of discourse, so that something, true or false, can be said about it, without picking out the object by appeal to any of its properties. To repeat Ruth Barcan Marcus's characterization, a proper name performs the semantic function of referring "without being tied to any particular characterization of the object". When we utter, for instance, "John Stuart Mill was a vegetarian", "John Stuart Mill" just conjures up the individual at the end of a chain of communication, so that we can attribute being vegetarian to him. The truth or falsity of what we say when we utter that sentence, i.e., the utterance's truth conditions, depend on that individual, and on whether he was, or was not, a vegetarian, so the contribution of the name to what is said, to *the proposition expressed* by the utterance, is just that individual.

But, observe that when we use proper names, we do not always manage to refer. Having discovered Neptune, Le Verrier was completely sure it had to be yet another planet that was causing anomalies in the orbit of Mercury. He and other astronomers even started using the name "Vulcan", thinking that they were indeed referring to a planet.[24] But there was no such planet. Yet, for quite some time Le Verrier and many others were using "Vulcan" as confidently as they were using "Neptune" – as confidently as we use "Aristotle" or "Julius Caesar". The point is that, far-fetched as in the latter two cases it may seem, proper names that we often use may fail to refer. Now, this generates a few problems for direct reference theories. For one thing, if the function of a name is precisely to be a stand-in for its referent, making it a subject of discourse and so on, it would appear that *empty* names have no function in language; competent speakers should dismiss them as mere meaningless noises, like the sound of snapping fingers. But they do not; surely "Vulcan" did not sound to Le Verrier like a meaningless noise when he was using the name, not even when, after pointing his telescope and finding empty space, he proclaimed "I must have made a mistake, Vulcan does not exist".

And, for another thing, if a name contributes its referent to what is said by an utterance of a sentence, an empty name contributes nothing, so it is as if, in uttering "Vulcan is causing anomalies in the orbit of Mercury", Le Verrier was not saying anything at all.[25]

Empty names do not appear to cause such problems for a descriptivist approach. First, the fact that a name fails to refer does not make it a meaningless noise, for the same reason that "the present King of France" or "the largest prime number" are not mere noises, even though they do not denote, i.e., they also fail to pick out an individual. Those descriptions continue to be meaningful because, as we have explained, they have parts that are themselves meaningful, even if no object is presently King of France and there are an infinite number of primes. As for the second problem, since definite descriptions are complex symbols that have other symbols as parts, they contribute the meanings of those parts to propositions too, so the problem of there being no contribution to what is said by an utterance of a sentence containing a non-denoting description does not arise. So, there are issues here specifically for theories of direct reference to address.[26]

Now, about the first problem, Donnellan has noted that what makes a name common currency in a community and, we could add, what makes it cognitively significant for a speaker in that community, is the fact that there is a chain of communication, a network of uses of the name. The chain itself may fail to be grounded in an initial act of referring. A name may be introduced, and then passed around, as a prank or by honest mistake, caused by a perceptual error, or by, as in the case of Le Verrier, because the introducer is convinced that there is a yet undiscovered object that satisfies certain specifications. The difference between a referring name and an empty one is that, in the latter case, as Donnellan puts it, the chain "ends in a block",[27] and speakers may come to discover this, as when Le Verrier finally faces the darkness of space where he expected to find a planet. But the chain of communication exists nevertheless, and its existence is what explains that speakers in a community do not dismiss empty names as mere noises; take your own perspective as a speaker: the name "Aristotle" has arrived to you from another user, and its arrival is independent of whether it is a referring name or not.

But, what does a theory of direct reference say about the contribution of an empty name to a proposition? Let us think first of how things are supposed to work in problem free cases: when a speaker utters "Plato was a Greek philosopher", according to direct reference theory, she says about a certain individual, Plato, the man at the end of the chain of communication that leads to the speaker's use of the name, that he is was a Greek philosopher. What the speaker says, the proposition expressed by her utterance, consists of an attribution of a property to an object. The proposition our speaker expresses is true, for it is a fact in the world that Plato was a Greek philosopher. But a speaker can also succeed in attributing a property to an object and express a false proposition. For instance, our speaker attributes the property of being a playwright to Jane Austen when she utters "Jane Austen was a playwright", but the proposition she expresses is false, for it is not a fact that Jane Austen was a playwright.

With this conception of what propositions are and of how facts in the world make them true or false, the view that a sentence containing an empty name does not express a proposition is, arguably, less far-fetched than it *prima facie* appears to be. For, after all, a speaker who utters "Vulcan is a planet" is attributing the property of being a planet to nothing at all. This does not mean that the speaker just produces meaningless noises, noises that are going to be equated to sounds like, say, snoring, by the rest of the members of her community: what makes her utterance significant is the fact that she is using a name, for which a chain of communication exists, plus all the connotations that, as mentioned before, speakers associate with the words that are common currency in their community. Her utterance is significant for it is made up of words that are part of a language; it just does not have a *propositional content*, something that can be evaluated for truth or falsity.[28]

Experimental Data and the Theory of Reference

The original case against descriptivism relied crucially on arguments such as Kripke's and Donnellan's error and ignorance arguments. Those arguments exploited our intuitions as competent speakers in order to establish that a speaker refers to the bearer of a name even if he does not associate correct nor uniquely identifying information in the form of a description. Thus, a speaker refers to Einstein when he uses "Einstein", even if he attaches to the name the description "the inventor of the atomic bomb", and he would refer to Gödel when he uses "Gödel" even if the descriptive information he has about Gödel – that he proved the incompleteness of arithmetic – were false, even if, unbeknownst to practically all of us, Gödel had actually stolen the proof from a man called "Schmidt", an obscure mathematician who appeared dead under mysterious circumstances. Supposing the latter, completely fictional, story to be true, Kripke convincingly contended, a speaker who uses "Gödel" still refers to Gödel, not to Schmidt, even though "the mathematician who proved the incompleteness of arithmetic" is a description that applies to Schmidt and not to Gödel.

Recently some philosophers have taken issue with Kripke's contention, and have argued that there is cultural variation in the way people react to Kripke's story: whereas the conclusion that in the fictional circumstance envisaged speakers who use "Gödel" refer to Gödel is accepted by a majority of Westerners, people in other cultures, East Asians for instance, display considerably stronger descriptivist leanings. Edouard Machery, Ron Mallon, Shaun Nichols and Stephen Stich compared the responses of a group of Westerner students in the US and a group of East Asian students in Hong Kong to the Gödel story.[29] In their study they gave the participants the following two choices:

> When John [a speaker in the envisaged situation] uses the name "Gödel", is he talking about:
> (A) the person who really discovered the incompleteness of arithmetic? or
> (B) the person who got hold of the manuscript and claimed credit for the work?

Machery and colleagues report that a significant majority of Westerners chose (B), thus revealing leanings towards Kripke's causal-historical account, whereas most of the Hong Kong participants chose (A), thus revealing descriptivist leanings.

The significance of those experimental findings has been debated. There are other studies that do not seem to support the conclusion.[30] Moreover, some philosophers have argued that the data that Machery *et al.* rely on does not take into account some of the strongest arguments by Kripke in favour of the causal-historical picture; so although their results are somewhat interesting and puzzling, they do not constitute a serious threat for the theory.[31] And there is a question as to the adequacy of the data that Machery *et al.* collect. In their study they ask participants what, on their view, a given speaker refers to when he uses a name, and it would seem that the data that should constitute the input for semantic theorizing about reference are data about how speakers use names and other referential expressions, not data about how speakers think other speakers use those expressions.[32]

In any case, and independently of the ultimate relevance of these results, the discussion around the use of experiments in the theory of reference has opened up a debate about an issue that used to be of concern to philosophers of language, and that was for some time somewhat abandoned: the debate about the empirical evidence on which the theory of reference and, in general, the theory of meaning is supposed to rely on.[33]

Notes

1. Bertrand Russell, *The Philosophy of Logical Atomism*. La Salle, Open Court, 1985: 111–12. See also "Knowledge by Acquaintance and Knowledge by Description". *Mysticism and Logic*. Totowa: Barnes and Noble, 1917: 152–67 (p. 163).
2. "Common words, even proper names, are usually really descriptions. That is to say, the thought in the mind of a person using a proper name correctly can generally only be expressed explicitly if we replace the proper name by a description." "Knowledge by Acquaintance and Knowledge by Description". *Mysticism and Logic*. Totowa: Barnes and Noble, 1917, p. 156.
3. Gottlob Frege, "On Sense and Reference", 1892, n. 2.
4. See John Searle, "Proper Names", *Mind* 67, 1958: 166–73, for a defence of the view that the referent of a name is the object that satisfies a sufficient number of the definite descriptions in a cluster associated with the name. See also Paul Ziff, "About 'God'" (*Philosophic Turnings*. New York: Cornell University Press. 1966: 93–102). Whether Frege himself was a descriptivist is a matter of some controversy. Gareth Evans (*The Varieties of Reference*, Oxford: Oxford University Press, 1982, chapter 1), John McDowell ("On the Sense and Reference of a Proper Name", *Mind* 86, 1977: 159–85) and other *neo-Fregean* philosophers have argued that Fregean senses of proper names are *object dependent* in that it is the referent that determines the sense. That would make senses of proper names radically different from other senses, and in particular from senses of definite

descriptions, since in general the sense of a term determines the referent, according to Frege.

5. See Perry's review of Howard Wettstein's *The Magic Prism* in *Philosophical Books*, 47, 2006: 34–9.

6. Kripke's lectures were published, with a Preface and Addendum, by Harvard University Press (Cambridge, MA.: 1982); Donnellan's paper appeared in *Synthese*, 21, 1970: 335–8.

7. Michael Dummett, *Frege: Philosophy of Language*. London: Duckworth, 1973, especially chapter 5. See also the second edition (1981) in which Dummett addresses Kripke's response.

8. See Scott Soames's "The Modal Argument: Wide Scope and Rigidified Descriptions" (*Noûs*, 32, 1998: 1–22, reprinted in volume 2 of Soames's *Philosophical Essays*. Princeton, NJ: Princeton University Press, 2009) for arguments against *widescopism* and other forms of descriptivism. Proponents of widescopism have, nevertheless, defended the view against some details of Soames's argument (although, in my view, not against the substance of Kripke's initial 1982 response). See, for example, David Sosa's discussion of Soames's paper in "Rigidity in the Scope of Russell's Theory" (*Noûs*, 35, 2001: 1–38), and more recently David Hunter's, "Soames and Widescopism" in *Philosophical Studies*, 123, 2005: 231–41. See also chapter 2 of Scott Soames, *Beyond Rigidity*. New York: Oxford University Press, 2002, for responses; and Ben Caplan's "Against Widescopism", *Philosophical Studies*, 125, 2005: 167–90.

9. See Alvin Plantinga, "The Boethian Compromise", reprinted in Alvin Plantinga and Matthew Davidson (eds), *Essays in the Metaphysics of Modality*. Oxford: Oxford University Press, 2003: 122–39; and Felicia (Diana) Ackerman, "Proper Names, Propositional Attitudes and Nondescriptive Connotations", *Philosophical Studies*, 1979: 55–69.

10. See again Scott Soames, "The Modal Argument: Wide Scope and Rigidified Descriptions", *Noûs*, 32, 1998: 1–22, reprinted in volume 2 of Soames's *Philosophical Essays*, Princeton, NJ: Princeton University Press, 2009; and chapter 2 of *Beyond Rigidity*, New York: Oxford University Press, 2002. See also Robin Jeshion, "Descriptive Descriptive Names", in M. Reimer and A. Bezuidenhout (eds), *Descriptions and Beyond*, Oxford: Oxford University Press, 2004: 591–613. For a more recent variant of the view that equates names to rigidified descriptions – incorporating also some anti-descriptivist elements – see Philipp Pettit, "Descriptivism, Rigidified and Anchored", *Philosophical Studies*, 118, 2004: 323–38.

11. This has come to be known as "the argument from ignorance", as presented by Kripke. Keith Donnellan makes the same point, arguing that being in possession of a description is not necessary for reference to occur.

12. This has come to be known as "the argument from error", as presented by Kripke. Donnellan puts forward similar considerations when he argues that being in possession of a description is not sufficient for the name to refer to the entity that satisfies the description.

13. The quotes are from "Possibilia and Possible Worlds", *Grazer Philosophische Studien*, 25–26, 1985–86: 107–33, and "Does the Principle of Substitutivity Rest on a Mistake?", A. Anderson and R.M. Martin, *The Logical Enterprise*, New Haven: Yale University Press, 1973: 31–8.

14 *A System of Logic*, 1843. Book II, chapter 11, § 5.
15. I have argued for this view in "The Question of Rigidity in New Theories of Reference", *Noûs*, 37, 2003: 161–79.
16. A name can also be introduced using a description. Urbain Le Verrier introduced the name "Neptune" to refer to the planet that caused certain anomalies in the orbit of Uranus. Acknowledging that a name can be introduced via a description is not a concession to descriptivism: the description is not what is passed from link to link of the communication chain. Users of the name can refer to Neptune in complete ignorance of the description that was originally used to fix its reference.
17. Some philosophers have argued that cases such as "Madagascar" pose a serious problem for the causal-historical picture, but this may be due to an over-restrictive interpretation of the claim that the referent is the object at the end of the chain of communication, or to a very strict interpretation of the picture of a dubbing ceremony. Obviously changes in meaning and reference do occur, and those changes are traceable to either intentional introduction of new uses for words (new dubbings, so to speak), or a gradual process also explicable in terms of how words are transmitted from link to link. See Gareth Evans, "The Causal Theory of Names", *Proceedings of the Aristotelian Society*, Supplementary Volume 47, 1973: 187–208; and Michael Devitt and Kim Sterelny, *Language and Reality*, Oxford: Blackwell, 1987, esp. chapter 4.
18. See Michael Devitt, "Singular Terms", *Journal of* Philosophy, 71, 1974: 183–205, and *Designation*, New York: Columbia University Press, 1981. See also Joseph Almog's "Semantical Anthropology", *Midwest Studies in Philosophy*, vol. ix, 1984: 479–89, for a discussion of the role of chains of communication.
19. For an in-depth discussion and defence of the view, see Frederick Kroon, "Causal Descriptivism", *Australasian Journal of Philosophy*, 65, 1987: 1–17; a similar line has been endorsed more recently by Manual García-Carpintero in "A Presuppositional Account of Reference-Fixing", *Journal of Philosophy*, 97, 2000: 109–47.
20. Even general terms, terms such as "gold" or "tiger", have been treated by some semanticists using the model of descriptions. The idea is that a general term applies to whatever instances satisfy associated descriptive information. Thus, for instance, "tiger" applies to things that fit the profile "large striped feline" or something similar. Since we are focusing on reference we will not discuss descriptivism about general terms here and the reaction of proponents of direct reference theories. Influential anti-descriptivist arguments as regards general terms can be found in Hilary Putnam's "Meaning and Reference", *Journal of Philosophy*, 70, 1973: 699–711.
21. Kaplan's manuscript was widely circulated in the 1970s. It appeared eventually, with "Afterthoughts", in J. Almog, J. Perry and H. Wettstein (eds), *Themes from Kaplan*, New York: Oxford University Press, 1984: 481–563.
22. In "Frege on Demonstratives", *The Philosophical Review*, 86, 1977: 474–97. John Perry applies to indexicals an argument reminiscent of Donnellan's argument about the non-necessity and non-sufficiency of descriptive information in the determination of the reference of a name. As Perry puts it, a speaker can be amnesiac, lack any information about herself, and still refer to herself when she

utters "I am lost". Similarly, a delusional speaker who thinks he is Hume may have a very rich descriptive profile that fits Hume perfectly. Yet, when he says "I wrote the *Treatise*" he is saying something false about himself. He does not manage to refer to Hume.

23. "Knowledge by Acquaintance and Knowledge by Description", *Mysticism and Logic*, Totowa: Barnes and Noble, 1917: 163.

24. We should be careful in characterizing the phenomenon that occupies us here. We are not talking about uses of names in fiction or to talk about fiction. The status of fictional discourse is an extremely interesting and complex topic, but here we are focusing rather on cases where a speaker intends to refer, assumes she is talking about a real object, and fails to do so. Le Verrier mistakenly thought that he was talking about a real planet when he used "Vulcan".

25. For a catalogue of the problems that empty names pose for theories of direct reference, and ways of addressing those problems, see David Braun, "Empty Names", *Noûs*, 27, 1993: 449–69. See also Marga Reimer, "The Problem of Empty Names", *Australasian Journal of Philosophy*, 79, 2001: 491–506.

26. Observe that neo-Fregeans who contend that names express object-dependent senses also face similar issues.

27. See Keith Donnellan, "Speaking of Nothing", *The Philosophical Review*, 83, 1974: 3–31.

28. In "Empty Names", David Braun argues that the speaker expresses a *gappy* proposition, rather than no proposition at all.

29. Edouard Machery, Ron Mallon, Shaun Nichols and Stephen Stich, "Semantics, cross-cultural style", *Cognition*, 92, 2004: B1–B12.

30. Barry Lam (in "Are Cantonese Speakers really Descriptivist? Revising cross-cultural semantics", *Cognition*, 2010) reports results that suggest that Cantonese speakers have the same causal-historical intuitions as Western English speakers. The results of a more recent study by Machery himself suggest a high level of intra-cultural, not cross-cultural variation (Edouard Machery, Christopher Y. Olivola and Molly De Blanc, "Linguistic and metalinguistic intuitions in the philosophy of language", *Analysis*, 69, 4, 2009: 689–94.

31. See Michael Devitt, "Experimental Semantics" (*Philosophy and Phenomenological Research* 82 (2): 418–435).

32. See Genoveva Martí, "Against semantic multi-culturalism", *Analysis*, 69, 2009: 42–8, and the ensuing discussion: E. Machery, C. Olivola and M. de Blanc, "Linguistic and Metalinguistic Intuitions in the Philosophy of Language", *Analysis*, 69, 2009: 689–94, and G. Martí, "Empirical Data and the Theory of Reference", in M. O'Rourke ed. *Topics in Contemporary Philosophy*, Vol. 10, Cambridge, MA: The MIT Press, forthcoming.

33. Classical sources in this debate are Rudolf Carnap, "Meaning and Synonymy in Natural Languages", Supplement D of *Meaning and Necessity*, 2nd edition. Chicago: The University Press, 1956; and W. V. O. Quine, *Word and Object*, Cambridge, MA: The MIT Press, 1960 (especially chapter 2).

6 Intensional Contexts

Michael Nelson

A general substitution principle is valid in classical quantificational logic (QL). If we stipulate that the *reference* of an individual constant is an individual, the *reference* of a predicate is the set of objects that it is true of, and the *reference* of a sentence is its truth value, then we can say that in QL co-referring expressions of any of these types are substitutable *salva veritate*. The language of QL is *extensional*.

QL has these attractive features because of its semantics. An interpretation I of a set of formulae Σ in the language of QL consists of an assignment of a non-empty set of individuals as the domain D, which can be conceived as the objects the language is about, an assignment, for each individual constant in the formulae of Σ, of exactly one individual from D, and an assignment of an n-tuple of individuals from D for each n-place predicate Φ^n in the formulae of Σ, called the *extension of* Φ^n in I. (There are interpretations with empty domains and empty individual constants in free but not classical QLs.) We define truth in terms of a notion of satisfaction. We define an *objectual* notion of satisfaction as follows. A sequence of objects $<1, ..., n>$ from D of I <u>satisfies</u> in I a condition $\Phi^n(x_1...x_n)$ just in case $<1, ..., n>$ is in the extension of Φ^n in I. We can then employ this notion of satisfaction to define truth for an atomic sentence as follows: $\Phi^n(\alpha_1...\alpha_n)$, where Φ^n is an n-place predicate letter and $\alpha_1...\alpha_n$ are individual constants, is true in I just in case the sequence of values of $\alpha_1...\alpha_n$ in I, which is an n-tuple of objects from D, satisfies the condition $\Phi^n(x_1...x_n)$ in I (and hence is in the extension of Φ^n in I). For simplicity, suppose our only primitive quantifier is the existential quantifier $\exists x$. We then define truth for a quantified sentence in terms of the notion of satisfaction as follows. A quantified formula $\exists x \Psi x$ is true in I just in case there is some object 1 in the domain D of I that satisfies Ψx in I. The truth-functional operators are defined in the standard way in terms of their truth tables.

One particular version of the substitution principle is the substitution of co-referring individual constants. Suppose that α_1 and α_2 are two individual constants that have the same value 1 in I. Then, for any pair of formulae γ, φ in the language of QL such that γ differs from φ exactly in the replacement of an occurrence of α_1 in γ for an occurrence of α_2, γ is true in I if and only if φ is true in I. This follows immediately from our definitions. For simplicity, suppose

125

that γ and φ are atomic sentences containing a 1-place predicate Φ^1. Then γ is true in I just in case the value of α_1 in I – i.e., **1** – satisfies Φ^1x. φ is true in I just in case the value of α_1 in I – i.e., **1** – satisfies Φ^1x. So, γ is true in I if and only if φ is true in I. So, in QL individual constants with the same value are inter-substitutable *salva veritate*. Indeed, substitutions of predicates with the same extension (within an interpretation) preserve truth value (within that inter-pretation) and substitutions of sentences, even when they are sub-formulae of larger formulae, with the same truth value (within an interpretation) preserve truth value (within that interpretation). Of course, these substitutions do not obtain across interpretations. Just because α_1 and α_2 have the same value in I does not entail that they have the same value in every interpretation I'. Indeed, if α_1 and α_2 are nonlogical, then there is an interpretation in which they have different values. The substitution principle only obtains within an interpretation.

Extensionalism is a sign of expressive shortcomings. A host of important notions – the notions of necessity (logical, metaphysical, and causal), the notions of belief and desire, temporal notions, among others – cannot be expressed within a purely extensional framework with individuals as the values of singular terms and variables. This is clearest when sentences with the same truth value are inter-substitutable. While it is true that I am wearing shorts, it is not necessary. But if truths are substitutable for truths regardless of the linguistic context in which they are embedded, then we could move from the true 'It is necessary that 2=2' to the false 'It is necessary that I am wearing shorts', substituting the true 'I am wearing shorts' for the true '2=2'. Necessary truth would, in that case, collapse to material truth. Any modal logic with such a principle would be equivalent to its non-modal base and hence wouldn't be a modal logic worth its salt, containing a wholly redundant operator with no new expressive power. Given our assumption that sentences refer to their truth values, modelling necessity (and the other notions mentioned above) requires moving to an intensional language.

Intensional logics promise to model expressions that are sensitive to more than just their references. Quotation is a clear, non-controversial example. Even though "Maya Angelou" and "Marguerite Johnson" co-refer, (1) below is true and (2) is false.

(1)   'Maya Angelou' has 11 letters.

(2)   'Marguerite Johnson' has 11 letters.

We can say that the occurrences of the names in (1) and (2) are *nonreferential*, following Quine's terminology (Quine 1980). The occurrences of those same terms in (3) and (4) below, on the other hand, are *referential*.

(3)   Maya Angelou wrote autobiographies.

(4)   Marguerite Johnson wrote autobiographies.

(3) is true if and only if (4) is true, as both names refer to the same object and both sentences ascribe the same property to that one object. While a purely extensional logic can hope to model sentences like (3) and (4), it is less helpful with intensional contexts.

Quotation is only one non-extensional context. We have already seen that modal contexts are also intensional. So too are temporal contexts – while it is true both that I am sitting and that I have skin, only one of these is always, or at least as long as I am alive, let's hope, true – causal contexts, and propositional attitude contexts. Whereas a quotational context is sensitive to the identity of expressions within its scope, it is plausible to think that the other contexts on our list are sensitive to the *meaning* of those expressions. Making this precise requires taking meanings seriously. Ignoring context-sensitivity, where the same sentence with a constant linguistic meaning expresses different things in different contexts, such as the sentence "I am happy", the meaning of a sentence is a proposition. Two sentences can both have the same truth value and yet different meanings; they can express different propositions. It is plausible to think that the above contexts are sensitive not only to the truth values of the sentences within their scope, as for example the truth-functions are, but to the *propositions expressed by* the sentences within their scope. Standard modal and temporal logics are built on this very idea. (5) below is true while (6) is false, even though both of their embedded sentences are true.

(5)   It is necessary that 2=2.

(6)   It is necessary that I am wearing shorts.

The embedded sentence of (5) expresses a different proposition from the embedded sentence of (6) and 'it is necessary that' is sensitive to the proposition expressed by the sentence it governs. The first expresses a proposition that is necessarily true while the second expresses a proposition that is only contingently true.

While modal contexts are intensional, in the sense that sentences with the same truth value are not always intersubstitutable, it may be that proper names are intersubstitutable within modal contexts. Whether this is so depends on a number of important issues, and fully exploring this issue is beyond the scope of the present essay. We will have to settle with a quick sketch of a set of theses that lead to such a view.

The first thesis is the thesis of direct reference. It is easiest to state this thesis if we assume that propositions are structured. Then the thesis of direct reference is the view that simple sentences with proper names express singular propositions, where a proposition is singular with respect to some individual i just in case it is about i in virtue of having i as a self-representing constituent. Proper names are directly referential, expressing as their sole semantic content their references. A consequence of this view is that two simple sentences with co-referring proper names express the same singular proposition. The second thesis concerns the semantics of the modal operator. In short, the modal operator is *only* sensitive to the proposition expressed by the embedded sentence it operates on, and not its mode of expression.

These two theses entail that a substitution principle for co-referring proper names is valid for modal contexts. This is because substituting co-referring proper names within a modal context will not affect the proposition the embedded sentence expresses, by the first thesis. And by the second thesis, the modal itself is only sensitive to the proposition expressed by the embedded sentence it operates on. So the substitution will not affect the truth value of the whole. So, in so far as we accept the above theses, we are committed to the claim that co-referring proper names, but not sentences with the same truth value, are intersubstitutable within modal environments.

In the following sections we shall look at a particular instance of an intensional context – namely, propositional attitude constructions – in more detail, spelling out a variety of positions.

Propositional Attitudes

Our partial list of intensional contexts included propositional attitude constructions, which include verbs such as "believe", "desire", "hope" and "intend", on at least some of their uses. The primary focus of this chapter is propositional attitude verbs. The standard, though not universal, view of such verbs is that they express relations between agents and propositions, where propositions are language-independent entities that are the primary bearers of truth value, what are expressed by sentences (or perhaps utterances of sentences), and the objects of beliefs, desires, wishes, etc. I shall assume a number of controversial theses concerning these expressions. The first is *propositionalism*, according to which sentences (or sentences in context or utterances of sentences – I will remain neutral on issues concerning the primary bearers of semantic content) express propositions in virtue of which they are true or false and propositions are the contents of cognitive (and some conative) attitudes. This may seem like a trivial assumption; they are, after all, called *propositional* attitudes. But accepting the assumption is to set aside a wide range of alternative accounts that historically have been very influential. Among the most important are *sententialist* accounts of the attitudes, according to which sentences (or utterances) are the primary bearers of truth values and the objects of the attitudes. Sententialists about the attitudes maintain that believing that grass is green or wanting world peace, for example, is a matter of believing-true the sentence "Grass is green" or desiring-true the sentence "There is world peace". (See, for example, Carnap 1958, Quine 1956, Davidson 1967, 1968, and Higginbotham 1991.)

Here is a problem for sententialism. (See Church 1950.) Intuitively we can report an agent's attitude using sentences that the agent herself would not use to express the attitude we are reporting. One clear case of this is reporting the attitudes of nonlinguistic beings. "Look, the cat thinks the mouse is still behind the books." This seems true on the basis of the cat's behaviour, but it is pretty implausible that the cat believes-true the sentence "The mouse is still behind the books". The same point can be made by considering English reports of the attitudes of non-English speakers. We may know that Jonas wants a bike and truly report that fact by saying "Jonas wants a bike". But if Jonas only speaks Swedish, this is not because Jonas wants-true the English sentence "Jonas has a bike". Finally, sometimes we report English speakers' beliefs using English sentences they would not use to express their beliefs. For example, I can truly say, "Bill believes that I am stepping on his toes", as I stand on his toes. But it is quite dubious that this is because he believes-true the sentence "I am stepping on his toes". I would report that latter state by saying, "Bill believes that he is stepping on my toes".

In all of these cases, it would seem that the report is true because the embedded sentence (the sentence in the that-clause of the report; the sentence "The mouse is still behind the books", for example) *expresses* something in the mouth of the reporter that the agent of the report bears the appropriate attitude to. Bill may believe-true the sentence "He is stepping on my foot" that, in his mouth, expresses the same thing as the sentence "I am stepping on his foot" expresses in my mouth. But it seems that what relates these sentences (or sentence-tokens) is the fact that they express the same proposition, which leads us back to propositionalism. Some sententialists have introduced a notion of same-saying, claiming that an attitude report is accurate in so far as the embedded sentence, as used by the reporter, same-says some sentence the agent of the report believes- (or desires-, or etc.) true. (See Davidson 1968 and Lepore and Loewer 1989.) The same-saying relation should not be taken as a primitive. But then in virtue of what do two utterances same-say? When they express the same proposition? If so, we are back to propositionalism. And it is hard to see how else to explicate the same-saying relation. Finally, introducing a same-saying relation will not help with the first problem of reports to non-linguistic beings, such as non-human animals and young children.

The issues are complex and there is more to say. I don't pretend to have established my first assumption. But I do think that I have offered some motivation for accepting it.

Second, I shall assume a *structural* version of propositionalism, according to which propositions have a structure, much like the syntactic structure of the sentences that express them. (It is a further thesis, and one we shall consider below, whether or not the structure of the proposition expressed by a sentence or utterance of a sentence must match the syntactic structure of the sentence itself. My assumption here is neutral on this issue.) This rules out views according to which propositions are sets of possible worlds or functions from possible worlds to truth values (see Lewis 1972, 1986 and Stalnaker 1981, 1984, 1987, 1988) or situations (see Barwise and Perry 1983). While these views are widely assumed in formal semantics, there are powerful reasons to think that they are incapable of doing justice to thought and reasoning. (See, for example, Soames 1985.) That 2+2=4 and that arithmetic is incomplete are true in the same set of worlds – namely, all mathematically possible ones. But most five-year olds know the first, while few know, or even are capable of grasping, the second. Furthermore, someone may well be reasoning rationally, given her conceptions, in judging true a necessarily false proposition. For example, Hilbert judged true the impossible when he thought that mathematics could be finitely axiomatized with a provably consistent system, but he was not irrational. Mathematical knowledge builds on itself and it was primarily through working on the Hilbert programme that Gödel was able to prove his incompleteness theorems. Now suppose that Hilbert had believed that $2 \neq 2$. Then he would have been irrational. In that case, he believed something *overtly* impossible. So, it is one thing to believe that mathematics is finitely axiomatized with a provably consistent system and another to believe that $2 \neq 2$. Our judgments of rationality, of when someone is failing to judge as they ought, requires making this distinction. So, it seems that these are different propositions, in which case propositions are not sets of worlds or situations. The contents of our attitudes are much more fine-grained than what either the possible worlds semanticist or situation theorist give us. Again, I do not take this to establish the second assumption, but I do think that it motivates it. (We'll return to this form of argument below in Frege's Puzzle.)

With all of these assumptions made, one might think that I have defined myself into a unique spot in the landscape of positions. But plenty of interesting issues remain. And our assumptions can help us better focus on and articulate those issues.

The first issue concerns the contents of sentences and the contents of attitudes. Is the content of a sentence and the content of an attitude ever a singular proposition, or are the contents of sentences and the contents of attitudes always fully conceptualized? A singular proposition about me to the effect that I am sitting, for example, contains me and the property **sitting**.

The proposition that the author of this chapter is sitting, on the other hand, plausibly does not contain me as a constituent but rather a conceptualization of me, as the author of this chapter. This latter proposition concerns me in virtue of my satisfying the condition of uniquely authoring this chapter and it is this condition and not me that forms the proposition itself. The former proposition concerns me in virtue of having me as a directly representing constituent. If sentences of natural language express singular propositions, then there are expressions in natural language that are directly referential. Their semantic contents are exhausted by their references. Referentialists claim that there are singular propositions and they are the contents of sentences and of our cognitive states. Fregeans deny this. This debate forms our first issue.

The second issue concerns whether or not a substitution principle is valid for proper names (and indexicals and demonstratives) that occur within the context of propositional attitude verbs. From the fact that Hesperus is Phosphorus, does it follow that anyone who believes that Hesperus is Hesperus believes that Hesperus is Phosphorus? This question forms our second issue.

The two issues are related. The most powerful arguments against a direct reference theory rest on a very robust set of intuitions seeming to support the invalidity of the substitution principle. In what follows I shall present some of the main positions on these issues.

Frege's Puzzle

Allen Stewart Konigsberg was born in New York City in 1935. By the age of 15, he was selling his jokes to a newspaper. By the age of 18, he enrolled in NYU, but soon dropped out. He went on to write, produce and act in some 30 films. Jane remembers the boy of her early years, the boy she called "Allen Konigsberg". But she lost track of him as an early teenager. Still, she thinks of him often. She also thinks of the quirky film director who goes under the name "Woody Allen". She doesn't realize, it seems, that they are one and the same. "If only I knew what became of Allen Konigsberg," she often says to husband. "He was always building things. He's probably an engineer. Nothing creative. Not a filmmaker, that's for sure … Hey, let's go see Woody Allen's new movie."

On the basis of Jane's linguistic behaviour, it is plausible that the following are true.

(7)   Jane believes that Woody Allen is a filmmaker.

(8)   Jane believes that Allen Konigsberg is not a filmmaker.

(9)   Jane does not believe that Allen Konigsberg is a filmmaker.

Grant, for the time, that (7)–(9) are true. Then the principle that co-referring singular terms within the scope of a propositional attitude-ascribing verb are substitutable *salva veritate* is invalid. For suppose otherwise. Then, as "Woody Allen" and "Allen Konigsberg" are co-referring, this principle would allow us infer (10) from the truth of (9).

(10)   Jane does not believe that Woody Allen is a filmmaker.

But (10) is the contrary of (7), which we have already assumed is true. So (10) is false. Contradiction.

The substitution principle also allows us to infer the truth of (11) from the truth of (7).

(11)   Jane believes that Allen Konigsberg is a filmmaker.

But if both (8) and (11) are true, then Jane believes a proposition and its negation. This is because the embedded sentence in (11) – i.e., (12) – is the contrary of the embedded sentence in (8).

(12)   Allen Konigsberg is a filmmaker.

Rational people do not, at the same time, believe a proposition and its negation. Jane would, in that case, not fulfil the requirements of good believing. But that is not terribly plausible, as no amount of pure reflection is likely to reveal to her the mistake she is making. Her mistake is not like the mistake of the person who believes that there can be a barber who shaves all and only those who do not shave themselves, for example. While this contradiction does not wear its contradictory nature on its sleeve, careful reflection of what would be involved in such a situation, and wondering who shaves the barber himself, reveals to the thoughtful person the mistake. The charge of irrationality, of not believing as one should, sticks in this case but not in Jane's. But then Jane does not believe a proposition and its negation. So, the truth of (11) does not follow from the truth of (8). As (8) is true, (11) is false. So, co-referring names are not substitutable within the scope of "believe". (In distinguishing these two aspects of the puzzle, the one involving believing and not believing and the other involving an intuitively rational agent believing a proposition and its negation, I am following Kripke 1979.)

Frege's puzzle is based on the more basic insight that sentences that differ only in the substitution of one co-referring name for another, such as (12) and (13), differ in *cognitive value*.

(13)   Woody Allen is a filmmaker.

To say that such pairs of sentences differ in cognitive value is to say that competent, reflective agents can rationally accept one while rejecting the other. This difference is at the heart of Frege's puzzle. It is very tempting to think that the difference entails a difference in content, or proposition expressed. (12) and (13) express different propositions, which accounts for the different attitudes competent, reflective agents can take towards them. But if that is so, then they do not express singular propositions, as they would in that case express the same proposition. Moreover, proper names such as "Woody Allen" are not directly referential. Their content must be other or more than their bare references.

Fregean Solution

A Fregean solution to our puzzle takes appearances for granted. (12) and (13) differ in cognitive value and express different propositions and (7)–(9) are true and (10)–(11) are false. (7) and (11) report different beliefs. For (7) to be true, Jane must stand in the belief relation to the proposition (Woody Allen is a filmmaker). For (12) to be true, Jane must stand in the belief relation to the proposition (Allen Konigsberg is a filmmaker). The Fregean claims that these are distinct propositions. (12) and (13), while referentially equivalent, express distinct propositions, as they express propositions that contain different *modes of presentation* of Woody Allen. A single object can be presented to an agent in many different ways. An agent can believe of a single object that it is such and such under one mode of presentation but not under another. These beliefs then have distinct contents. This is the heart of Frege's distinction between sense and reference. (See Frege 1948, 1956.)

The Fregean solution is comprised of two distinctive theses. The first is that differences in cognitive value correspond to differences in thought or proposition expressed. The second is that differences in pairs of sentences such as (7) and (12) – that is, pairs of propositional attitude-ascribing sentences that differ only in the co-referring subject position expression in the embedded sentence that intuitively differ in truth value – are to be explained in terms of their ascribing different belief contents to the agent, the one of which the agent believes and the other of which she does not. So, it is because (12) and (13) express different propositions – propositions about, to be sure, the same individual to the effect that he is a filmmaker and hence propositions with the same referential content – that they have different cognitive values. And it is because believing that Woody Allen is a filmmaker is distinct, in virtue of its content, from believing that Allen Konigsberg is a filmmaker that (7) is consistent with (9).

One way of making more precise a broadly Fregean solution, one based on the two distinctive claims identified above, is to accept the Russellian claims that ordinary proper names are "disguised definite descriptions", definite descriptions express descriptive conditions, and co-designating definite descriptions can express different descriptive conditions. Then (12) and (13) can be seen as expressing different but referentially equivalent propositions, each concerning Woody Allen himself. For simplicity, let's say that a name is short for its own metalinguistic description. Then "Allen Konigsberg" is short for "the person named 'Allen Konigsberg'" and "Woody Allen" is short for "the person named 'Woody Allen'". (This is not what Russell thought.) (12) and (13) can then be regimented as something as follows. (Let "$[\iota x \Phi x]\Psi x$" represent "The Φ is Ψ" and let "Ax" abbreviate "x is named 'Allen Konigsberg'", "Wx" abbreviate "x is named 'Woody Allen'", and "Fx" abbreviate "x is a filmmaker".)

(12$_R$) $[\iota x A x]Fx$

(13$_R$) $[\iota x W x]Fx$

These are distinct propositions. (See Manuel Garcia-Carpintero's chapter in this volume for details on Russell's theory of definite descriptions.) Moreover, it is possible for a rational, linguistically competent person to not realize that the person named "Allen Konigsberg" is the person named "Woody Allen". So, we have an account of the consistency of (7)–(9) and why substitution of co-referring proper names within the scope of propositional attitude verbs fails. Such substitutions can affect the identity of the belief being reported by changing the content of the embedded singular term.

Problems for the Fregean Solution

The Fregean solution faces several problems. Here I shall discuss three.

The first problem arises from a detail in Frege's own version of the view. Frege thought that the substitution principle is valid, even for expressions within the scope of attitude verbs. The name "Woody Allen" is co-referential with the name "Allen Konigsberg" as they occur in simple sentences such as (12) and (13). But as they occur in complex sentences such as (7) and (8), he claimed that they are not co-referential. In simple sentences, the names refer to the man himself and express a mode of presentation or sense. Inside the scope of an attitude verb, however, they refer to their customary senses, not the man himself. As the customary sense of "Woody Allen" is distinct from the customary sense of "Allen Konisberg", their references in (7) and (8) are distinct. Propositional attitude verbs induce, then, a reference shift. Terms that occur within their scope refer to their customary senses.

Some have found plausible a principle of *semantic innocence,* according to which the linguistic context of an expression does not change its reference. (Davidson 1968 is the classic source. See also Barwise and Perry 1983.) Semantic innocence seems to be required, furthermore, to explain cross-attitudinal anaphoric reference. Consider, for example, the following sentence.

(14)   Woody Allen directed *Vicki Barcelona* and Jane believes that he starred in it.

The pronoun "he" in (14) occurs within the scope of the attitude verb "believe" but is anaphoric on the occurrence of "Woody Allen", which occurs outside the scope of that verb. So, the occurrence of "Woody Allen" in (14) refers to the man himself. A standard theory of anaphoric relations would dictate that the reference of the occurrence of "he" in (14) is determined by the reference of the term that it is anaphoric on. So, the occurrence of "he" in (14) refers to the man too. But that conflicts with Frege's claim that propositional attitude verbs induce a reference shift, in which case one would expect "he", as it occurs in (14), to refer to its customary sense, whatever that may be.

Attitudinal anaphora, then, challenges the Fregean claim that attitude verbs induce a reference shift and supports semantic innocence. While the Fregean might attempt to defend the reference shifting view by offering a more complex theory of cross-attitudinal anaphora, in which the reference of "he" is some sense of the reference of the expression upon which it is anaphoric, as opposed to the reference of that expression, it is important to see that Fregeanism itself is independent of the reference shift view. This is because the core insights of Frege's solution, namely that different co-referring names have different senses and that this difference in sense is relevant to the difference in the thoughts agents have in cases in which they suffer from an identity confusion, can be embedded in a theory consistent with semantic innocence. The key is to claim that propositional attitude verbs are sensitive not only to the references of the expressions in their scope but also to their senses. We then have the same effects of reference shifts without claiming that the expressions themselves refer to the customary senses.

The Fregean claims that (12) and (13) express different propositions. She can then say that propositional attitude verbs themselves are sensitive to the senses of the terms within their scope. (12) and (13), although having the same referential content, will then not be intersubstitutable within the scope of propositional attitude verbs. There is no need to claim that the embedded terms themselves shift their references. The occurrence of "Woody Allen" in (7) refers to Woody Allen, just as it does in (12). So, an objection to Fregeanism that rests on semantic innocence is not successful, as semantic innocence is compatible with Fregeanism.

There are two further problems with Fregeanism that I shall consider. The first I will call the problem of sameness of sense and the second the problem of descriptivism. These threaten Fregean positions more generally.

The problem of sameness of sense can be seen by returning to (14). It seems to me that (14) is true. But what are the truth conditions for (14)? In particular, is there some specified way in which Jane must think of Woody Allen under which she judges that he starred in *Vicki Barcelona*? It's hard to see how that could be. Unlike (7), in which it is at least not implausible to think that the term "Woody Allen" specifies some type of way under which Jane must think of Woody Allen under which she judges that he is a filmmaker, it is not plausible to think that the occurrence of "Woody Allen" in (14) specifies one particular way. If that is not clear, then note that (14) would seem to entail (15) below, as "Woody Allen" occurs outside the scope of an intensional verb.

(15) Allen Konigsberg directed *Vicki Barcelona* and Jane believes that he starred in it.

If (14) were to require for its truth that Jane think of Woody Allen in a particular sort of way, then (15) must require for its truth that Jane think of Woody Allen in that same particular sort of way. Otherwise it is hard to see how the one could entail the other and vice versa. But that is implausible. How could both (14) and (15) require that Jane think of Woody Allen in the same way when the different singular terms, by the Fregean's own lights, express different senses?

The fundamental problem that this brings out is that some belief attributions do not seem to require for their intuitive truth that the believer think about the relevant objects in any way that is systematically related to the complement clause of the belief attribution. This same point can be made with indexicals and demonstratives. Consider the following sentence, as spoken by Woody Allen.

(16) Jane believes that I am a filmmaker.

It is clear that the truth of (16) does not require that Jane believe something that she would express by uttering the sentence "I am a filmmaker". To report that belief, Woody Allen would use (17).

(17) Jane believes that she herself is a filmmaker.

So, the truth of (16) does not require that Jane be disposed to express her belief using the embedded sentence of (16). But it is also clear that the truth of (16) does not require that Jane be disposed to express her belief using a sentence with an expression that is systematically related to the first-person pronoun.

For example, it is implausible that she must be disposed to utter the sentence "You are a filmmaker" in Woody Allen's presence. She might not be in a position to use the second-person pronoun, not being in the right relations to Woody Allen. Or, she might be in Woody Allen's presence but not recognize him as the person who created all the films she associates with the name "Woody Allen". What (16) seems to report, instead, is that Jane have some belief with the equivalent referential content to Woody Allen's utterance of "I am a filmmaker". There seems to be no more fine-grained specification of a required way of thinking of Woody Allen for (16) to be true. At the very least, there is not systematic, context-independent, fine-grained way of thinking of Woody Allen that is involved in (16)'s truth-conditions. While these problems may be surmountable, they show that how the complement clause of an attitude-ascribing sentence intuitively represents how the agent conceives of the entities the attitude is about is not a straightforward manner. It is implausible that there is a stable way of thinking of the reference that all competent speakers associate with a name such that any attitude-ascribing sentence with that name in the subject position of its complement clause is true only if the agent has a belief under that way of thinking of the reference.

The final problem I shall consider is the problem of descriptivism. I have described Fregeanism as the view that differences in cognitive value (between sentences such as (12) and (13), for example) are to be explained in terms of a difference in proposition expressed and intuitive differences in the truth value of referentially equivalent propositional attitude-ascribing sentences (such as (9) and (10), for example) are to be explained in terms of a difference in the thought content ascribed. Descriptivism is a thesis about the semantics of proper names, according to which the semantic content of a proper name is given by some definite description. While there is not a direct connection between the two theses, descriptivism promises a concrete way of establishing the two distinctive theses of Fregeanism. And descriptivism is subject to a famous and influential set of objections – namely, Saul Kripke's anti-descriptivism arguments (Kripke 1981) and Strawson's reduplication argument (Strawson 1959). Kripke's primary three arguments against descriptivism, the modal objection, the second the semantic objection, and the final the epistemological objection, are discussed in Genoveva Marti's chapter in this volume on "Reference", so I shall not discuss them here. But I shall discuss Strawson's reduplication argument.

Strawson's Argument

First some terminology. To identify an object is to have the capacity to think determinately about that very object. Descriptive identification requires possessing knowledge about some descriptive condition that object satisfies. Demonstrative identification is more direct, being grounded in real-world connections one bears to the object as opposed to one's conception of the object and its relations. Strawson then argues that thought about the external world requires a primitive form of demonstrative identification. This conclusion conflicts with a thoroughgoing form of descriptivism, according to which all our thought involves only descriptive identification of individuals.

Suppose that we lived in a reduplication universe, in which there is a distant region of the universe that is qualitatively indiscernible from our region of the universe. I am sitting at my desk, thinking about my computer. On the other side of the universe, there is a qualitatively identical set of happenings. Intuitively, I am thinking about the computer in front of me and my qualitative twin is thinking about the computer in front of him, and, intuitively, these are distinct things. (The claim that there are two people, two desks, and two computers is disputed by some; see, for example, O'Leary-Hawthorne 1995. They claim that objects are bundles of immanent universals and so what seems like two distinct, spatiotemporally separate, qualitatively indiscernible objects is really one object at some spatiotemporal distance from itself. I assume without argument that this is wrong.) If all identification were descriptive, this would not be possible, as there is no purely qualitative descriptive condition that only my computer satisfies. So, if all identification is descriptive, then the occupants of the massive reduplication universe do not have any thoughts determinately about the particulars in their surroundings, including themselves. This is implausible.

Strawson maintains that objects in our immediate perceptual environment can be identified directly – demonstratively – as *that*. As I am sitting in front of my computer, I can directly and demonstratively identify that object in virtue of my perceptual relation to it. I do not need to conceive of any relations that that object uniquely bears. Rather, it is sufficient for it to simply be the case that that object is uniquely perceptually related to me for me to be able to identify it. Because I am perceptually related to my computer and my twin to his, we can each succeed in demonstratively identifying our respective computers and thinking determinate thoughts about them.

I think that the reduplication argument shows that global descriptivism is false. It shows that we think about at least some particulars directly or demonstratively. But it leaves open *what* entities we think about demonstratively. It does not support Strawson's view that we think demonstratively about the objects in our perceptual environment. To see why, consider the view that we think demonstratively only about our occurrent sense-data (Russell 1910, 1912). As my sense-data are numerically distinct from my twin's, the description *the computer that is a causal source of that sense-datum* is satisfied by my computer instead of by my twin's. This view respects the intuition that the inhabitants of a reduplication world think determinately about particulars in their environments. So, the reduplication argument, while establishing the need for *some* irreducible demonstrative thoughts, leaves open the scope of demonstrative thought. (For more on the nature of singular thought, see the essays collected in Jeshion 2010.)

The reduplication argument challenges global descriptivism. But how does the reduplication argument challenge Fregeanism? Let me sketch a line of argument. Grant that the reduplication argument shows that there is an irreducible form of demonstrative thought about some particulars. In so far as it is possible to misidentify those particulars, then there will be Frege cases that are not susceptible to a Fregean solution. This is because there won't be distinct contents available, as our thought is referential with respect to those particulars. This problem is clearest if we consider the Strawsonian view, according to which the objects with which we are perceptually related are demonstratively identified. Clearly it is possible to misidentify mid-sized objects of perception. I can perceive the computer and not realize that it is the same as the object I earlier perceived. If my thought about the computer is demonstrative, then we cannot explain the confusion in terms of a difference in mode of presentation that leads to different thought contents. So, there are a set of Frege cases for which the Strawsonian cannot offer a Fregean solution. We may then suspect that the non-Fregean account of these cases can be applied to all Frege cases.

Referentialism Reconsidered

The above problems may suggest a return to referentialism. But Frege's puzzle challenges the referentialist. As we have seen, the intuitions supporting the puzzle strongly suggest that pairs of sentences such as (12) and (13) express different propositions. But if that is so, then what they express goes beyond their referential contents. The referentialist can't have that. What can be said, then, about those supporting intuitions?

There are two main referentialist strategies. The first employs the distinction between what is said by an utterance of a sentence and what is pragmatically implicated. The key is that, while utterances of referentially identical propositional attitude-ascribing sentences say the same thing, they often pragmatically implicate different information with differing truth values. The hope is that the intuitions generating Frege's puzzle can be fully accounted for in terms of this pragmatically implicated information. On this strategy, (7) and (9) are mutually inconsistent. The intuition that they are consistent is to be explained in terms of the information that ordinary utterances of those sentences pragmatically implicate. The second strategy rests on the claim that propositional attitude-ascribing sentences are context-sensitive. On this strategy, (7) and (9) are consistent, despite the fact that they both involve the same singular proposition (**o** is a filmmaker), where **o** is Woody Allen himself. The sentences involve an indexical element with different values. My saying, "I am hungry", and your saying, "I am not hungry", is perfectly consistent, because those utterances do not express a proposition and its negation, as the different uses of "I" express different contents. The contextualist claims that a similar, although less overt, phenomenon occurs with utterances of (7) and (9).

Let's begin with the first strategy. Much of what we communicate by our utterances is indirect. We are rarely fully direct, let alone fully explicit, about everything we mean. We say just enough to get our meaning across, relying on our audience to infer and fill in the rest. You ask me, as we are watching an NBA championship game, which team I am cheering for. I respond, "I live in LA". I have communicated that I am cheering for the Lakers. But I haven't said as much. What I said was that I live in LA. I rely upon you to infer that I am cheering for the Lakers, using your background knowledge that people living in LA tend to be Lakers fans. This inference was driven by the fact that I would be unresponsive to your question if I merely meant that I live in LA, as you didn't ask me about that, and yet I am clearly intending you to take me as being responsive. This is a clear case of the phenomenon H.P. Grice studied in his work on conversational implicatures. (See Grice 1975, 1978, 1981.)

According to proponents of the first referentialist strategy, a similar story holds for our uses of propositional attitude-ascribing sentences. (Proponents of this view include Bealer 1982, §39; Berg 1983; Braun 1998, 2000, 2001a, 2001b; McKay 1981, 1991; Nelson 2002, 2005; Reddam 1982; Richard 1983, 1987; Salmon 1986, 1989, 1995a; Soames 1987, 1989, 1995; and Tye 1978. Bealer has changed his view; see his 1993. Richard has also changed his view in 1989. Soames has also modified his view, although less drastically than the other three, in his 2002.) Although all utterances of (7) and (11) say the same thing, typical utterances of those sentences will communicate distinct information. On first pass we can say that this is because an utterance of a propositional attitude-ascribing sentence suggests something about the way in which the agent holds the attitude that she does, suggesting, in the case of an utterance of (11), that the agent would express her belief being reported by uttering (12), the embedded sentence. So, on this view, while (7) and (11) both report that Jane stands in the belief relation to the singular proposition (**o** is a filmmaker), a typical utterance of (7) suggests that she would express this belief by uttering the sentence "Woody Allen is a filmmaker", which is true, while a typical utterance of (11) suggests that she would express this belief by uttering the sentence "Allen Konigsberg is a filmmaker", which is false.

We saw above that the intuitive truth of a propositional attitude-ascribing sentence does not track the attitude the agent takes towards the very sentence embedded in that propositional attitude-ascribing sentence. To accommodate, the proponent of the first referentialist strategy needs a more plausible metaphysics of belief.

John Perry distinguished what an agent believes (the belief content) and how she believes it (the belief state). Perry (1977) argued against the Fregean's identification of belief contents, the *what* of belief, with belief states, the *how* of belief. Perry argued that an adequate account of indexicals and demonstratives in attitudes requires distinguishing these two aspects of acts of thinking and recognizing that they can vary independently. On Perry's view, we believe contents by being in belief states while embedded in a given environment. We can believe different contents in different environments by being in the same belief state – for example, when I issue a thought I would express by uttering "Today is Tuesday" on Tuesday, I entertain one thought content, and another on Wednesday, even though I am in the same type of belief state – and we can believe the same content in different environments by being in the different belief states – for example, I entertain the same content I entertained on Tuesday by issuing on Wednesday a thought I would express by uttering "Yesterday was Tuesday". These differences in environment do not need to be conceptualized by the agent for them to make a difference to her cognitive states. Perry (1977) identified belief states (what he there called "senses") with what he called roles and what Kaplan called character. In later work (see in particular his 1980, 1990, 1997, and 1998), Perry gives this identification up and individuates belief states in terms of their narrow functional role, in terms of the relationships to other cognitive states, perceptions and action executions.

While the details need to be fleshed out, we can employ this framework to say that utterances of propositional attitude-ascribing sentences pragmatically convey information about the type of belief state the agent is in by virtue of what she believes what she believes. A typical utterance of (7), then, pragmatically conveys information concerning the belief state Jane is in in virtue of which she stands in the belief relation to the singular proposition that Woody Allen is a filmmaker. A typical utterance of (11) pragmatically conveys different information concerning Jane's belief state in virtue of which she stands in the belief relation to that same singular proposition. This pragmatically implicated information can differ in truth value and so promises to account for the intuition that (7) is true and (11) false, even though those sentences always express the same proposition in any context.

Many find it unacceptable to reject the intuition that (7) is true and (11) is false. The referentialist, however, can accept that intuition. What the referentialist must reject is that (7) and (11) involve ascribing to Jane beliefs with different contents. But there may be other differences between (7) and (11) that the referentialist can appeal to. Namely, the referentialist can claim that (7) and (11) specify distinct belief states, using the terminology introduced above, and that that difference affects the semantic content of (7) and (11). This constitutes the second referentialist strategy; what I shall call the contextualist strategy.

Before developing this strategy further, let's pause to contrast it with what has come before. As a neutral terminology, let's say that (7) indicates a distinct belief state from (11) in virtue of which we intuit that (7) is true and (11) false. The Fregean maintains that this difference maps onto a difference in content. The referentialist, on the other hand, maintains that there is no difference in content but only a difference in the belief state by way of which the agent believes the content she does. The contextual referentialist maintains that this difference in indicated belief state affects the truth of (7) and (11). That is, for the contextual referentialist, this difference is semantically relevant, as propositional attitude-ascribing sentences are semantically sensitive to the indicated state. The pragmatic referentialist, on the other hand, thinks that this difference is not semantically relevant. Propositional attitude-ascribing sentences are semantically insensitive to the indicated state, although information about the indicated state is often pragmatically communicated as some kind of implicature.

Let's return to developing the contextualist strategy. I begin with Crimmins and Perry's version of the strategy. (See Crimmins and Perry 1989, Crimmins 1992a, 1992b, 1995a, 1995b.) Crimmins and Perry argue that propositional attitude reports involve "unarticulated constituents" that concern how the subject of the report believes what she (allegedly) believes. A typical utterance of (7) expresses a truth while a typical utterance of (11) expresses a falsehood. The first involves implicit reference to one way Jane has of thinking of Woody Allen and the second to a distinct way Jane has of thinking of Woody Allen. Because Jane believes the singular proposition (Woody Allen is a filmmaker) in the first way and not the second, the two sentences will typically express different propositions that diverge in truth value.

Extra-linguistic context determines what way of grasping is implicitly referred to by an utterance of a propositional attitude-ascribing sentence. The complement clause (and not just the referents or semantic contents of the expressions of the complement clause) are typically relevant to what way of grasping is implicitly referred to. So, although substitution of co-referring names does not affect the proposition the propositional attitude-ascribing sentence claims the believer to believe, as it does on the Fregean view, in some cases it affects what way of grasping is implicitly referred to and hence is capable of affecting truth value of a propositional attitude-ascribing sentence.

Crimmins and Perry's view has been subject to criticism. (For a sampling, see Bach 1993, Clapp 1995, Reimer 1995, Richard 1993, Rieber 1995, and Saul 1992. Crimmins responds to some of these objections in his 1992 and 1995. Schiffer objects to Crimmins and Perry's view in his 1992 and 1994 on the basis that "believes" and other propositional attitude verbs do not express three-place relations, as their view requires. Ludlow responds to Schiffer's "logical form" objection in his 1995 and 1996. Schiffer responds to Ludlow in his 1996.) I shall here present only one objection, in order to motivate another version of the second referentialist strategy to be discussed below.

Although the issues are complex and quickly draw us into general and delicate issues in the philosophy of language, many are drawn to what we can call a *principle of linguistic constraint*, according to which contextual supplementation of what's said is always traceable to some syntactic element. (See, for example, Stanley 2000, 2002 for a defence of this constraint. Recanati 2002 and Carston 2002 defend unarticulated constituents.) This principle is incompatible with the existence of unarticulated constituents. One reason to accept the principle is that it helps to delimit information that is conveyed by an utterance but not part of what is said by the sentence uttered in a way that solves, in a principled way, an overgeneration problem that threatens theories violating linguistic constraint. While one can, given the correct conversational setting, use the sentence "2+2=4" to communicate that one is going to the store, the sentence itself does not say that. A plausible explanation of why is that nothing in the sentence contributes the relevant components of that communicated piece of information. Crimmins and Perry's view is inconsistent with this principle, as they argue that "believes" is syntactically two-place even though it expresses a three-place relation.

This motivates a search for an account according to which the information encoded by utterances of belief sentences is sensitive to how the subject of the report grasps the proposition, while insisting that the proposition grasped is just a singular proposition, without making ways of grasping unarticulated constituents. We can build up to such a view by looking at a view developed by Mark Richard 1990, 1993, 1995. Like Crimmins and Perry, Richard offers a semantics of propositional attitude reporting sentences that treats them as context-sensitive, is (quasi-)referentialist (I return to this below), and yet blocks intersubstitution of co-referring names within the scope of propositional attitude verbs. Unlike Crimmins and Perry, however, Richard does not claim that "believe" (and its fellow propositional attitude verbs) expresses a three-place relation and does not appeal to unarticulated constituents. Richard's view is thus consistent with the principle of linguistic constraint. The key to Richard's view is his claim that "believe" is context-sensitive, expressing different relations in different contexts.

According to Richard, sentences express what he calls Russellian annotated matrices (RAMs). These are represented as tuples of pairs of linguistic expressions and their "Russellian interpretations". (Richard notes that, strictly speaking, we don't want a linguistic expression but rather some kind of internal representation, akin to Crimmins and Perry's ideas and notions.) The pairs are called annotations. RAMs serve as both the semantic contents of sentences and the contents of beliefs. According to Richard's account, (7), for example, is true relative to some context c and a world of evaluation w just in case Jane has a thought in w that is properly represented (relative to the standards in effect in c) by the sentence "Woody Allen is a filmmaker". The conversational setting generates restrictions on what expressions are proper translations of the representations of the alleged believer. Richard calls these restrictions correlation functions. Correlation functions map annotations (used by the belief reporter) onto (sets of) annotations (employed in the alleged believer's beliefs). As there are contexts in which "Woody Allen is a filmmaker" and "Allen Konigsberg is a filmmaker" are associated with different restrictions, we cannot substitute "Allen Konigsberg" for "Woody Allen" in (7) and preserve truth. Jane may well have a thought that can be appropriately represented, given the restrictions in place in the context, by the first sentence but not the second. So, there is no problem in saying that (7) is true while (11) is false.

Richard's view is not purely referentialist. This is because, on his view, the contents of beliefs are not singular propositions. Instead, the content of the belief that Woody Allen is a filmmaker contains the pair of Woody Allen himself and something that plays the role of a mode of presentation – the annotation. But Richard's view can be altered to retain its core features while being referentialist, treating the contents of beliefs (and the contents of sentences containing proper names) as singular propositions. The resulting view is in many ways superior to Richard's own. Begin by assuming the Perry-inspired metaphysics of belief sketched earlier, in which we distinguish belief contents from belief states. We can then conceive of Richardian correlation functions as maps from complement clauses to belief states, preserving content. The content of both (12) and (13) is the singular proposition (Woody Allen is a filmmaker). Jane believes that proposition in virtue of being in a belief state related to "Woody Allen is a filmmaker" but not "Allen Konigsberg is a filmmaker". So, in a belief-ascribing context in which the complement clauses are intended to represent the way by which the agent believes what she is claimed to believe, (7) is true and (11) is false. The view promises to offer a more plausible account of when two agents "believe the same thing", which Richard's own fine-grained account of the contents of attitudes cannot, as our intuitions about when two agents count as believing the same thing are often insensitive to differences in how agents believe what they believe.

Any view like Richard's faces a serious problem: The problem of conflicting restrictions. (See Sider 1995, Soames 1995.) To build up to the objection, consider cases in which a speaker is ascribing beliefs to different agents. It may be common ground that those agents conceive of matters differently. In such a case, the speaker may intend the same complement clause to represent different types of belief states for different agents. Suppose that Bob and Susan are looking at a picture of Bill Clinton. Bob might then use the complement clause "that he (pointing at the picture) was president" to represent a first-person belief state when ascribing beliefs to Bill Clinton and a different type of belief state when ascribing beliefs to George Bush. After all, we can imagine Frege-style cases in which the type of belief state Bob intends to specify might be essential to the point of his speech.

Now the problem of conflicting restrictions. Suppose that the ascriber is confused about the identities of the subject of the report. So, for example, suppose that Jane is ascribing beliefs to Woody Allen and Allen Konigsberg. Because of her identity confusions, she takes herself to be ascribing beliefs to two different people, depending on how she conceives of Woody Allen. But then we can imagine circumstances, similar to the ones with Bob and Susan described above, in which her intentions generate conflicting restrictions on a single complement clause. So, for example, Jane might intend "he", pointing at a frame shot from *Annie Hall*, in "that he lives in New York" to represent a first-person state when ascribing beliefs to Woody Allen and a third-person belief state when ascribing beliefs to Allen Konigsberg. So, when Jane says, "Woody Allen believes that he lives in New York", she intends to convey that Woody Allen has a first-person belief to the effect that Woody Allen lives in New York, and when she says, "Allen Konigsberg believes that he lives in New York", she intends to convey that Allen Konigsberg has a third-person belief to the effect that Woody Allen lives in New York. This is problematic for Richard because these restrictions conflict and so there is no correlation function that respects all the operative restrictions. As a result, any belief attribution Jane might make in such a conversational setting to Woody Allen / Allen Konigsberg with a complement clause containing "he" as subject is false. Even "Woody Allen believes that he is self-identical" is false. This is intuitively unacceptable.

Richard responded to this problem (1995) by claiming that, when there are conflicting restrictions operative in a context, a relevant sentence is true in the context just in case it is true on every resolution of the conflict. As the sentence "Woody Allen believes that he is self-identical" is true on any resolution of the conflict, the sentence is counted as true, on this modified view. Nelson 2002, 2005 criticises Richard's response, arguing that it still does not accommodate all intuitive truth-value judgments, as it still counts false some utterances that are intuitively true. This is because one of the conflicting restrictions may clearly be the operative restriction, as far as what the speaker intends to be conveying is concerned. One aim of Richard's view is to present a semantics that corresponds to the information intuitively conveyed by an utterance of a sentence, which in these cases is the information the speaker intends to convey.

Consider, for example, our case from above. Jane intends to be ascribing beliefs to Woody Allen, whom she conceives of as the very person in the photo she is pointing at. She says, "Woody Allen believes that he lives in New York", intending to ascribe a first-person belief to Woody Allen. Let us suppose that he has such a belief. But let us suppose that he does not have a third-person belief to the effect that he lives in New York. Then, as we are imagining Jane's context to be one in which conflicting restrictions are in effect, Richard's response counsels us to see whether or not the attribution is true on every resolution of the conflict. As it is not, the sentence is not true. But this does not respect intuitions regarding what Jane intends to convey, which is the true information that Woody Allen has a first-person belief to the effect that he lives in New York.

This problem will infect any semantic theory that aims to correspond directly to the information that is intuitively conveyed by utterances of propositional attitude-ascribing sentences. That is because any such account must deal with cases in which the attributor is confused about the identities of those to whom she is ascribing attitudes. In that case, what she intends to convey will be sensitive to the manner in which the agent of the ascription (as opposed to the object of the attitude, in a standard Frege-style case) is conceived. Then the subject-position of the attitude-ascribing sentence itself, as opposed to the subject position of the embedded sentence in the complement clause, is not open to substitution *salva veritate*. That is an undesirable result, as it is a violation of the principle of non-contradiction. These considerations suggest that we should not demand our semantics of propositional attitude-ascribing sentences to correspond to the information intuitively conveyed by utterances of those sentences. This in turn offers reason to prefer our first referentialism strategy above, even though it involves abandoning deeply held intuitions concerning the truth of attitude-ascribing sentences.

Propositional attitude ascriptions are but one instance of intensional contexts. Our focus here has been on them, shortchanging other intensional contexts such as modal and temporal operators, because they raise some of the most perplexing and far-reaching of problems. We have surveyed the main competing structured propositionalist views. We have seen Fregean views, according to which all thought about an object is under a mode of presentation, and so there are distinct thoughts about some object to the effect that it is such and such, depending on how the object is conceived. We have seen that, while this view is well-suited to handle standard Frege cases, the view faces several difficulties. While some differences in how an agent conceives of the object of her belief do seem to matter to our intuitive judgments of the truth value of a propositional attitude ascription, as standard Frege cases demonstrate, other differences do not, as is witnessed by indexical beliefs and single attributions to multiple agents. The referentialist cuts belief contents more coarsely. On the referentialist's view, for a core set of beliefs, differences in ways of conceiving of the object of the belief are irrelevant to what is believed. The difficulties for the Fregean are virtues for the referentialist. But the referentialist must work to offer an account of Frege cases. We surveyed two referentialist strategies for dealing with this problem. According to the first, the intuitive response to Frege cases rests on conflating what is merely conveyed with what the sentence uttered says. While utterances of (7) and (11) typically convey different information, the first being true and the second false, the sentences always say the same thing. According to the second referentialist strategy, the intuitive response to Frege cases is correct, but does not entail that the complement clauses of (7) and (11) pick out different propositions. On this view, there is more to an accurate belief-ascribing sentence than merely specifying the proposition believed; it must also accurately represent *how* the agent believes what she believes. We surveyed several techniques for how the referentialist can do this, from appealing to hidden indexicals and unarticulated constituents to postulating context sensitivity in the attitude verb itself, claiming that the verb picks out different relations in different contexts.

Bibliography

Bach, K. (1993), "Sometimes a great notion: A critical notice of Mark Crimmins's *Talk about Beliefs*", *Mind and Language* 8: 431–41.

—(1994), *Thought and Reference*. New York: Oxford University Press.

—(1997), "Do belief reports report beliefs?", *Pacific Philosophical Quarterly* 78: 214–41.

Barwise, J. and Perry, J. (1983), *Situations and Attitudes*. Cambridge, MA: The MIT Press.

Bealer, G. (1982), *Quality and Concept*. Oxford: Oxford University Press.

—(1993), "A solution to Frege's puzzle", *Philosophical Perspectives* 7: 17–60.

Berg, J. (1983), *Pragmatics and the Semantics of Belief*. Ph.D dissertation, UCLA.

Braun, D. (1991), "Proper names, cognitive contents, and beliefs", *Philosophical Studies* 62: 289–305.

—(1998), "Understanding belief reports", *Philosophical Review* 107: 555–95.

—(2000), "Russellianism and psychological generalizations", *Noûs* 34: 203–36.

—(2001a), "Russellianism and prediction", *Philosophical Studies* 105: 59–105.

—(2001b), "Russellianism and explanation", *Philosophical Perspectives* 14: 253–89.

—(2006a), "Illogical, but rational", *Noûs* 40: 376–9.

—(2006b), "Now you know who Hon Oak Yun is", *Philosophical Issues* 16: 24–42.

Burge, T. (1977a), "Kaplan, Quine, and suspended belief", *Philosophical Studies* 31: 197–203.

—(1977b), "*De re* belief", *Journal of Philosophy* 74: 338–62.

—(1986), "On Davdison's 'Saying that'", in E. LePore (ed.) *Truth and Interpretation: Perspectives on the Philosophy of Donald Davidson*. Oxford: Blackwell, 190–210.

Carnap, R. (1958), *Meaning and Necessity: A Study in Semantics and Modal Logic*, 2nd, enlarged, paperback edition. Chicago: The University of Chicago Press. (Originally published in 1947.)

Carston, R. (2002), *Thoughts and Utterances: The Pragmatics of Explicit Communication*. Oxford: Blackwell.

Castañeda, H.-N. (1966), "'He': A study in the logic of self-consciousness", *Ratio*, 8: 130–47.

—(1967), "Indicators and quasi-indicators", *American Philosophical Quarterly* 4: 85–100.

Chisholm, R. (1981), *The First Person*, Minneapolis: University of Minnesota Press.

Church, A. (1950), "On Carnap's analysis of statements of assertion and belief", *Analysis* 10: 97–9.

Clapp, L. (1995), "How to be direct and innocent: A criticism of Crimmins and Perry's theory of attitude ascriptions", *Linguistics and Philosophy* 18: 529–65.

—(2002), "Davidson's program and interpreted logical forms", *Linguistics and Philosophy* 25: 261–97.

Crimmins, M. (1992a), *Talk about Beliefs*. Cambridge, MA: The MIT Press.

—(1992b), "Context in the attitudes", *Linguistics and Philosophy* 14: 185–98.

—(1993), "So-labeled neo-Fregeanism", *Philosophical Studies* 69: 265–79.

—(1995a), "Notional specificity", *Mind and Language* 10: 464–77.

—(1995b), "Contextuality, reflexivity, iteration, logic", *Philosophical Perspectives* 9: 381–439.

Crimmins, M. and Perry, J. (1989), "The prince and the phone booth: Reporting puzzling beliefs", *Journal of Philosophy* 86: 685–711.

Davidson, D. (1967), "Truth and meaning", *Synthese* 17: 304–23.

—(1968), "On saying that", *Synthese* 19: 130–46.

Dummett, M. (1973), Frege: Philosophy of Language. London: Duckworth.

—(1981), The Interpretation of Frege's Philosophy. London: Duckworth.

—(1991), *The Logical Basis of Metaphysics*. Cambridge, MA: Harvard University Press.

Fitch, G. (1984), "Two aspects of belief", *Philosophy and Phenomenological Research* 45: 87–101.

—(1987), *Naming and Believing*. Dordrecht: Reidel.

Forbes, G. (1989), *Languages of Possibility*. Cambridge: Basil Blackwell.

—(1990), "The indispensability of Sinn", *Philosophical Review* 99: 535–63.

—(1993), "Reply to Marks", *Philosophical Studies* 69: 281–95.

—(1996), "Substitutivity and the coherence of quantifying in", *Philosophical Review* 105: 337–72.

—(2000), "Objectual attitudes", *Linguistics and Philosophy* 23: 141–83.

—(2002), "Intensionality", *Supplement to the Proceedings of the Aristotelian Society* 76: 75–99.

Frege, G. (1904), "Correspondence with Russell", in N. Salmon and S. Soames (eds), *Propositions and Attitudes*. Oxford: Oxford University Press, p. 56.

—(1948), "Sense and reference", *Philosophical Review* 57: 209–30. (Originally published in 1892.)

—(1956), "The thought: A logical inquiry", *Mind* 65: 289–311. (Originally published in 1918.)

Grice, H. P. (1975), "Logic and conversation", in P. Cole and J. Morgan (eds), *Syntax and Semantics* 3: 41–58. (Originally delivered as William James lectures at Harvard University in 1967.)

—(1978), "Further notes on logic and conversation", *Syntax and Semantics* 9: 113–28.

—(1981), "Presupposition and conversational implicature", in P. Cole (ed.) *Radical Pragmatics*, New York: Academic Press, 183–98.

Higginbotham, J. (1991), "Belief and logical form", *Mind and Language* 6: 344–69.

Jeshion, R. (ed.) (2010), *New Essays on Singular Thought*. Oxford: Oxford University Press.

Kaplan, D. (1969), "Quantifying in", *Synthese* 19: 178–214.

—(1970), "What is Russell's theory of descriptions?", in W. Yourgrau, A. Breck and H. Bondi (eds), *Physics, Logic, and History*, New York: Plenum, 277–88.

—(1977/1989), "Demonstratives", in J. Almog, J. Perry and H. Wettstein (eds), *Themes from Kaplan*, Oxford: Oxford University Press, 481–563.

—(1986), "Opacity", in L. Hahn and P. Schilpp (eds), *The Philosophy of W. V. Quine*, La Salle: Open Court, 229–89.

Kripke, S. (1979), "A puzzle about belief", in A. Margalit ed. *Meaning and Use*, Dordrecht: Reidel, 239–83.

—(1980), *Naming and Necessity*, Oxford: Blackwell. (Originally delivered as a series of lecture at Princeton University in 1970.)

Larson, R. and P. Ludlow. (1993), "Interpreted logical forms", *Synthese* 95: 305–55.

Larson, R. and G. Segal. (1995), *Knowledge of Meaning: Semantic Value and Logical Form* Cambridge, MA: The MIT Press.

Lepore, E. and Loewer, B. (1989), "You can say that again", *Midwest Studies in Philosophy* 14: 338–56.

Lewis, D. (1972), "General semantics", in D. Davidson and G. Harman (eds), *Semantics of Natural Language*, Dordrecht: D. Reidel, 169–218.

—(1979), "Attitudes *de dicto* and *de se*", *Philosophical Review* 88: 513–43.

—(1981), "What puzzling Pierre believes", *Australasian Journal of Philosophy* 59: 283–9.

—(1986), *On the Plurality of Worlds*. Oxford: Basil Blackwell.

Ludlow, P. (1995), "Logical form and the hidden indexical theory: A reply to Schiffer", *Journal of Philosophy* 92: 102–7.

—(1996), "The adicity of 'believes' and the hidden indexical theory", *Analysis* 56: 97–101.

—(2000), "Interpreted logical forms, belief attribution, and the dynamic lexicon", in M. Jaszczolt ed. *The Pragmatics of Propositional Attitude Reports*, Oxford: Elsevier Science, 31–42.

McKay, T. (1981), "On proper names in belief ascriptions", *Philosophical Studies* 39: 287–303.

—(1986), "His burning pants", *Notre Dame Journal of Formal Logic* 27: 393–400.

—(1991), "Representing de re beliefs", *Linguistics and Philosophy* 14: 711–39.

Nelson, M. (2002), "Descriptivism defended", *Noûs* 36: 408–36.

—(2005), "The problem of puzzling pairs", *Linguistics and Philosophy* 28: 319–50.

O'Leary-Hawthorne, J. (1995), "The bundle theory of substance and the identity of indiscernibles", *Analysis* 55: 191–6

Perry, J. (1977), "Frege on demonstratives", *Philosophical Review* 86: 474–97. (Contained in Perry 1993 and 2000.)

—(1979), "The problem of the essential indexical", *Noûs* 13: 3–21. (Contained in Perry 1993 and 2000.)

—(1980), "Belief and acceptance", *Midwest Studies in Philosophy* 5: 533–42. (Contained in Perry 1993 and 2000.)

—(1990), "Self-notions", *Logos* 11: 17–31.

—(1993), *The Problem of the Essential Indexical*, Oxford: Oxford University Press.

—(1997), "Rip Van Winkle and other characters", *The European Review of Analytical Philosophy* 2: 13–39. (Contained in Perry 2000.)

—(1998), "Myself and I", in M. Stamm ed. *Philosophie in Synthetischer Absicht*, Stuttgart: Klett-Cotta, 83–103. (Contained in Perry 2000.)

—(2000), *The Problem of the Essential Indexical*. Expanded edition, Stanford: CSLI.

—(2001), *Reference and Reflexivity*, Stanford: CSLI.

Plantinga, A. (1974), *The Nature of Necessity*, Oxford: Clarendon.

—(1978), "The Boethian compromise", *American Philosophical Quarterly* 14: 129–38.

Quine, W. (1956), "Quantifiers and propositional attitudes", *Journal of Philosophy* 53, 177–87.

—(1980), "Reference and modality" (2nd revised version), in *From a Logical Point of View*. 2nd edition, revised printing, New York: Harper and Row, 139–49. (Originally published in 1953.)

Recanati, F. (1993), *Direct Reference: From Language to Thought*. Oxford: Blackwell.

Reddam, P. (1982), *Pragmatics and the Language of Belief*. Ph.D dissertation, USC.

Reimer, M. (1995), "A defense of de re belief reports", *Mind and Language* 10: 446–63.

Richard, M. (1983), "Direct reference and ascriptions of belief", *Journal of Philosophical Logic* 12: 425–52.

—(1987), "Attitude ascriptions, semantic theory, and pragmatic evidence", *Proceedings of the Aristotelian Society* 87: 243–62.

—(1988), "Taking the Fregean seriously", in D. Austin ed. *Philosophical Analysis*. Dordrecht: Kluwer, 219–39.

—(1989), "How I say what you think", *Midwest Studies in Philosophy* 14: 317–37.

—(1990), *Propositional Attitudes: An Essay on Thoughts and How We Ascribe Them*. Cambridge University Press.

—(1993a), "Attitudes in context", *Linguistics and Philosophy* 16: 123–48.

—(1993b), "Sense, necessity and belief", *Philosophical Studies* 69: 243–63.

—(1993c), "Boër and Lycan's Knowing Who", *Noûs* 27: 235–42.

—(1995), "Defective contexts, accommodation, and normalization", *Canadian Journal of Philosophy* 25: 551–70.

—(1997), "Propositional attitudes", in B. Hale and C. Wright (eds.), *A Companion to Philosophy of Language*. Oxford: Blackwell, 197–226.

—(2001), "Seeking a Centaur, adoring Adonis: Intensional transitives and empty terms", *Midwest Studies in Philosophy* 25: 103–127.

Russell, B. (1903), *The Principles of Mathematics*. Cambridge: Cambridge University Press).

—(1904/1988), "Correspondence with Frege", in N. Salmon and S. Soames (eds), *Propositions and Attitudes*. Oxford: Oxford University Press, 57.

—(1905), "On denoting", *Mind* 14: 479–93.

—(1910), "Knowledge by acquaintance and knowledge by description", *Proceedings of the Aristotelian Society* 11: 108–28.

—(1912), *The Problems of Philosophy*, Oxford: Oxford University Press.

Sainsbury, M. (1993), "Russell on names and communication", in A. D. Irvine and G. A. Wedeking (eds), *Russell and Analytic Philosophy*, Toronto: The University of Toronto Press, 3–21.

Salmon, N. (1981), *Reference and Essence*. Princeton, NJ: Princeton University Press.

—(1985), "Reflexivity", *Notre Dame Journal of Formal Logic* 27: 401–29.

—(1986), *Frege's Puzzle*. Cambridge, MA: The MIT Press.

—(1989), "Illogical belief", *Philosophical Perspectives* 3: 243–85.

—(1992), "Reflections on reflexivity", *Linguistics and Philosophy* 14: 53–63.

—(1995a), "Being of two minds: Belief with doubt", *Noûs* 29: 1–20.

—(1995b), "Relational belief", in P. Leonardi and M. Santambrogio (eds), *On Quine: New Essays*, Cambridge: Cambridge University Press, 206–28.

—(1997), "Is de re belief reducible to de dicto?", in A. Kazmi ed. *Meaning and Reference* (*The Canadian Journal of Philosophy* Supplementary Volume 23), 85–110.

—(2006), "The resilience of illogical belief", *Noûs* 40: 369–75.

Saul, J. (1993), "Still an attitude problem", *Linguistics and Philosophy* 16: 423–35.

—(1996), *The Problem with Attitudes*. Ph.D dissertation, Princeton University.

—(1997), "Substitution and simple sentences", *Analysis* 57: 102–8.

—(1998), "The pragmatics of attitude ascription", *Philosophical Studies* 92: 363–89.

—(1999a), "The road to hell: Intentions and propositional attitude ascription", *Mind and Language* 14: 356–75.

—(1999b), "The best of intentions: Ignorance, idiosyncrasy, and belief reporting", *Canadian Journal of Philosophy* 29: 29–48.

Schiffer, S. (1977), "Naming and knowing", *Midwest Studies in Philosophy* 2: 28–41.

—(1987a), "The 'Fido'-Fido theory of belief", *Philosophical Perspectives* 1: 455–80.

—(1987b), *Remnants of Meaning*. Cambridge,MA: The MIT Press.

—(1990), "The mode-of-presentation problem", in C. Anderson and J. Owens (eds), *Propositional Attitudes*, Stanford: CSLI.

—(1992), "Belief ascription", *Journal of Philosophy* 89: 499–521.

—(1994), "A paradox of meaning", *Noûs* 28: 279–24.

—(1996), "The hidden-indexical theory's logical-form problem: A rejoinder", *Analysis* 56: 92–7.

—(2006), "A problem for a direct-reference theory of belief reports", *Noûs* 40: 361–8.

Sider, T. (1995), "Three problems for Richard's theory of belief ascriptions", *Canadian Journal of Philosophy* 25: 487–513.

Soames, S. (1985), "Lost innocence", *Linguistics and Philosophy* 8: 59–72.

—(1987), "Substitutivity", in J. Thomson ed. *On Being and Saying*, Cambridge, MA: The MIT Press, 99–132.

—(1989a), "Direct reference, propositional attitudes and semantic content", *Philosophical Topics* 14: 44–87.

—(1989b), "Semantics and semantic competence", *Philosophical Perspectives* 3: 575–96.

—(1992), "Truth, meaning, and understanding", *Philosophical Studies* 65: 17–35.

—(1995), "Beyond singular propositions", *Canadian Journal of Philosophy* 25: 514–49.

—(2002), *Beyond Rigidity: The Unfinished Semantic Agenda of Naming and Necessity*, New York: Oxford University Press.

—(2003), *Philosophical Analysis in the Twentieth Century, Volume II: The Age of Meaning*. Princeton, NJ: Princeton University Press.

Sosa, D. (1996), "The import of the puzzle of belief", *Philosophical Review* 105: 373–434.

—(2001), "Rigidity in the scope of Russell's theory", *Noûs* 35: 1–38.

Sosa, E. (1970), "Propositional attitudes de dicto and de re", *Journal of Philosophy* 67: 883–96.

Stalnaker, R. (1981), "Indexical belief", *Synthese* 49: 129–42.

—(1984), *Inquiry*. Cambridge, MA: The MIT Press.

—(1987), "Semantics for belief", *Philosophical Topics* 14: 177–90.

—(1988), "Belief attribution and context", in R. Grimm and D. Merril (eds), *Contents of Thought*, Tucson: University of Arizona, 146–81.

Stanley, J. (1997a), "Rigidity and content", in R. Heck ed. *Language, Thought, and Logic: Essays in honour of Michael Dummett*, Oxford: Oxford University Press, 131–56.

—(1997b), "Names and rigid designation", in B. Hale and C. Wright (eds), *Companion to the Philosophy of Language*, Oxford: Blackwell, 555–86.

—(2002), "Modality and what is said", *Philosophical Perspectives* 16: 321–44.

Strawson, P. F. (1959), *Individuals: An essay in descriptive metaphysics*. London: Methuen.

Taschek, W. (1988), "Would a Fregean be puzzled by Pierre?", *Mind* 97: 99–104.

—(1992), "Frege's puzzle, sense, and information content", *Mind* 101: 767–92.

—(1995a), "Belief, substitution, and logical structure", *Noûs* 29: 71–95.

—(1995b), "On belief content and that-clauses", *Mind and Language* 10: 274–98.

—(1997), "Putting Pierre and Peter in context: On ascribing beliefs", in D. Jurtronic-Tihomirovic ed. *The Maribor Papers in Naturalized Semantics*, Maribor: Maribor.

—(1998), "On ascribing beliefs: Content in context", *Journal of Philosophy* 95: 323–53.

7 Context Dependence

Kent Bach

All sorts of things are context-dependent in one way or another. What it is appropriate to wear, to give or to reveal depends on the context. Whether or not it is all right to lie, harm, or even kill depends on the context. If you google the phrase "depends on the context", you'll get several hundred million results. This chapter aims to narrow that down. In this context the topic is context dependence in language and its use.

It is commonly observed that the same sentence can be used to convey different things in different contexts. That is why people complain when something they say is "taken out of context" and insist that it be "put into context", because "context makes it clear" what they meant. Indeed, it is practically a platitude that what a speaker means in uttering a certain sentence, as well as how her audience understands her, "depends on the context". But just what does that amount to, and to what extent is it true?

Philosophers and linguists often say that certain words (and sentences containing them) are *context-sensitive*, that what they express is *context-dependent*, as if it is perfectly obvious what context dependence is. It is not. So we will need to ask what context is, what depends on it, and what this dependence involves. Answers to these questions are not straightforward. It turns out that there is more than one kind of context and that different sorts of things depend on each. At least they seem to, for, as we will see, much of what passes for context dependence is really something else. Looking at what goes on in specific cases suggests that much of what is done in context is not done by context.

Why should we look into these questions? There are two main theoretical reasons, though we will not dwell on them. First, context sensitivity poses a challenge to the common view that the meaning of a sentence determines its truth-condition. This is the assumption underlying the widespread view that the goal of semantics is to give a systematic theory of the truth-conditions of sentences. However, a truth-conditional semantics has to reckon with the fact that the semantic contents of context-sensitive expressions vary from one context of utterance to another, and that is possible only if the meanings of context-sensitive expressions determine *how* their semantic contents vary with the context. One complication, as we will see, is that many sentences do not seem to have truth-conditions, even relative to contexts.

The second worry, related to the first, is that context sensitivity might undermine the principle of compositionality. This is the common methodo-logical assumption that the semantic properties of complex expressions are determined by those of their constituent expressions and how these are related syntactically. If this principle did not hold, so it is thought, we could not under-stand, much less knowingly produce, any of the virtually unlimited number of sentences we have not previously encountered. Here the challenge is to show how the contents of complex expressions are determined by the contents of their possibly context-sensitive constituents. In some cases, the semantics of the complex expression creates problems for compositionality. To see this, just compare the meanings of "water lily" and "tiger lily" or of "child abuse" and "drug abuse".

There are more down-to-earth reasons for investigating context sensitivity. If the words in a language all had unique and determinate meanings (no ambiguity or vagueness) and fixed references (no indexicality), and if using language were simply a matter of putting one's thoughts into words, under-standing an utterance would merely be a matter of deciphering whatever words the speaker uttered. But language and our use of it to communicate are not as straightforward as that. Some expressions, most obviously pronouns, such as "I", "they" and "this", and temporal terms such as "today" and "next week", do not have fixed references. For example, when I use "I" it refers to me, but when you use it it refers to you. Moreover, we often speak inexplicitly, non-literally, or indirectly, and in each case what we mean is distinct from what can be predicted from the meanings of the expressions we utter. We can leave something out but still mean it, use a word or phrase figuratively, or mean something in addition to what we say. We can even do all three at once.

Here's an example. Suppose you have a friend whose neighbour is well known to be an incompetent doctor. Your friend complains about a chronic cough, and you say, "You should see someone today, but not that genius next door". You meant, let's assume, that your friend should see a doctor that very day for a diagnosis, but not the incompetent neighbour. You probably meant also that he could well have a serious medical condition.

What is the role of context in this case? It does not determine what you meant. Your communicative intention determines that. What context does do is provide information that your friend could use, presuming you intend him to, to figure out what you meant. In that connection context plays a merely evidential role. However, it seems that context can play a more direct, semantic role, at least in connection with such words as "I" and "today". They are context-sensitive, in that their contents, what they contribute to the contents of sentences in which they occur, depend on the context in which they are used.

After discussing how this is so in these paradigm cases, we will look at a wide range of other sorts of expressions that have also been claimed to be context-sensitive. To evaluate such claims, which fall under the general rubric of *contextualism*, we will need to ask whether it is the content of the expression itself that varies from one context of utterance to another and, crucially, whether it does so because of features of the context. This question rarely gets asked. Rather, contextualists tend to use phrases such as "context-dependent" and "context-sensitive" freely and uncritically, as if it is obvious that what is done in context is done by context and equally obvious how. The primary aim of this chapter is to encourage the reader not to take the "obvious" for granted.

1. Introduction: Two kinds of context, two roles for context

One thing should be understood from the start. To hold that certain terms are context-sensitive is not to deny that they have dictionary meanings. The claim is *not* that their meanings vary with the context. It is that their standing meanings determine their contents as a function of contexts of their use. After all, we wouldn't look words up in the dictionary if they didn't have (fairly) stable meanings. To be sure, we recognize that a great many are ambiguous and expect their dictionary entries to give their distinct meanings separately. But ambiguity is not context dependence. Take the ambiguous words "press" and "suit" as they occur in the sentence "A tailor pressed a suit in court". It might seem in a certain context that the speaker is using it to mean that the tailor sued someone, but this does not show that "press" and "suit" are context-sensitive. For she could instead, however improbably, have used the sentence to mean that the tailor ironed a suit of clothes in a courtroom (for convenience, I will generally use "<u>s</u>he" for the <u>s</u>peaker and "<u>h</u>e" for the <u>h</u>earer). Context cannot prevent that, although she might not be understood unless she clarified how she was using her words. In some cases, the context may leave that open, as with this sentence in a letter of recommendation: "I enthusiastically recommend this candidate with no qualifications whatsoever".

This sentence, as it might occur in a letter of recommendation, illustrates a different point:

(1)   Mr Tully is a clear and forceful speaker.

If the letter is for the job of radio announcer, the writer surely means that Mr Tully has an important qualification for the job. On the other hand, if the letter is for a radiologist job, the writer could well use (1) to imply that Mr Tully is a poor candidate. In neither case does the context determine what the writer means in uttering (1) – that is a matter of her intention – but it does determine what the reader could reasonably take her to mean.

There are different things a speaker might be doing in uttering this sentence:

(2)   The cops will break up the party.

Suppose there's a boisterous party going on very late at night in an otherwise quiet neighbourhood. One can imagine different circumstances in which (2) could be used to, and be taken by the hearer to, make a prediction, issue a threat, make a promise, issue a warning or give an order. For example, a nearby resident, confident in the impatience of another neighbour and in the responsiveness of the police, might utter (2) to her husband to make a prediction. That impatient neighbour, tired of the noise, might call the police, and the responding officer might use (2) to promise that the police will break up the party. And if the impatient neighbour happens to be the mayor, she might call the police chief and use (2) to give an order.

These last examples fall under the domain of pragmatics (see Chapter 8), and the issues they raise will not be pursued here. However, it is important to point out that the role of context in these cases is different from the role it plays with expressions that are semantically sensitive to context. Indeed, two different kinds of context are involved. *Narrow context* consists of matters of objective fact to which the determination of the semantic contents of certain expressions are sensitive. *Broad context* is the conversational setting, the mutual cognitive context or salient common ground. It includes the current state of the conversation (what has just been said, what has just been referred to, etc.), the physical setting (if the parties are face to face), salient personal knowledge, and relevant broader common knowledge. Playing a pragmatic role in communication (on whether it could also play a semantic role, see Section 3.1), broad context includes the information that the speaker exploits to make what she means evident to the hearer and, if communication is to succeed, that the hearer takes into account, on the assumption that he is intended to, to figure out what the speaker means.

This difference is often overlooked. For example, Stalnaker, although he contrasts propositions semantically expressed by (context-sensitive) sentences and pragmatic effects of speakers' utterances, treats semantic and pragmatic context sensitivity on a par:

> How should a context be defined? This depends on what elements of the situations in which discourse takes place are relevant to *determining what propositions are expressed by context-dependent sentences and to explaining the effects of various kinds of speech acts.* The most important element of a context, I suggest, is the common knowledge, or presumed common knowledge and common assumptions of the participants in the discourse. A speaker inevitably takes certain information for granted when he speaks as the common ground of the participants in the conversation. It is this information which he can use as a resource for the communication of further information, and

against which he will expect his speech acts to be understood. (Stalnaker 1999: 67; my emphasis)

However, being used as a resource for communication is very different from determining what propositions are expressed. The pragmatic role of context is to provide a basis, as intended by the speaker, for the hearer to figure out what the speaker means. A speaker's communicative intention is reasonable to the extent the hearer can be expected to recognize it on the basis of what she says and the fact that she says it in the context. However, it does not literally determine, in the sense of fixing, what the speaker means. Rather, it enables the hearer to determine, in the sense of ascertaining, what she means.

This characterization suggests that broad context imposes a rational constraint on the speaker's communicative intention. However, it would be misleading to say that this constraint determines what a speaker should intend, given that she says a certain thing. After all, a speaker can try to communicate anything she pleases. The constraint, rather, is this: *given* what she intends to communicate, she should say something that, even if she is not being fully explicit, makes evident to the hearer what she aims to convey. In order to understand the speaker, the hearer relies on the assumption that she intends him to be able to figure out what this is, and to do that he must take into account contextual facts that he can reasonably take her as intending him to take into account (see Grice 1989, chs 2 and 14, and Bach and Harnish 1979, chs 1 and 5).

In the remainder of this chapter we take up a variety of examples of expressions that have been thought to be context-sensitive. Many turn out not to be. In some cases, this is because the source of the contextual variation is not the expression itself but the open range of possible ways in which speakers can use simple sentences containing that expression. In Section 2 we will discuss so-called *indexicals*, some of which, such as "I" and "today", do seem to be context-sensitive in a straightforward way, and compare them with demonstratives, whose contextually variable uses seem to depend on the speaker's intention in using the expression, not on the context in which the expression is used. We will also briefly consider the claim that certain sentences that would otherwise not have truth-conditions contain "hidden indexicals", whose values are somehow provided by context and thereby complete the proposition being expressed. Then, in Section 3, we will discuss various issues about speaker intentions, contexts of utterance, and the relationship between the two. Do intentions really trump contexts, or is intention part of context? Finally, in Section 4, we will take up more examples, mostly involving various kinds of adjectives that have been thought to be context-sensitive.

One aim of this chapter is to show that many supposed cases of context sensitivity are really instances of something else, which I call *semantic incompleteness*.

That is, many sentences containing such expressions fall short of expressing a proposition and are therefore not capable of being true or false, even relative to a context. The idea of semantic incompleteness is straightforward if you think in terms of structured propositions rather than truth-conditions, as built up out of objects, properties and relations (see Kaplan 1989a). Since these are made up of building blocks assembled in a particular way, it makes sense to suppose that in some cases such an assemblage, put together compositionally from a sentence's constituents according to its syntactic structure, might fail to comprise a proposition (see Bach 1994b and Soames 2009). That is because, although this comprises the entire semantic content of the sentence, it lacks at least one constituent needed for it to be true or false and to be the content of a thought or a statement. Even so, like a mere phrase (see Stainton 2006), a semantically incomplete sentence can be used to *assert* a proposition.

2. Indexicals: Automatic, discretionary and hidden

The common philosophical term for contextually shifty terms is "indexical". The obvious examples of indexicals are pronouns ("she", "we", "you", "they", etc.) and demonstratives ("this", "those", "there", etc.), but there are also temporal terms, such as "now" and "today", "last week", and "three days ago", as well as discourse indexicals, notably "the former" and "the latter". Pronouns also function as discourse indexicals, when used anaphorically, as linguists say, to refer back to previously mentioned items (for a thorough discussion, see Neale 2006). In fact, anaphoric pronouns illustrate one of our main themes, as with these examples:

(3)   a. A cop arrested a robber. He was wearing a badge.
        b. A cop arrested a robber. He was wearing a mask.

It is natural to suppose that in (3a) "he" refers to the cop and in (3b) to the robber. It is natural all right, but not inevitable. The speaker of (3a) could be using "he" to refer to the robber, and the speaker of (3b) could be using it to refer to the cop. Such speakers would probably not be understood correctly, at least not without enough stage setting to override commonsense knowledge about cops and robbers, but that would be a pragmatic mistake. Nevertheless, the fact that "he" could be so used suggests that it is the speaker's intention, not the context, which determines that in (3a) it refers to the cop and in (3b) to the robber. The same point applies to these examples with two anaphoric pronouns:

(4)   a. A cop arrested a robber. He took away his gun.

b. A cop arrested a robber. He used his gun.
c. A cop arrested a robber. He dropped his gun.
d. A cop arrested a robber. He took away his gun and escaped.

In (4a), presumably "he" would be used to refer to the cop and "his" to the robber, whereas in (4b) both would be used to refer to the cop, in (4c) both would be used to refer to the robber, and in (4d) "he" would be used to the robber and "his" to the cop. However, given the different uses of the pronouns in what is essentially the same linguistic environment, what explains these differences in reference can only be the speaker's intention, not the narrow context. It is a different, pragmatic matter how the audience figures out the references, and that depends on the broad, communicative context, which comprises the extralinguistic information to be taken into account. If the speaker does not correctly anticipate the hearer's inference, her references will be misunderstood.

2.1 Automatic indexicals

Matters are different with those indexicals that refer independently of the speaker's intention. Suppose you said (5) to me,

(5)   I am relaxed today.

The word "I", the present tense form of the verb, and the word "today", as you are using them, refer to you and the time and day when you spoke. Indeed, they seem to do so automatically, not because of your intention. That is why Perry calls them "automatic" rather than "discretionary" indexicals. What they refer to depends not on what you intend to refer to but "on meaning and public contextual facts" (Perry 2001: 58). So, if instead *I* had uttered (5) and had done so on the following day, the references would have been to me and to a different day, and again the references would have been automatic. Also, if I were then to remind you what you said the previous day, I would use different indexicals and utter (6), not (7).

(6)   You said you were relaxed yesterday.

(7)   You said I am relaxed today.

It is a fact about the standing meaning of "I" that, as used on a given occasion, it refers to its user and a fact about the meaning of "today" that, as used on a given occasion, it refers to the day it is used. These facts about their meanings are essentially rules for their use. The stable meaning of the expression, or what Kaplan (1989a) calls its *character*, determines what contextual parameter fixes its reference, or what Kaplan calls its semantic *content*. This was just illustrated by the difference between "I" and "today". The content (reference) of each varies, as a matter of its respective linguistic meaning, with a certain sort of fact about the context. Moreover, as Kaplan argues, the terms' characters (meanings) do not enter into the semantic contents of sentences in which the terms occur. Rather, their references enter in (Braun (2008) argues similarly regarding demonstrative phrases, such as "that guy"). So if the day after you uttered (5) I spoke (8) to you,

(8)   You were relaxed yesterday.

I would be saying the same thing you said the day before. That is, despite their lexical differences, sentence (5) as uttered by you on one day and sentence (8) as spoken by me to you the next day would have the same semantic contents, in that what it takes for them to be true depends on the same thing, your being relaxed on the day in question. The rules for the use of "you" and "yesterday" are different from those for "I" and "today" but in the situations described their respective contents are the same.

2.2 Discretionary indexicals

Terms such as "now", "then", "here", "we", "you", "she" and "that" seem to differ in how they work from "I", "today" and "last week". Just compare "now" with "today". Whereas the reference of "today" as used on a given occasion is straightforwardly the day of that use, the reference of "now" is not straightforwardly the time of its use. This is because the extent of that time is not fixed. Is it strictly the moment that "now" is used, or can the time in question be a larger duration that includes that moment? One might insist that it is strictly the moment of use and that any larger duration merely including that moment is not, strictly speaking, the reference of "now".

That might seem plausible until one considers "here". The analogous claim would be that "here" as used on a given occasion refers to the place of that use. But which place is that? What is the spatial analogue of the moment of utterance, even if we exclude regions that extend beyond the speaker's body? The location of the speaker's mouth, her complete vocal apparatus, her entire body?

The situation is similar with "we", but also interestingly different. For not only can the extent of the reference be larger or smaller, it can be disparate. "We" can be used on a given occasion to refer to a plurality (or group) that includes the speaker, but which plurality is that? It could include the intended audience, but it might not, as when one person speaks on behalf of a group of people not present.

What determines the reference? A first thought is that the context does, but does it? On second thought, it seems that the speaker's referential intention does the trick. What context does is to impose rational constraints on that intention and on the hearer's inference as to what that intention is. This contrasts with what determines the references of "I", "today" and "last week", as used on a given occasion. A specific, objective fact about the context (the identity of the speaker in the case of "I" and the time of the utterance with "today" and "last week") determines the reference. In Section 3 we look more deeply into intentions and contexts in connection with uses of demonstratives such as "this" and "that".

2.3 Hidden Indexicals?

Several types of sentences raise an interesting issue. As used in a given context, they seem intuitively capable of being true or false – they seem to express definite propositions – and yet they seem to be missing something necessary for that. To account for this it has been suggested that they contain a "hidden indexical". This phrase was introduced by Schiffer (1977: 31–36) to address the longstanding philosophical puzzle about belief reports. We will take up some less puzzling cases.

Weather and other environmental reports

So-called weather reports have attracted considerable attention ever since they were first discussed by Perry (1986) in connection with his notion of "unarticulated constituent", his phrase for an element in the proposition expressed by the speaker that does not correspond to any expression in the uttered sentence. The debate has focused on "It is raining", but there are similar sentences, some of which pertain to aspects of the environment other than the weather:

(9)   It is raining.

(10) It is windy.

(11) It is noisy.

(12) It is eerie.

These sentences do not specify a location where it is said to be raining or whatever. Moreover, they do not seem to say merely that it is raining (windy, etc.) somewhere or other, although this is a matter of some debate (see Recanati 2002, Stanley 2002 and Taylor 2001), at least in the case of (9). This line seems far less plausible with the other sentences, especially (12). It seems that these sentences, as they stand, do not fully express propositions (are not true or false), even given the time of utterance. That is, it seems that a location where it is being said to be windy, noisy or eerie needs to be understood. This is not a general requirement, as Taylor points out with examples such as "John is dancing". That sentence expresses a proposition even though dancing must take place at a location. However, something is missing in what sentences (10)–(12) express, with the semantically empty "it" as subject. Compare them with "Chicago is windy", "Midtown Manhattan is noisy" and "Carlsbad Caverns is eerie". Speakers uttering sentences such as (9)–(12) must intend some location as part of what they mean. It is as if they uttered a richer sentence, one that included a locative phrase, as here:

(9+)   It is raining in St. Andrews.

(10+) It is windy in Chicago.

(11+) It is noisy in midtown Manhattan.

(12+) It is eerie in Carlsbad Caverns.

These sentences do express propositions, and speakers could use (9)–(12) to convey these propositions, but only in the right contexts, where they can reasonably expect to be taken to be talking about the location in question.

Do (9)–(12) contain a hidden indexical, something like "(in) x", for the unspecified location that a speaker must mean? That is an interesting linguistic question. Recanati (2004) and Stanley (2005a) have continued their debate about whether contextualism, to be defensible, must take the form of *indexicalism* (this is Recanati's term for the view that Stanley defends). However, neither addresses the underlying question of how context does what each assumes it does, whether it is to provide values for hidden indexicals or merely to supply unarticulated constituents.

Regarding this interesting linguistic question, the main reason for positing a hidden indexical is to account for the meaning of sentences such as (13a), as represented in (13b):

(13)   a. Wherever John is on his vacation, it rains.
       b. Wherever(x) John is on his vacation, it rains in x.

That is, we seem to need the variable to account for the variation in the place, indicated by "wherever", where it is said to be raining. Moreover, so the so-called *binding argument* goes, if the variable is present because of a quantifier needing a variable to bind, as in (13), the variable is present, functioning as an indexical, in the absence of a quantifier, as in (9). However, this argument does not seem to work for (14) and (15):

(14)   Whenever John is on his vacation, it rains.

(15)   Whenever John doesn't have his umbrella, it rains.

In these cases the variation in location is understood, but there is nothing in the sentence ("whenever" has replaced "wherever") to require that location be marked syntactically.

Terms with missing complements

A similar situation arises with certain expressions that can be used without what linguists call *complements*, as in these sentences:

(16)   Ronnie is ready.

(17)   Lynn is late.

Because one can't be just plain ready or just plain late (being ready and being late are relations, not properties) and these sentences do not indicate what Ronnie and Lynn are being said to be ready or late for, these sentences seem not to express propositions and not capable of being true or false. Yet these sentences are perfectly usable. How can that be?

Borg (2004) and Cappelen and Lepore (2005) maintain that these sentences do express propositions but not the ones they are used to assert. For example, Borg thinks that (16) expresses the proposition that Ronnie is ready for something or other, even though it cannot be used to assert that proposition. Cappelen and Lepore think that it expresses the "minimal" proposition that Ronnie is ready, full stop. Their critics (in Preyer and Peter 2005) doubt that there is such a proposition (one can't be just plain ready), and some suggest that (16) must be context-sensitive, perhaps with a hidden variable whose value is what Ronnie is being said to be ready for. Even if there is such a variable, rather than merely an unarticulated constituent, for reasons we have seen the context does not provide that value.

The most economical approach denies that (16) and (17) express propositions, whereas the following augmented versions of these sentences, with the extra material in italics, do express propositions (given a time of utterance):

(16+) Ronnie is ready *to go to school.*

(17+) Lynn is late *for work.*

A speaker can reasonably use (16) or (17) to assert the propositions expressed by (16+) and (17+) even without specifying what she means Ronnie is ready to do or what Lynn is late for, provided she does so in a context in which the hearer can figure out what she is trying to convey. Context does not determine what completes the proposition, but enables the hearer to figure out how the speaker intends it to be completed (see Bach 1994b).

Relational terms

Relational terms, such as "neighbour", "fan", "enemy", "local" and "foreign", are so-called, unsurprisingly, because they seem to involve a relation to something. You can't just be a neighbour, full stop, but only a neighbour of others. You can't just be a fan; you have to be a fan of something, such as a team or a performer. You can't be an enemy, full stop, but only an enemy of a person or a group. That is why sentences such as the following seem semantically incomplete and have been thought to contain hidden indexicals:

(18)   Oliver is a neighbour.

(19)   Oscar is a fan.

(20)   Osama was an enemy.

They seem to be missing something present in these augmented versions:

(18+) Oliver is a neighbour *of the Joneses.*

(19+) Oscar is a fan *of FC Barcelona.*

(20+) Osama was an enemy *of Obama.*

Does this show that who the person is being said to be a neighbour, fan or enemy of is determined *by* the context? No, it shows only that this is determined *in* the context. When someone utters a sentence such as one of these, what she means must include such relational information. Whether or not sentences (18)–(20) contain hidden variables, context does not determine what fills the gap.

Perspectival terms

A similar point applies to perspectival terms, such as "left", "distant", "horizon", "faint" and "occluded". Sentences such as the following seem to be semantically incomplete for essentially the same reason as the previous three, and have also been thought to contain hidden indexicals:

(21)   The post office is on the left.

(22)   One can see a ship on the horizon.

(23)   The old firehouse is occluded by an apartment building.

In these cases there is no explicit indication of a perspective and, since something can't just be on the left, full stop, be on the horizon, full stop, etc., the explicitly expressed semantic contents of these sentences seem to be sub-propositional. In contrast, the semantic contents of their explicitly completed counterparts are fully propositional:

(21+)   The post office is on the left after you cross the intersection of 1st and Main.

(22+)   From the top of the hill one can see an island on the horizon.

(23+)   From the post office the old firehouse is occluded by an apartment building.

Once again context does not determine what fills the gap. Rather, it provides information to help the hearer to figure out how the speaker intends the gap to be filled.

We have certainly not settled the questions of whether sentences such as (9)–(23), the ones considered in this section, contain hidden indexicals or are merely used to convey propositions with unarticulated constituents, but either way they are semantically incomplete. That does not mean that they are context-sensitive. Unfortunately, the tests that Cappelen and Lepore (2005: ch. 7) and Cappelen and Hawthorne (2009: ch. 2) have proposed for context sensitivity fail to discriminate between that and semantic incompleteness.

3. Context and intention

Some philosophers see no important difference between contents that are "determined by the speaker's intentions and those that are determined solely by the non-intentional features of the context of utterance (such as the speaker, time, and place). ... [Yet] no substantive or even remotely interesting issue depends upon this distinction" (Cappelen 2007: 8). However, the examples considered so far suggest that the role of the speaker's intention is to determine what the speaker means, not the contents of expressions the speaker uses. And where expression content is determined, as in the case of automatic indexicals, it is determined by (narrow) context, without the help of the speaker's intention. However, some have argued that certain aspects of what of we have been treating as broad context, such as relevance and salience, are capable of playing a role in determining the contents of certain expressions. And others have argued that the speaker's intention can itself play such a role and should be construed as an aspect of narrow context, hence that the role of context of the semantically relevant sort is not limited to automatic indexicals. In this section we will take up several of these arguments and look at the role of intention in the use of demonstratives, the paradigm of discretionary indexicals.

3.1 Context vs. intention

Gauker (2007; 2010) has argued that what is contextually salient or relevant, along with several other "accessibility" factors, can and do help determine semantic content. This is in the spirit of Lewis's (1979, 1980) liberal conception of the semantic role of context, on which even contextually apt standards of precision can play such a role. Gauker in effect treats salience and relevance as elements of narrow context, not merely factors for hearers to take into account to figure out what the speaker means. But how can these factors bear on *semantic* content unless the meanings of the expressions in question somehow require them to play such a role? Gauker's proposal must in effect treat meaning as character in Kaplan's sense, but not limited to matters of objective fact as the speaker and time of utterance.

This sort of proposal invites the following objection, stated originally by Bach (1994a: 176–9) and forcefully put by Schiffer:

> Meaning-as-character may initially seem plausible when the focus is on a word such as "I", but it loses plausibility when the focus is on other pronouns and demonstratives. What "contextual factors" determine the referent of the pronoun "she" in a context of utterance? ... Evidently, the meaning of "she" (very roughly speaking) merely constrains the speaker to

refer to a female. We do not even have to say that it constrains the speaker to refer to a contextually salient female, since the speaker cannot intend to refer to a particular female unless he expects the hearer to recognize to which female he is referring, and the expectation of such recognition itself entails that the speaker takes the referent to have an appropriate salience. What fixes the referent of a token of "she" are the speaker's referential intentions in producing that token, and therefore in order for Kaplan to accommodate "she", he would have to say that a speaker's referential intentions constitute one more component of those n-tuples that he construes as "contexts". The trouble with this is that there is no work for Kaplanian contexts to do once one recognizes speakers' referential intentions. The referent of a pronoun or demonstrative is always determined by the speaker's referential intention. (Schiffer 2005: 1141)

Schiffer's argument applies not only to personal pronouns such as "she" (and obviously to demonstratives) but also to expressions of any other sort for which salience or relevance is thought to play a content-determining role (in the sense of fixing content, not merely ascertaining it). The only exception is automatic indexicals.

It is important to appreciate that Schiffer's argument does not bear on the pragmatic, that is epistemic and normative, role of context, construed broadly to include salience, relevance and so on. For these factors do constrain what a speaker can *reasonably* intend. However, that role should not be confused with the semantic role of actually determining content. As Fodor and Lepore explain, "Since the speaker's access to the interpretation of his utterance is epistemically privileged, nothing about the background of an utterance is metaphysically constitutive of its interpretation. The function of background knowledge in interpretation is (only) to provide premises for the hearer's inferences about the speaker's intentions" (2005: 10).

Instead of appealing to salience and relevance, which are properties that rational speaker intentions exploit but which cannot plausibly be regarded as actually fixing semantic content, one might argue that the speaker's intention fills the semantic gap. Stokke (2010) defends "intention-based semantics", according to which the speaker's intention is itself an element of narrow context, hence capable of determining semantic content. Focusing specifically on demonstrative reference, he argues that the speaker's intention in using a demonstrative determines its reference.

However, there is a problem with this proposal. Perhaps unaware of the ambiguity of the phrase "demonstrative reference", which can mean either reference by a demonstrative or reference by a speaker in using a demonstrative, Stokke evidently conflates the two. At best, his proposal renders reference by the demonstrative itself as derivative, with no theoretical importance of its own. As

Neale puts the point, in the spirit of Strawson (1950), "referring is an intentional act, something *speakers* do, [and] talk of an *expression* itself referring, and even talk of an expression referring relative to an utterance, a speech act, a 'context', or a 'tokening', is, at best, derivative" (Neale 2007: 254). That is, we can always *stipulate* that to say that when the speaker's intention determines what the speaker is referring to, the expression thereby refers to it. But what's the point of such a stipulation? It just trivializes intention-based semantics for demonstratives.

There is a deeper problem, pertaining to the speaker's intention. If the speaker intends to use a demonstrative to refer to a certain object, she does so with the audience in mind. She uses "that" to enable her audience to focus on the intended object, and does so with the intention that he take that as the object she is talking about. But this is part of her overall communicative intention in uttering the sentence in which "that" occurs. As such, it is essentially an audience-directed, hence pragmatic intention. The speaker does not have a separate semantic intention that the word "that" itself refer to the object she is using it to refer to. As far as reference to that object is concerned, there is just her one pragmatic intention. And recognizing that intention is all the hearer has to do for the reference to be conveyed. It is not the word "that" but the speaker's *use* of it that manifests her referential intention and triggers the hearer's inference to what she intends to refer to.

3.2 Intentions or demonstrations?

But is it really the speaker's intention that determines demonstrative reference? Kaplan (1989a) initially thought it was the speaker's demonstration (at least an implicit one, when there is no gesture but a particular object is uniquely salient), but later (Kaplan 1989b) he decided that it was the speaker's "directing intention", so-called because it guides the act of demonstration (if there is one) of a certain object. The demonstration, Kaplan now thought, plays merely the pragmatic role of facilitating communication by making clear to the hearer what the speaker intends to be referring to (Braun 1996 modified Kaplan's account of the character of demonstratives that finessed the difference between intentions and demonstrations). Reimer (1991) subsequently argued that Kaplan shouldn't have changed his mind. Her argument relies mainly on cases where the intention and the demonstration diverge. In one example the speaker uses "that dog" with the intention of referring to Fido but, as Fido is frolicking around with other dogs, she inadvertently points to Spot. It seems that she is thus referring to Spot, contrary to her intention. This is clear from the fact that she would be speaking falsely if she said, "That dog is Fido". The explanation for this, according to Reimer, is that what is controlling is not the intention but the act of demonstration.

We can agree with Reimer that what the speaker says in this example is false and that this is because the reference is indeed to Spot. However, as Bach (1992) argued, that is because the relevant intention on the part of the speaker is to refer to the dog she is pointing at. She believes that the dog she is pointing at is Fido – that's why she says "That dog is Fido" – and to that extent intends to refer to Fido. However, the intention that the hearer is to recognize, the one whose recognition is essential to the success of the speaker's act of communication, is the intention to refer to the dog she is pointing at. And *this* intention *is* decisive in determining the reference. That is because when demonstrating something, the speaker intends the hearer to think of a certain item *as* the one she is pointing at and thereby intending to be talking about. If she intended the hearer to think of the dog as Fido, she could not have thought she was providing him with new information. She would have been telling him that this dog, Fido, was Fido. So, although she failed to refer to the dog she intended to refer to, in so far as she intended to refer to Fido, she succeeded in referring to the dog she intended to demonstrate and did demonstrate, the one she was pointing at. The former intention can be trumped by the demonstrative gesture, but the latter cannot be.

3.3 Context of *utterance?*

At the beginning we assumed that some indexicals, such as "I" and "today", are automatic (rather than discretionary) and that the context of utterance determines their references. However, there are exceptional cases, such as the standard answering machine message "I am not here now" and the similar office door message "I will not be in my office today". The most obvious part of the problem is that the intended time associated with "now", "today" or the present tense is not the time of speaking or writing. Not only that, the speaker (or writer) need not be the right person (the recorded message might have come with the telephone, and a colleague might have posted the note). Similar situations arise with advertisements, signs, wills, fictional and historical narratives, stenographers and translators.

Such examples suggest that the context of utterance (the agent and the time of the utterance) does not always determine the reference, or else that the notion of utterance context must be construed more abstractly. Either way, the question arises of how the relevant notion of context ties in with the meanings of words such as "I", "now" and "today". That is, what could it be about the meaning of "I" that makes it refer to the person being called or the occupant of the relevant office? And what could it be about the meanings of "now" and "today" that could make them refer to the time of the call or the day of the visit to the office. In defence of the standard appeal to context of utterance, one might appeal to the distinction between the semantic content of the sentences in which they were originally uttered and the contents they are to be taken to have when heard by a caller or read by a visitor. To defend such a view, one would have to argue that these are not literal uses of the sentences in question, or at least that they are to be treated as if they were being uttered at the time they are encountered. However, such moves would require invoking intentions and thereby viewing these indexicals as less automatic and more discretionary than standardly supposed.

To address this problem, or at least the part involving "I", Dodd and Sweeney (2010) refine the notion of agent of the context. They consider different versions of the answering machine and Post-it Note examples and argue that in some cases the agent of the context can be someone other than the person who actually produced the token of "I". In these as in standard cases, "I" automatically refers to the agent of the context. In other cases "I" doesn't refer at all. For example, if I take an "I will be back soon" note left from yesterday on my neighbour's door and put it on my door, I am the agent of the context. But if my neighbour, knowing that I am away but will return soon, puts her note on my door, I am not the agent of the context. In this case, "I" does not manage to refer to me, although it is naturally taken as if it does.

4. Adjectives and other additional examples

So far we have attended mainly to the prime candidates for context sensitivity, indexicals and demonstratives, and to several specific sorts of sentences thought to contain hidden indexicals. Now we will take up several kinds of adjectives that have been claimed to be context-sensitive. After that we will mention a few other candidates.

4.1 Gradable adjectives

There are thousands of gradable adjectives, and they fall into two broad categories. *Relative* adjectives, exemplified by "tall", "old", "fast" and "smart", are the more abundant by far. Less common but still plentiful are *absolute* adjectives, such as "flat", "empty", "pure" and "dry". Relative adjectives apply in degrees but, unlike absolute adjectives, not to any maximal degree. There are no ultimate degrees of tallness, oldness, etc. Even fastness, though presumably limited in fact by the speed of light, is not limited by the semantics of "fast". Nothing can be completely or perfectly tall, old, fast or smart. In contrast, absolute adjectives, as their name would suggest, apply to maximal degrees. Even if, as a matter of physical fact, a surface cannot be perfectly flat and a container cannot be completely empty, these phrases, "perfectly flat" and "completely empty", make perfectly good semantic sense.

Relative adjectives

Let us begin with relative adjectives, as they occur in sentences such as these:

(24)   No jockey is tall.

(25)   Richard Hughes is tall.

(26)   Fido is old.

(27)   Michael Phelps is fast.

All of these sentences may seem true. In particular, (24) seems true. Yet Irish jockey Richard Hughes is 5'10", and that makes him tall for a jockey. Does that make (25) true and (24) false? Not if "tall" is construed as a context-sensitive term. But is that the right way to look at it? The key thing to notice is that tallness is not a property. One cannot be just plain tall. Richard Hughes is tall for a jockey but not tall for an adult Caucasian man – being tall for a jockey is a property he has, and being tall for an adult Caucasian man is a property he lacks. So it would seem that both (24) and (25), as well as (26) and (27), are semantically incomplete, are not capable of being true or false.

Could (24) and (25) still be true or false, albeit only relative to comparison classes (jockeys, adult men, etc.)? Kennedy (2007) points out that, strictly speaking, the relativization of a gradable adjective is to a standard, not necessarily to a comparison class (even with a specified comparison class, as in "tall for a jockey", a standard is still needed). Even so, when we relativize explicitly, usually it is to comparison classes rather than to standards, as in these augmented versions of (24)–(27):

(24+) No jockey is tall for an adult human.

(25+) a. Richard Hughes is tall for a jockey.
          b. Richard Hughes is tall for an adult Caucasian man.

(26+) Fido is old for a dog.

(27+) Michael Phelps is fast for a swimmer.

(25+a) and (25+b) are relativized to different comparison classes, and express different propositions, one true and one false (notice that what makes the difference is the additional phrase, not the word "tall", whose role is the same in both). Speakers can use (25) to convey one of those (or similar) propositions. Which one she succeeds in conveying depends on the context, in the broad sense in which the proposition she can reasonably expect to be taken to convey and the hearer can reasonably take her to convey depends on what information is mutually available. In some cases it will be necessary to explicitly mention the intended comparison class. (It should be noted that relative adjectives are generally vague, and vagueness might seem to involve a different sort of apparent context dependence. How that is treated depends on one's theory of vagueness, far too big a topic to take up in this chapter. It is briefly discussed in Chapter 12.)

Absolute adjectives

Absolute adjectives, unlike relative ones, apply to maximal degrees. There is a maximal degree to which, for example, a surface can be flat, a container can be empty, a sample of gold can be pure, or a cloth can be dry. So it might seem that sentences such as the following determinately express propositions and are perfectly capable of being true or false.

(28)   Pool tables are flat.

(29)   Some freight cars are empty.

(30)   The gold in Fort Knox is pure.

(31)   My raincoat is dry.

However, it is debatable whether such predicates have to apply to the maximal degree for sentences such as these to be true (never mind whether they can apply maximally in the real world). For example, even though pool tables are not perfectly flat, it seems that (28) is true. It may seem that such sentences can be true if the relevant predicate applies closely enough, but Unger (1975) argued that something can be flat (empty, pure, dry) only if nothing can be flatter (emptier, purer, drier) than it. However, he later conjectured that these two contrasting views, which he dubbed *contextualism* and *invariantism*, are equally tenable (Unger 1984). Only on a contextualist view are sentences such as (28)–(31) semantically context-sensitive; on an invariantist view they are not. If invariantism is correct, such sentences are categorically true only if their predicates apply completely or perfectly, and categorically false otherwise. This means that uses of them are pragmatically context-sensitive. Lasersohn (1999) describes their uses as blessed with "pragmatic halos", which may be larger or smaller depending how tolerant or exacting their use. Utterances of them can be treated as true if they are close enough to applying maximally (as if they included an implicit "approximately", "for all practical purposes", or the like), but what counts as close enough varies. A pool table can be flat for all practical purposes if it is level enough and smooth enough for playing an unimpeded game of pool, assuming that's the relevant purpose, but an airport runway can be less flat and still count as flat for its purpose.

Why did Unger (1984) suggest that there is no objective basis for deciding between the two views on terms such as "flat" and "empty"? He pointed out that appealing to intuitions is inconclusive because they point in both directions. For example, it is intuitively plausible that something can be flat only if nothing can be flatter than it, and that phrases such as "nearly flat" and even "almost perfectly flat" imply not flat. On the other hand, it seems that phrases such as "perfectly flat" and "completely flat" are not redundant, hence that they are stronger than unmodified "flat". So Unger doubted that the conflict between contextualism and invariantism about absolute adjectives can be resolved. However, we should remember that "contextualism" is not really the right term for the first view, since it does not really claim that context determines the standard for applying the term.

4.2 Terms for response-dependent properties

A special case of gradable adjectives are those, such as "edible", "scary" and "comfortable", used to ascribe *response-dependent* properties. These properties are so-called because they apply to things or substances because of the effects that these things or substances have on other things (so they are better described as relations than properties). The terms that express them are generally relative adjectives, but some, such as "lethal", are absolute. They are worth singling out here because they might seem to be context-dependent quite apart from being standard-relative (and vague). Consider sentences such as these:

(32) Some roots are edible.

(33) Horror movies are scary.

(34) Wassily chairs are comfortable.

These sentences are used to indicate a certain responsiveness (sensitivity or sensibility), either biological or psychological. With edibility, obviously this responsiveness is biological, but typically when a speaker makes a statement using a sentence such as (32) it reflects the responsiveness of her biological type, that is, *Homo sapiens*. With scariness and comfortableness, although biologically based, it is primarily psychological, a matter of how things of the relevant sorts, horror movies or Wassily chairs in the above examples, are experienced. Things are not edible, scary or comfortable, full stop, but only relative to animals or people. This suggests that sentences such as (32)–(34) are not context-sensitive but, rather, semantically incomplete. That does not mean, of course, that they cannot be used to convey propositions.

Typically, but not necessarily, statements made in using sentences such as (32)–(34) are from the speaker's perspective, perhaps generalized to include a group of which the speaker takes herself to be typical. If advised that most men are not scared by horror movies, a female speaker might retreat and claim that horror movies are scary to most women. Perhaps more realistically, the intended group comprises people such as the speaker or perhaps people with sensibilities like the speaker's.

These observations suggest that sentences such as the above, if they are to express propositions, need to be augmented in ways such as these:

(32+) a. Some roots are edible *for humans.*
      b. Some roots are edible *for goats.*

(33+) a. Horror movies are scary *to people like me.*
      b. Horror movies are scary *to small children.*

(34+) a. Wassily chairs are comfortable, *at least to people of my size and shape.*
      b. Wassily chairs are comfortable *to people with strong backs.*

These sentences express propositions that speakers of the semantically incomplete sentences (32)–(34) might mean. Typically, but not necessarily, statements made in using (32)–(34) are from the speaker's perspective, perhaps generalized to include a group of which the speaker takes herself to be typical as to response. The augmented (a) sentences express such propositions. However, as the (b) sentences illustrate, the intended group need not include the speaker. It is not difficult to imagine contexts, say in response to a question about whether little Billy should watch *Halloween 5*, in which a rational speaker uttering (33) is likely to mean, and a rational listener is likely to take the speaker to mean, that horror movies are scary to small children. However, this does not show that the context determines that this is what is meant. Note, finally, that the speaker may not have a precise communicative intention when uttering a sentence such as (32)–(34), in which case there is no proposition that the speaker determinately means (see Buchanan 2010).

4.3 Predicates of personal taste

The above problems are exacerbated for *predicates of personal taste*, a special case of adjectives for response-dependent properties. They include such adjectives as "fun", "tasty", "thrilling" and "funny". They do not express absolute properties but, so it is sometimes thought, properties that are relative to a judge or to an assessor (see Lasersohn 2005 and MacFarlane 2005). However, arguably they are experiencer-relative, since whether or not something is, say, fun or tasty depends on how it affects the person, on what sort of experience it causes, not on the judgment or assessment that the person makes on the basis of that experience (see Glanzberg 2007). Statements made using simple, unrelativized versions of sentences containing predicates of personal taste are typically made from the speaker's perspective:

(35)   Pineapples are tasty.

(36)   Rafting through the Grand Canyon is thrilling.

(37)   Jon Stewart is funny.

However, a speaker can also adopt the perspective of someone else or some group, as perhaps in uttering these sentences with the same predicates:

(38)   Alpo is tasty.

(39)   Skydiving is thrilling.

(40)   Three Stooges movies are funny.

Someone uttering (38) is likely to mean that Alpo is tasty to dogs, or perhaps to her own dog, not to herself. Someone uttering (39), say if she were explaining why some people engage in skydiving, could well mean that skydiving is thrilling to people not afraid to do it, and someone might utter (40) with the perspective of French people in mind, say if she were explaining why *Les Trois Imbeciles* are still popular in France. It is always possible, and to ensure successful communication often necessary, to make the relevant perspective explicit, by uttering a sentence relativized to that perspective, as with these more elaborate versions of (38)–(40):

(38+) Alpo is tasty to dogs.

(39+) Skydiving is thrilling to people not afraid to do it.

(40+) The Three Stooges are funny to French people.

In some cases it is unnecessary to specify the experiencers from whose perspective being tasty, thrilling or funny is being considered. For example, if you are asking someone whether something is tasty, thrilling or funny, or you are reporting that someone finds something tasty, thrilling or funny, normally you are asking for or reporting how it is from their perspective.

Lasersohn (2005) and Stephenson (2007) have proposed relativist accounts of sentences such as (35)–(40), according to which such sentences express propositions that are not true or false absolutely but only relative to judges or assessors. Leaving aside general challenges to the idea of relative truth (see Glanzberg (2009) and Soames (2011), and several contributions to García-Carpintero and Kölbel (2008)), Boghossian (2006) and Wright (2008) have raised doubts that truth relativism in a given area, such as where predicates of personal taste are involved, can amount to anything more than property relativism in that area. Their basic idea is that certain ostensibly monadic properties, as expressed by one-place predicates, are actually relational. This is supported by our observation that when the relatum is actually specified, as in the sentences in (38+)–(40+), there is no question of relative truth. Once we take those sentences into account, we can see, by subtraction as it were, that (38)–(40) are semantically incomplete. Instead of supposing that they express propositions whose truth is judge- or experiencer-relative, we can reject the presupposition that they express propositions at all. This leaves open, of course, what speakers do when they use such sentences. They may or may not have a particular perspective in mind, and they may or may not be understood as asserting something that involves a particular perspective, but these are separate questions, questions about using unrelativized sentences containing predicates of personal taste. As sentences, (35)–(40) are no different from the ones containing terms for response-dependent properties or, for that matter, other relative adjectives.

4.4 Odds and ends

We have discussed a variety of types of expressions that are or at least have been thought to be context-sensitive. The following list includes them and a few more, which, due to space limitations, cannot be taken up here:

- automatic indexicals: *I, today, next week, last year* [tense]
- discretionary indexicals and demonstratives: *we, she, they, you, now, here, then, there, that, those*
- weather and other environmental reports: *(It is) raining, hot, humid, windy, noisy, eerie, crowded*

- expressions that can be used without complements: *ready, late, finish, strong enough, legal, eligible, incompetent, experienced, applicable, relevant, difficult*
- relational terms: *neighbour, fan, enemy, local, foreign, employee, mentor*
- perspectival terms: *left, distant, up, behind, foreground, horizon, faint, occluded*
- gradable adjectives, both relative and absolute: *tall, old, fast, smart; flat, empty, pure, dry*
- terms for response-dependent properties: *edible, poisonous, scary, nauseating, comfortable*
- predicates of personal taste: *fun, funny, thrilling, boring, tasty, delicious, tasteful, cute, sexy, cool*
- possessive phrases, adjectival phrases, noun-noun compounds: *John's car, John's hometown, John's boss, John's company; fast car, fast driver, fast tyres, fast time; water lily, tiger lily; child abuse, drug abuse; vitamin pill, diet pill, sleeping pill, pain pill*
- subsentential utterances: *"A shark!", "In the cupboard", "Scalpel!", "Water!", "Coffee or tea?"*
- prepositions: *in, on, to, at, for, with*
- light verbs: *do, have, put, get, go, make, take, give*
- implicit temporal, spatial, and quantifier domain restriction
- certain philosophically interesting terms: *know, might, probable, necessary, explain, and, or, if, obligatory, permissible, ought, free, responsible*

Finally, some philosophers and linguists have suggested that all, or at least a vast preponderance, of sentences are context-sensitive, irrespective of which particular words they contain (Searle 1978, Sperber and Wilson 1986, Travis 2000, Carston 2002, Recanati 2004). *Radical contextualism* is based on intuitions about the truth-values of utterances of a given sentence in various contexts. By describing various contexts in which the same sentence can be used to mean different things, as evidenced by intuitions that in some contexts an utterance of the sentence is true and in others false, these writers conclude that the meaning of the sentence, even if it contains no obviously indexical expressions, is context-sensitive.

There are three problems with this line of reasoning (for more detailed discussion see Bach 2005: 29–34). First of all, the most that it shows is that a great many sentences are semantically incomplete. It does not show that they are context-sensitive. Secondly, the sentences usually considered are not random sentences but, rather, sentences of the typically short sort that people use in everyday speech. Even if those sentences are semantically incomplete, and even if that showed that they are context-sensitive, it does not follow that there aren't other, more elaborate sentences, one for each context, whose utterance would have made what the speaker meant fully explicit. And there are a lot more of those longer, more elaborate sentences than there are of the short sentences that motivate the line of reasoning in the first place. Thirdly, this line of argument has a rather drastic implication. If it worked not only for the short sentences under consideration but also for the more elaborate ones, we would have to conclude that thoughts are essentially ineffable. That is because the argument would show that no amount of elaboration, of spelling out the thought the speaker is trying to express, could ever make that thought fully explicit. Perhaps some would welcome this consequence, but it seems to be an unfortunate consequence of the radical contextualist position.

It takes a lot to show that expressions of a given type are context-sensitive. It is not enough to point out that what a speaker means when using the expression can be different in different contexts. It has to be the content of the expression itself that varies, and it has to be the context, in a way determined by the meaning of the expression, that makes the difference. The fact that a sentence does not express a proposition independently of the context does not show that it is context-sensitive and that which proposition it expresses depends on the context. For it might not express a proposition at all. What passes for a sentence's "intuitive" content is often the proposition a speaker uses it to convey.

Appendix: Guide to Further Reading

To look more deeply into the topics touched on in this chapter and into some relevant ones omitted for reasons of space, the reader should consult the references listed below.

Adjectives and context sensitivity: Unger (1984), Lahav (1989), Ludlow (1989), Heal (1997), Kennedy (2007), Glanzberg (2007), Reimer (2002), Rothschild and Segal (2009)

Binding argument: Partee (1989), Stanley and Szabó (2000), Bach (2000), Cappelen and Lepore (2005: ch. 6), Stanley (2005b), Cappelen and Hawthorne (2007), Cohen and Rickless (2007), Neale (2007: 354–8), Elbourne (2008), Sennet (2008)

Context and compositionality: King and Stanley (2005), Fodor and Lepore (2005), Pagin (2005), Recanati (2010: ch. 1)

Contexts and intentions (and demonstrations), Lewis (1979; 1980), Kaplan (1989a; 1989b), Reimer (1992), Bach (1992), Braun (1996), García-Carpintero (1998), Stalnaker (1999), King (2001), Fodor and Lepore (2005), Bach (2005; 2006a), Gauker (2007), Åkerman (2010), Gauker (2010), Montminy (2010), Mount (2010), Stokke (2010)

Contextualism (epistemic), Preyer and Peter, eds. (2005, Part I)

Contextualism (semantic), Strawson (1950), Searle (1978; 1980), Lewis (1979), Sperber and Wilson (1986), Travis (2000), Bezuidenhout (2002), Carston (2002), Recanati (2004; 2010)

Hidden indexicals (variables, arguments) and unarticulated constituents: Perry (1986), Stanley (2000), Taylor (2001), Recanati (2002), Stanley (2002), Martí (2006), Neale (2007), Hall (2008), Recanati (2010, ch. 4), Landau (2010)

Hidden indexicals and belief reports: Schiffer (1977: 31–36; 1992), Richard (1990), Crimmins (1992), Bach (1997)

Indexicals and their diverse uses: Smith (1989), Sidelle (1991), Predelli (1998), Corazza et al. (2002), Romdenh-Romluc (2002), Weatherson (2002), Predelli (2002), Corazza (2006), Mount (2008), Åkerman (2009), Egan (2009), Stevens (2009), Dodd and Sweeney (2010), Recanati (2010: ch. 6)

Pragmatic intrusion (into semantic content), Levinson (2000), Recanati (2004), King and Stanley (2005), Korta and Perry (2008)

Relative truth: Kölbel (2002), Lasersohn (2005), MacFarlane (2005), Stephenson (2007), Wright (2007), García-Carpintero and Kölbel, eds. (2008), Cappelen and Hawthorne (2009), Glanzberg (2009), Soames (2011), Egan and Weatherson, eds. (2011: Intro. and chs. 4–8)

Semantic incompleteness/underspecification: Atlas (1989: Ch. 2), Bach (1994b), Recanati (2004), Atlas (2005), Stainton (2006), Soames (2009), and works listed under "Contextualism (semantic)" above

Semantic minimalism vs. contextualism: Unger (1984), Borg (2004), Cappelen and Lepore (2005), Bach (2005; 2006b), Montminy (2006), Preyer and Peter, eds. (2007)

Vagueness and context sensitivity: Raffman (1996), Lasersohn (1999), Fara (2000), Stanley (2003), Shapiro (2006), Kennedy (2007)

References

Åkerman, Jonas (2009), "A plea for pragmatics", *Synthese* 170: 155–67.

—(2010), "Communication and indexical reference", *Philosophical Studies* 149: 355–66.

Atlas, Jay David (1989), *Philosophy Without Ambiguity*, Oxford: Oxford University Press.

—(2005), "Semantical underdeterminacy", in *Logic, Meaning, and Conversation*, Oxford: Oxford University Press, pp. 3–44.

Bach, Kent (1992), "Intentions and demonstrations", *Analysis* 52: 140–46.

—(1994a), *Thought and Reference*, pbk. edn, Oxford: Oxford University Press.

—(1994b), "Conversational impliciture", *Mind and Language* 9:124–62.

—(1997), "Do belief reports report beliefs?" *Pacific Philosophical Quarterly* 78: 215–41.

—(2000), "Quantification, qualification, and context: A reply to Stanley and Szabo", *Mind and Language* 15: 262–83.

—(2005), "Context ex machina", in Z. Szabó ed. *Semantics vs. Pragmatics*, Oxford: Oxford University Press, pp. 15–44.

—(2006a), "What does it take to refer?" in E. Lepore and B. Smith (eds), *The Oxford Handbook of Philosophy of Language*, Oxford: Oxford University Press: pp. 516–54.

—(2006b), "The excluded middle: Semantic minimalism without minimal proposi-tions", *Philosophy and Phenomenological Research* 73: 435–42.

Bach, Kent, and Robert Harnish (1979*)*, *Linguistic Communication and Speech Acts*, Cambridge, MA: MIT Press.

Bezuidenhout, Anne (2002), "Truth-conditional pragmatics", *Philosophical Perspectives* 16: 105–34.

Boghossian, Paul (2006), "What is relativism?" in P. Greenough and M. Lynch (eds), *Truth and Realism*, Oxford: Oxford University Press, pp. 13–37.

Borg, Emma (2004), *Minimal Semantics*, Oxford: Oxford University Press.

—(2007), "Minimalism versus contextualism in semantics", in G. Preyer and G. Peter (eds), *Context Sensitivity and Semantic Minimalism: New Essays on Semantics and Pragmatics*, Oxford: Oxford University Press, pp. 546–71.

Braun, David (1996), "Demonstratives and their linguistic meanings", *Noûs* 30: 145–73.

—(2008), "Complex demonstratives and their singular contents", *Linguistics and Philosophy* 31: 57–99.

Buchanan, Ray (2010), "A puzzle about meaning and communication", *Noûs* 44: 340–71.

Cappelen, Herman, and John Hawthorne (2007), "Locations and binding", *Analysis* 67: 95–105.

—(2009), *Relativism and Monadic Truth*, Oxford: Oxford University Press.

Cappelen, Herman, and Ernie Lepore (2005), *Insensitive Semantics: A Defense of Semantic Minimalism and Speech Act Pluralism*, Oxford: Blackwell.

—(2007), "The myth of unarticulated constituents", in M. O'Rourke and C. Washington (eds), *Situating Semantics: Essays In Honor of John Perry*, Cambridge, MA: MIT Press, pp. 199–214.

Carston, Robyn (2002), *Thoughts and Utterances: The Pragmatics of Explicit Communication*, Oxford: Blackwell.

Cohen, Jonathan and Samuel Rickless (2007), "Binding arguments and hidden variables", *Analysis* 67: 65–71.

Cohen, L.J. (1971), "Some remarks on Grice's views about the logical particles of natural language", Y. Bar-Hillel ed. *Pragmatics of Natural Language*, Dordrecht: Reidel, pp. 50–68.

Corazza, Eros (2006), "On the alleged ambiguity of 'now' and 'here'," *Synthese* 138: 289–313.

Corazza, Eros, William Fish and Jonathan Gorvett, J. (2002), "Who is I?" *Philosophical Studies* 107: 1–21.

Crimmins, Mark (1992), *Talk about Beliefs*, Cambridge, MA: MIT Press.

Dodd, Dylan and Paula Sweeney (2010), "Indexicals and utterance production", *Philosophical Studies* 150: 331–48.

Egan, Andy (2009), "Billboards, bombs, and shotgun weddings", *Synthese* 251–79.

Egan, Andy, and Brian Weatherson (eds) (2011), *Epistemic Modality*, Oxford: Oxford University Press.

Elbourne, Paul (2008), "The argument from binding", *Philosophical Perspectives* 22: 89–110.

Fara, Delia Graff (2000), "Shifting sands: An interest-relative theory of vagueness", *Philosophical Topics* 20: 45–81 (originally published under the name "Delia Graff").

Fodor, Jerry and Ernie Lepore (2005), "Out of context", *Proceedings and Addresses of the American Philosophical Association* 78: 3–20.

García-Carpintero, Manuel (1998), "Indexicals as token-reflexives", *Mind* 107: 529–64.

García-Carpintero, Manuel, and Max Kölbel (eds) (2008), *Relative Truth*, Oxford: Oxford University Press.

Gauker, Christopher (2007), "No tolerance for pragmatics", *Synthese* 175: 359–71.

—(2010), "Contexts in formal semantics", *Philosophy Compass* 5: 568–78.

Glanzberg, Michael (2007), "Context, content, and relativism", *Philosophical Studies* 136: 1–29.

—(2009), "Semantics and truth relative to a world", *Synthese* 166: 281–307.

Grice, Paul (1989), *Studies in the Way of Words*, Cambridge, MA: Harvard University Press.

Hall, Alison (2008), "Free enrichment or hidden indexicals?" *Mind & Language* 23: 426–56.

Heal, Jane (1997), "Indexical predicates and their uses", *Mind* 106: 619–40.

Kaplan, D. (1989a), "Demonstratives", in J. Almog, J. Perry and H. Wettstein (eds), *Themes From Kaplan*, Oxford: Oxford University Press, pp. 481–563.

—(1989b), "Afterthoughts", in J. Almog, J. Perry and H. Wettstein (eds), *Themes From Kaplan*, Oxford: Oxford University Press, pp. 565–614.

Kennedy, Christopher (2007), "Vagueness and grammar: The semantics of relative and absolute gradable adjectives", *Linguistics and Philosophy* 30: 1–45.

King, Jeffrey (2001), *Complex Demonstratives: A Quantificational Account*, Cambridge, MA: MIT Press.

King, Jeffrey, and Jason Stanley (2005), Semantics, Pragmatics, and the Role of Semantic Content, in Z. Szabó ed., *Semantics vs. Pragmatics*, Oxford: Oxford University Press, pp. 111–64.

Kölbel, Max (2002), *Truth Without Objectivity*, London: Routledge.

Korta, Kepa, and John Perry (2008), "The pragmatic circle", *Synthese* 165: 347–57.

Lahav, Ran (1989), "Against compositionality: the case of adjectives", *Philosophical Studies*, 55: 111–29.

Landau, Idan (2010), "The explicit syntax of implicit arguments", *Linguistic Inquiry* 41: 357–88.

Lasersohn, Peter (1999), "Pragmatic halos" *Language* 75: 522–51.

—(2005), "Context dependence, disagreement, and predicates of personal taste", *Linguistics and Philosophy* 28: 643–86.

Levinson, Stephen (2000), *Presumptive Meanings: The Theory of Generalized Conversational Implicature*, Cambridge, MA: MIT Press.

Lewis, David (1979), "Scorekeeping in a language game", *Journal of Philosophical Logic* 8: 339–59.

—(1980), "Index, context, and content", in S. Kanger and S. Ohman (eds), *Philosophy and Grammar*, Dordrecht: Reidel, pp. 79–100

Ludlow, Peter (1989), "Implicit comparison classes", *Linguistics and Philosophy* 12: 519–33.

MacFarlane, John (2005), "Making sense of relative truth", *Proceedings of the Aristotelian Society* 105: 321–39.

Martí, Luisa (2006), "Unarticulated constituents revisited", *Linguistics and Philosophy* 29: 135–66.

Montminy, Martin (2006), "Semantic content, truth-conditions and context", *Linguistics and Philosophy* 29: 1–26.

—(2010), "Context and communication: A defense of intentionalism", *Journal of Pragmatics* 42: 2910–18.

Mount, Allyson (2008a), "The impurity of 'pure' indexicals", *Philosophical Studies* 138: 193–209.

—(2008b), "Intentions, gestures, and salience in ordinary and deferred demonstrative reference", *Mind and Language* 23: 145–64.

Neale, Stephen (2006), "Pronouns and anaphora", in M. Devitt and R. Hanley (eds), *The Blackwell Guide to the Philosophy of Language*, Oxford: Blackwell, pp. 335–73.

—(2007), "On location", in M. O'Rourke and C. Washington (eds), *Situating Semantics: Essays in Honor of John Perry*, Cambridge, MA: MIT Press, pp. 251–395.

Pagin, Peter (2005), "Compositionality and context", in G. Preyer and G. Peter (eds), *Contextualism in Philosophy: Knowledge, Meaning, and Truth*, Oxford: Oxford University Press, pp. 303–48.

Partee, Barbara (1989), "Binding implicit variables in quantified contexts", in C. Wiltshire, B. Music and R. Graczyk (eds), *CLS 25: Papers from the Twenty Fifth Meeting of the Chicago Linguistic Society*, Chicago: Chicago Linguistic Society, pp. 342–65.

Perry, John (1986), "Thought without Representation", *Proceedings of the Aristotelian Society*, Supp. Vol. 60: 263–83.

—(2001), *Reference and Reflexivity*, Stanford: CSLI Publications.

Predelli, Stefano (1998), "I am not here now", *Analysis* 58: 107–15.

—(2002), "Intentions, indexicals, and communication", *Analysis* 62: 310–16.

Preyer, Gerhard, and Georg Peter (eds) (2005), *Contextualism in Philosophy: Knowledge, Meaning, and Truth*, Oxford: Oxford University Press.

—(2007), *Context Sensitivity and Semantic Minimalism: New Essays on Semantics and Pragmatics*, Oxford: Oxford University Press.

Raffman, Diana (1996), "Vagueness and context-sensitivity", *Philosophical Studies* 81: 175–92.

Ravin, Yael, and Claudia Leacock (eds) (2000), *Polysemy: Theoretical and computational approaches*, Oxford: Oxford University Press.

Recanati, François (2002), "Unarticulated constituents", *Linguistics and Philosophy* 25: 299–345.

—(2004), *Literal Meaning*, Cambridge: Cambridge University Press.

—(2010), *Truth-conditional Pragmatics*, Oxford: Oxford University Press.

Reimer, Marga (1992), "Do demonstrations have semantic significance?" *Analysis* 51: 177–83.

—(2002), "Do adjectives conform to compositionality?" *Philosophical Perspectives* 16: 183–98.

Richard, Mark (1990), *Propositional Attitudes: An Essay on Thoughts and How We Ascribe Them*, Cambridge: Cambridge University Press.

Romdenh-Romluc, Komarine (2002), "Now the French are invading England!" *Analysis* 62: 34–41.

Rothschild, Daniel, and Gabriel Segal (2009), "Indexical predicates", *Mind & Language* 24: 467–93.

Schiffer, Stephen (1977), "Naming and knowing", *Midwest Studies in Philosophy* 2: 28–41.

—(1992), "Belief ascription", *Journal of Philosophy* 89: 499–521.

—(2005), "Russell's theory of descriptions", *Mind* 114: 1135–83.

Searle, John (1978), "Literal meaning", *Erkenntnis* 13: 207–24.

—(1980), "The background of meaning", in J. R. Searle, F. Kiefer and M. Bierwisch (eds), *Speech Act Theory and Pragmatics*, Dordrecht: Reidel, pp. 221–32.

Sennet, Adam (2008), "The binding argument and pragmatic enrichment, or, why philosophers care even more than weathermen about 'raining'," *Philosophy Compass* 3: 135–57.

Shapiro, Stewart (2006), *Vagueness in Context*, Oxford: Oxford University Press.

Sidelle, Alan (1991), "The answering machine paradox", *Canadian Journal of Philosophy* 21: 525–39.

Smith, Quentin (1989), "The multiple use of indexicals", *Synthese* 78: 167–91,

Soames, Scott (2009), "The gap between meaning and assertion", in *Philosophical Essays, Volume 1, Natural Language: What It Means and How We Use It*, Princeton, NJ: Princeton University Press, pp. 278–97.

—(2011), "True at", *Analysis* 71: 124–33.

Sperber, Dan, and Deirdre Wilson (1986), *Relevance: Communication and Cognition*, Cambridge, MA: Harvard University Press.

Stainton, Robert (2006), *Words and Thoughts: Subsentences, Ellipsis, and the Philosophy of Language*, Oxford: Oxford University Press.

Stalnaker, Robert (1999), *Context and Content: Essays on Intentionality in Speech and Thought*, Oxford: Oxford University Press.

Stanley, Jason (2000), "Context and logical form", *Linguistics and Philosophy* 23: 391–434.

—(2002), "Making it articulated", *Mind and Language* 17: 149–68.

—(2003), "Context, interest-relativity, and the sorites", *Analysis* 63: 269–80.

—(2005a), "Review: François Recanati, *Literal Meaning*", *Notre Dame Philosophy Reviews*, available online at http://ndpr.nd.edu/news/24857-literal-meaning/

—(2005b), "Semantics in context", in G. Preyer and G. Peter (eds), *Contextualism in Philosophy: Knowledge, Meaning, and Truth*, Oxford: Oxford University Press, pp. 221–53.

Stanley, Jason, and Zoltán Gendler Szabó (2000), "On quantifier domain restriction", *Mind and Language* 15: 219–61.

Stephenson, Tamina (2007), "Judge dependence, epistemic modals, and predicates of personal taste", *Linguistics and Philosophy* 30: 427–525.

Stevens, Graham (2009), "Utterance at a distance", *Philosophical Studies* 143: 213–221.

Stokke, Andreas (2010), "Intention-sensitive semantics", *Synthese* 175: 383–404.

Strawson, P.F. (1950), "On referring", *Mind* 59: 320–44.

Szabó, Zoltán Gendler (2001), "Adjectives in context", in I. Kenesei and R. M. Harnish (eds), *Perspectives on Semantics, Pragmatics, and Discourse*, Amsterdam: John Benjamins, pp. 119–46.

Taylor, Kenneth (2001), "Sex, breakfast and descriptus interruptus", *Synthese* 128: 45–61.

Travis, Charles (2000), *Unshadowed Thought*, Cambridge MA, Harvard University Press.

Unger, Peter (1975), *Ignorance: A Case for Scepticism*, Oxford: Oxford University Press.

—(1984), *Philosophical Relativity*, Minneapolis: University of Minnesota Press.

Weatherson, Brian (2002), "Misleading indexicals", *Analysis* 62: 308–10.

Wright, Crispin (2008), "Relativism about truth itself: Haphazard thoughts about the very idea", in Manuel García-Carpintero and Max Kölbel (eds), *Relative Truth*, Oxford: Oxford University Press, pp. 157–85.

8 Pragmatics

François Recanati

Pragmatics and Ordinary Language Philosophy

Semantics, the study of meaning, and pragmatics, the study of language in use, are two important areas of linguistic research that owe their shape to the groundwork of philosophers. Although the two disciplines are complementary, the philosophical movements out of which they grew were very much in competition. In the middle of the twentieth century, there were two opposing "camps" within the analytic philosophy of language. The first camp – "ideal language philosophy", as it was then called – was that of the pioneers, Frege, Russell and the logical positivists. They were, first and foremost, logicians studying formal languages and, through them, "language" in general. Work in this tradition (especially that of Frege, Russell, Wittgenstein, Carnap, Tarski and later Montague) gave rise to contemporary formal semantics. The other camp was that of so-called "ordinary language philosophers", who advocated a more descriptive approach and emphasized the "pragmatic" nature of natural language as opposed to, say, the "language" of *Principia Mathematica*. Their own work (especially that of Austin, Strawson, Grice and the second Wittgenstein) gave rise to contemporary pragmatics.

The pragmatic investigations undertaken by ordinary language philosophers had been notably anticipated by various researchers belonging to other traditions (phenomenologists such as Marty or Reinach, linguists such as Bally or Gardiner, psychologists such as Bühler, and anthropologists such as Malinowski). However, what influenced ordinary language philosophers most was the conception of language advocated by "ideal language philosophers", which they reacted strongly to.

Central in the ideal language tradition had been the equation of, or at least the close connection between, the meaning of a sentence and its truth-conditions. This truth-conditional approach to meaning is one of the things which ordinary language philosophers found quite unpalatable. Their own emphasis was on the distinction between "language" and "speech" (Gardiner 1932) and, correlatively, between "sentence" and "statement" (Austin 1950, Strawson 1950). It is the sentence (a unit of "language") that has meaning, according to ordinary language philosophers; whereas it is the statement made by uttering the sentence in a particular context that has truth-conditions. The sentence itself does not have truth-conditions. Truth can only be predicated of sentences indirectly, via the connections between the sentence and the speech act it can be used to perform. Rather than equating the meaning of a sentence with its alleged truth-conditions, some philosophers in the pragmatic tradition have suggested equating it with its "speech act potential" (which may include, as a proper part, a certain truth-conditional potential; see Alston 1964, 2000).

Suppose that we posit abstract objects, namely "propositions", which are essentially true or false. Then the point made by ordinary language philosophers can be put by saying that sentences do not express propositions *in vacuo*, but only in the context of a speech act. Given that the same sentence can be used to make different speech acts with different contents, the "proposition" which is the content of the speech act must be distinguished from the linguistic meaning of the sentence *qua* unit of the language ("sentence meaning"). It must also be distinguished from the contextually determined meaning of a particular utterance of the sentence ("utterance meaning"), for this includes much more than merely the propositional content of the speech act performed in uttering the sentence. Utterance meaning includes a rich non-truth-conditional component: Besides the proposition it expresses, an utterance conveys indications concerning the type of the speech act being performed, the attitudes of the speaker, the place of the utterance within the discourse, its presuppositions, and so forth. Moreover there is a secondary layer of meaning which includes the contextual implications of the speech act, and in particular what Paul Grice, himself an ordinary-language philosopher, called the "conversational implicatures" of the utterance.

Speech Acts

Speech act theory (Austin 1975, Searle 1969) is concerned with communication – not communication in the narrow sense of the transmission of information, but communication in a broader sense which includes the issuing of orders, the asking of questions, the making of apologies and promises, etc. According to the theory, a speech act is more than merely the uttering of a grammatical sentence endowed with sense and reference. To speak is also to *do* something in a fairly strong sense – it is to perform what Austin called an "illocutionary act". In performing an illocutionary act, a speaker takes on a certain role and assigns a corresponding role to the hearer. By giving an order, the speaker expresses his desire that the hearer follow a certain course of conduct and presents himself as having the requisite authority to oblige the hearer to follow the course of conduct in question simply because it is the speaker's will. The social role taken on by the speaker who gives an order is embodied in the organizational notion of "superior rank". Austin stressed such institutional embodiments of illocutionary roles in order to show that language itself is a vast institution incorporating an array of conventional roles corresponding to the range of socially recognized illocutionary acts. From this point of view, assertion, the act of making a statement, is only one illocutionary act among many others.

Illocutionary acts (including assertions) have "felicity conditions" – conditions that must be contextually satisfied for the illocutionary act to be successfully performed. The study of felicity conditions is a central concern of speech act theory, along with the taxonomy of illocutionary acts. But the most central concern, perhaps, relates to the characterization of the very notion of an illocutionary act. Illocutionary acts are generally introduced ostensively, by examples – as I did above; and they are distinguished both from the act of merely saying something ("locutionary" act) and from the act of causing something to happen by saying something ("perlocutionary" act, e.g. frightening, convincing, etc.). The nature of the intermediate category of "illocutionary acts" remains a matter of debate, however. The pioneers of speech act theory, Austin and Searle, advocated an institutional or conventional approach. In this framework the illocutionary acts performed in speech, like the acts that are performed in games (e.g. "winning a set" in tennis), are governed by rules, and exist only against a background of conventions. But an alternative, "intentionalist" view, originating from Grice (1957) and Strawson (1964), developed and has been for some time the dominant trend in speech act theory (see communicative intentions on pages 199–200).

Contextual Implications

The notion of a contextual implication itself is a speech-act theoretic notion. If, beside the meaning or content of an utterance, there is another realm, viz. that of the illocutionary act the utterance serves to perform, then along with the implications of what is said there will be a further set of implications derivable from the utterance, namely the implications of the illocutionary act itself. Some of these "pragmatic" implications are fairly trivial. Thus, according to ordinary language philosophers, it is a rule of the language game of assertion that whoever asserts something believes what she says and has some evidence for it; even the liar, who does not obey this rule, has to pretend that she does if she wants to participate in the game. This rule generates pragmatic implications: By asserting something and therefore engaging in the language game, the speaker "implies" that she obeys the rules of the game and, therefore, that she believes whatever she is asserting. The speaker cannot disavow these implications of her speech act without "pragmatic contradiction". A pragmatic contradiction is a conflict between what an utterance says and what it pragmatically implies.

Thus Moore's famous paradoxical utterance, "It is raining but I do not believe it", is not self-contradictory in the logical sense: the state of affairs it describes is logically possible. But the speaker's asserting that it rains implies that she believes it, and this contradicts the second part of the utterance. (The twin notions of pragmatic implication and pragmatic contradiction or "pragmatic paradox" have been used to illuminate a variety of philosophical issues, including the nature of Descartes's *cogito*.)

Less trivial are the contextual implications discussed by Grice under the label "conversational implicatures" (Grice 1989). According to Grice, the speaker making an utterance does not merely imply that she respects the rules of the language game; among the pragmatic implications of the utterance, we find a number of additional assumptions contextually required in order to maintain the supposition that the rules of the game are being observed. Suppose that I am asked whether I will go out; I reply, "It is raining". As I said above, it is a rule of assertion that the assertor believes what he says and has sufficient evidence for it. By virtue of this rule, my utterance implies that I believe that it is raining, and that I have some evidence for my assertion. Considered as an answer to a question, my utterance also implies that it provides the information requested by the addressee, for it is a rule of the Question-and-Answer language game that the answerer must provide the requested piece of information. Now in order to maintain the supposition that the speaker's utterance actually provides the requested information, additional premises are needed, for example the assumption that the speaker will not go out if it rains. In conjunction with this contextual assumption, the utterance implies that the speaker will not go out, thereby providing a negative answer to the question. In so far as they serve to restore the utterance's conformity to the rules of the game, the conclusion that the speaker will not go out and the contextual assumption through which it is derived are further pragmatic implications of the utterance. Grice called them "conversational implicatures". Contrary to the more trivial pragmatic implications, they can be disavowed by the speaker without pragmatic contradiction (at least if there is another way of making the utterance compatible with the supposition that the rules of the game are being respected). This distinguishing feature of conversational implicatures is referred to as their "cancelability". Implicatures that are not disavowed are legitimately taken as part of what the utterance communicates. They constitute a second layer of meaning, additional to what is literally said. Grice's theory of layers of meaning has proved very fruitful both in linguistics and in philosophy. Its strategic importance will be stressed below (see pages 198–99).

Non-Truth-Conditional Aspects of Meaning

Like pragmatic implications, non-truth-conditional aspects of meaning are easy to account for if speech is considered as a rule-governed activity (Stenius 1967). What is the meaning of, say, the imperative mood? Arguably, the sentences "You will go to the store tomorrow at 8", "Will you go to the store tomorrow at 8?" and "Go to the store tomorrow at 8" represent the same state of affairs. The difference between them is pragmatic rather than descriptive; it relates to the type of illocutionary act performed by the utterance. Thus the imperative mood indicates that the speaker, in uttering the sentence, performs an illocutionary act of a "directive" type. (Such an act is governed by the rule that if the speaker performs a directive act with content P, the addressee is to make it the case that P.) To account for this "indication", which does not belong to the utterance's descriptive or propositional content, we can posit a rule or convention to the effect that the imperative mood is to be used only if one is performing a directive type of illocutionary act. This rule gives conditions of use for the imperative mood. By virtue of this rule, a particular token of the imperative mood in an utterance **u** indicates that a directive type of speech act is being performed by **u**. This (token-reflexive) indication conveyed by the token follows from the conditions of use that govern the type, which conditions of use constitute the linguistic meaning of the type (Recanati 1987: 15–17).

Pragmatic indications are a species of pragmatic implication: they are what the use of a particular expression pragmatically implies, by virtue of a certain condition of use conventionally associated with the expression. In contrast to more standard pragmatic implications, however, pragmatic indications are linguistically encoded, via the condition of use conventionally associated with the expression. Grice called such conventional pragmatic implications "conventional implicatures", as opposed to conversational implicatures (Grice 1989). Whether they concern the type of the illocutionary act, as in the example I have given, or some other aspect of the context of utterance, pragmatic indications can always be accounted for in terms of conditions of use. They are "use-conditional" aspects of meaning. Their exploration is one of the empirical tasks of semantics construed as the study of linguistic meaning under all its aspects. (See Potts 2005 for recent developments in this area.)

Indexicals

Use-conditional meaning is not incompatible with descriptive content, in the sense that one and the same expression can be endowed with both. There are expressions that have a purely use-conditional meaning and do not contribute to truth-conditional content. Illocutionary markers such as the imperative mood, or discourse particles such as "well", "still", "after all", "anyway", "therefore", "alas", "oh" and so forth, fall into this category. Thus the following utterances have the same truth-conditional content, and are distinguished only by the pragmatic indications they respectively convey:

Well, Peter did not show up
Still, Peter did not show up
After all, Peter did not show up
Therefore, Peter did not show up
Alas, Peter did not show up
Oh, Peter did not show up

But there are also expressions that have a two-layered meaning. Indexicals are a case in point. A rule of use is clearly associated with indexicals: thus "I" is governed by a convention of use – it is to be used to refer to oneself. By virtue of this conventional rule, a use **u** of "I" token-reflexively indicates that it refers to the speaker of **u**. But **u** also contributes to the utterance's truth-conditional content. "I" being a directly referential expression, its truth-conditional contribution (its "content") is its actual referent, not the rule of use that contextually determines the referent (Kaplan 1989a).

Beside the horizontal distinction between truth-conditional and non-truth-conditional aspects of meaning, we see that there is a vertical distinction between two levels of meaning for indexical expressions (Strawson 1950, Kaplan 1989a). At the first level – corresponding to the linguistic meaning of the expression-type – we find the rule of use conventionally associated with the expression. At the second level – corresponding to the context-dependent semantic value of the token – the rule of use determines the expression's "content".

Levels of Meaning

The two distinctions we have made, between truth-conditional and non-truth-conditional aspects of meaning on the one hand, and between levels of meaning on the other hand, cross-cut each other. In the same way as the truth-conditional content of an indexical sentence is context-dependent and, therefore, belongs to the second level of meaning, the pragmatic indications conveyed by an expression governed by a rule of use also are context-dependent and belong to the second level of meaning. In other words, a distinction must be made between the rule of use (first level of meaning) and the pragmatic indications it contextually generates, just as we distinguish between the rule of use and the truth-conditional content it contextually determines.

That pragmatic indications, though conventional, are context-dependent is shown by examples such as (1):

(1)   The weather is nice, but I have a lot of work

The conjunction "but" is governed by a certain condition of use which distinguishes it from "and". According to Ducrot, "but" is to be used only if the following conditions are contextually satisfied (Ducrot 1972: 128ff):

  (i)   The first conjunct (P) argues in favour of a certain conclusion r;
  (ii) The second conjunct (Q) argues in favour of not-r;
  (iii) Q is considered stronger than P, i.e. the whole utterance argues in favour of not-r.

Uttering (1) pragmatically implies that the conditions of use associated with "but" are satisfied, i.e. that there is a conclusion r such that the first conjunct argues in favour of r and the second conjunct provides a stronger reason to conclude that not-r. But the pragmatic implication conveyed by a particular utterance of (1) is much more specific. In context, the variable "r" is assigned a particular interpretation, e.g. *we should go for a walk*. (1) therefore pragmatically implies something like (2):

(2)   We should not go for a walk (because of all the work I have to do), despite the nice weather.

In so far as it is context-dependent and conveyed by the token, this pragmatic implication is to be located at the second level of meaning, alongside the content of indexicals. Even in a case in which the pragmatic indication is fully conventional and not in need of contextual specification, it is conveyed by the token, not by the type. Thus a particular use **u** of the pronoun "I" indicates that it (**u**) refers to the speaker of **u**. This token-reflexive indication is distinct from the rule of use, to the effect that for all x, if x is a token of "I" it must be used to refer to the speaker of x.
    The picture is further complicated by the Gricean distinction between what is literally said and what is non-literally or indirectly communicated. We end up having a three-fold distinction between the following layers of meaning:

  First level: rules of use ("character", in Kaplan's framework)
  Second level: truth-conditional content + pragmatic indications
  Third level: conversational implicatures

The need for a third level of meaning comes from the fact that the contextual process responsible for conversational implicatures (and non-conventional pragmatic implications in general) takes the second-level meaning of the utterance as input. When an expression is governed by a condition of use, using that expression pragmatically implies that the condition is satisfied. But conversational implicatures, in contrast to conventional implicatures, are not generated by virtue of a condition of use directly associated with a particular linguistic expression; they are normally generated by virtue of conversational norms which concern the content of utterances rather than the expressions which are used to convey that content. For example, a speaker should not say what he believes to be false ("maxim of quality", in Grice's terminology); as a result, saying that P pragmatically implies that the speaker believes that P. The generation of this pragmatic implication presupposes that the proposition expressed has been identified: from the fact that the speaker has said that P, together with the default assumption that the maxim of quality is respected, we can infer that the speaker believes that P. The implicature-generating process therefore deserves to be called a "secondary pragmatic process" (Recanati 1993, 2004). There are three basic levels of meaning, with the context controlling the transition from the first one to the second and from the second to the third. The proposition expressed by the utterance must first be contextually identified (primary pragmatic process) in order for the non-conventional pragmatic implications to be derived (secondary pragmatic process).

Open Texture

For ordinary language philosophers, the truth-conditional or "descriptive" content of an utterance is a property of the speech act, not a property of the sentence. A sentence only has truth-conditions in the context of a speech act. This is so not merely because of indexicality – the fact that the reference of some words depends on the context of utterance in a systematic way. Indexicality is only one form of context-dependence. There is another one, no less important, which affects the sense (the conditions of application) of words rather than their reference. According to Austin and Wittgenstein, words have clear condi-tions of application only against a background of "normal circumstances" corresponding to the type of context in which the words have been used in the past. There is no "convention" to guide us as to whether or not a particular expression applies in some extraordinary situation. The reason for this is that the application of words ultimately depends on there being a sufficient similarity between the new situation of use and past situations. The relevant dimensions of similarity are not fixed once for all – this is what generates "open texture" (Waismann 1951). Ultimately, it is the context of utterance which deter-mines which dimension of similarity is relevant, hence which conditions have to be satisfied for a given expression to apply (Recanati 2004: ch. 9). It follows that the sense of ordinary descriptive words is context-dependent, like the reference of indexicals, though not quite in the same way. On this "contextualist" approach advocated by Travis (1975, 1981, 2008) and Searle (1978, 1983), truth-conditions cannot be ascribed to sentence-types but only to utterances. Contextualism was a central tenet in the pragmatic conception of language developed by ordinary language philosophers (though some atypical ordinary language philosophers, such as Grice, rejected it).

The Semantics/Pragmatics Distinction

If much of contemporary pragmatics derives from the work of ordinary language philosophers, the name "pragmatics" – contrasted with "semantics" – was coined by a philosopher in the ideal language tradition, Charles Morris (Morris 1938). The general conception associated with Morris's distinction (hereafter "the traditional conception") has been very influential, though it is now outdated.

On the traditional conception, the semantics/pragmatics distinction rests on two more basic distinctions: (a) semantics studies the relations between words and the world (i.e., what words *denote* or *represent*), while pragmatics studies the relations between words and their users (e.g. what words are used to *do*); (b) semantics deals with the standing meaning which expression-types possess in virtue of the conventions of the language, while pragmatics is concerned with what *the speaker* means when she utters something *in a particular context*. On this conception, the linguistic meaning of the sentence is taken to *be* its representational content, and the context is taken to contribute only information pertaining to "the relations between the words and their users".

As we have seen, however, the equation of the meaning of the sentence with its representational content cannot be accepted, for two reasons:

1 Because of indexicality, open-texture, etc., sentences represent a specific state of affairs only in context; their representational content depends on some features of their context of use, hence it cannot be equated with the context-independent meaning of the sentence-type.
2 There are use-conditional as well as truth-conditional aspects of the meaning of sentence-types. To account for them, it seems we must give up the purely truth-conditional conception of semantics and make room for a non-truth-conditional component within the latter.

Faced with each of these objections, there have been attempts to defend the traditional conception, or at least its spirit. As for the first objection, it has been argued that the conventional meaning of a sentence determines its representational content, even if it does so only "with respect to context". The role context plays in the determination of content is said to be minimal, in contrast to the role it plays in the determination of speaker's meaning. As for the second, there have been attempts to force use-conditional aspects of meaning into the mould of truth-conditional semantics. Take, for example, the imperative mood. One can use the pragmatic equivalence between the imperative "Close the door!" and the "explicit performative" "I ask you to close the door" to support the claim that non-declarative sentences have a declarative paraphrase through which they can be given a truth-conditional analysis (see Lewis 1970: 54–61).

None of these attempts have been quite successful. As for the first, the sharp distinction between speaker's meaning and "what is said" has been called into question. It has been shown that we need to appeal to what the speaker means (what he "has in mind") to fix the value of indexicals, hence the content of what is said (see page 196). Even the "minimalist principle", according to which context comes into play in the determination of semantic content only when some expression conventionally requires it, has been questioned. (On these debates, see Carston 2002; Borg 2004; Recanati 2004, 2010; Cappelen and Lepore 2005; Predelli 2005; Stanley 2007.) As for the second, it is commonly acknowledged nowadays that not all aspects of linguistic meaning are descriptive or truth-conditional.

With the downfall of the traditional conception, the semantics/pragmatics distinction has lost much of its bite, and different authors draw it differently. (Some authors propose to dispense with it altogether – see e.g. Cappelen 2007.) Still, there is some continuity with the traditional conception. As the "Pragmatics vs Semantics" entry of the *Handbook of Pragmatics* (Horn and Ward 2004) puts it, the more context-dependent an aspect of meaning is, and the less descriptive or truth-conditional it is, the less we are tempted to call it "semantic" and the more we are tempted to call it "pragmatic". But nothing more specific than that can be said without relying on stipulation, and for that reason the "border wars" over the semantics/pragmatics interface are often suspected of being verbal disputes.

Context and Propositional Attitudes

The descriptive component of sentence meaning can be equated with a function from contexts to propositions (Stalnaker 1970, 1999; Kaplan 1989a). The "context" is often construed as a package of various situational factors relevant to determining the semantic values of the context-sensitive constituents of the sentence. (See the next two sections below, pages 196–98, for an alternative notion of context.) Thus the place of utterance, the identity of the participants in the speech episode and the time of utterance are among the factors on which the proposition expressed by an indexical sentence depends. It would be a mistake, however, to hold that only such "external" (i.e. non-intentional) features of the situation of utterance have a role to play in the determination of what is said. In many cases, what the speaker "has in mind" is the relevant factor. Thus "John's book" can mean the book that John wrote, the book that he bought, the book he is reading, or whatever. The sentence in which the expression "John's book" occurs expresses a definite proposition only when a particular relation between John and a certain book has been contextually determined, but there is no "rule" which enables the interpreter to determine the latter except that it must be the relation which the speaker "has in mind". Likewise, in the case of demonstratives, one of the crucial contextual factors seems to be the referential intention that the speaker manifests by the utterance of the demonstrative and the associated gestures (Kaplan 1989b; Bach 1992).

This suggests that the context against which an utterance is interpreted includes factors such as the intentions, expectations, beliefs and other propositional attitudes of the speaker and her audience. Especially important, on that sort of view, are the beliefs that are shared and "mutually known" to be shared; they constitute a "common ground" which can be exploited in discourse (Stalnaker 1999, 2002; Clark 1992). This introduces us to the topic of "presupposition" which is generally mentioned, along with speech acts, indexicals and implicatures, as one of the central issues in pragmatics.

Presupposition

There is a basic sense in which presupposing is a pragmatic attitude towards a proposition – the attitude consisting in taking it for granted. The "context" is sometimes defined as a set of presuppositions in this sense, i.e. a set of propositions that are taken for granted at a given point in discourse (see e.g. Karttunen 1974; Stalnaker 1974). In order to be part of the context thus defined, a presupposition must not only be shared by the participants in the speech episode, but also recognized by them to be so shared.

Beside the pragmatic notion of presupposition (where presupposing is something a speech participant does), is there also a purely semantic notion, where presupposing is something which a sentence does? For example, does the sentence "John stopped teaching undergraduates" carry the presupposition that John used to teach undergraduates as part of its semantic content?

The semantic notion of presupposition has been questioned on two grounds. First, it has been pointed out that presuppositions, like conversational implicatures, seem to be defeasible or cancelable. This might suggest that the basic, pragmatic sense is the only sense we can give to the notion of presupposition. Sentences do not have presuppositions; only the participants in a speech episode can presuppose something. This conclusion, however, is too strong, for the conventional nature of (some) presuppositions is manifest and well-documented. Arguably, what the defeasibility of presuppositions shows is not that presuppositions are non-conventional – no one doubts that some presup-positions are encoded and belong to the linguistic meaning of expressions – but rather that they can be overridden if certain conditions are satisfied (Gazdar 1979).

Another issue is whether presuppositions affect the truth-conditional content of utterances and should be characterized primarily in semantic terms. According to Stalnaker, that need not be the case. Like pragmatic indications in general, the linguistic presuppositions associated with certain expressions (e.g. the verb "stop" in the previous example) can be construed as conditions of use or constraints on the context. The linguistic presupposition encoded by the verb "stop" is a certain constraint on the context, namely the requirement that the speaker of the context presuppose a certain proposition, or (if the context is directly construed as a set of propositions or "common ground") the requirement that it contain a certain proposition, namely the proposition that John used to teach undergraduates. An utterance of "John stopped teaching undergraduates" is appropriate or felicitous only in a context in which this constraint is satisfied.

Interpretation and Context-Change

The notion of "context" as common ground that features in discussions of presupposition makes it possible to see the relation between context and content as two-way rather than one-way. The proposition expressed, which depends on the context, itself changes the context. According to dynamic theories of discourse, the content of an assertion is normally fed into the context against which the next utterance will be interpreted (Karttunen 1974; Stalnaker 1978; Kamp 1985; Heim 1988). The context of interpretation constantly changes – Stalnaker speaks of an "everchanging context" – because it evolves as discourse proceeds. Thus it is possible for the context to shift in the middle of an utterance. This possibility is taken to account for a number of puzzling facts, including the defeasibility of presuppositions in complex sentences (see Schlenker 2008 for a critical discussion, and for a revised version of the pragmatic approach to the "projection problem" pioneered by Stalnaker).

If the proposition expressed by an utterance is normally fed into the context, the assumption that this proposition has been expressed always becomes part of the context as a result of the interpretation of the utterance. It is this assumption, together with the default assumption that the speaker respects the norms of conversation (plus various other assumptions included in the context), which make it possible to infer the conversational implicatures that enrich the overall meaning of the utterance. It follows that the contextual changes induced by an utterance by virtue of its expressing a certain proposition affect not only the interpretation of the utterances that follow, but equally the overall meaning of the very utterance responsible for the contextual change.

Another sort of context-change induced by an utterance has been described by David Lewis (1979). Sometimes the default assumption that the speaker respects the norms of conversation prevents the utterance from being interpreted with respect to the context at hand because, if it were so interpreted, it would violate the norms in question. This leads to a modification of the context in order to reach a more satisfactory interpretation. Thus if the utterance presupposes that P, and P is not part of the context at hand, it is introduced into the context in order to render the utterance conform to the norms ("accommodation").

The Strategic Importance of Conversational Implicatures

If semantics and pragmatics both study the contextual determination of the proposition expressed (in so far as it depends both on the linguistic meaning of the sentence and on the context), conversational implicatures fall within the sole domain of pragmatics, for they are not constrained by the linguistic meaning of the sentence in the way the proposition expressed is. Yet the theory of implicatures has important consequences for semantics. Thanks to Grice's theory, many intuitive aspects of meaning can be put into the "pragmatic wastebasket" as implicatures, rather than treated as genuine data for semantics. Take, for example, the sentence [P or Q]. It can receive an inclusive or an exclusive interpretation. Instead of saying that "or" is ambiguous in English, we may consider it as unambiguously inclusive, and account for the exclusive reading by saying that in some contexts the utterance conversationally implicates that [P] and [Q] are not both true. When there is such a conversational implicature, the overall meaning of the utterance is clearly exclusive, even though what is strictly and literally said corresponds to the logical formula [P v Q]. It is here that the complementary character of semantics and pragmatics is particularly manifest. Semantics is simplified because a lot of data can be explained away as "implicatures" rather than genuine aspects of the (literal) meaning of the utterance.

Grice's theory of implicatures has been extremely popular among semanticists precisely because it enables the theorist, when certain conditions are satisfied, to shift the burden of explanation from semantics to pragmatics. From this point of view, the most interesting notion is that of a generalized conversational implicature (Grice 1989; Gazdar 1979; Levinson 2000). When a conversational implicature is generalized, i.e. generated by default, it tends to become intuitively indistinguishable from semantic content. Grice's theory has taught the semanticist not to take such "semantic" intuitions at face value. Even if something seems to be part of the semantic content of an utterance, the possibility of accounting for it pragmatically, in terms of conversational implicature, must always be considered.

Grice's theory is important also because it has provided an influential argument against the contextualism professed by ordinary language philosophers. For example, Strawson had claimed that the truth-conditions of [P and Q] in English are contextually variable: the notion of temporal succession, or that of causal connection, or a number of other suggestions concerning the connection between the first and the second conjunct can enter into the interpretation of [P and Q], depending on the context (Strawson 1952: 81–2). "They got married and had many children" means that they had children after getting married; "Socrates drank the hemlock and died" means that he died as result of drinking the hemlock. Those aspects of the interpretation are very much context-sensitive; yet they affect the utterance's truth-conditions. The truth-conditions of [P and Q], therefore, are not fixed by a rigid rule, but depend on the context. As against this view, Grice has argued that the truth-conditions of [P and Q] are fixed and context-independent. [P and Q] is true if and only if [P] and [Q] are both true. Thus "They got married and had many children" would be true, even if they had the children before getting married. To be sure, the utterance conveys the suggestion that the children came after the marriage. But this suggestion is nothing other than a conversational implicature, according to Grice. It does not affect the utterance's semantic content – its literal truth-conditions. Grice criticised his fellow ordinary language philosophers for confusing the truth-conditions of an utterance with its total significance. Though controversial (Travis 1985; Recanati 1994, 2004), this argument has been very popular, and it has played a major role in the subsequent downfall of ordinary language philosophy.

Communicative Intentions

The pioneers of pragmatics (e.g. Malinowski and Austin) used to insist on the social dimension of language as opposed to its cognitive or representational function. As pragmatics developed, however, it is the psychological dimension of language use that came to the forefront of discussions, in part as a result of Grice's work on meaning and communication.

In his famous 1957 article, Grice defined a pragmatic notion of meaning: the notion of someone's meaning something by a piece of behaviour (a gesture, an utterance, or whatnot). Grice's idea was that this pragmatic notion of meaning was basic and could be used to analyse the semantic notion, i.e. what it is for a linguistic expression to have meaning. Strawson soon pointed out that Grice's pragmatic notion of meaning could also be used to characterize the elusive notion of an illocutionary act (Strawson 1964). In the section Speech acts (page 188), we mentioned the view that illocutionary acts are essentially conventional acts (like the acts which owe their existence to the rules of a particular game). This conventionalist approach was dominant in speech act theory until Strawson established a bridge between Grice's theory of meaning and Austin's theory of illocutionary acts. Illocutionary acts, in the new framework, can be analysed in terms of the utterly non-mysterious notion of a perlocutionary act.

A perlocutionary act consists in bringing about certain effects by an utterance. For example, by saying to you "It is raining", I bring it about that you believe that it is raining. Now, according to the suggested analysis, to perform the illocutionary act of asserting that it is raining is (in part) to make manifest to the addressee one's intention to bring it about, by this utterance, that the addressee believes that it is raining. (This is not the full story, of course.) An illocutionary act therefore involves the manifestation of a corresponding perlocutionary intention. But there is a special twist that the suggested analysis inherits from Grice's original conception of meaning: the intention must be made manifest in a specially "overt" manner. Not only must the speaker's intention to bring about a certain belief in the addressee be revealed by his utterance, but his intention to reveal it must also be revealed, and it must be revealed in the same overt manner. This characteristic (if puzzling) feature of overtness is often captured by considering the revealed intention itself as reflexive: A communicative intention, i.e. the type of intention whose manifestation constitutes the performance of an illocutionary act, is the intention to achieve a certain perlocutionary effect (e.g. bringing about a certain belief in the addressee) via the addressee's recognition of this intention. The notion of "mutual knowledge" (Lewis 1969; Schiffer 1972), at work in the characterization of common ground (see Context and propositional attitudes, page 196), is also relevant to the characterization of overtness.

The Intentional-Inferential Model

Even though the conventionalist approach to communication is still alive (as witnessed by, e.g., Millikan, 1998), the Grice–Strawson "intentionalist" approach has gained wide currency in pragmatics. Typical in this respect are the neo-Gricean theories offered by Bach and Harnish (1979) and Sperber and Wilson (1995). They have put forward an inferential model of communication intended to supersede the "code model" inspired by Shannon and Weaver.

According to the code model, communication proceeds as follows. The speaker wishes to communicate a certain content; she encodes the content in question into a sentence, using the grammar of the language as a "code", pairing contents and sentences (possibly with respect to a context of utterance). The interpreter, by virtue of his knowledge of the same grammar (and, perhaps, of the context), is capable of decoding the sentence and recovering the intended content.

The alternative, inferential model of communication is very different. An utterance is seen as a meaningful action, i.e. an action that provides interpreters with evidence concerning the agent's intentions. What distinguishes communicative acts from other meaningful actions is what can be inferred from the evidence: A communicative act is an act that provides evidence of a certain communicative intention on the part of the speaker. In other words, the speaker's intention to communicate something is what explains his utterance, considered as a piece of behaviour. From this point of view, the content of the communicative act – what is communicated – is the total content of the communicative intentions that can be inferred from it. Let us call this the utterance's communicative meaning, distinct from the literal or conventional meaning of the sentence (determined by the code, i.e. the grammar). Understanding is essentially an inferential process in this framework, and the conventional meaning of the sentence provides only part of the evidence used in determining the communicative meaning of the utterance.[1]

Notes

1. This chapter is a lightly updated and shortened version of the entry "Pragmatics" that appeared in the 1998 *Routledge Encyclopedia of Philosophy*.

References

Alston, W. (1964), *Philosophy of Language*, Englewood Cliffs, NJ: Prentice Hall.
—(2000), *Illocutionary Acts and Sentence Meaning*, Ithaca, NY: Cornell University Press.
Austin, J. (1950/1971), "Truth", in J. Austin, *Philosophical Papers*, 2nd edn, Oxford: Clarendon Press, pp. 117–33.
—(1971), *Philosophical Papers*, 2nd edn, Oxford: Clarendon Press.
—(1975), *How to Do Things with Words*, 2nd edn, Oxford: Clarendon Press.
Bach, K. (1992), "Paving the Road to Reference", *Philosophical Studies* 67: 295–300.
Bach, K. and Harnish, M. (1979), *Linguistic Communication and Speech Acts*, Cambridge, MA: MIT Press.

Borg, E. (2004), *Minimal Semantics*, Oxford: Clarendon Press.

Bühler, K. (1990), *Theory of Language*, trans. by D. Goodwin, Amsterdam: J. Benjamins.

Cappelen, H. (2007), "Semantics and Pragmatics: Some Central Issues", in G. Preyer and G. Peter (eds), *Context-Sensitivity and Semantic Minimalism*, Oxford: Clarendon Press, pp. 3–22.

Cappelen, H. and Lepore, E. (2005), *Insensitive Semantics*, Oxford: Blackwell.

Carston, R. (2002), *Thoughts and Utterances: The Pragmatics of Explicit Communication*, Oxford: Blackwell.

Clark, H. (1992), *Arenas of Language Use*, Chicago: The University of Chicago Press and CSLI.

Davis, S. (ed.) (1991), *Pragmatics: A Reader*, New York: Oxford University Press.

Ducrot, O. (1972), *Dire et ne pas dire: principes de sémantique linguistique*, Paris: Hermann.

Gardiner, A. (1932), *The Theory of Speech and Language*, Oxford: Clarendon Press.

Gazdar, G. (1979), *Pragmatics: Implicature, Presupposition and Logical Form*, New York: Academic Press.

Grice, P. (1957), "Meaning", *Philosophical Review* 66: 377–88.

—(1989), *Studies in the Way of Words*, Cambridge: Cambridge University Press.

Heim, I. (1988), "On the Projection Problem for Presuppositions", reprinted in S. Davis ed. *Pragmatics: A Reader*, New York: Oxford University Press, pp. 397–405.

Horn, L. (2005), "The Border Wars: A Neo-Gricean Perspective", in K. von Heusinger and K. Turner (eds), *Where Semantics Meets Pragmatics: the Michigan Papers*, Oxford: Elsevier, pp. 21–48.

Horn, L. and Ward, G. (eds) (2004), *Handbook of Pragmatics*, Oxford: Blackwell.

Kamp, H. (1985), "Context, Thought and Communication", *Proceedings of the Aristotelian Society* 85: 239–61.

Kaplan, D. (1989a), "Demonstratives", in J. Almog, H. Wettstein and J. Perry (eds), *Themes from Kaplan*, New York: Oxford University Press, pp. 481–563.

—(1989b), "Afterthoughts", in J. Almog, H. Wettstein and J. Perry (eds), *Themes from Kaplan*, New York: Oxford University Press, pp. 565–614.

Karttunen, L. (1974), "Presupposition and Linguistic Context", *Theoretical Linguistics* 1: 181–94.

Levinson, S. (2000), *Presumptive Meanings: The Theory of Generalized Conversational Implicature*. Cambridge, MA: MIT Press.

Lewis, D. (1969), *Convention*, Cambridge, MA: Harvard University Press.

—(1970), "General Semantics", *Synthese* 22: 18–67.

—(1979), "Scorekeeping in a Language-Game", *Journal of Philosophical Logic* 8: 339–59.

Malinowski, B. (1923/1949), "The Problem of Meaning in Primitive Languages", supplement to C. Ogden and I. A. Richards, *The Meaning of Meaning*, 10th edn, London: Routledge, pp. 296–336.

Millikan, R. (1998), "Proper Function and Convention in Speech Acts", in L. Hahn ed. *The Philosophy of P.F. Strawson*, La Salle: Open Court, pp. 25–43.

Morris, C. (1938), *Foundations of the Theory of Signs*, Chicago: University of Chicago Press.

Potts, C. (2005), *The Logic of Conventional Implicatures*, Oxford: Oxford University Press.

Predelli, S. (2005), *Contexts: Meaning, Truth, and the Use of Language*, Oxford: Oxford University Press.

Recanati, F. (1987), *Meaning and Force: The Pragmatics of Performative Utterances*, Cambridge: Cambridge University Press.

—(1993), *Direct Reference: From Language to Thought*, Oxford: Basil Blackwell.

—(1994), "Contextualism and Anti-Contextualism in the Philosophy of Language", in S. Tsohatzidis, *Foundations of Speech Act Theory: Philosophical and Linguistic Perspectives*, London: Routledge, pp. 156–66.

—(2004), *Literal Meaning*, Cambridge: Cambridge University Press.

—(2010), *Truth-Conditional Pragmatics*, Oxford: Oxford University Press.

Schiffer, S. (1972), *Meaning*, Oxford: Clarendon Press.

Schlenker, P. (2008), "Be Articulate! A Pragmatic Theory of Presupposition Projection", *Theoretical Linguistics* 34: 157–212.

Searle, J. (1969), *Speech Acts*, Cambridge: Cambridge University Press.

—(1978/1979), "Literal Meaning", in J. Searle, *Expression and Meaning*, Cambridge: Cambridge University Press, pp. 117–36.

—(1979), *Expression and Meaning*, Cambridge: Cambridge University Press.

—(1983), *Intentionality*, Cambridge: Cambridge University Press.

Sperber, D. and Wilson, D. (1995), *Relevance: Communication and Cognition*, 2nd edn, Oxford: Basil Blackwell.

Stalnaker, R. (1970), "Pragmatics", *Synthese* 22: 272–89.

—(1974/1991), "Pragmatic Presuppositions", reprinted in S. Davis ed. *Pragmatics: A Reader*, New York: Oxford University Press, pp. 471–82.

—(1978/1999), "Assertion", reprinted in R. Stalnaker, *Context and Content*, Oxford: Oxford University Press, pp. 78–95.

—(1999), *Context and Content*, Oxford: Oxford University Press.

—(2002), "Common Ground", *Linguistics and Philosophy* 25: 701–21.

Stanley, J. (2007), *Language in Context*, Oxford: Clarendon Press.

Stenius, E. (1967), "Mood and Language-Game", *Synthese* 17: 254–74.

Strawson, P. (1950/1971), "On Referring", in P. Strawson, *Logico-Linguistic Papers*, London: Methuen, pp. 1–27.

—(1952), *Introduction to Logical Theory*, London: Methuen.

—(1964/1971), "Intention and Convention in Speech Acts", in P. Strawson, *Logico-Linguistic Papers*, London: Methuen, pp. 149–69.

—(1971), *Logico-Linguistic Papers*, London: Methuen.

Travis, C. (1975), *Saying and Understanding*, Oxford: Basil Blackwell.

—(1981), *The True and the False: the Domain of the Pragmatic*, Amsterdam: J. Benjamins.

—(1985), "On What is Strictly Speaking True", *Canadian Journal of Philosophy* 15: 187–229.

—(2008), *Occasion-Sensitivity: Selected Essays*, Oxford: Oxford University Press.

Tsohatzidis, S. (1994), *Foundations of Speech Act Theory: Philosophical and Linguistic Perspectives*, London: Routledge.

Waismann, F. (1951), "Verifiability", in A. Flew ed. *Logic and Language*, 1st series, Oxford: Basil Blackwell, pp. 17–44.

Wittgenstein, L. (1953), *Philosophical Investigations*, Oxford: Basil Blackwell.

9 Semantic Normativity and Naturalism[1]

José L. Zalabardo

Kripke's Normativity Argument

In *Wittgenstein on Rules and Private Language*, Saul Kripke presented an argument, inspired by his reading of Wittgenstein, against the possibility of facts as to what someone means by a linguistic expression. The argument proceeded by considering a series of proposals as to what these facts might consist in, arguing in each case that the candidate account of meaning facts was unsatisfactory.

A proposal that figures prominently in Kripke's argument is the dispositional account of meaning. According to the dispositional account, the conditions of correct use associated with the meaning of an expression are determined by speakers' dispositions: how it would be correct to use an expression, as meant by a speaker, is determined, on this account, by how the speaker is disposed to use the expression.

Kripke raised several objections to dispositionalism. One that has received much attention in the literature arises from the normative status of facts about correct use. Here are some representative passages, focusing on the case of the meaning of the sign "+":

> The dispositionalist gives a *descriptive* account of this relation [between the meaning I ascribe to "+" and how I am disposed to answer the question "68 + 57 = ?"]: if "+" meant addition, then I will answer "125". But this is not the proper account of the relation, which is *normative*, not descriptive. The point is *not* that, if I meant addition by "+", I *will* answer "125", but rather that, if I intend to accord with my past meaning of "+", I *should* answer "125". [...] the relation of meaning and intention to future action is *normative*, not *descriptive* (Kripke 1982: 37).

> A candidate for what constitutes the state of my meaning one function, rather than another, by a given function sign, ought to be such that, whatever in fact I (am disposed to) do, there is a unique thing that I should

203

do. Is not the dispositional view simply an equation of performance and correctness? (Kripke 1982: 24).

The interpretation of these and related passages is by no means straightforward, but many have read them as advancing arguments that apply to semantics lines of reasoning originally aimed at naturalistic accounts of ethical concepts (Boghossian 1989; Wright 1984; Blackburn 1984; McDowell 1984). In this chapter I am going to consider two of these lines of reasoning. I am not going to be concerned with the question whether they can be plausibly attributed to Kripke.[2] My goal will be to determine whether these lines of reasoning can be construed as providing cogent arguments against semantic naturalism.

The Naturalistic Fallacy

The first line of reasoning that I want to consider is based on the thought that there is an unbridgeable logical gap between statements about how things are and statements about what someone should do. David Hume appears to endorse this thought in the following famous passage of the *Treatise*:

> In every system of morality, which I have hitherto met with, I have always remark'd, that the author proceeds for some time in the ordinary ways of reasoning, and establishes the being of a God, or makes observations concerning human affairs; when all of a sudden I am surpriz'd to find, that instead of the usual copulations of propositions, *is*, and *is not*, I meet with no proposition that is not connected with an *ought*, or an *ought not*. This change is imperceptible; but is however, of the last consequence. For as this *ought*, or *ought not*, expresses some new relation or affirmation, 'tis necessary that it shou'd be observ'd and explain'd; and at the same time that a reason should be given; for what seems altogether inconceivable, how this new relation can be a deduction from others, which are entirely different from it (Hume 1978: 469).

Hume is here presenting a thought about arguments from premises about how things are to conclusions about what someone should do. The thought appears to be that these arguments cannot be deductive, or, as I propose to construe the thought initially, that they cannot be underwritten exclusively by logic and conceptual analysis.

We can formulate the thought as concerning the character of the inferential principles that can validate these arguments. I am going to refer to the principles that concern us as *prescriptive principles*. Prescriptive principles will be statements of the form:

1. $(\forall x)(\forall S)(\phi(x, S) \supset S$ should/shouldn't do $x)$

where S ranges over subjects and x over actions, and ϕ is a propositional function that describes an action and possibly a subject and the relationship between subject and action.

I want to concentrate on a particular type of prescriptive principles – those in which the description from which a prescription is derived doesn't include the ascription to the subject of a desire, goal or pro-attitude. For this purpose I am going to introduce a distinction between hypothetical and categorical prescriptive principles. We shall say that a prescriptive principle is *hypothetical* just in case in order for x and S to satisfy ϕ, S needs to have some desire, goal or pro-attitude. That is, if x and S satisfy ϕ, there is a desire, goal or pro-attitude that S has, such that in its absence x and S wouldn't satisfy ϕ. A prescriptive principle will be *categorical* if it is not hypothetical.

Thus, the obligations expressed by categorical prescriptive principles are independent of the subject's volitions. However, they are subject to be overridden by the demands placed on the subject's behaviour by other prescriptive principles. Let's focus on an instance of 1 specifying conditions under which you should do x. Even if it were true, and even if S and x satisfied ϕ, it might be that, all things considered, S should not do x, if for S to do x would be incompatible with what other prescriptive principles demand of S.

I want to formulate the thought that we cannot deduce a conclusion about what someone should do from premises about how things are as a claim about the status of categorical prescriptive principles. I shall refer to the claim as *Hume's thought*:

> *Hume's thought*: Categorical prescriptive principles cannot be established solely by means of logic and conceptual analysis.

Notice that Hume's thought is in principle neutral on whether or not there are true categorical prescriptive principles. On the one hand, an advocate of Hume's thought can maintain that there are true categorical prescriptive principles, so long as she doesn't take them to be derivable by logic and conceptual analysis. On the other hand, an advocate of Hume's thought can deny the existence of true categorical prescriptive principles. The rejection of categorical prescriptive principles can take two forms. One possibility is to deny the existence of facts as to what one should do over and above what follows from hypothetical prescriptive principles. The other is to assert the existence of categorical prescriptive facts, while denying that they supervene on descriptive facts. On this view, when S should do x there isn't a description of S and x such that whenever an action and a subject satisfy the description the subject should perform the action.

Hume's thought can be seen as posing an insuperable obstacle to the provision of naturalistic analyses of ethical notions. Suppose the following is a conceptual truth about moral rightness:

2.   If it would be morally right for you to perform an action, then in principle (i.e. unless the obligation is overridden by other imperatives) you should perform the action.

Now consider a naturalistic analysis of the concept of moral rightness, according to which there is a (categorical) description N of a relationship between an action and a subject such that for an action and a subject to satisfy this description is what it means for it to be morally right for the subject to perform the action. This analysis would result in a straightforward violation of Hume's thought. $(\forall x)(\forall S)(N(x, S) \supset S$ should do $x)$ would be a true categorical prescriptive principle derivable from the conceptual analysis of moral rightness. If Hume's thought is correct, and if it is analytic that one should do what's morally right, then no naturalistic (categorical) analysis of moral rightness can be correct.

This is not as serious a blow to ethical naturalism as it might sound, since contemporary ethical naturalists don't typically see themselves as providing conceptual analyses of ethical concepts. They see themselves more commonly as trying to disclose the hidden essence of ethical concepts, not unlike the way in which science discloses the hidden essence of water or gold. On this conception of the task, a naturalistic account of an ethical concept would express a metaphysically necessary truth that could only be established *a posteriori*.

If a naturalistic account of moral rightness is conceived along these lines, it will no longer license violations of Hume's thought, since it won't allow us to establish $(\forall x)(\forall S)(N(x, S) \supset S$ should do $x)$ by conceptual analysis. As far as I can see, the only way to counter this move would be to strengthen Hume's thought in order to rule out the possibility of deriving categorical prescriptive principles from metaphysically necessary truths:

> *Hume's thought (second version)*: Categorical prescriptive principles cannot be established solely by means of logic, conceptual analysis or metaphysical necessities.

I am not going to discuss the plausibility of either version of Hume's thought. Instead I am going to assume for the sake of the argument that the second version of the principle is correct, in order to address the question, whether we can obtain from this a cogent argument against semantic naturalism.

The Normativity of Linguistic Meaning

Discussion of the consequences of Hume's thought for semantics has generally focused on naturalistic accounts of the relation pairing each predicate with the property whose instances satisfy the predicate, as meant by a speaker at a time. When a predicate, as meant by a speaker, is related in this way to a property, I shall say that the predicate *refers* to the property, or that the speaker *refers* to the property by the predicate. Using this notion of predicate reference, we can now define predicate satisfaction as follows:

3.   P, as meant by S, is *satisfied* by a just in case a instantiates the property to which S refers by P.

Suppose now that the following is a conceptual truth about predicate meaning:

4.   If P, as meant by S, is satisfied by a, then S should apply P to a.

It follows that for every predicate P, subject S and object a, the following is a conceptual truth:

5. $(\forall x)(\forall S)(x$ is an ascription of P to a by S & P, as meant by S, is satisfied by a $\supset$ S should do x$)^3$

Now consider a naturalistic analysis of predicate reference, according to which there is a natural relation ρ between predicates, properties and speakers such that for P, Π and S to be ρ-related is what it means for S to mean Π by P. And let N be the naturalization of predicate satisfaction that results from the following definition: $N(S, P, a)$ iff $\rho(P, \Pi, S)$ & $\Pi a.^4$ Now the analysis of predicate reference will enable us to derive the following from 5:

6. $(\forall x)(\forall S)(x$ is an ascription of P to a by S & $N(S, P, a) \supset$ S should do x$)$

Clearly, the antecedent of 6 is a description of x and S, on the plausible assumption that being an ascription of P to a is a description of x. Then it follows that 6 is a categorical prescriptive principle. Furthermore, if predicate reference were correctly analysable in terms of ρ, 6 would be a true categorical prescriptive principle derivable by conceptual analysis, and we would have a violation of Hume's thought. Hume's thought appears to rule out naturalistic analyses of predicate reference. The same situation will ensue if we think of the claim that predicate reference is ρ as a necessary *a posteriori* truth, so long as we invoke the second version of Hume's thought.

One could try to resist this line of reasoning, as presented, by objecting to

4. The problem is that it requires the subject to ascribe P to every object that satisfies it. This is, in general, not a possibility. Hence, on the assumption that ought implies can, 4 cannot express a genuine prescription (see Hattiangadi 2006: 226). There are several ways in which the argument might be modified to overcome this objection. An appealing possibility is to replace 4 with an injunction against ascribing P to objects that don't satisfy it:

7. ($\forall$x)($\forall$S)(x is an ascription of P to a by S & P, as meant by S, is not satisfied by a $\supset$ S shouldn't do x)

7 doesn't fall foul of the ought-implies-can principle, since refraining from ascribing P to objects that don't satisfy it is in principle within S's powers. And 7, together with a naturalistic analysis of predicate reference will yield a violation of Hume's thought similar to 6.

   However, one could object to 7, as well as 4, on different grounds. One could argue that there simply is no categorical obligation for speakers to speak the truth or to refrain from speaking falsehoods. For speakers who have this as their goal, 7 is a legitimate maxim, but to those who have no desire to avoid saying falsehoods, 7 doesn't apply. If this is right, then to get a universally valid principle we need to replace 7 with a claim along the following lines:

8. ($\forall$x)($\forall$S)(x is an ascription of P to a by S & P, as meant by S, is not satisfied by a & S wants to avoid saying what's false $\supset$ S shouldn't do x)

I think that the status of 8 as a conceptual truth is unobjectionable. However, 8 would not bring naturalistic accounts of predicate reference into conflict with Hume's thought. It would indeed force us to treat the following as a conceptual/metaphysical truth:

9. ($\forall$x)($\forall$S)(x is an ascription of P to a by S & ~N(S, P, a) & S wants to avoid saying what's false $\supset$ S shouldn't do x)

The problem is that, while 9 is a prescriptive principle, it is obviously of the hypothetical variety, and Hume's thought is not violated by treating hypothetical prescriptive principles as conceptual truths.[5]

   It is important to bear in mind that this objection to 7 cannot simply rest on the possibility that the demands that it makes on the subject's behaviour might be outweighed by other prescriptive principles, as this would be compatible with 7, on our understanding of prescriptive principles. The claim is that these demands apply only to those that have a certain desire, and this is the sure sign that the categorical prescriptive principle is illegitimate.[6]

Another approach to developing the argument against naturalistic accounts of predicate reference would be to focus on prescriptive principles that express, not an obligation to speak the truth, or to refrain from speaking falsehoods, but an obligation to speak in ways that express the meanings that we want to convey.[7] This approach comes to prominence when we reflect on the contrast between factual mistakes, e.g., applying a predicate to an object that doesn't instantiate the property that the predicate refers to, and semantic mistakes, e.g., applying to an object a predicate that doesn't refer to the property that the speaker wants to attribute to the object. The claim that mistakes of the second kind are to be avoided can be expressed along the following lines:

10. $(\forall x)(\forall S)$(x is an ascription of P to a by S & S refers to Π by P & S wants to avoid attributing Π to a in x $\supset$ S shouldn't do x)

The claim that 10 is a conceptual truth has more plausibility than the corresponding claim for 7. However, 10 doesn't bring naturalist accounts of predicate reference into conflict with Hume's thought. If predicate reference can be analysed in naturalistic terms, and if a parallel naturalistic treatment is available of the notion of which property a subject wants to attribute with a given predicate ascription, then 10 is undeniably a prescriptive principle. But just as clearly, given that its antecedent mentions S's desire to avoid attributing a certain property to the object of predication, 10 is a prescriptive principle of the hypothetical kind, and, as we know, Hume's thought is not in conflict with the conceptual status of hypothetical prescriptive principles.

The Normativity of Mental Content

The normative character of semantic notions can also be invoked to undermine naturalistic accounts, not of linguistic meaning, but of mental content, and shifting our attention to the mind might remove some of the obstacles encountered in the linguistic version of the enterprise. This is not a fundamental change of subject matter. It would be surprising if semantic notions were to receive independent explications in the linguistic and the mental realm. Rather, we should expect that one set of notions is explicated in terms of the other. The only remaining question is whether our semantic theory treats linguistic meaning or mental content as fundamental, and while both options have advocates, starting with the mental is the favoured route among semantic naturalists.[8]

According to the representational theory of mind, the primary bearers of mental content are syntactically specifiable mental items analogous to linguistic expressions. On this account, we will have a category of mental representations that play the same role in the composition of thoughts that the predicates of a language play in the composition of sentences. The mental event of attributing a property to an object will consist, on this account, in tokening in a certain way a mental predicate that refers to this property.[9]

If we assume this picture of mental representation, we can easily develop a mental version of the argument we presented above against naturalistic accounts of predicate reference. However, this assumption is not indispensable.[10] We can also formulate a version of the argument for mental content that doesn't presuppose the representational theory of mind. The argument would be based on the thought that the following claim is a conceptual truth:

11. $(\forall x)(\forall S)(x$ is a mental attribution by S of Π to a & $\sim\Pi a \supset S$ shouldn't do x)

If this thought is correct, it will pose an obstacle to any naturalistic account of the notion of mental attribution of properties, whether or not the account construes the notion as involving syntactically identifiable types, along the lines of the representational theory of mind. Any such account would turn 11 into a conceptually true categorical prescriptive principle, in violation of Hume's thought.

Notice that 11 is the restriction to a class of beliefs with a particularly simple structure of the prescription not to believe falsehoods – to believe only truths – to which I'm going to refer as the *truth prescription*. Hence our question is, in effect, whether we can derive the truth prescription from logic, conceptual analysis or metaphysics.

Some authors have suggested that even if 11 were a conceptual truth, it wouldn't follow directly that mental content is normative in a sense that would pose an obstacle to a naturalist account of the notion. The thought is that the conceptual truth of 11 might in principle manifest the normative character, not of mental content, but of belief.[11]

We can see the issue more clearly if we focus on the version of 11 that we can formulate if we assume the representational theory of content:

12. $(\forall x)(\forall S)(x$ is an ascription by S of mental predicate M to a & M refers to Π & $\sim\Pi a \supset S$ shouldn't do x)

The thought is that the conceptual character of 12 could be made compatible with Hume's thought *either* by rejecting the possibility of a naturalistic account of the reference of mental predicates (the second conjunct) *or* by rejecting such an account of the notion of a mental state being an ascription of a mental predicate (the first conjunct). In the terminology used by advocates of the representational theory of mind, this is the contrast between accounts of mental content and accounts of propositional attitudes.

The idea, then, is that the semantic naturalist can accept Hume's thought and the conceptual character of 12, so long as she is prepared to forgo a naturalistic account of the notion of a mental state being an ascription of a mental predicate – of a mental predicate being "tokened in the belief mode".

This point is, strictly speaking, correct, but I suspect the naturalist won't find this route particularly appealing. The problem concerns the status that the resulting position would accord to facts about which mental states token a given predicate in the belief mode. These facts would have to be construed as non-descriptive, but this construal would have to be made compatible with a naturalistic account of facts about which property each mental predicate refers to. I am not going to explore the issue here, but it is hard to see how these views could be combined into an appealing package. I shall assume, accordingly, that if we could establish the conceptual status of 11, Hume's thought would be rendered incompatible with a naturalistic account of mental content.

Clearly, for the anti-naturalist it's not enough to establish the conceptual truth of a hypothetical imperative concerning mental attributions of properties, making the obligation to avoid attributing Π to objects that don't instantiate it contingent on S having the desire to avoid believing falsehoods. Another unpromising avenue would be to ground the obligation to avoid false mental property attributions on the untoward practical consequences of believing falsehoods. For we cannot expect to establish the practical undesirability of believing falsehoods exclusively on logical, conceptual or metaphysical considerations, unless a pragmatist account of truth is adopted. On any non-pragmatist account of truth, the connection between true belief and the promotion of our goals will be a contingent matter. The anti-naturalist needs to establish on conceptual/metaphysical grounds a categorical obligation to refrain from believing what's false, independent of the subject's volitions or of the practical consequences of such beliefs.

Shah and Velleman on Why we Should Believe the Truth

The most prominent recent attempts to establish the truth prescription on conceptual grounds are due to Nishi Shah and David Velleman. They consist in two separate arguments, each presented in the first instance by one of these authors individually, but later developed jointly in co-authored work. My goal in this section is to provide an assessment of Shah and Velleman's arguments, summarizing a more detailed discussion that I have presented elsewhere (Zalabardo 2010).

I want to start by considering Shah's argument for the truth prescription. It is based on the contention that accepting the truth prescription is a condition for possessing the concept of belief. He writes: "it is one of the conditions for possessing the concept of belief that one accept the prescription to believe that p only if p is true" (Shah 2003: 470). It follows from this that "a competent user of the concept of belief must accept the prescription to believe that p only if p is true for any activity that he conceives of as belief-formation" (Shah 2003: 470).

It is important to understand the contrast between Shah's contention and the claim that accepting the truth prescription is a condition for having beliefs. Shah is very careful to point out that his argument doesn't establish the latter claim. His argument concerns the conditions for having the concept of belief, not the conditions for forming beliefs, and, as Shah concedes, having the concept of belief is not required for forming beliefs.

This point renders the connection between Shah's contention and the truth prescription slightly problematic. If accepting the prescription were a condition for having beliefs, the link would be straightforward: all believers would be subject to the prescription because those who didn't accept it wouldn't count as believers. But with Shah's claim things are slightly more complicated, since, according to him, someone who doesn't accept the truth prescription might still count as a believer. It would seem, then, that Shah's claim would establish the truth prescription only for subjects who have the concept of belief. But this restriction won't protect the naturalist from the consequences of Hume's thought. All it means is that Shah's claim will ground a prescription of the following form:

13. $(\forall x)(\forall S)(x$ is a mental attribution by S of Π to a & S has the concept of belief & $\sim\Pi a \supset S$ shouldn't do x)

Since the naturalist can also be expected to endorse a descriptive account of who counts as having the concept of belief, her naturalistic account of mental property attribution will turn 13 into a categorical prescriptive principle, thus bringing it into conflict with Hume's thought.

Thus, for Shah, you are not conceiving of an attitude as belief unless you accept the prescription to avoid falsehood in it. Shah defends this claim with an inference-to-the-best-explanation argument. He argues that there is a phenomenon that would be adequately explained by the view that the concept of belief requires accepting the truth prescription, but would otherwise go unexplained, or receive only inferior explanations. The explanandum that plays this role in his argument is a phenomenon to which he refers as the *transparency* of *doxastic deliberation*. Doxastic deliberation is "deliberation about what to believe" (Shah 2003: 447), and the transparency of doxastic deliberation is the following feature of this activity:

> The deliberative question *whether to believe that p* inevitably gives way to the factual question *whether p*, because the answer to the latter question will determine the answer to the former. That is, the only way to answer the question *whether to believe that p* is to answer the question *whether* p (Shah and Velleman 2005: 499).

According to Shah, treating acceptance of the truth prescription as necessary for having the concept of belief enables us to provide a satisfactory explanation of transparency, but if this view is rejected transparency will go unexplained. Here is how Shah proposes to explain transparency:

> [...] a competent user of the concept of belief must accept the prescription to believe that p only if p is true for any activity that he conceives of as belief-formation. Because one accepts this prescription insofar as one is deliberating about *whether to believe that p*, determining *whether p is true* will be immediately imperative, to the exclusion of any other question, for anyone who entertains the deliberative question *whether to believe that p* (Shah 2003: 470).

Shah's thought is that, since doxastic deliberation involves conceiving of the cognitive activity that it generates as belief formation, it requires accepting the truth prescription for this activity, and this makes the question whether to believe that p give way to the question whether p.

Shah's opponent is someone who thinks that accepting the truth prescription is not necessary for having the concept of belief – that you could in principle count as having the concept of belief even if you adhered to doxastic policies that are incompatible with the truth prescription, e.g. having only beliefs that maximize your overall utility. I am going to refer to this position as *relativism*.[12]

In order for Shah's argument to succeed, he needs to achieve two goals. First, he needs to convince the relativist that transparency is a genuine phenomenon for which an explanation is needed. Second, he needs to convince us that treating acceptance of the truth prescription as necessary for the concept of belief affords a better explanation of transparency than any available to the relativist.

Shah's first task then is to convince the relativist that transparency is a real phenomenon calling for an explanation. Notice that transparency postulates the existence of two different enterprises: on the one hand, the cognitive enterprise of trying to answer the question whether p and, on the other, the deliberative enterprise of trying to answer the question whether to believe that p. Transparency is the phenomenon that obtains if the latter enterprise immediately gives way to the former.

But on the conception of the deliberative enterprise that the relativist can

213

be expected to endorse at the outset, transparency doesn't seem to hold. For the relativist, we try to answer the question whether to believe that p by trying to determine whether believing that p would satisfy our doxastic criteria. For someone who subscribes to the truth prescription, this will consist in trying to answer the question whether p, but someone who subscribes to an alternative doxastic prescription, e.g. to believe only what maximizes her utility, would try to answer the deliberative question by trying to answer a different factual question – whether believing p would maximize her utility (call this enterprise *utilitarian reflection*). On this conception of doxastic deliberation, it is not generally a transparent enterprise.

Thus, establishing that transparency is a genuine phenomenon requires invoking a different account of doxastic deliberation. Shah and Velleman make a proposal to this effect in their joint paper. To deliberate about whether to believe that p, Shah and Velleman tell us, is to engage "in reasoning that is aimed at issuing or not issuing in one's believing that *p* in accordance with the norm for believing that *p*" (Shah and Velleman 2005: 502).[13] As we have seen, Shah needs to show that utilitarian reflection doesn't count as doxastic deliberation on p. In light of this construal of the deliberative enterprise, Shah would achieve this goal if he could show that utilitarian reflection cannot be aimed at issuing (or not issuing) in your believing that p in accordance with the norm for believing that p.

In a different paper, Shah seems to put forward an argument that would yield this conclusion. He writes:

> In the sense I have in mind, deliberating whether to believe that p entails intending to arrive at belief as to whether p. If my answering a question is going to count as deliberating whether to believe that p, then I must intend to arrive at belief as to whether p just by answering that question. I can arrive at the belief just by answering the question whether p; however, I cannot arrive at the belief just by answering the question whether it is in my interest to hold it (Shah 2006: 482).

Here Shah seems to argue that the reason why I cannot aim at arriving at a belief as to whether p through utilitarian reflection is that I cannot achieve this goal just by means of utilitarian reflection.

This argument relies on a questionable principle to the effect that an activity cannot aim at an outcome if it can't bring it about. But even if we concede this principle to Shah, his reasoning runs into trouble. Let's assume for the sake of the argument that the only activity that can enable me to arrive at a belief as to whether p in the requisite way is answering the question whether p, and that it follows from this that answering the question whether p is the only activity that can be aimed at issuing or not issuing in belief as to whether p. On Shah and Velleman's construal of doxastic deliberation, this outcome would entail that the enterprise is transparent.

The problem for Shah is that the argument that he has used to establish transparency can also be used as a seemingly adequate explanation of the phenomenon that doesn't rest on the assumption that accepting the truth prescription is necessary for having the concept of belief. The alternative explanation would go as follows: (a) trying to answer the question whether p is the only activity that can enable me to arrive, in the requisite way, at a belief as to whether p; (b) it follows from this that it is the only activity that can be aimed at issuing or not issuing in a belief as to whether p, and (c) this entails, in turn, that doxastic deliberation can only take the form of trying to answer the question whether p, as transparency requires. In trying to convince his opponent that transparency is a real phenomenon, Shah has also supplied her with a seemingly adequate explanation of it. Hence Shah has failed to convince the relativist that transparency is a genuine phenomenon that can only be explained by the assumption that accepting the truth prescription is necessary for having the concept of belief. Therefore he has failed to provide a cogent argument for the legitimacy of 11 (or 13).

Let me turn now, more briefly, to the argument originally developed by David Velleman. He has argued that "[...] an attitude doesn't qualify as a belief unless it [...] has a tendency to be constrained by input in ways designed to ensure that it is true" (Velleman 2000: 255). It would follow from this that abiding by the truth prescription is necessary for having beliefs.

Velleman defends this view by contending that, unless we introduce this condition in our definition of belief, we won't be able to distinguish beliefs from other cognitive attitudes, such as imaginings and assumings (Velleman 2000: 247). The alternative that he considers is the motivational account of belief, which seeks to account for belief in terms of the dispositions to behaviour that beliefs motivate.

Velleman is undoubtedly right to claim that other cognitive attitudes besides belief can motivate behaviour. But this is not enough to establish his point. He needs to argue that, say, assuming or imagining that p has *the same* motivational role as believing that p, and I can't see that he provides adequate support for this point. To take one of the examples Velleman considers, imagining that you are an elephant as part of a game of make-believe may motivate you to behave in certain ways, but I don't think one can plausibly claim that it motivates you to behave in exactly the same ways as *believing* that you are an elephant would.[14] And so long as the motivational role of belief is different from the motivational roles of other propositional attitudes, it will be possible in principle to use these differences to single out belief, obviating the need to introduce regulation for truth in our account. I conclude that Velleman's argument doesn't provide adequate support for the claim that having beliefs requires abiding by the truth prescription.

Stability[15]

As I have argued in the preceding section, I think that Shah and Velleman have failed to support the claim that there is a universal prescription to believe only truths. I am not aware of any other extant proposals that succeed in this enterprise. However, there is an area that I think holds some promise for the view. In this section I want to sketch a line of reasoning that might go some way towards establishing 11 on purely conceptual grounds. I am going to argue that the doxastic policy based on the prescription expressed by 11 doesn't have many coherent alternatives.

Let me refer to the doxastic criterion according to which S should believe that p just in case p satisfies condition C (written Cp) as *the C-criterion*.[16] And let's say that S has adopted the C-criterion as her doxastic policy just in case, for every proposition p on which she wants to form an opinion, S aims to bring it about that she believes that p if and only if Cp. I am going to argue that the conditions that a criterion has to satisfy in order to generate an adequate doxastic policy might confer on the truth criterion a special status.

Consider first the effect that your doxastic policies can be expected to have on your practical policies. Suppose that your policy as to when to do ϕ is to do ϕ on occasion x just in case x satisfies condition C. What you end up doing in pursuit of this policy on a particular occasion (whether you ϕ or you don't ϕ) will depend on the belief that you form as to whether C is satisfied. Hence, if your nominal policy as to whether to ϕ is to do so just in case C is satisfied, your effective policy will be to do so just in case you believe that C is satisfied.

If you subscribe to the truth criterion, this point doesn't have any remarkable consequences: you aim to ϕ on occasion x just in case you believe Cx, but you aim to believe Cx just in case Cx. Hence your overall policy is still to ϕ on occasion x just in case Cx. Things are different, however, if you subscribe to a doxastic criterion other than the truth criterion. Then the policy of ϕing on occasion x just in case you believe Cx doesn't immediately collapse into the policy of ϕing on occasion x just in case Cx. Suppose that, for propositions concerning whether C is satisfied, your doxastic policy is the D-criterion (to believe p just in case Dp) Then your effective criterion with respect to ϕ will be to ϕ on occasion x just in case the proposition Cx satisfies condition D (written DCx). In this way, which doxastic policy you adopt will affect your effective practical policies. Suppose, e.g., that your nominal dietary policy is to eat something just in case it is good for you, but your doxastic policy with respect to whether a food is good for you is to believe that it is just in case this makes you feel good about yourself. Then your effective dietary policy will be to eat something just in case believing that it is good for you makes you feel good about yourself.

Doxastic policies can have this kind of effect, not only on practical policies, but also on other doxastic policies. Suppose that your nominal doxastic policy with respect to a proposition p is to believe p just in case Cp, but your doxastic policy with respect to the proposition Cp is to believe it just in case it satisfies condition D. Then your effective doxastic policy with respect to p will be to believe it just in case DCp – or rather to believe p just in case DCp satisfies your doxastic criterion for *this* proposition …

These considerations have important consequences when we focus on global doxastic policies – policies determining the circumstances under which a subject would believe *any* proposition. Suppose that you have adopted a doxastic policy based on the C-criterion. Then you will aim to believe p just in case Cp, but you will aim to believe Cp just in case CCp, and so on ad infinitum. In this case, what will be your effective doxastic policy with respect to p?

Whether this question can receive a satisfactory answer depends on the behaviour of C. Let's say that the C-criterion is *completely stable* just in case, necessarily, for every p, Cp if and only if p. If the C-criterion is completely stable, we can plausibly argue that the infinite regress generated by a global doxastic policy doesn't pose a problem. When the C-criterion is applied to p, it dictates that you should believe that p just in case Cp, i.e., by the stability of the C-criterion, just in case p. When the scope of the criterion is extended to Cp, the verdict that it yields for p doesn't change. It dictates that you should believe that p just in case you should believe that Cp, and you should believe that Cp just in case CCp. Hence, by two applications of the stability of the C-criterion, we have that you should believe that p just in case p. By the same reasoning, if we extend the scope of the C-criterion along this hierarchy any number of times, the same verdict will ensue – you should believe that p just in case p. This suggests that, when the criterion is applied along the whole infinite hierarchy, we will obtain the same outcome: you should believe that p if and only if p. Hence the infinite regress won't prevent the policy from issuing a verdict for every proposition.

In other cases, though, the regress will be problematic. Let me use $C^0(p)$ to denote p, and for every n, let $C^{n+1}(p)$ denote $CC^n(p)$. Let me say that C is *ultimately unstable* just in case, for every n there is an m greater than n such that it is not the case that necessarily $C^{m+1}(p)$ just in case $C^m(p)$. If C is ultimately unstable, then adopting a global doxastic policy based on the C-criterion will have disastrous consequences. No matter how far along the hierarchy we extend the application of the criterion, the verdict that we have reached at that point concerning whether one should believe p might be reversed at some later point as we continue to extend the scope of the criterion. At no point will we reach a definitive verdict that can't be reversed further along the hierarchy.

In these circumstances, we seem forced to conclude that the criterion doesn't yield a verdict on whether one should believe that p when it is applied to the whole infinite hierarchy. Hence an ultimately unstable criterion won't sustain a coherent global doxastic policy.

This is unquestionably an auspicious outcome for supporters of the truth prescription. The truth criterion is completely stable. Hence the infinite regress generated by global doxastic policies won't pose a problem for the policy based on the truth criterion. Furthermore, one could plausibly argue that the truth criterion is the only completely stable doxastic criterion. Let's assume this is right. Then, if completely stable criteria were the only doxastic criteria for which the regress doesn't pose a problem, we would have found a way of vindicating the idea that the truth prescription applies universally: only doxastic policies compatible with it would seem to overcome the problem.

However, this is not quite right. Completely stable criteria are not the only doxastic criteria to survive the regress, as they are not the only doxastic criteria that are not ultimately unstable. The C-criterion is *ultimately stable* (i.e. not ultimately unstable) just in case there is an n such that, for every m greater than or equal to n, necessarily $C^{m+1}(p)$ just in case $C^m(p)$. Now, completely stable criteria are ultimately stable for n = 0. But criteria that are ultimately stable only for higher values for n are not completely stable. Nevertheless, the reasoning that we have presented to show that completely stable criteria do not face a problem with the regress generated by global doxastic policies could be used to establish this result for every ultimately stable criterion. If the C-criterion is ultimately stable for n, then once the scope of the criterion has been extended to the nth term of the hierarchy, the verdict that it yields concerning whether one should believe that p will not be changed by further extensions. The policy will continue to dictate that one should believe that p just in case $C^n(p)$. In light of this, we can conclude that this is the verdict that the policy will sanction when the criterion is applied to the whole infinite hierarchy. Every ultimately stable doxastic criterion can avoid the difficulty posed by the infinite regress.

Are there any ultimately stable criteria that are not completely stable? I want to suggest that there might be at least one. It is certainly not the case for every p and every possible state of information that the evidence supports p just in case p. Misleading evidence is a distressingly common occurrence. It follows that the evidence criterion is not completely stable. Nevertheless one could plausibly argue that, necessarily, for every p and every possible state of information, the evidence supports p just in case the evidence supports the proposition that the evidence supports p. The right-to-left direction of this biconditional is fairly uncontroversial, as evidence for the hypothesis that there is evidence for p surely counts as evidence for p. And the left-to-right direction also has some plausibility. For one could argue that it is in the nature of evidence to be accessible. And this would seem to entail that the evidence won't support p unless there is evidence that it does. If this reasoning is correct, the evidence criterion will be ultimately stable (for n = 1).

In any case, even if the evidence criterion is ultimately stable, and even if other ultimately stable criteria exist, the line of reasoning that I have sketched has to count as a partial victory for the universality of the truth prescription. Most doxastic policies incompatible with it are ultimately unstable, and hence unsuitable as global doxastic policies. Take, for example, doxastic criteria based on the practical consequences of belief. It seems reasonable to suppose that it is not the case necessarily for any proposition p and subject S that believing that p maximizes S's utility just in case S's utility is maximized by the belief that believing that p maximizes her utility.

However, the discredit that the argument brings on ultimately unstable criteria has limits. There is nothing wrong, as far as the argument goes, with assessing beliefs with an ultimately unstable criterion, so long as we don't try to base our own doxastic policy on it. Even their use as the basis for a doxastic policy is not ruled out by the argument, so long as its scope is suitably restricted. I can use an ultimately unstable criterion for p, for the proposition that this criterion is satisfied by believing that p, and so on. All that's needed is that sooner or later we reach a point in this sequence beyond which my doxastic policy is based on an ultimately stable criterion.

The Open-Question Argument

Let me turn now to the second line of reasoning against semantic naturalism that I want to consider in this paper. Kripke's appeal to the normative character of meaning has sometimes been seen as putting forward a version of the open-question argument. The argument was originally presented by G.E. Moore against the possibility of defining or analysing good. Moore writes:

> The hypothesis that disagreement about the meaning of good is disagreement with regard to the correct analysis of a given whole, may be most plainly seen to be incorrect by consideration of the fact that, whatever definition be offered, it may be always asked, with significance, of the complex so defined, whether it is itself good (Moore 1903: 15).

Moore is happy to accept that there may be necessary and sufficient conditions for something being good. What he doesn't accept is that these conditions could be taken as defining or analysing *good*. The reason that the quoted passage gives for this is that we can meaningfully ask whether these conditions are sufficient or, presumably, necessary for being good.

The argument features prominently the notion of whether it is possible to ask meaningfully whether, say, maximizing utility is good. I propose to construe this notion in terms of whether or not having a certain belief involving a concept is a necessary condition for this to be the concept of *good*. In linguistic terms, the question is whether having a belief expressible with a sentence involving a predicate, say "good", is a necessary condition for this predicate to mean *good*. On this construal, the question "Is C good?" could not be meaningfully asked if someone who doesn't believe that C is a sufficient condition for the satisfaction of "good" cannot mean *good* by "good". Having this belief shouldn't be taken to require entertaining the proposition in consciousness. The belief could be manifested instead in your linguistic dispositions by your unwillingness to contemplate the possibility of withholding "good" from something that you believe to satisfy C.

We can now provide a formulation for the open-question argument, concentrating again on the concept *morally right*:[17]

14.   For every description D, it is possible for someone who means *morally right* by "morally right" to believe, for some action x, both D(x) and "~Morally right (x)".[18]

15.   If satisfying D is analytically sufficient for being morally right, then, for every x, believing D(x) and "~Morally right (x)" is incompatible with meaning *morally right* by "morally right".

Therefore:

16.   For every description D, satisfying D is not analytically sufficient for being morally right.

And a parallel argument can be formulated against the possibility of analysing predicate satisfaction:

17.   For any description D, it is possible for someone who means *satisfies* by "satisfies" to believe, for some S, P, a, both D(S, P, a) and "~satisfies (S, P, a)".

18.   If satisfaction of D by S, P and a is analytically sufficient for a satisfying P, as meant by S, then for all S, P, a, believing D(S, P, a) and "~satisfies (S, P, a)" is incompatible with meaning *satisfies* by "satisfies".

Therefore:

19.   For every description D, D(S, P, a) is not analytically sufficient for a satisfying P, as meant by S.

Clearly, the cogency of each of these arguments depends on whether we are capable of providing adequate support for its first premise. We shall address this point later on. But a more immediate problem is that even if these arguments succeeded in establishing their conclusions, the naturalist could easily dismiss them as irrelevant to her project. As we mentioned above, contemporary naturalists don't typically see themselves as providing analytically necessary and sufficient conditions for the satisfaction of concepts. Instead, they tend to see the satisfaction of the concepts they are accounting for as connected by a necessary *a posteriori* link to the conditions that figure in the account. The model for this conception of their task is the semantics of natural kind terms as explicated by Saul Kripke and Hilary Putnam (Kripke 1980; Putnam 1975b). On this conception of naturalist accounts, an account of "morally right" or "satisfies" will seek to achieve the kind of understanding of, say, "water" provided by the discovery that water is H_2O. Clearly, on this conception of the enterprise, the conclusion of an open-question argument has no power to undermine an account of what determines the satisfaction conditions of "water". The point is made very clearly by Gilbert Harman for the case of ethics:

> [...] as it stands the open question argument is invalid. An analogous argument could be used on someone who was ignorant of the chemical composition of water to "prove" to him that water is not H_2O. This person will agree that it is not an open question whether water is water but it is an open question, at least for him, whether water is H_2O. Since this argument would not show that water is not H_2O, the open question argument in ethics cannot be used as it stands to show that for an act to be an act that ought to be done is not for it to have some natural characteristic C (Harman 1977: 19).

On our construal of the notion of what counts as an open question, Harman's point is that the satisfaction conditions of "water" are determined by H_2O, even though meaning water by "water" does not require believing that being H_2O is necessary for satisfying "water".

A similar point is made by Scott Soames concerning the effect of the argument on naturalistic accounts in semantics:

> [...] I am willing to grant that the skeptic might be right in maintaining that claims about what I meant are not a priori consequences of nonintentional truths. If it were clear that any necessary consequence of a set of claims P was also an a priori consequence of P, then this admission would provide the sceptic with just what he needs; for then he could force me to admit that claims about meaning might not be necessary consequences of nonintentional truths. [...] However, this argumentative strategy fails. Thanks to the work of Kripke and others, it has become clear that many

221

necessary consequences of propositions are not a priori consequences of them. Consequently, my admission that claims about meanings may not be a priori consequences of nonintentional truths need not undermine my belief that they are necessary consequences of those truths (Soames 1998: 231).

Thus what these authors are proposing is that naturalists can sidestep the open-question argument by modelling the connection between their explicanda and their explicantia on the connection between natural-kind terms and the properties that determine their satisfaction conditions. Analysis of the concept *water* doesn't suffice for determining that it is satisfied by samples of H_2O. Similarly, for the enlightened naturalist, analysis won't suffice for determining that *morally right* is satisfied by, say, actions that maximize utility, or that *refers* is satisfied by a predicate and a property whenever, say, tokenings of the latter cause tokenings of the former under normal conditions. It follows that even if these naturalistic accounts are correct, the descriptions "x maximizes utility" or "tokenings of x cause tokenings of y under normal conditions" won't provide counterexamples to the conclusion of the open-question argument.

This point strikes me as incontestable. I want to suggest, however, that the antinaturalist might still have some room for manoeuvre. Going back to *water*, the point that the description H_2O is not analytically sufficient for the satisfaction of *water* is not open to question. But the antinaturalist might accept this point, as she should, and still contend that the behaviour of *water* as a natural-kind term renders other descriptions analytically sufficient for its satisfaction. Let me follow Putnam in using the term *operational definition* to refer to the array of criteria that a speaker (or a community) uses for applying a natural-kind term (Putnam 1975b). On the standard account of the semantics of a natural-kind term, the property to which it refers is singled out as the underlying kind present in most samples in the speaker's environment that satisfy her operational definition for the term.

My suggestion is that the antinaturalist could argue that the fact that the reference of a natural-kind term is determined in this way is discoverable by analysis – independently of any fact that can be ascertained only by empirical investigation. We need empirical research to ascertain which property plays this role, but not to ascertain that the property that plays this role, if there is one, will determine the extension of the term. But if this is correct, it turns out that there is, after all, a description that is analytically sufficient for the satisfaction of *water* – namely, *x is an instance of the kind, if there is one, present in most of the samples in the speaker's environment that satisfy her operational definition of water.*[19]

Providing adequate support for the claim that this description should be treated as analytically sufficient for the satisfaction of *water* lies well beyond the scope of this paper.[20] What I am arguing is that *if* this claim could be adequately established, then the threat of the open-question argument to naturalist accounts would be reinstated. For the naturalist would have to explain how, say, maximizing utility, is singled out as the property that determines the extension of *morally right*. This explanation may or may not be the same as the one given for *water*, but in either case it can be expected to invoke a second-order property M whose satisfaction by *utility maximization* confers on the latter its extension-fixing role. And if the connection between *morally right* and M can be claimed to be analytic, we will have, as in the case of *water*, an analytically sufficient description: *x is an instance of the property, if there is one, that satisfies M.*[21] The same situation could be claimed to obtain in semantics. Once again, a second-order property T would have to be invoked to explain how, say, *tokenings of x cause tokenings of y under normal conditions* is singled out for the role of fixing the extension of *refers*. And if the connection between T and *refers* is analytic, we will appear to have an analytically sufficient description: *being a predicate-property pair instantiating the relation, if there is one, that satisfies T.*

Hence, even if *morally right* and *refers* are treated as natural-kind terms, they will have analytically sufficient descriptions. Therefore, invoking this semantic model won't enable the enlightened naturalist to sidestep the conclusion of the open-question argument. Her account will still be in conflict with the conclusion of the argument.

Normativity?

In the preceding section I have argued that the conclusion of an open-question argument for a concept C might still be in conflict with a naturalistic account of C, even if the account is construed along the lines of the natural-kind model. Obviously this would pose a threat for the naturalist only if the argument were sound, and the soundness of the argument in each case cannot be plausibly asserted until support is provided for its first premise – the principle that there is no description that has to be believed to be sufficient for the satisfaction of the concept by anyone who has the concept. I want to close by considering briefly how this principle could be supported in ethics and in semantics.

The standard approach to this task in ethics is to appeal to the normative dimension of ethical concepts. For the case of *good*, Darwall, Gibbard and Railton express the thought in the following terms:

> Attributions of goodness appear to have a conceptual link with the guidance of action, a link exploited whenever we gloss the open question "Is P really good?" as "Is it clear that, other things being equal, we really ought to, or must, devote ourselves to bringing about P?" (Darwall, Gibbard, and Railton 1992: 117).

For *morally right*, the same thought is expressed by 2, above (page 207).

This link enables us to invoke the intuition that it is perfectly possible to imagine, for any action description, someone who accepts the description but doesn't think that the action ought to be performed. As Darwall, Gibbard and Railton put it:

> Our confidence that the openness of the open question does not depend upon any error or oversight may stem from our seeming ability to imagine, for any naturalistic property R, clear-headed beings who would fail to find appropriate reason or motive for action in the mere fact that R obtains (or is seen to be in the offing) (Darwall, Gibbard, and Railton 1992: 117).

These considerations suggest an argument for 14 with the following premises:

20.   For every action description D, it is possible to believe, for some x, both Dx and that x does not have to be done.

21.   You don't mean *morally right* by "morally right" unless, for every x, if you believe that x doesn't have to be done, you believe "~Morally right (x)".

For predicate reference we might try the same approach, deriving 17 from the following premises:

22.   For any description D, it is possible to believe, for some S, P and a, both D(S, P, a) and that S doesn't have to ascribe P to a.

23.   You don't mean *satisfies* by "satisfies" unless, for all S, P, a, if you believe that S doesn't have to ascribe P to a then you believe "~satisfies (S, P, a)".

Notice, though, that this approach would take us back to the difficulties that we encountered trying to use Hume's thought to undermine semantic naturalism. For 23 and related principles would have no plausibility unless the truth prescription could be established by conceptual analysis.

However, I want to suggest that invoking the normativity of meaning at this point is not mandatory. The alternative that I want to put forward, in closing, is that the role that normativity plays in the ethical case could be played in semantics by disquotation. What we would need to invoke is the claim that having the concept of satisfaction requires believing that a is not satisfied by P, as meant by you, whenever you believe ~Pa. This claim would supply the argument with the following premise:

24.	You don't mean *satisfies* by "satisfies" unless, for all P, a, if you believe ~Pa you believe "~satisfies (I, P, a)".[22]

Now, to complete the argument for 17 we would only need to argue that for any description D, it is possible to believe D(I, P, a) while not believing Pa. This would give us the following principle:

25.	For any description D, it is possible to believe, for some P and a, both D(I, P, a) and ~Pa.

And 25 and 24 would establish 17 in the same way in which 20 and 21 establish 14. Following this approach we would be able to mount a version of the open-question argument in semantics that doesn't rely on the assumption that meaning is normative.

Notes

1.	I am grateful to Mario Gómez Torrente, Christopher Jay, Mark Kalderon, Genoveva Martí, Mike Martin and the editors of this volume.
2.	In Zalabardo 1997 I argued against this attribution.
3.	In *an ascription of P to a*, as I am using the phrase, S asserts that a satisfies P.
4.	Here and elsewhere I use predicative terms as singular terms in propositions in which they figure as objects of predication.
5.	Notice that the same objection would apply to a version of the argument that replaced the objective obligation expressed by 7 with a subjective obligation: $(\forall x)(\forall S)(x$ is an ascription of P to a by S & S believes that P, as meant by her, is not satisfied by a $\supset$ S shouldn't do x)
6.	This point is made in Hattiangadi 2006. See Whiting 2007 for a reply.
7.	This approach is discussed in Wikforss 2001: 209–12.
8.	This is the approach associated with Paul Grice. See Grice 1957.
9.	See, for example, the Appendix to Fodor 1987.
10.	See in this connection the debate between Colin McGinn and Paul Boghossian. McGinn (1984: 147) argued that it was not possible to raise a problem of the normativity of mental content analogous to the problem of the normativity of linguistic meaning. Boghossian (1989: 514) offers a reply that rests on the assumption that mental content has syntactically identifiable bearers. I am suggesting that this assumption is unnecessary.
11.	Boghossian (2003: 41–5) offers an interesting discussion of this issue.
12.	The position is independent of relativism about truth. It is a view about the goal of cognition, which is perfectly compatible with a non-relativist notion of truth.
13.	See also Shah 2006: 489.
14.	Velleman appears to concede that the behavioural outcome will be different in each case (Velleman 2000: 272), but he claims that the differences are due not to a difference in the underlying behavioural disposition, but to the presence

in the case of imagining of countervailing beliefs. However, he doesn't offer an argument for explaining the difference in this way, rather than as arising from different behavioural dispositions.

15. This section can be skipped without loss of continuity.
16. I am using propositions as their own names.
17. I am not claiming that Moore would have applied to *morally right* the argument that he develops for *good*.
18. Believing "f(x)", for some x, is believing the proposition expressed by a substitution instance of "f(x)".
19. Notice that the analyticity of this connection is compatible with the possibility that different speakers have different operational definitions of *water*, so long as, in their respective environments, they all track the presence of H_2O.
20. Putnam, for one, thinks that it's not possible to obtain analytically sufficient conditions for the satisfaction of a natural-kind term (Putnam 1975b), but the difficulties that he raises for the candidates that he considers (Putnam 1975a) do not invalidate my proposal.
21. An account of moral concepts along these lines has been defended by Frank Jackson. See Jackson 1997.
22. "I" here is the first-person pronoun.

References

Blackburn, Simon (1984), "The Individual Strikes Back", *Synthese* 58: 281–302.
Boghossian, Paul (1989), "The Rule-Following Considerations", *Mind* 98: 507–49.
—(2003), "The Normativity of Content", *Philosophical Issues* 13: 31–45.
Darwall, Stephen, Allan Gibbard, and Peter Railton (1992), "Toward *Fin de siècle* Ethics: Some Trends", *Philosophical Review* 101: 115–89.
Fodor, Jerry A. (1987), *Psychosemantics. The Problem of Meaning in the Philosophy of Mind*. Cambridge, MA: MIT Press.
Grice, H. P (1957), "Meaning", *Philosophical Review* 66: 377–88.
Harman, Gilbert (1977), *The Nature of Morality. An Introduction to Ethics*. New York: Oxford University Press.
Hattiangadi, Anandi (2006), "Is Meaning Normative?" *Mind and Language* 21: 220–40.
Hume, David (1978), *A Treatise of Human Nature*. 2nd edn. Oxford: Clarendon Press.
Jackson, Frank (1997), *From Metaphysics to Ethics: A Defense of Conceptual Analysis*. Oxford: Oxford University Press.
Kripke, Saul (1980), *Naming and Necessity*. Oxford: Blackwell.
—(1982), *Wittgenstein on Rules and Private Language*. Oxford: Blackwell.
McDowell, John (1984), "Wittgenstein on Following a Rule", *Synthese* 58: 325–63.
McGinn, Colin (1984), *Wittgenstein on Meaning*. Oxford: Basil Blackwell.
Moore, G. E (1903), *Principia Ethica*. Cambridge: Cambridge University Press.
Putnam, Hilary (1975a), "Is Semantics Possible?" In *Mind, Language and Reality. Philosophical Papers, Volume 2*. Cambridge: Cambridge University Press.
—(1975b), "The Meaning of 'Meaning'", In *Mind, Language and Reality. Philosophical Papers, Volume 2*. Cambridge: Cambridge University Press.

Shah, Nishi (2003), "How Truth Governs Belief", *Philosophical Review* 112: 447–82.

—(2006), "A New Argument for Evidentialism", *Philosophical Quarterly* 56: 481–98.

Shah, Nishi, and J. David Velleman (2005), "Doxastic Deliberation", *Philosophical Review* 114: 497–534.

Soames, Scott (1998), "Skepticism about Meaning: Indeterminacy, Normativity, and the Rule-Following Paradox", *Canadian Journal of Philosophy Supplementary Volume* 23: 211–49.

Velleman, J. David (2000), "On the Aim of Belief", In *The Possibility of Practical Reason*. Oxford: Clarendon Press.

Whiting, Daniel (2007), "The Normativity of Meaning Defended", *Analysis* 67: 133–40.

Wikforss, Åsa Maria (2001), "Semantic Normativity", *Philosophical Studies* 102: 203–26.

Wright, Crispin (1984), "Kripke's Account of the Argument against Private Language", *Journal of Philosophy* 81: 759–77.

Zalabardo, José L (1997), "Kripke's Normativity Argument", *Canadian Journal of Philosophy* 27 (4), 467–88.

—(2010), "Why Believe the Truth? Shah and Velleman on the Aim of Belief", *Philosophical Explorations* 13: 1–21.

10 Analyticity, Apriority, Modality

Albert Casullo

In the introduction to his *Critique of Pure Reason*, Immanuel Kant introduces a conceptual framework that involves three distinctions: the epistemic distinction between *a priori* and empirical (or *a posteriori*) knowledge; the metaphysical distinction between necessary and contingent propositions; and the semantic distinction between analytic and synthetic propositions. Kant utilizes his framework to pose four questions: (1) What is *a priori* knowledge? (2) Is there *a priori* knowledge? (3) What is the relationship between the *a priori* and the necessary? (4) Is there synthetic *a priori* knowledge? In response, he (1965: 43) maintains that *a priori* knowledge is "independent of experience", contrasting it with *a posteriori* knowledge, which has its "sources" in experience. He offers two criteria for *a priori* knowledge: necessity and strict universality; and argues that, since mathematical propositions are necessary, mathematical knowledge is *a priori*. Kant's claim that necessity is a criterion of the *a priori* entails

(K1)   All knowledge of necessary propositions is *a priori*,

but not

(K2)   All propositions known *a priori* are necessary.

Finally, Kant maintains that all propositions of the form "All A are B" are either analytic or synthetic: analytic if the predicate is contained in the subject; synthetic if it is not. Utilizing this distinction, he argues that

(K3)   All knowledge of analytic propositions is *a priori*; and

(K4)   Some propositions known *a priori* are synthetic.

In support of (K4), Kant claims that the predicate terms of "7 + 5 = 12" and "The straight line between two points is the shortest" are not contained in their respective subjects.

Kant's conceptual framework and the four questions that he poses within it are at the centre of much current philosophical discussion. First, there is disagreement over how to articulate Kant's characterization of *a priori* knowledge and whether that characterization, however articulated, is adequate. Second, the most fundamental division in contemporary philosophy is between those who accept and those who reject the existence of *a priori* knowledge. Kant's supporting argument plays a central role in the debate. Third, Saul Kripke rejects both (K1) and (K2), but his examples of necessary *a posteriori* knowledge and contingent *a posteriori* knowledge remain controversial. Finally, the denial of (K4) by proponents of logical empiricism and W.V. Quine's subsequent rejection of the analytic/synthetic distinction continue to dominate discussions of *a priori* knowledge.

The Concept of *a priori* Knowledge

Kant's characterization of the *a priori* is not fully articulated. He does not spell out the sense in which *a priori* knowledge must be "independent" of experience or the sense in which *a posteriori* knowledge has its "source" in experience. It is generally accepted that, by a source of knowledge, Kant means a source of justification. So the Kantian conception of *a priori* knowledge comes to:

(APK) S knows *a priori* that p if and only if S's belief that p is justified *a priori* and the other conditions on knowledge are satisfied; and

(APJ) S's belief that p is justified *a priori* if and only if S's justification for the belief that p does not depend on experience.

(APJ) has been criticised from two directions. First, some maintain that it is not sufficiently informative; it tells us what *a priori* justification is not, but not what it is. Hence, Laurence BonJour (1985) rejects the Kantian conception of *a priori* justification in favour of the traditional rationalist conception:

(AP1) S's belief that p is justified *a priori* if and only if S intuitively "sees" or apprehends that p is necessarily true.

Alvin Plantinga (1993) and BonJour (1998) offer variants of (AP1). Second, others maintain that the sense of "dependence" relevant to *a priori* justification requires articulation, and have offered two competing accounts. Albert Casullo (2003) endorses

(AP2) S's belief that p is justified *a priori* if and only if S's belief that p is non-experientially justified (i.e., justified by some non-experiential source).

Hilary Putnam (1983) and Philip Kitcher (1983) favour

(AP3) S's belief that p is justified *a priori* if and only if S's belief that p is non-experientially justified and cannot be defeated by experience.

(AP1) and (AP3) face serious objections.

The term "see" is used metaphorically in (AP1). Let us assume that it shares one basic feature with the literal use of "see": "S sees that p" entails "S believes that p". Hence, (AP1) has the consequence that if S's belief that p is justified *a priori* then S believes that p is necessarily true. This consequence faces two problems. Suppose that Sam is a mathematician who believes some generally accepted theorem T on the basis of a valid proof. Presumably, Sam's belief is justified. But suppose that Sam is also a serious student of philosophy who has come to doubt the cogency of the distinction between necessary and contingent propositions and, as a consequence, refrains from modal beliefs. It is implausible to maintain that Sam's belief that T is not justified *a priori* merely because of his views about a controversial metaphysical thesis. (AP1) is also threatened with a regress. It entails that if S's belief that p is justified *a priori* then S believes that necessarily p. Must S's belief that necessarily p be justified? If not, it is hard to see why it is a necessary condition of having an *a priori* justified belief that p. If so, then presumably it is justified *a priori*. But in order for S's belief that necessarily p to be justified *a priori*, S must believe that necessarily necessarily p, and the same question arises with respect to the latter belief. Must it be justified or not? Hence, (AP1) either faces an infinite regress of justified modal beliefs or is committed to the view that having an unjustified belief that necessarily p is a necessary condition of having a justified belief that p.

(AP3) is also open to serious objection. Kripke (1980) and Kitcher (1983) maintain that an adequate conception of *a priori* knowledge should allow for the possibility that a person knows empirically some proposition that he or she can know *a priori*. (AP3) precludes this possibility. Assume that

(A)   S knows empirically that p and S can know *a priori* that p.

From the left conjunct of (A), it follows that

(1)   S's belief that p is justified$_k$ empirically,

where "justified$_k$" abbreviates "justified to the degree minimally sufficient for knowledge". Consider now the empirical sources that have been alleged to justify mathematical propositions: counting objects, reading a textbook, consulting a mathematician, and computer results. Each of these sources is fallible in an important respect. The justification each confers on a belief that p is defeasible by an empirically justified overriding defeater; that is, by an empirically justified belief that not-p. If S's belief that p is justified by counting a collection of objects and arriving at a particular result, then it is possible that S recounts the collection and arrives at a different result. If S's belief that p is justified by a textbook (mathematician, computer result) that states that p, then it is possible that S encounters a different textbook (mathematician, computer result) that states that not-p. In each case, the latter result is an empirically justified overriding defeater for S's original justification. Hence, given the fallible character of empirical justification, it follows that

(2)   S's empirical justification for the belief that p is defeasible by an empirically justified belief that not-p.

(2), however, entails that

(3)   S's belief that not-p is justifiable$_d$ empirically,

where "justifiable$_d$" abbreviates "justifiable to the degree minimally sufficient to defeat S's justified$_k$ belief that p". Furthermore, the conjunction of (AP3) and the right conjunct of (A) entails

(4)   It is not the case that S's non-experiential justification$_k$ for the belief that p is defeasible by S's empirically justified belief that not-p.

(4), however, entails that

(5)   It is not the case that S's belief that not-p is justifiable$_d$ empirically.

The conjunction of (3) and (5) is a contradiction. Hence, (AP3) is incompatible with (A). (AP2), however, is compatible with (A) since the conjunction of (AP2) and the right conjunct of (A) does not entail (4). Since both the traditional rationalist conception and the Putnam–Kitcher articulation of the Kantian conception of *a priori* justification are open to serious objections which (AP2) avoids, (AP2) provides the superior articulation of the concept of *a priori* justification.

The Existence of *a priori* Knowledge

Traditional apriorism: Kant

Kant offers the most influential traditional argument for the existence of *a priori* knowledge. Kant (1965: 43) holds that necessity is a criterion of the *a priori*: "if we have a proposition which in being thought is thought as *necessary*, it is an *a priori* judgment; ... " He (1965: 52) then goes on to argue that "mathematical propositions, strictly so called, are always judgments *a priori*, not empirical; because they carry with them necessity, which cannot be derived from experience." Kant's argument, the *Argument from Necessity*, can be presented as follows:

(N1) Mathematical propositions are necessary.

(N2) One cannot know a necessary proposition on the basis of experience.

(N3) Therefore, one cannot know mathematical propositions on the basis of experience.

The phrase "know a necessary proposition" in (N2) masks some important distinctions:

(A)   S knows the *truth-value* of p just in case S knows that p is true or S knows that p is false.

(B)   S knows the *general modal status* of p just in case S knows that p is a necessary proposition (i.e., necessarily true or necessarily false) or S knows that p is a contingent proposition (i.e., contingently true or contingently false).

(C)   S knows the *specific modal status* of p just in case S knows that p is necessarily true or S knows that p is necessarily false or S knows that p is contingently true or S knows that p is contingently false.

(A) and (B) are logically independent: one can know one but not the other. One can know that the Goldbach Conjecture is either necessarily true or necessarily false but not know whether it is true or false. Similarly, one can know that the Pythagorean Theorem is true, but not know whether it is necessarily true or contingently true. The specific modal status of a proposition is just the conjunction of its *truth-value* and its general modal status. Therefore, one cannot know the specific modal status of a proposition unless one knows both its *truth-value* and its general modal status.

We can now distinguish two readings of (N2):

(N2A) One cannot know the *truth-value* of a necessary proposition on the basis of experience; and

(N2B) One cannot know the *general modal status* of a necessary proposition on the basis of experience.

Kant (1965: 52) supports (N2) with the observation that "Experience teaches us that a thing is so and so, but not that it cannot be otherwise." This observation supports (N2B) but not (N2A), since Kant allows that experience can provide evidence that something is the case, but denies that it can provide evidence that something must be the case. The conclusion of the argument, however, is that knowledge of the *truth-value* of mathematical propositions, such as that 7 + 5 = 12, is *a priori*.

Kant's argument, the *Kantian Argument*, can now be articulated as follows:

(N1) Mathematical propositions are necessary.

(N2B) One cannot know the *general modal status* of a necessary proposition on the basis of experience.

(N3A) Therefore, one cannot know the *truth-value* of mathematical propositions on the basis of experience.

The Kantian Argument turns on this principle:

(KP) If the general modal status of p is knowable only *a priori*, then the *truth-value* of p is knowable only *a priori*.

(KP), however, is false. If one can know only *a priori* that a proposition is necessary, then one can know only *a priori* that a proposition is contingent. The evidence relevant to determining the latter is the same as that relevant to determining the former. For example, if one determines that "2 + 2 = 4" is necessary by trying to conceive of its falsehood and failing, one determines that "Kant is a philosopher" is contingent by trying to conceive of its falsehood and succeeding. But from the fact that one can know only *a priori* that the proposition "Kant is a philosopher" is contingent, it does not follow that one can know only *a priori* that the proposition "Kant is a philosopher" is true. Clearly, it is knowable *a posteriori*.

Roderick Chisholm (1977) suggests the following reformulation of the Argument from Necessity, the *Modal Argument*:

(N1)   Mathematical propositions are necessary.

(N2B) One cannot know the *general modal status* of a necessary proposition on the basis of experience.

(N3B) Therefore, one cannot know the *general modal status* of mathematical propositions on the basis of experience.

The Modal Argument faces a different problem. Why accept (N2B)? Kant maintains that experience can teach us only what is the case. But a good deal of our ordinary practical knowledge and the bulk of our scientific knowledge provide clear counterexamples to the claim. My knowledge that my pen will fall if I drop it does not provide information about what is the case for the antecedent is contrary-to-fact. Scientific laws are not mere descriptions of the actual world. They support counterfactual conditionals and, hence, provide information beyond what is true of the actual world. In the absence of further support, (N2B) should be rejected.

Moderate Apriorism: Logical Empiricism

A second strategy for defending the existence of *a priori* knowledge is offered by proponents of logical empiricism, such as A. J. Ayer (1952) and Carl Hempel (1972), who reject John Stuart Mill's contention that knowledge of basic mathematical propositions, such as that $2 \times 5 = 10$, is based on induction from observed cases. Both draw attention to the fact that, if one is justified in believing that some general proposition is true on the basis of experience, then contrary experiences should justify one in believing that the proposition is false. But no experiences would justify one in believing that a mathematical proposition, such as that $2 \times 5 = 10$, is false. Suppose, for example, that one were to count what appear to be five pairs of shoes and arrive at the result that there were only nine shoes. Ayer (1952: 75–6) contends that

> [o]ne would say that I was wrong in supposing that there were five pairs of objects to start with, or that one of the objects had been taken away while I was counting, or that two of them had coalesced, or that I had counted wrongly. One would adopt as an explanation whatever empirical hypothesis fitted in best with the accredited facts. The one explanation which would in no circumstances be adopted is that ten is not always the product of two and five.

Since Ayer maintains that we would not regard any experiences as evidence that a mathematical proposition is false, he concludes that no experiences provide evidence that they are true.

Ayer's argument, the *Irrefutability Argument*, can be stated as follows:

(A1) No experiences provide evidence that mathematical propositions are false.

(A2) If no experiences provide evidence that mathematical propositions are false, then no experiences provide evidence that they are true.

(A3) Therefore, no experiences provide evidence that mathematical propositions are true.

Ayer's example provides very weak support for (A1) because (a) it does not take into account the number of experiences that confirm the proposition in question, (b) it involves only a single experience that disconfirms the proposition, and (c) the hypotheses which are invoked to explain away the disconfirming experience as apparent are not subjected to independent empirical test. In a situation where there is a strong background of supporting experiential evidence for an inductive generalization and an isolated disconfirming experience, it is reasonable to discount the disconfirming experience as apparent and to explain it away on whatever empirical grounds are most plausible. But it does not follow that the generalization in question cannot be disconfirmed by experience.

In order to provide stronger support for (A1), Ayer's example must be revised as follows: increase the number of experiences that disconfirm the proposition so that it is large relative to the number of experiences that confirm it; and subject the hypotheses invoked to explain away the disconfirming experiences as apparent to independent tests that fail to support them. Let us now suppose that one has a very large number of experiences that disconfirm the proposition that $2 \times 5 = 10$ and, furthermore, that empirical investigations of the hypotheses invoked to explain away these disconfirming experiences as apparent produce very little, if any, support for the hypotheses. Given these revisions, Ayer can continue to endorse premise (A1) only at the expense of holding empirical beliefs that are at odds with the available evidence.

Inductive Radical Empiricism: Mill

Radical empiricism is the view that denies the existence of *a priori* knowledge. One strategy for denying the existence of *a priori* knowledge is to offer radical empiricist accounts of those domains of knowledge that proponents of the *a priori* allege to be knowable only *a priori*. Since mathematical knowledge has received the most attention, we will focus on it. Radical empiricist accounts of mathematical knowledge fall into two broad categories: inductive and holistic.

John Stuart Mill (1973) offers an inductive empiricist account of mathematical knowledge. Inductive empiricism with respect to a domain of knowledge involves two theses: (1) some propositions within that domain are epistemically more basic than the others, in the sense that the non-basic propositions derive their justification from the basic propositions via inference; and (2) the basic propositions are known by inductive inference from observed cases. Mill's primary thesis is that the basic propositions, the axioms and definitions, of arithmetic and geometry are known by induction from observed cases.

Mill's account faces serious objections, such as those offered by Gottlob Frege (1974). Let us assume, however, that these objections can be deflected and that Mill provides a defensible inductive empiricist account of mathematical knowledge. Does this show that mathematical knowledge is not *a priori*? If Mill's account is defensible, then it follows that Kant's claim that one cannot know mathematical propositions on the basis of experience is false. It does not follow, however, that the weaker claim that there is *a priori* knowledge of mathematical propositions is false. From the fact that one knows (or can know) mathematical propositions on the basis of experience, it does not immediately follow that one does not (or cannot) know mathematical propositions *a priori*.

Mill (1973: 231–2) addresses the gap in his argument with the following considerations:

> They cannot, however, but allow that the truth of the axiom, Two straight lines cannot inclose a space, even if evident independently of experience, is also evident from experience. ... Where then is the necessity for assuming that our recognition of these truths has a different origin from the rest of our knowledge, when its existence is perfectly accounted for by supposing its origin to be the same? ... The burden of proof lies on the advocates of the contrary opinion: it is for them to point out some fact, inconsistent with the supposition that this part of our knowledge of nature is derived from the same sources as every other part.

He attempts to close the gap by appealing to a version of the Explanatory Simplicity Principle: If a putative source of knowledge is not necessary to explain knowledge of the propositions within some domain, then it is not a source of knowledge of the propositions within that domain.

Mill's argument, the *Explanatory Simplicity Argument*, can be articulated as follows:

(M1) Inductive empiricism provides an account of mathematical knowledge based on inductive generalization from observed cases.

(M2) α is a source of knowledge for some domain D only if α is necessary to explain knowledge of some propositions within D.

(M3) Therefore, mathematical knowledge is not *a priori*.

The burden of the argument is carried by (M2), the Explanatory Simplicity Principle.

Casullo (2005) argues that the Explanatory Simplicity Principle is false because it rules out the possibility of a familiar form of epistemic overdetermination. The justification of some of our beliefs is overdetermined by different sources. There are some beliefs for which we have more than one justification, each of those justifications derives from a different source, and each, in the absence of the others, is sufficient to justify the belief in question. For example, I've misplaced my wallet and wonder where I might have left it. I suddenly recall having left it on the kitchen table last night. My recollection justifies my belief that my wallet is on the kitchen table. But, just to be sure, I walk out to the kitchen to check. To my relief, I see my wallet on the table. My seeing my wallet on the table also justifies my belief that my wallet is on the table. So here my justification is overdetermined by different sources. If the justification of my belief is overdetermined by two different sources, it follows that my belief is justified by two different sources. Hence, in the absence of an argument against the possibility of epistemic overdetermination by different sources, Mill's appeal to the Explanatory Simplicity Principle simply begs the question.

Holistic Radical Empiricism: Quine

Quine rejects inductive empiricism. He rejects the idea that there are basic mathematical propositions which, taken in isolation, are directly justified by observation and inductive generalization. Quine's account of mathematical knowledge is a version of holistic empiricism. Mathematical propositions are components of scientific theories. They are not tested directly against observation, but only indirectly via their observational consequences. Moreover, they don't have observational consequences in isolation, but only in conjunction with the other propositions of the theory. Hence, according to holistic empiricism, entire scientific theories, including their mathematical components, are indirectly confirmed or disconfirmed by experience via their observational consequences.

Our main concern is whether Quine's account of mathematical knowledge provides an argument against the existence of *a priori* knowledge. The argument of Quine's (1963) classic paper, "Two Dogmas of Empiricism", remains controversial. His attack is directed at a variant of Frege's conception of analyticity: a statement is analytic if it can be turned into a logical truth by replacing synonyms with synonyms. His primary target is the notion of *synonymy* and his leading contentions can be summarized as follows. First, synonymy cannot be explained in terms of definition, interchangeability *salve veritate*, or semantic rules. Second, the verification theory of meaning does provide an account of statement synonymy; but the theory presupposes radical reductionism, which is a failed programme. A vestige of that programme survives in the view that individual statements admit of confirmation or disconfirmation. Quine objects to this vestige since it lends credence to the idea that there are statements confirmed no matter what, which he (1963: 43) rejects on the grounds that "no statement is immune to revision".

There are two strands to Quine's argument. The first challenges the cogency of semantic concepts such as synonymy. The second challenges the remaining vestige of reductionism. Neither contention, however, is explicitly directed at *a priori* knowledge. Hence, if Quine's argument does present a challenge to the existence of *a priori* knowledge, then some additional premise is necessary that connects one of its explicit targets to the *a priori*.

One standard reading of Quine's argument is that his goal is to undermine the central tenet of logical empiricism,

(LE)   All *a priori* knowledge is of analytic truths,

by showing that the analytic/synthetic distinction is not cogent. Suppose we grant that (LE) is indeed Quine's target and that his arguments establish that the analytic/synthetic distinction is not cogent. It does not follow that either the claim of proponents of (LE) that there is *a priori* knowledge or their supporting argument for that claim is not cogent. Logical empiricists, such as Ayer, do not take (LE) to be constitutive of the concept of *a priori* knowledge. Moreover, they do not base their case for the existence of *a priori* knowledge on a premise, such as (LE), that involves the concept of analytic truth. They endorse the Kantian conception of *a priori* knowledge and base their case for *a priori* knowledge on the Irrefutability Argument. They then go on to offer independent arguments to show that propositions known *a priori* are analytic. Hence, Quine's argument establishes only that their thesis about the nature of the propositions known *a priori* is not cogent. But from this it does not follow that either their claim that there is *a priori* knowledge or their supporting argument for that claim is not cogent.

One might attempt to bolster Quine's argument by maintaining that (LE) is constitutive of the concept of *a priori* knowledge. If the concept of *a priori* knowledge involves the concept of analytic truth and the latter concept is incoherent, then the former is also incoherent. There are two ways in which the concept of *a priori* knowledge might involve the semantic concept of analytic truth: explicitly or implicitly. As we saw in section 1, neither Kant's conception of *a priori* knowledge, (APK), nor his conception of *a priori* justification, (APJ), explicitly involves the concept of analytic truth. The only plausible case for maintaining that the concept of *a priori* knowledge implicitly involves that concept is based on two premises: (1) the concept of *a priori* knowledge involves the concept of necessary truth; and (2) the concept of necessary truth is analysable in terms of the concept of analytic truth. Both premises are problematic since (APK) does not involve the concept of necessary truth, and there is no available analysis of the concept of necessary truth in terms of the concept of analytic truth.

Putnam (1983) proposes an alternative connection between Quine's contentions and the rejection of the *a priori*. He maintains that Quine's contentions are directed towards two different targets. His initial contentions are directed towards the semantic concept of synonymy. His later contentions, however, are directed towards the concept of a statement that is confirmed no matter what, which is not a semantic concept. It is an epistemic concept; it is a concept of apriority. Kitcher (1983: 80) endorses Putnam's reading of Quine's argument: "If we can know *a priori* that *p* then no experience could deprive us of our warrant to believe that *p*." Hence, the Putnam–Kitcher version of Quine's argument, the *Unrevisability Argument*, can be stated as follows:

(Q1)   No statement is immune to revision in light of recalcitrant experience.

(Q2)   If S's belief that p is justified *a priori*, then S's belief that p is not rationally revisable in light of any experiential evidence.

(Q3)   Therefore, no knowledge is *a priori*.

The argument fails. Premise (Q2) is open to the objection presented against (AP3) on pages 231–2.

The Relationship Between *a priori* Knowledge and Necessary Truth

Current interest in the relationship between *a priori* knowledge and necessary truth is due to Kripke (1971, 1980), who makes two striking epistemological claims:

(E1)   There are necessary *a posteriori* truths; and

(E2)   There are contingent *a priori* truths.

Kripke maintains that (E1) is a consequence of one of his primary metaphysical theses:

(MT) Identity statements involving proper names are necessarily true if true,

and that (E2) is a consequence of one of his primary semantic theses:

(ST)   A definite description that is employed to introduce a name fixes the reference of that name rather than providing its sense.

He also acknowledges that it is a widely held view, one that he associates with Kant, that

(K)   All knowledge of necessary truths is *a priori* and all *a priori* knowledge is of necessary truths.

Therefore, he argues against (K) in order to defuse a potential objection to (MT) and (ST).

In order to assess how Kripke's claims bear on Kant's account of the relationship between *a priori* knowledge and necessary truth, four preliminary observations are in order. First, (K) is the conjunction of two principles:

(K1)   All knowledge of necessary truths is *a priori*; and

(K2)   All *a priori* knowledge is of necessary truths.

Second, Kant's conception of *a priori* knowledge (KAP),

(KAP)S knows *a priori* that p if and only if S's justification for the belief that p is independent of all experience and the other conditions on knowledge are satisfied,

does not underwrite either (K1) or (K2) since necessity is not constitutive of (KAP). Third, Kant's contention that necessity is a criterion of *a priori* knowledge, where a criterion is a sufficient condition that is not constitutive of the concept of *a priori* knowledge, underwrites (K1). Fourth, neither Kant's conception of *a priori* knowledge nor his contention that necessity is a criterion of the *a priori* underwrites (K2). (K2) plays no role in the framework for discussing the *a priori* that Kant articulates in his introduction to the *Critique*.

Casullo (2010) maintains that (K2) draws its support from a different source, the traditional rationalist conception of *a priori* knowledge:

(RAP) S knows *a priori* that p just in case S intuitively "sees" (or apprehends) that p is necessarily true and the other conditions on knowledge are satisfied.

Since "'seeing' that p is necessarily true" entails "p is necessarily true", it follows from (RAP) that *a priori* knowledge is restricted to necessary truths. Therefore, only (E1) bears on Kant's account of the relationship between *a priori* knowledge and necessary truth.

Kripke initially provides two different examples in support of (E1): (a) statements in which an essential property is attributed to a physical object; and (b) identity statements involving different co-referential proper names. He later extends his discussion of identity statements to include theoretical identity statements. We will focus on (a) and (b). Let "a" be the name of a particular lectern and "F" be the property of being made of wood. Suppose that someone knows that Fa – i.e., that this lectern is made of wood. Such knowledge is *a posteriori* since one knows that something is made from wood as opposed to, say, water frozen from the river Thames on the basis of how it looks and feels. Yet, if Fa is true, it is necessarily true since F is an essential property of a. In any possible world in which a exists, a is F. Hence, one who knows that Fa has *a posteriori* knowledge of a necessary truth.

To assess the implications of Kripke's example, we must keep in mind that the expression "*a posteriori* knowledge of a necessary truth" is ambiguous since it does not distinguish between (A) *a posteriori* knowledge of the *truth-value* of a necessary proposition, (B) *a posteriori* knowledge of the general modal status of a necessary proposition, and (C) *a posteriori* knowledge of the specific modal status of a necessary proposition. Kripke's case is an example of *a posteriori* knowledge of the *truth-value* of Fa since one discovers via experience that the lectern is made of wood. What about knowledge of its general modal status? Here Kripke (1971: 153) is explicit in maintaining that we know by "*a priori* philosophical analysis" that if Fa is true, then it is necessarily true. Hence, Kripke's case is not an example of *a posteriori* knowledge of the general modal status of a necessary proposition. Kripke maintains that such knowledge is *a priori*. Finally, one who knows (*a posteriori*) that Fa and (*a priori*) that if Fa, then necessarily Fa can infer, and thereby know, that necessarily Fa. Knowledge that necessarily Fa is knowledge of the specific modal status of Fa. Since knowledge of the specific modal status of Fa is based (in part) on *a posteriori* knowledge of its truth, it is also *a posteriori*.

The same observations apply to Kripke's example of identity statements involving proper names. Since, according to Kripke, ordinary proper names, such as "Hesperus" and "Phosphorus", are rigid designators, each picks out the same object in all possible worlds in which it picks out any object. Therefore, if both pick out the same object in the actual world, both pick out the same object in all possible worlds in which they pick out any object. Hence, if "Hesperus is Phosphorus" is true, it is necessarily true. On the other hand, it was an astronomical discovery that Hesperus is Phosphorus. So, once again, Kripke has provided an example of *a posteriori* knowledge of the *truth-value* of a necessary proposition. Moreover, he (1980: 109) maintains that we know "by a priori philosophical analysis" that such identity statements are necessarily true if true. Hence, Kripke's case is not an example of *a posteriori* knowledge of the general modal status of a necessary proposition. Finally, one who knows (*a posteriori*) that Hesperus is Phosphorus and (*a priori*) that if Hesperus is Phosphorus, then necessarily Hesperus is Phosphorus can infer, and thereby know (*a posteriori*), that necessarily Hesperus is Phosphorus.

How does (E1) bear on Kant's account of the relationship between *a priori* knowledge and necessary truth? The question cannot be answered straightforwardly because neither Kant nor Kripke makes the appropriate distinctions. (K1) is ambiguous. There are two ways of reading it:

(K1A) All knowledge of the *truth-value* of necessary propositions is *a priori*; and

(K1B) All knowledge of the *general modal status* of necessary propositions is *a priori*.

Although Kant endorses both (K1A) and (K1B), the argument he offers in support of (K1) supports only (K1B). Kripke's examples of necessary *a posteriori* truths are examples of *a posteriori* knowledge of the *truth-value* of a necessary proposition. He, however, denies that they are examples of *a posteriori* knowledge of the general modal status of a necessary proposition. Hence, Kripke's claims challenge (K1A) but not (K1B).

Both Kant and Kripke contend that knowledge of the general modal status of propositions is possible. Yet Kripke's claim that there are necessary *a posteriori* truths presents a significant challenge to that contention. Prior to his arguments to the contrary, most held the false belief that necessary *a posteriori* truths, such as that Hesperus is Phosphorus, are contingent truths. Moreover, there remains a strong intuition that appears to support that false belief. This suggests that modal intuitions are systematically unreliable and that they result in widespread error regarding the general modal status of propositions. Such widespread error, in turn, threatens modal knowledge.

Kripke recognizes the challenge to his position and responds to it in a manner that is hospitable to modal knowledge. Kripke maintains that, given that Hesperus is Phosphorus, there is no possible world in which Hesperus is not Phosphorus. So it is false that it might turn out that Hesperus is not Phosphorus. Yet he (1980: 103) acknowledges that "this seems very strange because in advance, we are inclined to say, the answer to the question whether Hesperus is Phosphorus might have turned out either way." Kripke (1980: 103–4) attempts to resolve this tension as follows:

> The evidence I have before I know that Hesperus is Phosphorus is that I see a certain star or a certain heavenly body in the evening and call it "Hesperus", and in the morning and call it "Phosphorus". I know these things. There certainly is a possible world in which a man should have seen a certain star at a certain position in the evening and called it "Hesperus" and a certain star in the morning and called it "Phosphorus"; and should have concluded – should have found out by empirical investigation – that he names two different stars, or two different heavenly bodies. … And so it's true that given the evidence that someone has antecedent to his empirical investigation, he can be placed in a sense in exactly the same situation, that is a qualitatively identical epistemic situation, and call two heavenly bodies "Hesperus" and "Phosphorus", without their being identical. So in that sense we can say that it might have turned out either way. Not that it might have turned out either way as to Hesperus's being Phosphorus. Though for all we knew in advance, Hesperus wasn't Phosphorus, that couldn't have turned out any other way, in a sense.

Kripke (1980: 142) generalizes his answer to the puzzle as follows:

> Any necessary truth, whether a priori or a posteriori, could not have turned out otherwise. In the case of some necessary a posteriori truths, however, we can say that under appropriate qualitatively identical evidential situations, an appropriate corresponding qualitative statement might have been false.

So there is a sense in which a necessary *a posteriori* truth might have turned out to be false, but that sense does not entail that it is not a necessary truth.

There are two different senses in which p might turn out to be false or, alternatively, two senses in which it is possible that p is false. The first is metaphysical since it pertains to whether there is a possible world in which p is false. The second is epistemic since it pertains to whether the falsehood of p (or, more precisely, p*, where p* is the appropriate qualitative analogue to p) is compatible with one's qualitative evidence. According to Kripke, where p is a necessary *a posteriori* truth and one has an intuition that p might turn out to be false, one does not have an intuition that the falsehood of p is metaphysically possible. Instead, such an intuition, when properly understood and accurately reported, is an intuition that the falsehood of p is epistemically possible. In other words, where E is one's original qualitative evidence for p, one has the intuition that the falsehood of p* is compatible with E*, where p* is a qualitative statement that appropriately corresponds to p and E* is an evidential situation that is appropriately qualitatively identical to E. Therefore, the intuition does not call into question the necessary truth of p.

Kripke's account is hospitable to modal knowledge for two reasons. First, when modal intuitions are properly understood and accurately reported, the modal beliefs that they support are true. Modal error arises when one confuses epistemic possibility with metaphysical possibility. Second, modal error is tractable in that (a) it is systematic and widespread only in the case of *a posteriori* necessities, but (b) Kripke's account identifies the source of the error, which enables us to avoid it or, at least, to correct it. These features of modal intuition align it favourably with other fallible sources of knowledge, such as perception.

Two-dimensional semantics occupies a prominent place in the contemporary discussion of modal knowledge. One of its virtues, according to its proponents, is that it provides a perspicuous account of the two types of possibility distinguished by Kripke. David Chalmers (2006: 59) lucidly summarizes the two-dimensional approach as follows:

> The core idea of two-dimensional semantics is that there are two different ways in which the extension of an expression depends on possible states of the world. First, the actual extension of an expression depends on the character of the actual world in which an expression is uttered. Second, the counterfactual extension of an expression depends on the character of the counterfactual world in which the expression is evaluated. Corresponding to these two sorts of dependence, expressions correspondingly have two sorts of intensions, associating possible states of the world with extensions in different ways.

The two sorts of intensions, according to Chalmers (2006: 59), yield two different ways of thinking about possibilities:

> In the first case, one thinks of a possibility as representing a way the actual world might turn out to be: or as it is sometimes put, *one considers a possibility as actual*. In the second case, one acknowledges that the actual world is fixed, and thinks of a possibility as a way the world might have been but is not: or as it is sometimes put, *one considers a possibility as counterfactual*.

The two different ways of thinking about possibilities can result in different extensions being assigned to an expression relative to a possible world. Consider again the possible world described by Kripke, in which someone sees a certain star in a certain position in the evening sky and calls it "Hesperus", and also sees a certain star in a certain position in the morning sky and calls it "Phosphorus", but the two stars are not identical. If we think of this possibility as counterfactual, then "Hesperus" and "Phosphorus" both pick out Venus given that both pick out Venus in the actual world. Hence, in that world considered as counterfactual, Hesperus is Phosphorus. Moreover, in any world considered as counterfactual, "Hesperus" and "Phosphorus" both pick out Venus given that both pick out Venus in the actual world. So there is no world, considered as counterfactual, in which Hesperus is not Phosphorus. On the other hand, if we think of Kripke's possibility as actual, then "Hesperus" and "Phosphorus" pick out different objects. Hence, in that world considered as actual, Hesperus is not Phosphorus. So, thinking of possibilities as counterfactual, captures the sense in which it could not have turned out that Hesperus is not Phosphorus; but thinking of them as actual captures the sense in which, for all we knew in advance, it might have turned out that Hesperus is not Phosphorus.

Synthetic *a priori* Knowledge

Kant's most enduring contribution to the controversy surrounding *a priori* knowledge is his defence of

(K4)   Some propositions known *a priori* are synthetic.

The literature on the *a priori* over the past 150 years is dominated by this issue. In addressing that literature, one question immediately arises: Why is the existence of synthetic *a priori* knowledge *epistemologically* significant? Kant regards it as significant because it sets the stage for his primary theoretical undertaking, which is to answer the question: How is synthetic *a priori* knowledge possible? Kant's question, however, is puzzling in one respect. Having established that there is *a priori* knowledge, he is in a position to pose the question: How is *a priori* knowledge possible? The fact that he deems it necessary to draw the analytic/synthetic distinction and to defend (K4) indicates that Kant does not think that *a priori* knowledge *in general* is problematic. In particular, he views analytic *a priori* knowledge as unproblematic.

   If synthetic *a priori* knowledge is epistemologically problematic but analytic *a priori* knowledge is not, then they must differ in some way. What, according to Kant, is the difference? Kant maintains that knowledge of analytic propositions requires only possession of the relevant concepts and the principle of contradiction. Synthetic *a priori* knowledge, however, requires more. For example, in order to know that $7 + 5 = 12$, Kant (1965: 53) maintains: "We have to go outside

245

these concepts, and call in the aid of the intuition which corresponds to one of them." Synthetic *a priori* knowledge raises special epistemological problems because of its alleged source in intuition.

The significance of (K4) is rooted in the assumption that the source of synthetic *a priori* knowledge is different from the source of analytic *a priori* knowledge. Kant, however, does not defend this assumption. Although he maintains that knowledge of analytic propositions requires only knowledge of the principle of contradiction and the content of concepts, he does not explicitly address the source of such knowledge. Since he does not explicitly address the source of analytic *a priori* knowledge, Kant has no basis for claiming that the source of such knowledge is different from the source of synthetic *a priori* knowledge, let alone that the latter is epistemologically more problematic than the former. Consequently, the epistemological significance of (K4) is presupposed rather than established.

Reactions to (K4) fall into three broad categories. Those in the first endorse (K4) but take issue with some of Kant's examples. Frege, for example, agrees that the truths of geometry are synthetic *a priori* but maintains that the truths of arithmetic are analytic. Those in the second reject (K4). Logical empiricists, such as Ayer, argue that alleged examples of synthetic *a priori* truths are either analytic or *a posteriori*. The reactions in the third category, which draw their inspiration from Quine, deny the cogency of the analytic/synthetic distinction and, *a fortiori*, the cogency of (K4). The epistemological import of these reactions is minimal.

Frege endorses (K4), but contends that the truths of arithmetic are analytic. His defence of this contention requires a modification of Kant's conception of analytic truth. Frege (1974: 4ᵉ) explicates the concept, with respect to mathematical propositions, in terms of features of their proof: "If, in carrying out this process [of following the proof of a proposition], we come only on general logical laws and on definitions, then the truth is an analytic one." The resulting conception of analytic truth is broader than Kant's. It does not restrict such truths to those in which the predicate is contained in the subject. Any mathematical truth whose proof consists solely of general logical laws and definitions qualifies as analytic.

Armed with this broader conception of analyticity, Frege's project is to demonstrate

(F1)   All arithmetic truths are analytic.

This project faces a number of formidable technical obstacles. But we will assume that they can be overcome in order to assess its epistemological consequences. A successful demonstration of (F1) has no significant epistemological consequences. A demonstration that all arithmetic truths can be proved from general logical laws and definitions, taken by itself, tells us little about knowledge of those truths since it is silent with respect to the issue of how one knows the primitive general laws, definitions, and logical principles employed in such proofs. In particular, (F1) is compatible with the claim that the truths of arithmetic are knowable only via intuition.

One might suggest that although (F1) fails to establish that arithmetic knowledge is not grounded in intuition, it does have a significant consequence regarding such knowledge. (F1) establishes that if knowledge of logic and definitions does not have its source in intuition then knowledge of arithmetic does not have its source in intuition. This result is significant since it establishes that there is a uniform explanation of knowledge of logic, definitions, and arithmetic.

The claim that (F1) establishes that there is a uniform explanation of knowledge of logic, definitions, and arithmetic rests on an unsubstantiated assumption: the only route to arithmetic knowledge is through proof from general logical laws and definitions. This assumption has an unwelcome consequence. It entails a wide-ranging scepticism with respect to the elementary truths of arithmetic. If the only route to arithmetic knowledge is through proof from general logical laws and definitions then very few, if any, have such knowledge.

Kant took for granted that most literate adults know *a priori* that $7 + 5 = 12$, and set out to provide an account of such knowledge. If most literate adults have such knowledge, then there must be a route to it other than the type of proof envisioned by Frege. Therefore, Frege fails to show that there is a uniform explanation of the typical literate adult's knowledge of logic, definitions, and arithmetic. There are two possible explanations of the typical literate adult's knowledge of arithmetic: either its source is the same as the source of knowledge of logic and definitions, or it is different. If it is the same, then Frege's programme for establishing (F1) is unnecessary. If it is different, then we are still faced with the problem of explaining how such knowledge is possible. If Kant is right about the scope of *a priori* arithmetic knowledge, then Frege fails to provide an explanation of such knowledge.

Ayer (1952: 73) rejects (K4) on the grounds that either we must "accept it as a mysterious inexplicable fact" that there is synthetic *a priori* knowledge, or we must "accept the Kantian explanation which ... only pushes the mystery a stage further back." Instead, he endorses

(LE)   All *a priori* knowledge is of analytic truths,

which he regards as epistemologically significant because it provides an explanation of *a priori* knowledge that is free of the mystery that plagues Kant's account.

Ayer (1952: 78) rejects Kant's account of the analytic/synthetic distinction, and offers an alternative: "a proposition is analytic when its validity depends solely on the definitions of the symbols it contains, and synthetic when its validity is determined by the facts of experience." Ayer's conception of analyticity is broader than Kant's since it does not restrict analytic propositions to those whose predicate is contained in the subject. Any proposition that is true in virtue of the definitions of the symbols it contains qualifies as analytic.

Ayer's (1952: 78–9) most explicit defence of (LE) is presented in the context of discussing logical truths:

> [T]he proposition "Either some ants are parasitic or none are" is an analytic proposition. For one need not resort to observation to discover that there either are or are not ants which are parasitic. If one knows what is the function of the words "either", "or", and "not", then one can see that any proposition of the form "Either *p* is true or *p* is not true" is valid, independently of experience.

His argument can be stated as follows:

(AJ1) One need not resort to observation to discover that there either are or are not ants which are parasitic.

(AJ2) Therefore, the proposition "Either some ants are parasitic or none are" is an analytic proposition.

(AJ1) is an epistemological premise: it asserts that the proposition in question can be known *a priori*. (AJ2), however, is a semantic conclusion: it asserts that the proposition in question is analytic. The validity of the argument depends on the following principle, which links the epistemic premise and the semantic conclusion:

(AJ3) All propositions knowable *a priori* are analytic.

Hence, Ayer's defence of (LE) is circular.

Suppose we grant (AJ2). Does (AJ2) provide an explanation of *a priori* knowledge of logical truths? If we return to the previously cited passage, Ayer offers the following premise in support of (AJ1):

(AJ4) If one knows what is the function of the words "either", "or", and "not", then one can see that any proposition of the form "Either *p* is true or *p* is not true" is valid, independently of experience.

Ayer explains *a priori* knowledge of logical truths in terms of an ability to "see" that they are true independently of experience. The sense of "see" invoked by Ayer to explain knowledge of logical truths is not the literal sense. His explanation appeals to a metaphorical sense of "see" that is not further explained. Therefore, Ayer's explanation, like Kant's appeal to intuition, "only pushes the mystery a stage further back".

Quine's rejection of the cogency of the analytic/synthetic distinction has been widely viewed as challenging the existence of *a priori* knowledge. We have examined two lines of argument in support of that view (see pages 239–40) and concluded that both fail. There is, however, another argument, the *Explanatory Argument*, which draws its inspiration from Quine and challenges the existence of *a priori* knowledge:

(E1)   A theory of knowledge has two goals: (a) to articulate the sources and extent of human knowledge; and (b) to explain how those sources generate the knowledge in question.

(E2)   Therefore, if a theory of knowledge endorses a category of knowledge but cannot explain how that knowledge is possible, then the theory is unacceptable.

(E3)   The only available non-mysterious explanation of how *a priori* knowledge is possible involves the analytic/synthetic distinction.

(E4)   But Quine has shown that the distinction is incoherent.

(E4)   Therefore, a theory of knowledge that endorses the *a priori* is unacceptable.

The Explanatory Argument focuses attention on the explanatory requirements of an adequate theory of knowledge. Its central premise is (E3). Although widely endorsed, there is little support for (E3). As we saw earlier, however, neither Kant's nor Frege's nor Ayer's conception of analyticity offers much in terms of an explanation of *a priori* knowledge.

Nevertheless, the challenge posed by the Explanatory Argument remains. A theory of knowledge endorsing the *a priori* must offer some explanation of how such knowledge is possible. Once we recognize that the concept of analyticity offers little in terms of explanatory power, we are in a position to recognize that the explanatory problem goes beyond the coherence of the analytic/synthetic distinction. The more general problem that must be addressed is how *a priori* knowledge is possible.

Kant's introduction of the analytic/synthetic distinction, along with the assumption that the source of analytic *a priori* knowledge is different from and more problematic than the source of synthetic *a priori* knowledge, is largely responsible for the continued controversy surrounding the existence of *a priori* knowledge. By focusing attention on the question of how synthetic *a priori* knowledge can be possible, Kant initiated a tradition whose primary preoccupation was with the *semantic* questions of whether there is a cogent analytic/synthetic distinction, how to draw that distinction, and which propositions fall into each category. Providing answers to these semantic questions, however, will not settle the controversy over the existence of *a priori* knowledge. The question that must be addressed to resolve that controversy is the more general *epistemological* question: How is *a priori* knowledge possible?

References

Ayer, A. J. (1952), *Language, Truth and Logic*, New York: Dover Publications.

BonJour, Laurence (1985), *The Structure of Empirical Knowledge*, Cambridge MA: Harvard University Press.

—(1998), *In Defense of Pure Reason*, Cambridge: Cambridge University Press.

Casullo, Albert (2003), *A Priori Justification*, New York: Oxford University Press.

—(2005), "Epistemic Overdetermination and A Priori Justification", *Philosophical Perspectives* 19: 41–58.

—(2010), "Knowledge and Modality", *Synthese* 172: 341–59.

Chalmers, David (2006), "The Foundations of Two-Dimensional Semantics", in M. Garcia-Carpintero and J. Macia (eds), *Two-Dimensional Semantics*, Oxford: Oxford University Press.

Chisholm, R. M. (1977), *Theory of Knowledge*, 2nd edn, Englewood Cliffs, NJ: Prentice-Hall.

Frege, Gottlob (1974), *The Foundations of Arithmetic*, 2nd edn, revised, trans. J. L. Austin, Evanston: Northwestern University Press.

Hempel, Carl (1972), "On the Nature of Mathematical Truth", in R. C. Sleigh ed. *Necessary Truth*, Englewood Cliffs: Prentice-Hall.

Kant, Immanuel (1965), *Critique of Pure Reason*, trans. Norman Kemp Smith, New York: St Martin's Press.

Kitcher, Philip (1983), *The Nature of Mathematical Knowledge*, New York: Oxford University Press.

Kripke, Saul (1971), "Identity and Necessity", in M. K. Munitz ed. *Identity and Individuation*, New York: New York University Press.

—(1980), *Naming and Necessity*, Cambridge MA: Harvard University Press.

Mill, John Stuart (1973), *A System of Logic*, J. M. Robson ed. Toronto: University of Toronto Press.

Plantinga, Alvin (1993), *Warrant and Proper Function*, New York: Oxford University Press.

Putnam, Hilary (1983), "'Two Dogmas' Revisited", in *Realism and Reason: Philosophical Papers, Vol. 3*. Cambridge: Cambridge University Press.

Quine, W. V. (1963), "Two Dogmas of Empiricism", in *From a Logical Point of View*, 2nd edn, revised, New York: Harper and Row.

11 New Directions in the Philosophy of Language[1]

Max Kölbel

Much recent work in the philosophy of language has been concerned in one way or another with questions concerning the interaction between the standing meaning of expressions and the context in which they are used. There are at least two different types of source for this renewed interest in context dependence. On the one hand, there are long-standing controversies concerning the right treatment of context and about the scope and viability of traditional semantics (see Chapter 7, Context Dependence, in this volume). On the other hand, there are a number of philosophical controversies outside natural language semantics in which appeal to some kind of context dependence has played a role, and which drive an interest in corresponding semantic issues concerning context dependence. All these areas seem to converge on a certain complex of problems, and these in turn point towards foundational and methodological uncertainty in semantics and philosophy of language. Independently, methodological reflection is receiving impetus from a general philosophical trend to reflect on method ("Metaphilosophy"), and this is leading to a renewed interest in foundational debates about the empirical status of semantics and the correct treatment of context dependence. I shall briefly adumbrate the kinds of questions that are in play, and how they interact. I shall then move on to discuss a series of further, related topics, which seem recently to attract the interest of researchers.

Double Index Semantics

Standard treatments of context-dependent expressions such as "I", "she", "tomorrow" and "here" follow the model of a double index semantics (Kamp 1971; Kaplan 1977; for more details, see Chapter 7, pages 159–66 in this volume). On this model, the same expression can express different *contents* in different *contexts of use* – which content this is is determined by the expression's *character*, i.e. (part of) its stable linguistic meaning. Thus, if the sentence "I am hungry now" is used in a certain context, it will express about the utterer *of* that context and the time *of* that context, that the former is hungry at the latter. In other words, the semantic properties of sentences are treated as *characters*, i.e. functions from contexts of use to semantic contents, where semantic contents in turn are (or at least determine) functions from *circumstances of evaluation* to truth-values. (In Kaplan 1977, contexts are ordered sequences consisting of an agent, a place, a time and a world, such that at the time, the agent is at the place at the world. Circumstances are ordered sequences consisting of a world, a time and possibly further parameters such as a location.) Correspondingly, subsentential expressions have characters that ensure that sentences will have appropriate characters and express the appropriate contents in context.

A double index semantics of this kind can be seen as predicting the truth-values of actual and potential utterances in the following oversimplified way. Suppose an act of uttering a sentence *s* occurs *at* a context *c*. The semantics will assign to *s* a character, i.e. a function from context to content. The utterance is then treated as expressing the content that is the value of *s*'s character for *c* as argument. This content of *s* at *c* can now be evaluated with respect to the circumstance of evaluation determined by *c*. The semantics predicts the utterance to have that truth-value, i.e. the value of the content of *s* at *c* for the circumstance *of c* as argument (see Kaplan 1977: 522).

On this simplified understanding of the Kaplanian framework, whenever one utterance of a sentence is true and another utterance of the *same* sentence is false, then the two utterances must have occurred at different contexts of use. The divergence of truth-value must have arisen in one of two ways: either the sentence expresses two different contents at the different contexts, or, while it expresses the same content in the different contexts, this content receives different values with respect to the different circumstances of evaluation corresponding to these contexts. Thus, to give names to the two possibilities, any sentence that can be uttered now truly and now not, must exhibit either *context-sensitivity* or *circumstance-sensitivity* (see Chapter 7, and see Recanati, 2007: 34). For example, if we have an earlier and a later utterance of "Obama is asleep", one true, one false, then this could be due to the respective contexts determining different semantic contents, one about the time at which the earlier utterance occurred, and one about the time at which the later utterance occurred (in the case of tensed sentences, King 2003, e.g., follows this model). This would be a case of context-sensitivity. Alternatively, it might be a case of circumstance-sensitivity: while the semantic content expressed by "Obama is asleep" in the two utterances is the same, the relevant circumstance of evaluation is different in the two cases: the first utterance's truth-value is the value of this shared content with respect to the time of the first utterance, while the second utterance's truth-value is the value of this shared content with respect to the time of the second utterance (in the case of tensed sentences, Kaplan 1977 and Recanati 2007, e.g., follow this model).

Grice's Buffer: What is Said and Implicatures

This view of the predictions generated by a semantics in a Kaplanian framework is, however, questionable, for there are several different ways in which a given utterance can be evaluated for truth, and different such ways can result in different evaluations: for example one can evaluate the utterance in a literal or in a non-literal way, one can evaluate a message directly expressed or one that is indirectly conveyed. Take one of the examples from Chapter 7: an utterance of "He is a genius" could express a literal message that is false, yet an ironical message that is true. Which of these is to serve as a datum to be predicted by a semantic theory? Again, if the sentence is uttered in response to the question "Can he solve this problem?", then it may well convey the content that the referent of "he" can solve the problem. Accordingly, the utterance may be judged to be true if he is indeed able to solve the problem – even if he is not a genius. We could even encounter both phenomena at once: an ironical use of "he is a genius" in response to the question whether he can solve the problem.

It seems clear that our description of the semantic properties of the expressions involved in the sentence "He is a genius" should not need to make special provision for each and every message that this sentence could be used to convey. This would make the task of semantics impossible. It seems that we should articulate more carefully which data we take semantic theories to predict. We might insist that there is a good sense in which all these utterances, whether ironical or indirect, depend for their truth-value only on whether the referent of "he" is a genius. What they *strictly and literally* say is the same. It seems a more reasonable and feasible task for a compositional semantic theory to predict the truth-value of what utterances say strictly and literally.

It was Grice (1989: especially chs. 2 and 15) who pioneered and explored the potential of this thought and tried to make it fruitful for semantics. He introduced the technical notion of *what is said* by an utterance and contrasted it with what is merely *implicated*. He tried to provide a general theory of conversation that would explain how language users convey ("implicate") information over and above what their utterances "say". According to Grice, language exchanges are governed by a number of cooperative principles or "conversational maxims" that participants will be expected to adhere to. The general maxim requires participants in a conversation to make their contributions "such as is required, at the stage at which it occurs, by the accepted purpose … of the talk exchange in which [they] are engaged" (Grice 1989: 26). What an utterance conveys, or in Grice's words, what it "conversationally implicates", can be worked out or inferred by appeal to these maxims. Another example: if I say "My watch looks like a Rolex", you may reasonably conclude that my watch is not in fact a Rolex. Grice's theory allows us to offer a semantics of this sentence according to which the content it expresses is compatible with the watch in fact *being* a Rolex, and to explain the reasonableness of the inference in terms of the audience's assumption that I observe Grice's cooperative principle (see Chapter 8, Pragmatics, in this volume for more details).

Grice's theory of conversational implicatures was originally meant to shield traditional compositional semantics from the difficulty that, given the right circumstances, almost any sentence can be used to get across almost any message. Postulating an intermediate semantic content ("what is said") to be predicted by semantics, from which the ultimate message conveyed can be pragmatically inferred, allows us to maintain the systematicity and compositionality of semantics. However, there is today considerable controversy about the best implementation of Grice's ideas concerning what utterances *say*. Grice originally characterized his notion by saying (i) that what is said is closely related to the conventional meaning of the expressions used, and (ii) that what is implicated by an utterance can be worked out from what has been said, on the assumption that the cooperative principle is being adhered to. Nowadays many theorists doubt that semantic contents can meet both requirements. Some, such as Recanati (2001, 2004), have insisted that what is said by an utterance must be a proposition that is "available" to conscious thought, because it constitutes the input to a "process" of deriving conversational implicatures. As a consequence, these theorists argue, what is said (the semantic content) cannot be predicted by a standard semantic theory such as Kaplan's. In other words, the conventional semantic properties of the words used in an utterance are often not sufficient to determine, together with the Kaplanian context, what has been said by that utterance. Others, such as Bach (2001; Chapter 7 in this volume), have maintained that semantic contents (what is said) *are* predicted by semantic theories, but conclude that these contents (what is said) are often subpropositional or "semantically incomplete". Yet others stick to Grice's original position according to which the conventional meaning of the expressions used in an utterance, as described by the semantics, is sufficient to predict the semantic content (what is said) of the utterance given its Kaplanian context. In order to maintain this, some (Borg 2004; Cappelen and Lepore 2004) claim that there are such things as "minimal contents", while others (Stanley 2000 and Stanley and Szabó 2000) claim that there is more to the sentences used in the utterances in question than their superficial phonetic appearance suggests.

Without the simplifying assumption that semantic theories are directly predictive of our intuitions as to the truth-values of utterances of sentences, there are some deep methodological disagreements amongst semanticists. For there is no consensus as to what exactly "semantic contents" are, whether they are predictable merely on the basis of semantics and context, and how we can track semantic contents on the basis of empirical or quasi-empirical data.

Unarticulated Constituents and Compositionality

Disagreements about the appropriate notion of semantic content or what is said are directly linked to a debate about the question of whether there are so-called "unarticulated constituents" (a notion originating with Perry 1986). Thus, consider an utterance of the sentence "It is raining". Two simultaneous utterances of this sentence can concern different places, A and B, and thus (at least apparently) differ in truth-value. To what do we attribute the difference? It does not seem too promising to say that in fact the two utterances have the same truth-value and that the impression of a difference is created only by a conversational implicature. A more promising option is to claim that the utterances express different semantic contents: one a proposition about A and the other a proposition about B. Now, the defenders of unarticulated constituents (e.g. Carston 2002; Recanati 2004) will claim that no element of the sentence used has this location as its semantic value. This constituent of the semantic content is not "articulated" explicitly by any syntactic element of the expression type used. This view pits them against two different types of opponents. One type of opponent of unarticulated constituents (Stanley and Szabó 2000; Stanley 2000, 2007) will agree that the semantic contents expressed have a location as a constituent. But they claim that the sentence uttered does, at a deep syntactic level ("logical form"), contain a syntactic element that has the location as its semantic content. In this way, the location is, after all, articulated. On this view, the sentence "It is raining" exhibits standard context-sensitivity with respect to the place relevant for each utterance. The other type of opponent would deny that the content expressed has a location as a constituent. Yet another position, which plays hardly any role in this particular debate, would maintain that the semantic content of the two utterances is the same, but that it is a content that is circumstance-sensitive, so that the two different utterances are evaluated differently because the content they share is evaluated differently at the different circumstances of evaluation of each utterance (cf. Predelli 2005).

The contextualists' view that there are unarticulated constituents, i.e. that some constituents of semantic contents (what is said) do not correspond to any constituent of the expression type used, has led them to deny (in line with other deniers of compositionality such as Lahav 1989; Travis 1997) that there can be a compositional semantics, i.e. a theory that allows derivation of the meanings of complex expressions (in context) from the meanings (in context) of their constituent parts (Carston 2002; Recanati 2004; for some criticism see Pagin and Pelletier 2007). More recently one of the contextualists, Recanati, has explained that his semantics still respects certain compositionality constraints, such as for example the constraint that the semantic content of an utterance is determined by the *modulated* meanings of the syntactic parts of the utterance (Recanati 2010a: 44). An emerging minimal consensus about compositionality seems to be that (i) "compositionality" can be defined in many interesting yet significantly different ways and that (ii) meeting *some* compositionality constraints is in the background of any explanation of linguistic creativity (see Szabó 2007, and Pagin and Westerståhl 2010a and 2010b, for overviews and references to the literature).

To summarize, then, there is considerable debate about the nature of semantic contents and therefore about the *kind* of predictions a semantic theory for a natural language should be expected to provide. According to theorists such as Stanley and Szabó, the semantics for a language L provides information about the semantic properties of expressions of L which suffices to predict for each utterance of a sentence of L what its semantic content is, and this content is what has been said by the utterance and represents the starting point for deriving any conversational implicatures. In those cases where it seems that the same sentence is used to express different contents in different utterances without relevant variation in the context, these theorists postulate extra deep syntax and claim that strictly the sentences uttered were indexical in such a way that the variation in context brought about a difference in semantic content. The preferred strategy of another group (minimalists, Borg, Cappelen and Lepore) is to say that, just as the sentence is the same, the semantic content expressed is also the same. The appearance of a difference in semantic content is due to a difference in speech-act content, and speech-act content is largely independent of semantic content. Bach agrees that the sentence used has no hidden structure and determines the same semantic content in both cases, but according to him this content is not fully propositional (not semantically complete), for, on his view, propositions are evaluable in terms of truth (which these stable contents aren't), and semantically complete contents are propositions. Contextualists (Carston, Recanati), again, deny any extra hidden syntactic structure, but they insist that semantic contents are fully propositional and generated by "modulation" or "free enrichment" from sentences whose semantic properties by themselves underdetermine semantic content. A further position (Predelli 2005) tries to avoid all the problems raised by variations of semantic value from one utterance to another by pointing out that a Kaplanian semantics can be successful even if we have not been able to say exactly which sentence-context pairs are representative of, or model, any given utterance.

Contextualism and Relativism

In some areas outside of natural language semantics in a strict sense, questions of context dependence and correct assignment of semantic content, have recently become prominent. In epistemology, the term "contextualism" has a different sense and denotes a much debated view. Epistemological contextualists claim that whether a person can be truly said to know some proposition will depend on certain contextual factors. That is, the very same person with the same beliefs, evidence, information etc. can be truly said to know in one but not in another context of utterance. For example, according to the contextualist, it might be true in most ordinary contexts to say of Peter that he knows that he has hands. But in a context in which a sceptic has raised certain possibilities of error to salience, it's not true to say that he knows. The idea is that whether a thinker knows some proposition is relative to, say, standards of knowledge. Interesting from a semantic point of view is in this connection whether the epistemological contextualist wants to claim that the verb "to know" is to be treated like an indexical, i.e. as expressing a different relation between knowing subject and known proposition in different contexts of use, or whether it is to be treated as expressing the same relation each time, however, a relation that holds in relation to some standards, but not in relation to others. (See, e.g., Cohen 1986; DeRose 1992; Lewis 1996; as well as Hawthorne 2006; Stanley 2007; MacFarlane 2005a).

This debate about the purported context dependence of knowledge claims is motivated by specifically epistemological concerns, namely the problem of knowledge-undermining sceptical arguments. However, structurally similar debates have arisen in different areas, for different philosophical reasons. Thus, metaphysical and epistemological worries of a different kind have led to the view that evaluative claims or judgments of various sorts can be evaluated as true or false only in relation to certain parameters, such as a standard or a perspective (see, e.g., Kölbel 2003; Lasersohn 2005, 2008; Stephenson 2007; Stojanovic 2007; Francén 2007; MacFarlane forthcoming a; compare Chapter 7, Section 3 in this volume). Similarly, in metaphysical discussions about the nature of causation, one position has been to say that whether one event causes another depends on a purpose or contrast (see, e.g., Hitchcock 1996; Woodward 2003; Schaffer 2005, 2011). Again, whether something is possible in the epistemic sense or whether it is probable, is frequently claimed to depend on a state of information (e.g. Price 1983; Egan *et al.* 2005; MacFarlane forthcoming b; Yalcin 2007; Egan 2007, 2011). In each of these cases a semantic debate can be had concerning the precise nature of these dependencies (see Kölbel 2008 for a more detailed overview and some more references to the literature).

The basic data the theorists are trying to account for are very similar to the ones giving rise to debates, discussed above, about the right construal of semantic content: we have different utterances of the same sentence, which seem to receive different evaluations. But the sentence does not seem to be indexical on the surface. Here, as previously, the options are: (i) deny a difference in truth-value and explain the appearance of such a difference in other ways; (ii) concede a difference in truth-value while denying a difference in semantic content, by construing contents as receiving truth-values in relation to an extra factor; or (iii) postulate implicit syntax with indexical elements and thus concede (and explain) a difference in semantic content.

On certain assumptions, this seemingly technical issue in semantics can turn into a profound metaphysical divide. Suppose we say that reality is made up of all the true propositions, i.e. all the facts. Then anti-contextualists in category (i) and contextualists in category (iii) can maintain that reality is objective, that everyone faces the same facts. However, the second of these views will be committed to reality depending on standards for knowledge (standards of taste, explanatory contrasts, states of information, etc.); i.e. that in some areas of thought and speech, the contents of thought and speech do not have absolute truth-values and are not made true or false by objective facts (see Einheuser 2008; Wright 2008).

Reflection on so-called "relativist" approaches along the lines of (ii) have led some theorists to think about what it might be to *assert* a semantic content or proposition that varies in its truth-value not just with a possible world but also with a standard for knowledge, a state of information, a standard of taste, a contrast, and so on. In particular, the question has been raised whether a practice of asserting propositions makes sense if there is no single world, time, standard, state etc. with respect to which assertions will be evaluated as true or false (e.g. Kölbel 2002; MacFarlane 2005b; Recanati 2007; see also Evans 1985). MacFarlane (2003, 2008) has argued that, in the case of utterances concerning the contingent future, the semantic content of an utterance cannot be construed as having an absolute truth-value, roughly because this would conflict with the metaphysical view that the future is genuinely open. What norms, then, govern the practice of asserting such contents? This has also led to renewed interest in what it is to assert, or communicate with, propositions construed as sets of "centred worlds" within a Stalnakerian model of conversation (e.g. Egan 2007; Stalnaker 2008: ch. 3; Torre 2010; Ninan 2010; Einheuser forthcoming; Moss forthcoming; cf. Stalnaker 1978, 2002).

Vagueness and the sorites paradox, a field of research that has received enormous attention in recent years, is also relevant to these debates concerning the correct construal of semantic contents. Contextualists about vagueness propose that vague (i.e. sorites-prone) predicates should be construed as context-dependent in a very specific way, one which explains why it seems to us that a single grain or hair cannot turn a non-heap into a heap, or a bald man into one that isn't bald (Kamp 1981; Raffman 1996; Soames 1999; Shapiro 2006; Fara 2000, 2008). Some have construed this context-dependence as a kind of indexicality (Soames 1999), others have strenuously denied this (Raffman 2005; cf. Stanley 2003). Others have proposed "vague propositions" in analogy with tensed or contingent propositions, i.e. approach (ii) above (e.g. Kölbel 2011). A closely related field of enquiry within linguistics is the semantics of gradable adjectives, where the exact nature of the context-dependence of such adjective is discussed (e.g. Szabó 2001; Kennedy 1999).

Methodological and Foundational Uncertainties

Neither in philosophy of language and semantics of natural languages more narrowly construed, nor in other fields of philosophy with related interests, is there a consensus about a basic semantic framework within which to anchor claims about semantic content. It is therefore not surprising that, increasingly, theorists begin to make explicit their methodological assumptions about the theoretical aim of semantics and the framework within which to conduct it. Many, probably most, theorists operate with the assumption that semantic theories for natural languages *in some sense* model the competence of speakers of that language, and the minimum consensus about what competence involves seems to be knowledge of the conditions under which a sentence (in context) would be true (see Chapter 4, Theories of Meaning and Truth Conditions). In Barbara Partee's words: "semantic competence is widely considered to consist in knowledge of truth-conditions and entailment relations of sentences of the language" (Partee 2011: section 2). However, there is considerable variation as to any additional aspects of competence that semantic theories are to model.

Some, more traditionally minded, semanticists afford a fairly minimal role to semantics: all semantics does is predict or explain literal truth or correctness of utterances of sentences, as judged by competent speakers under idealized conditions of omniscience of the circumstances of utterance (e.g. Carnap 1955; Lewis 1980; Stanley 2007: Introduction). On this view, there would be little to choose between semantic theories that predict the same truth-conditions, except perhaps elegance or explanatory convenience. Others go further and claim that semantic theories are quite literally "known" by a mental faculty, the language module (Larson and Segal 1995). Some go so far as to hypothesize that semantic theories have "psychological reality" and should be viewed as detailed models of psychological processes of interpreting language. Carston (2002) explores the hypothesis that semantic theories model interpretive brain processes in such a way that they predict comparative processing speeds. Recanati (2004) claims that certain stages of utterance interpretation are "available" to consciousness. Paul Pietroski (2011) takes the cognitive conception of semantics much further in that he claims that the traditional truth-conditional conception of semantics has little value in empirical semantics. There is a further contrast between those who emphasize a dependence on current linguistic theory (Higginbotham 1985; Larson and Segal 1995; Heim and Kratzer 1998; Pietroski 2003; Stanley 2007) and those who envisage a more aprioristic approach for semantics (e.g.

Katz 1985; Soames 1985; Devitt 2003). For more details see Chapter 2, On the Nature of Language in this volume.

As reported above (Chapter 5, Reference), a new approach to method has also led some philosophers to question the so-called causal theory of reference, which had for a long time enjoyed the status of orthodoxy. Some philosophers have suggested that certain non-Western populations do not share the intuitions on which Kripke's famous arguments were based (see Machery *et al.* 2004). They have tried to establish this by experimental, i.e. questionnaire, methods. Moreover, they have found that there is a high degree of divergence even within the same cultural group (Machery *et al.* 2009). This novel methodology is by no means widely accepted, nor is the interpretation of the results of these experiments (see Chapter 5 in this volume, and also Hansen & Chemla forthcoming). However, the discussion is another manifestation of a new readiness to probe methodological assumptions.

Other Developments

This brings me to another relatively new development: independently of the challenges posed by the new experimental philosophers just mentioned, the current of those who want to resist Kripke's landmark arguments against "descriptivism" has grown. Even if this is not a mass movement, several philosophers have consistently taken up Dummett's line of resistance to Kripke and have developed forms of "causal descriptivism", the view that all expressions, including proper names, do express some minimal descriptive content – even if not the type of descriptive content that Kripke was envisaging. The suggestion, for example, is that the semantic content of a use of a name such as "John Smith" can be expressed by "the man who is at the beginning or source of the name-using practice to which this token of 'John Smith' belongs" (see, e.g., Stanley 1997; Noonan 2001; García-Carpintero 2006). In some cases this descriptivist view is part of a more general outlook that tries to revive and develop Frege's and Carnap's views on analyticity and apriority (e.g. Chalmers 2002, 2010). Similarly, opponents of Direct Reference theories of singular thought (see again Chapter 5, above) have been developing "latitudinarian" views of singular thought, as for example Sosa 1970, 1995, and Hawthorne and Manley (forthcoming).

This is not to say that the dominant view does not continue to be one that assigns a special non-descriptive role to a certain class of singular terms that includes proper names and demonstratives. These views are also being developed further, for example in Sainsbury 2005; Soames 2005; Recanati 2010b; Jeshion 2010.

These are some of the areas in which philosophers of language have recently been active, and in which no doubt we will see further developments in coming years. There are also many other areas of lively research activity in the philosophy of language that I have not been able to survey here, such as discussions of non-truth-conditional aspects of meaning (see, e.g., David Kaplan (ms)), the nature of presupposition (see, e.g., Schlenker 2009; von Fintel 2008), conventional implicature (see, e.g., Potts 2007), Davidson's programme (see, e.g., Lepore and Ludwig 2005), and dynamic semantics (see, e.g., Beaver 2001).

Note

1. The title of this chapter smacks of crystal ball gazing: pronouncing on which topics and views are currently fashionable, and where the spotlight of fashion might move next. It is true that I have not carried out a statistical analysis of recent research in philosophy of language, nor have I used any other systematic methods in arriving at a judgment of what might be the directions in which the philosophy of language is currently moving. Instead, what I will be doing is make some observations on some recent developments in the philosophy of language, developments that seem to me to reflect certain general trends. However, I claim neither authority nor objectivity nor exhaustiveness for my particular selection of focus. I am grateful to Manuel García-Carpintero for his help with parts of this chapter. The research leading to these results was supported by MICINN, Spanish Government, I+D+i programme, grant FFI2009-13436 and also CONSOLIDER INGENIO Programme, grant CSD2009-0056, as well as the European FP7 programme, grant no. 238128.

References

Bach, Kent (2001), "You Don't Say?", *Synthese* 128, 15–44.

Beaver, David (2001), *Presupposition and Assertion in Dynamic Semantics*. Stanford: CSLI.

Borg, Emma (2004), *Minimal Semantics*, Oxford: Oxford University Press.

Cappelen, Herman and Ernie Lepore (2004), *Insensitive Semantics*, Oxford: Blackwell.

Carnap, Rudolf (1955), "Meaning and Synonymy in Natural Languages", *Philosophical Studies* 6, 33–47.

Carston, Robyn (2002), *Thoughts and Utterances*, Oxford: Blackwell.

Chalmers, David J. (2002), "On Sense and Intension", *Philosophical Perspectives* 16, 135–82.

—(2010), "Constructing the World", The John Locke Lectures, delivered at the University of Oxford in May 2010. Available online at http://www.philosophy.ox.ac.uk/lectures/john_locke_lectures/past_lectures/

Cohen, Stewart (1986), "Knowledge and Context", *The Journal of Philosophy* 83, 574–83.

DeRose, Keith (1992), "Contextualism and Knowledge Attributions", *Philosophy and Phenomenological Research* 52, 913–29.

Devitt, Michael (2003), "Linguistics Is Not Psychology", in A. Barber ed. *Epistemology of Language*, Oxford: Oxford University Press, pp. 107–39.

Egan, Andy (2007), "Epistemic Modals, Relativism and Assertion", *Philosophical Studies* 133, 1–22.

—(2011), "Relativism about Epistemic Modals", in Steven D. Hales ed. *A Companion to Relativism*, Oxford: Blackwell.

Egan, A., J. Hawthorne and B. Weatherson (2005), "Epistemic Modals in Context", in G. Preyer and G. Peter (eds), *Contextualism in Philosophy*, Oxford: Oxford University Press, pp. 131–70.

Einheuser, Iris (2008), "Three Forms of Truth-Relativism", in Manuel Garcia-Carpintero and Max Kölbel (eds), *Relative Truth*, Oxford: Oxford University Press.

—(forthcoming), "Relativized Propositions and the Fregean Orthodoxy", *Philosophy and Phenomenological Research.*

Evans, Gareth (1985), "Does Tense Logic Rest on a Mistake?", in his *Collected Papers*, Oxford: Clarendon Press, pp. 341–63.

Fara, Delia Graff (2000), "Shifting Sands: An Interest-Relative Theory of Vagueness", *Philosophical Topics* 28, 45–81.

—(2008), "Profiling Interest Relativity", *Analysis* 68, 326–35.

Fintel, Kai von (2008), "What Is Presupposition Accommodation, Again?", *Philosophical Perspectives* 22, 137–70.

Francén, Ragnar (2007), *Metaethical Relativism: Against the Single Analysis Assumption.* Dissertation, University of Gothenburg.

García-Carpintero, Manuel (2006), "Two-Dimensional Semantics: A Neo-Fregean Interpretation", in M. García-Carpintero and J. Macià (eds), *Two-Dimensional Semantics*, Oxford: Oxford University Press, pp. 181–204.

García-Ramírez, Eduardo and Marilyn Shatz (2011), "On Problems with Descriptivism: Psychological Assumptions and Empirical Evidence", *Mind & Language*, 26, 53–77.

Grice, Paul (1989), *Studies in the Way of Words*, Cambridge, MA: Harvard University Press.

Hansen, Nathaniel and Emmanuel Chemla (forthcoming). "Experimenting on Contextualism".

Hawthorne, John (2006), *Knowledge and Lotteries*. Oxford: Oxford University Press.

Hawthorne, John and David Manley (forthcoming), *The Reference Book*, Oxford: Oxford University Press.

Heim, Irene and Angelika Kratzer (1998), *Semantics in Generative Grammar*, Oxford: Blackwell.

Higginbotham, James (1985), "On Semantics", *Linguistic Inquiry* 16, 547–93.

Hitchcock, Christopher Read (1996), "The Role of Contrast in Causal and Explanatory Claims", *Synthese* 107, 395–419.

Jeshion, Robin (2010), "Singular Thought: Acquaintance Semantic Instrumentalism and Cognitivism", in Robin Jeshion ed. *New Essays on Singular Thought*, Oxford: Oxford University Press, pp. 105–40.

Kamp, Hans (1971), "Formal Properties of 'Now'", *Theoria* 37, 227–74.

—(1981), "The Paradox of the Heap", in U. Mönnich ed. *Aspects of Philosophical Logic*, Dordrecht: Reidel, pp. 225–77.

Kaplan, D. (1977), "On Demonstratives", in J. Almog, J. Perry and H. Wettstein (eds), *Themes from Kaplan* (1989), Oxford: Oxford University Press, pp. 481–563.

Kaplan, David (nd), "The Meaning of 'Oops' and 'Ouch'". Unpublished ms.

Katz, Jerrold J. (1985), "Outline of a Platonist Grammar", in J. Katz ed. *The Philosophy of Linguistics*, Oxford: Oxford University Press, pp. 172–203.

Kennedy, Christopher (1999), *Projecting the Adjective: The Syntax and Semantics of Gradability and Comparison*, New York: Garland Press.

King, Jeffrey (2003), "Tense, Modality, and Semantic Values", *Philosophical Perspectives* 17, 195–245.

Kölbel, Max (2002), *Truth Without Objectivity*, London: Routledge.

—(2003), "Faultless Disagreement", *Proceedings of the Aristotelian Society* 104, 53–73.

—(2008), "Motivations for Relativism", in Manuel Garcia-Carpintero and Max Kölbel (eds), *Relative Truth*, Oxford: Oxford University Press, pp. 1–38.

—(2011), "Vagueness as Semantic", in R. Dietz and S. Moruzzi (eds), *Cuts and Clouds: Issues in the Philosophy of Vagueness*, Oxford: Oxford University Press, pp. 304–26.

Lahav, Ran (1989), "Against Compositionality: The Case of Adjectives", *Philosophical Studies* 57, 261–79.

Larson, Richard and Gabriel Segal (1995), *Knowledge of Meaning*, Cambridge, MA: MIT Press.

Lasersohn, Peter (2005), "Context Dependence, Disagreement, and Predicates of Personal Taste", *Linguistics and Philosophy* 28, 643–86.

—(2008), "Quantification and Perspective in Relativist Semantics", *Philosophical Perspectives* 22, 305–37.

Lepore, Ernest and Kirk Ludwig (2005), *Donald Davidson. Meaning, Truth, Language and Reality*, Oxford: Oxford University Press.

Lewis, David (1980), Index, Context, and Content, in Stig Kanger and Sven Öhman (eds), *Philosophy and Grammar*, Dordrecht: Reidel. Reprinted in David Lewis, *Papers in Philosophical Logic*, Cambridge: Cambridge University Press, 1998.

—(1996), "Elusive Knowledge", *Australasian Journal of Philosophy* 74, 549–67.

—(1998), *Papers in Philosophical Logic*, Cambridge: Cambridge University Press.

MacFarlane, John (2003), "Future Contingents and Relative Truth", *Philosophical Quarterly* 53, 321–36.

—(2005a), "The Assessment Sensitivity of Knowledge Attributions", in Tamar Szabo Gendler and John Hawthorne (eds), *Oxford Studies in Epistemology* 1, Oxford: Oxford University Press, pp. 197—233.

—(2005b), "Making Sense of Relative Truth", *Proceedings of the Aristotelian Society* 105, 321–39.

—(2008), "Truth in the Garden of Forking Paths", in Max Kölbel and Manuel García-Carpintero (eds), *Relative Truth*, Oxford: Oxford University Press.

—(forthcoming a), *Assessment sensitivity: relative truth and its applications*.

—(forthcoming b), "Epistemic Modals are Assessment-Sensitive", in Brian Weatherson and Andy Egan (eds), *Epistemic Modals*, Oxford: Oxford University Press.

Machery, E., Christopher Y. Olivola and Molly De Blanc (2009), "Linguistic and metalinguistic intuitions in the philosophy of language", *Analysis*, 69, 689–94.

Machery, E., R. Mallon, S. Nichols and S. Stich (2004), "Semantics cross-cultural style", *Cognition* 92, B1–B12.

Mallon, R., E. Machery, S. Nichols and S. Stich (2009), "Against arguments from referente", *Philosophy and Phenomenological Research*, 79, 332–56.

Martí, Genoveva (2009), "Against Semantic Multi-Culturalism", *Analysis* 69, 42–8.

Moss, Sarah (forthcoming), "Updating as Communication", *Philosophy and Phenomenological Research*.

Ninan, Dilip (2010), "De Se Attitudes: Ascription and Communication", *Philosophy Compass* 5, 551–67.

Noonan, Harold (2001), *Frege: a Critical Introduction*, Cambridge: Polity.

Pagin, Peter and Dåg Westerståhl (2010a), "Compositionality: Definitions and Variants", *Philosophy Compass* 5, 250–64.

—(2010b), "Compositionality: Arguments and Problems", *Philosophy Compass* 5, 265–82.

Pagin, Peter and Jeff Pelletier (2007), "Content, Context and Composition", in G. Peter and G. Preyer (eds), *Content and Context. Essays on Semantics and Pragmatics*, Oxford: Oxford University Press, pp. 25–62.

Partee, Barbara (2011), "Formal Semantics", in Patrick Colm Hogan ed. *The Cambridge Encyclopedia of the Language Sciences*, Cambridge: Cambridge University Press.

Perry, J. (1986), "Thought without Representation", *Proceedings of the Aristotelian Society, supplementary volume* 60, 137–52. Reprinted in J. Perry, *The Essential Indexical and Other Essays*, Oxford: Oxford University Press, 1993.

Pietroski, Paul (2003), "The Character of Natural Language Semantics", in Alex Barber ed. *The Epistemology of Language*, Oxford: Oxford University Press.

—(2011), "Minimal Semantic Instructions", in Cedric Boeckx ed. *Oxford Handbook of Linguistic Minimalism*, Oxford: Oxford University Press.

Potts, Christopher (2007), "Conventional Implicature: A Distinguished Class of Meanings", in G. Ramchand and Ch. Reiss (eds), *Oxford Handbook of Linguistic Interfaces*, Oxford: Oxford University Press, pp. 475–501.

Predelli, Stefano (2005), *Context: Meaning, Truth and the Use of Language*, Oxford: Oxford University Press.

Price, Huw (1983), "Does 'probably' modify Sense?", *Australasian Journal of Philosophy* 61, 396–408.

Quine, Willard Van Orman (1960), *Word and Object*. Cambridge, MA: MIT Press.

Raffman, Diana (1996), "Vagueness and Context Relativity", *Philosophical Studies* 81 175–92.

—(2005), "How to Understand Contextualism about Vagueness: Reply to Stanley". *Analysis* 65, 244–8.

Recanati, François (2001), "What is Said", *Synthese* 128, 75–91.

—(2004), *Literal Meaning*, Cambridge: Cambridge University Press.

—(2007), *Perspectival Thought*, Oxford: Oxford University Press.

—(2010a), *Truth-conditional Pragmatics*, Oxford: Oxford University Press.

—(2010b), "Singular Thought: in Defence of Acquaintance", in Robin Jeshion ed. *New Essays on Singular Thought*, Oxford: Oxford University Press, pp. 141–89.

Sainsbury, Mark (2005), *Reference without Referents*, Oxford: Oxford University Press.

Schaffer, Jonathan (2005), "Contrastive Causation", *Philosophical Review* 114, 327–58.

—(2011), "Causal Contextualisms", in Martijn Blaauw ed. *Contrastivism in Philosophy*, London: Routledge.

Schaffer, Jonathan and Joshua Knobe (forthcoming), "Contrastivism Surveyed", *Noûs*.

Schlenker, Philippe (2009), "Local Contexts", *Semantics & Pragmatics* 2, 1–78.

Shapiro, Stewart (2006), *Vagueness in Context*, Oxford: Oxford University Press.

Soames, Scott (1985), "Semantics and Psychology", in J. Katz ed. *The Philosophy of Linguistics*, Oxford: Oxford University Press, pp. 204–26.

—(1999), *Understanding Truth*, Oxford: Oxford University Press.

—(2005), *Reference and Descriptions: The Case against Two-Dimensionalism*. Princeton, NJ: Princeton University Press.

Sosa, Ernest (1970), "Propositional Attitudes De Dicto and De Re", *Journal of Philosophy* 67, 883–96.

—(1995), "Fregean Reference Defended", *Philosophical Issues* 6, 91–9.

Stalnaker, Robert (1978), "Assertion", in P. Cole ed. *Syntax and Semantics*, ix. *Pragmatics*, 315–22.

—(2002), "Common Ground", *Linguistics and Philosophy* 25, 701–21.

—(2008), *Our Knowledge of the Internal World*, Oxford: Oxford University Press.

Stanley, Jason (1997), "Names and Rigid Designation", in Bob Hale and Crispin Wright (eds), *A Companion to the Philosophy of Language*, Oxford: Blackwell, pp. 555–85.

—(2000), "Context and Logical Form", *Linguistics & Philosophy* 23: 391–434.

—(2003), "Context, Interest Relativity and the Sorites", *Analysis* 63, 269–81.

—(2006), *Knowledge and Practical Interests*, Oxford: Oxford University Press.

—(2007), *Language in Context: Selected Essays*, Oxford: Oxford University Press.

Stanley, Jason and Zoltan Szabó (2000), "On Quantifier Domain Restriction", *Mind and Language* 15, 219–61.

Stephenson, Tamina (2007), "Judge dependence, epistemic modals, and predicates of personal taste", *Linguistics and Philosophy* 30, 487–525.

Stojanovic, Isidora (2007), "Talking about Taste: Disagreement, Implicit Arguments and Relative Truth", *Linguistics and Philosophy* 30: 691–706.

Szabó, Zoltán (2001), "Adjectives in Context", in R. Harnish and I. Kenesei (eds), *Perspectives on Semantics, Pragmatics, and Discourse*, Amsterdam: John Benjamins, pp. 119–46.

—(2007), "Compositionality", in E.N. Zalta ed. *The Stanford encyclopedia of philosophy*. Available online at http://plato.stanford.edu/entries/compositionality/

—(2010), "The Determination of Content", *Philosophical Studies* 148, 253–72.

Torre, Stephan (2010), "Centered Assertion", *Philosophical Studies* 150, 97–114.

Travis, Charles (1997), "Pragmatics", in Bob Hale and Crispin Wright (eds), *A Companion to the Philosophy of Language*, Oxford: Blackwell.

Woodward, James (2003), *Making Things Happen: A Theory of Causal Explanation*, Oxford: Oxford University Press.

Wright, Crispin (2008), "Relativism about Truth Itself", in Manuel García-Carpintero and Max Kölbel (eds), *Relative Truth*, Oxford: Oxford University Press.

Yalcin, Seth (2007), "Epistemic Modals", *Mind* 116, 983–1026.

A–Z of Key Terms

The proper characterization of many of the following notions is controversial. Here we only purport to give the reader an initial impression of what the relevant notion is intended to encompass.

a priori vs. a posteriori (or empirical) knowledge: One has *a posteriori* or empirical knowledge of one's weight or the colour of the clothes people around one are wearing. *A priori* knowledge is supposed to be knowledge that we have without thus relying on experience, perceptual or even introspective. Usual candidates are the knowledge that every object is identical to itself, that two plus three equals five, or that no surface can be both red all over and green all over.

analytic vs. synthetic: *Analytic* statements are supposed to be statements true in virtue of the meaning of some of the constituent terms of the sentences with which they are made, and known to be so on the basis of understanding such terms. Purported examples are *all vixens are female foxes* or *all bodies are extended*. *Synthetic* statements are non-analytic ones.

bivalence: The view that propositions are either true or false, with no third alternative, even propositions that are contents of **vague** statements, statements with **empty names**, or about a possibly indeterminate **contingent future**.

causal-historical chain of communication: One's ability to use terms such as "Gustave Flaubert" or "bouillabaisse" or "palm tree" is acquired, through a specific causal process, from one's fellow speakers. The same applies, in turn, to the ability of those other speakers, and so on. In this way we can ideally trace different histories of use back to events in which those terms were first introduced for their use in linguistic communication ("initial baptisms"; events such as the ones in which, say, *iPhones* or newborns or pet animals acquire their names. This series of interconnected language users that goes back from a given use of a term to the original introduction of the term is called a "causal-historical chain".

causal theory of reference: The view that causal relations – such as *causal-historical chains of communication* – determine what uses of terms refer to; it contrasts with the **descriptivist** view that the reference is determined by identifying knowledge of the referents that competent speakers have, because the reference-determining causal relations are not supposed to be known by competent speakers.

(subjunctive) conditional: It is a common emotion to regret some things that happened, and to wish that they had been different; we typically express it by means of statements such as "if I had remembered to take my passport, I would not have missed the flight". These are *subjunctive conditionals*, in contrast with indicative conditionals such as "if he did not remember to take his passport, he had time enough to go back home and pick it up". Subjunctive conditionals are sometimes called "counterfactual conditionals", but the antecedent need not express anything contrary to fact: predictions are sometimes expressed by means of these conditionals, even when the antecedent is actually satisfied: "if he had caught measles, he would show exactly those symptoms".

compositionality: When we encounter a word for the first time, we have to look it up in the dictionary, or otherwise find out its meaning. However, much more frequently than we are aware of, we encounter sentences or phrases that we have never heard before, whose meanings we have no difficulty whatsoever in understanding. This seems to suggest that, while particular words or lexical items get their meaning, as it were, one by one, compound phrases and sentences get their meaning from the meaning of the constituent expressions and the syntactic manner of composition.

content (semantic, propositional): Utterances, given their linguistic meaning, allow us to perform different **speech-acts**, such as orders, promises or claims; some of them – as when one tells Peter, "Peter, return the book to the library today", when Peter replies "I promise I'll return the book to the library today", and an observer contends "Peter will return the book to the library today" – appear to represent things in the same way. This *content* or *proposition* potentially represented by different speech-acts (and also by different mental attitudes) is of course not something that must obtain in the actual world, for the order or the promise might well not be satisfied, and the claim might not be true, and still they would represent things in the same way; it is common to think of it as a **truth-condition**, *a condition that the world must meet*, for the order and the promise to be satisfied, or the claim to be true.

contextualism (about knowledge, in debates about semantic contents, etc.): Although there is a sense in which utterances of "I am hungry", made by different subjects, share a common meaning, it is natural to think that their **semantic content** is not the same: one may be true in complete independence of the other, because they represent different things; the conditions that should obtain in the world for each to be true are *prima facie* independent of each other.

In the example, it is natural to think that the expressions responsible for this are "I", and the present tense of the verb, which are context-dependent expressions: their contribution to **semantic content** depends on the *context* in which they are used, on who the speaker is in the context in the case of "I" or what the time of the context is in the case of the present tense. A contextualist view about a given piece of discourse purports to detect instances of context dependence in unexpected places. Thus, contextualists about "to know" contend that "Peter knows that the bank is open on Saturdays" expresses different semantic contents in different contexts, allowing for differences in truth-value; thus, in one context it may be the claim that Peter knows in-a-way-that-requires-very-little-evidence that the bank is open on Saturdays, and is thus true; in another that Peter knows it in-a-way-that-requires-very-strong-evidence, and hence is false.

contingent: Propositions (the contents of thought or speech) can be true or false depending on the state of the world. Some of these propositions are necessarily true, they cannot fail to obtain: e.g., (putting aside matters of vagueness) that *either there are at most two phones on the table, or there are three or more phones on the table*. Other propositions obtain, but not necessarily so, they might have failed to obtain: e.g., that *there are at most two phones on the table*. The latter are *contingent* propositions. In an extended sense, it is sometimes said that a being is necessary, when the proposition that it exists is necessary, or contingent, when that proposition is true, but not necessarily so.

convention: Some regularities in the behaviour of a group are essentially sustained by the (perhaps tacit) agreement of its members, because, although they serve a coordination function useful for the group, some alternative regularity might have been equally serviceable. Such regularities can be called "conventions". The agreement need not have been explicit, but might have been tacitly adopted after the group somehow stumbled on the regularity: the *convention* of driving on a particular side of the road might have been adopted in such a way.

conversational maxim: As Grice pointed out in elaborating his theory of *conversational* **implicatures**, conversations are rational activities, which are thereby subject to norms or principles determining when they are pursued rationally. Grice identified a "supermaxim", or more general regulating "cooperative principle": *Make your conversational contribution such as is required, at the stage at which it occurs, by the accepted purpose or direction of the talk exchange in which you are engaged*; and several submaxims developing further this general principle in ways more adequate for specific conversations, in particular those consisting of exchanges of information. One of these submaxims, however, sounds almost as general as the cooperative principle: Be relevant!

creativity: When it comes to language mastery, Chomsky and others have used "creativity" to refer to the fact, that we are able to produce and understand sentences and phrases we have never come across before. This fact is often taken as evidence for **compositionality**. The term can also be properly used to refer to our capacity to give to our sentences meanings they do not conventionally have, and to understand them when other speakers do so, as with metonymy and metaphor, conversational **implicatures** and indirect **speech-acts**.

denotation: Russell introduced this term in his discussion of *denoting phrases*, such as "every man", "a man", "the king of France", etc.; and some people reserve it for the entity satisfying a definite **description** (Neil Armstrong in the case of "the first person to set foot on the Moon"), but nowadays it is mostly used as synonymous with "**extension**".

descriptivism: The view that (uses of) names and other referential expressions, like indexicals such as "he" or "that book", are meaningful through their association with definite descriptions such as *the first heavenly body seen at dusk in the western sky*, or "the first person to set foot on the Moon", which identify their referent among all possible candidates. The "association" might be as tight as synonymy, or merely *reference-fixing* without synonymy.

determiner: A syntactic category of expressions including the definite article "the" and quantifiers such as "every", "some", "most", "the", etc. Determiners combine with common nouns to form noun phrases, as in "most dogs" or "some man".

direct reference: A claim such as *the capital of any democratic country is the seat of its parliament* is about Washington DC, but only indirectly so; the semantic **content** of the claim directly involves only properties such as *being a democratic country*, *being a capital*, plus the contribution of **determiners** such as *any* or *the*. Direct reference is the view that claims made with proper names and indexicals are directly about their referents, in that, even if those expressions are somehow associated with definite descriptions, it is the referents themselves, and not the properties expressed by such descriptions, that identify the **contents**.

double index semantics: Semantic **contents** are typically conditions that obtain in some **possible worlds** and not in others; they can thus be represented as functions from indexes (possible worlds) to truth-values. An assertion of one of these contents is true if the function yields truth when applied to the actual world, the value for the index supplied by the context in which the sentence is uttered. Operators such as *it is **possible** that* or *it is **necessary** that* change the index of evaluation: "possibly, snow is blue" (or, more simply, "snow might have been blue") is true of the actual world supplied by the context if *snow is blue* is true of some world, in this case a different one. Some expressions in the same category (modal expressions in this case), however, do not take their value from the index relative to which they are being evaluated as they appear embedded in a sentence, but always from the value provided by the context of utterance for the index. Thus, consider "actually" in "it is possible that snow is blue, even though snow is not actually blue". This is true of the actual world, as before, if *snow is blue, even though snow is not actually blue* is true with respect to some world *w*, again in this case not the actual one. However, to properly evaluate the part *snow is not actually blue*, we cannot consider the value that *snow is not blue* has with respect to *w*; we must establish the value it has with respect to *the actual world*, the value provided by the context of utterance. Something similar happens with temporal indexicals such as "now" or "today", if we treat contents of atomic sentences as functions from worlds and times to truth-values, and tenses such as the past or the future as operators over them: we need to keep track of the time of the context, because "now" or "today" are always interpreted relative to it, as shown by examples such as "some day it will be the case that the colour of snow is blue, although today (now) it is not blue". Dealing with these examples requires that our **semantics** has not just one index for the world or the time of evaluation, but two: one shiftable by operators such as "possibly" or "it will be the case that", another given by the context of utterance required to interpret indexicals such as "actually" and "now" no matter where they appear embedded in a complex sentence.

empiricism (logical, radical): Empiricists in general take perceptual experience and introspection as the fundamental source of knowledge and evidence, deflating the role of reason and *a priori* knowledge; most researchers in the "logical empiricism" movement starting around the Vienna Circle in the 1920s followed Carnap in accepting a special category of logical and mathematical truths, but they tried to explain them as *analytic* truths resulting from linguistic stipulations or **conventions**. Others follow Quine's more radical view, rejecting the category of *a priori* or *analytic* truths and knowledge altogether.

empty names: Names such as "Vulcan" or "Sherlock Holmes" that lack the kind of referent (**extension** or **denotation**) in the physical world that "Venus" or "Benjamin Franklin" do have (although, on some views, they do have referents, extensions or denotations, of a more abstract kind).

experimental semantics (pragmatics, philosophy): Linguists take for granted that speakers, they themselves in particular, have linguistic intuitions that are reliable indicators of the properties of the languages they investigate, and thus they typically rely on their own intuitions in setting up, confirming or disconfirming their theories. Experimental semantics is the resort to the empirically refined methodologies that psychologists, neurologists and cognitive scientists have devised in recent years to study in a more systematic way data for semantic theories – for instance, data about the truth-value of utterances relative to different situations. Experimental pragmatics does the same for data about **conversational implicatures**, **presuppositions**, **speech-acts**, etc.; experimental philosophy, for data relevant for philosophical accounts of knowledge, reference, moral value and obligation, etc.

extension: In providing a **compositional** characterization of the meaning contribution of sentential connectives such as "and", "or", "if … then …", Frege and Russell found that we should assume that sentences signify their truth-values, the True and the False on **bivalent** assumptions (they were considering formal languages, but they had in view at least some uses of those expressions in their natural languages). Similarly, in providing an account of the contribution of **quantifiers** such as "every", "some", etc., they found that we should assume that predicates such as "is a man" or "is Greek" signify their extensions, the class of objects (perhaps in a given domain of objects) of which they are true, and singular terms such as "Barack Obama" or "he" or even perhaps "the first man landing on the Moon", the objects to which they refer. Truth-values, extensions (in a domain) and referents are the extensions of sentences, predicates and singular terms, respectively; these expressions may of course have additional semantic values, but they are assigned extensions of the kind indicated in any promising semantic theory.

first-order logic (predicate logic): The logic of logical constants including the sentential connectives "not", "and", "if then", the quantifiers "for all" and "for some", and identity; i.e., the delineation of the class of validities determined by the meaning of such expressions, such as "all Greeks admire some poet, Socrates is Greek, therefore Socrates admires some poet".

formal language: A language whose syntax and semantics has been explicitly specified, using the resources of some mathematical metatheory such as set theory. The language of **first-order logic** is a good example.

formal semantic theory: A semantic theory that uses *formal languages* as idealized models ("frictionless planes") for natural languages, in the hope of thus making more perspicuous its essential semantic properties, abstracting away from semantically irrelevant features.

foundational vs. descriptive semantics: A *descriptive* semantics purports to characterize the semantic properties of a given language, mostly trying to perspicuously characterize its **compositional** structure: the **semantic values** of its lexical items, those of their relevant structural rules, and how they combine for complex expressions to have their resulting values. A *foundational* semantics purports to explain why a given language in fact has the descriptive semantics it does have (whether in virtue of **conventions** its speakers follow, in virtue of some intentions of its speakers, in virtue of deep properties of their mind/ brain, etc.).

Fregeanism: Frege defended different views, on the nature of numbers and of arithmetic in general, on logic, etc., and thus there are different forms of Fregeanism; but in philosophy of language contexts it usually refers to a **descriptivist** conception of reference.

illocutionary force: In **speech-acts**, **contents** are put forward with different constitutive *purposes*, *goals*, *points* or *forces*: as the content of an *assertion*, an *order*, a *promise* or a *request*. Not just any purpose that may be the point of a speech-act is an illocutionary force, for many purposes ("perlocutionary" ones) are not essential or constitutive of the speech-act as such, as for instance *frightening* the audience or *impressing* them.

implicature (conversational-, conventional-, generalized-): Technical term introduced by H.P. Grice. In making speech-acts, we sometimes convey or implicate contents additional to those constituting the **semantic content** of the expressions we issue; to use Grice's famous example, if in writing a letter of reference for a philosophy job one just says that the candidate is polite and has good handwriting, we convey that we do not take him or her to be commendable for the job. This is a *conversational implicature*, "particularized" in that it is essentially conveyed by particular utterances of the context. Appealing to his theory of implicatures (which essentially appeals to **conversational maxims**), Grice suggested that the natural language "and" has the same **semantic content** as its counterpart in **first-order logic**, and thus semantically lacks temporal implications: "he got sick and he took a pill" is synonymous with "he took a pill and he got sick"; the temporal implication is also a conversational implicature, in this case conveyed in almost any context and to that extent generalized. Finally, Grice suggested that "and" and "but" have the same semantic content; the implication in "p but q" that the truth of p is in some tension with that of q, absent in "p and q", is also an extra-semantic implicature, although in this case one conventionally associated with the expression. Recently different writers have made similar claims about pejoratives: "boche" would have the same semantic content as "German", the additional derogatory aspects being a conventional implicature.

indexical: An expression such as "I", "he" or "now", which yields a semantic content relative to properties of the **context** in which it is used. See **double index semantics** for some more details.

inferential role: A pattern of inferences associated with a given expression, perhaps as a matter of its meaning. For instance, the introduction rule (from p on the one hand and q on the other, infer p & q) and elimination rule (from p & q, infer p; from p & q, infer q) associated with **first-order logic** conjunction.

intension: Semantic theory must ascribe **extensions** to expressions. Expressions have different extensions with respect to different **possible worlds**; the intension of an expression is a function from worlds to extensions, which are also required for semantic purposes such as the account of the **modal** operators of **necessity**, **possibility** or **contingency**.

is–ought distinction: It is often thought that *normative* or *prescriptive* conclusions cannot be validly derived from purely *descriptive* premises. In other words, claims or judgments about what someone *ought* to do do not follow deductively or conceptually from claims or judgments about *what is the case as a matter of fact*. In a famous passage (*Treatise* III, I, I, 27), Hume articulates this principle by stating that *is* and *ought* are distinct relations, and that the latter does not follow by deduction from the former. Hence the term "is–ought distinction". → **naturalistic fallacy**

literal meaning: What an expression literally means on an occasion can be contrasted with what is communicated, for example, metaphorically, indirectly, ironically, as a conversational implicature, etc. Thus, when someone says "I have nothing to wear", they do not usually wish to convey that they have literally nothing whatsoever that they can wear, which is what their words literally mean. Rather, they are conveying something non-literally, e.g. that they don't have anything suitable to wear for the upcoming occasion, etc. This intuitive difference between literal and non-literal use of language is sometimes given a more specific theoretical role in theories about language, cf. Recanati's book *Literal Meaning* (2004).

mass term: Mass terms or mass nouns are used only in the singular. Examples: "milk", "gold", "pepper"; they typically apply to proper parts of what they apply to, proper parts thereof, and so on. They contrast with count nouns, such as "chair" or "tiger".

meaning theory: A theory that predicts or explains the meaning of linguistic expressions, i.e. those of their properties that allow one to communicate with them. One can distinguish between the theory of meaning in general, i.e. the study of linguistic meaning in abstraction of any particular language, and a theory of meaning for a particular language, such as Catalan or Swedish. A theory of meaning for a particular language is a theory that contains the information needed for understanding the language. General insights about what individual theories of meaning for particular languages would need to say will amount to insights about linguistic meaning in general.

modality (metaphysical, epistemic, deontic): In addition to allowing us to say how things are, many languages allow one to say how things can or might be, or how things cannot fail to be or must be. In the first case, one states a *possibility*, in the second, a *necessity*. Possibility and necessity are called "modalities", and languages that can express these are called "modal". Philosophers distinguish different species of necessity and possibility: it is physically possible that *p*, just if it is compatible with the laws of physics that *p*. It is physically necessary that *p* just if it is incompatible with the laws of physics that not-*p*. *Metaphysically* possible is what is compatible with the laws of metaphysics. Epistemically possible is what is compatible with what is known. The so-called *deontic* modalities concern what is compatible not with descriptive laws, but with prescriptive requirements, i.e. what is permitted and required respectively.

natural language: Natural languages are those languages that are acquired by infant humans in the natural way, e.g. English, Japanese, etc.; or local versions of English, Japanese, etc. (Sometimes, natural languages are acquired not in the natural way in infancy, but by arduous training in adulthood, e.g. when a native speaker of English takes Japanese classes.) Natural languages contrast with artificial languages, i.e. languages that have been designed, such as programming languages or the **formal languages** that logicians and theoretical linguists build as models.

naturalistic fallacy: The term "naturalistic fallacy" was introduced by G.E. Moore in his book *Principia Ethica* as a term for the (alleged) mistake made by anyone who thinks that "good" can be defined in natural terms. Moore used the "open question argument" to argue that no such definition can be correct. But the term "naturalistic fallacy" is also often used more loosely to denote any mistaken inference of prescriptive or normative conclusions from purely descriptive premisses. → **is–ought distinction**

necessity (metaphysical-, epistemic-, deontic): → **modality**

possibility (metaphysical-, epistemic-, deontic): → modality

possible world: In addition to the way the world actually is, there are many non-actual (counterfactual) ways the world might be. A possible world is a complete way the world might be. Thus, the actual world is one of the possible worlds. In modern semantics, the notion of a possible world (and similar notions, such as Carnap's state-descriptions) has been used in modelling or explaining various **modal** or **intensional** phenomena. Thus, necessity is often modelled as truth in all possible worlds, and belief is often modelled as the set of possible worlds that are regarded as "live possibilities". Standard intensions are functions from possible worlds to **extensions**. There is some controversy about the metaphysical status of possible worlds.

predicate: Traditional grammar distinguishes the *subject* and the *predicate* as the main parts of a *sentence*. Thus, in the sentence "Socrates is wise", "is wise" would be the predicate. More recent linguistics uses different syntactic categories, such as VP (verb-phrase) and NP (noun-phrase).

presupposition: When I say to you "Your inferiority complex has disappeared", then I am presupposing that you used to have an inferiority complex. Presupposing this is different from stating it, e.g. when I say "You used to have an inferiority complex. Now it has disappeared." Presuppositions also differ from other kinds of implication in their characteristic "projection" properties: presuppositions are preserved under a certain range of embeddings or modifications under which other implications are not preserved. Thus, the presupposition that you have an inferiority complex does not go away when I turn my initial claim into a question: "Has your inferiority complex disappeared?"; or when I embed it modally: "Possibly your inferiority complex has disappeared"; or even when I add a simple negation: "Your inferiority complex has not disappeared."

proposition: Propositions are theoretical abstract entities that have been postulated as the "objects" or "**contents**" of speech and thought. Thus it is said that when you desire that there be a revolution next year, and I suppose that there will be a revolution next year, and a third person believes and asserts that there will be a revolution next year, then the desire, the supposition, the belief and the assertion all share the same content, namely the proposition that there will be a revolution next year. There is philosophical controversy about the existence of propositions as well as about their nature. As to their nature, theorists are divided into those who want to construe propositions as sets of **possible worlds**, and those who prefer a theory of "structured propositions".

propositional attitude: Propositional attitudes are those mental states and mental acts that can or have been construed as involving a relation with a **proposition**. Similarly, many speech-acts are construed as *propositional acts.*

quantifier (generalized-, restricted-): Quantifiers are expressions that bind variables, such as the existential quantifier "∃*x*" and the universal quantifier "∀*x*" in classical logic. Roughly, if we have a **predicate** "exists", a formula "∃*x*: *x* exists" is true just if one of the values for the variable *x* in the domain of quantification is in the **extension** of "exists". Similarly, "∀*x*: *x* exists" is true if all the values of *x* in the domain meet this condition. Thus, quantifiers can be used to say something about the proportion of members of the domain that satisfy the **predicate** (or open sentence) to which the quantifier is applied. *Generalized* quantifier theory studies all possible quantifiers, whereas *restricted* quantifiers are quantifiers that relate two predicates (or open sentences) to one another: e.g. (Most *x*: F*x*) G*x* which would roughly be interpreted as: most things in the domain that satisfy F*x*, also satisfy G*x*. Restricted quantifiers allow a more faithful formal model of natural language quantifier phrases, such as "every woman" or "most politicians".

rationalism: Views that afford great importance to pure reason as a source of knowledge are often called "rationalism". The exact extent of the role of reason can vary from "some knowledge is acquired by reason alone" to " all knowledge is acquired by reason alone."

rigidity: An expression is called "rigid" if its **extension** does not vary from one **possible world** to another. Thus, Kripke has famously argued in *Naming and Necessity* (1982) that proper names are rigid: they name the same individual in all possible worlds.

Semantic normativity: The thesis that there are irreducible norms that govern the use of linguistic expressions is called a thesis of "semantic normativity".

semantic value: It was Frege's idea to employ the mathematical theory of functions in the description of languages, treating some expressions as referring to functions and others to arguments that are members of the domain of these functions. When one of the function-expressions, *e*1, is then syntactically applied to one of the argument-expressions, *e*2, the resulting compound expression *e*1(*e*2) refers to the value of the referent of *e*1 for the argument that is the referent of *e*2. This allowed Frege a systematic description of how the referents of compounds are determined by the referents of their parts and the way they are combined (→ **compositionality**). Frege used the theoretical notion of a "referent" in such a systematic description of a language, i.e. in a semantics. Other theorists later introduced the term "semantic value" as a generic term for the entities that are thus systematically assigned in a semantics.

semantics: A systematic description of a language that models at least an important aspect of the meaning-related properties of the expressions of that language. *Formal semantics* describes (and thereby stipulates) the meaning properties of some **formal language**. *Natural language semantics* provides a description of a fragment of a **natural language**, or perhaps designs **formal languages** that are supposed to model certain aspects of natural languages.

singular term: There is no generally agreed upon definition of "singular term". "John Stuart Mill" and "the inventor of logic" are usually thought of as examples of singular terms. By contrast, "philosopher" and "inventor" are usually classified as general terms. Mill (in *A System of Logic*, 1843, p. 17a) provides a definition that is a good guide: he says that a singular term (or, in Mill's terminology, "singular name") is a "name which is only capable of being truly affirmed, in the same sense, of one thing". By contrast, he defines "general term" as follows: "name which is capable of being truly affirmed, in the same sense, of each of an indefinite number of things". The proper semantic treatment of singular terms, in particular the question of whether they constitute a semantically homogeneous category, is historically amongst the most debated issues in the philosophy of language.

speech-act: Just like hitting a nail with a hammer is a kind of *action*, performed with a certain purpose by an agent, the use of language in communication can also be thought of as a type of action, which can be deliberate, serve a purpose, and be assessed in terms of its *rationality*. For example, the event which consists in a person uttering the words "One cheeseburger, please" in a fast food outlet qualifies as an action, just like his walking to the outlet or blowing his nose. It's the action of ordering a cheeseburger. By contrast, sneezing and breathing do not seem classifiable as actions. J.L. Austin is well-known for having distinguished many speech-act types, such as asserting, promising, commanding or asking.

substitutability salva veritate: "*Salva veritate*" is Latin for "under preservation of truth". So, to say that one expression is substitutable *salva veritate* for another means that substituting the one for the other will not affect the truth-value.

syntax: Syntax of a language defines or describes which expressions are well-formed. In the case of a formal language, this is a matter of definition. In the case of a natural language, this is a matter of providing a systematic or principled account of which expressions are grammatically correct. Thus, a syntax of English that predicts that "And coughed drank beer he" is well-formed would seem to be incorrect.

synthetic: Not **analytic**.

truth-condition: The truth-condition of a sentence (in context) is the condition under which it is true. The expression "truth-condition" is often used by adherents of truth-conditional semantics in order to characterize the semantic values of sentences (in context). However, the term masks a certain unclarity. It is often thought that a Tarski-style extensional semantic theory for a language *L* specifies the truth-conditions of sentences in *L* by generating a T-theorem of the form "*s* is T iff *p*" for each sentence *s* in *L*. However, truth-conditions could only figure as the semantic values of sentences if they go beyond what such theorems state.

truth-value: In some semantic theories, the **semantic values** of some expressions are "truth-values". Frege's original semantics treated sentences as having truth-values as their semantic value (referent). In Frege, there are only two truth-values: the True and the False. But in principle we could have more truth-values.

vagueness. Imagine a series of 400.001 men, starting with one with 0 hairs on his head, another with 1, and so on until the last one who has 400.000 hairs. The first is clearly bald, the last clearly non-bald. In between, we would find *borderline* cases for the application of "bald": men of whom it is unclear whether they are bald, and unclear whether they are not. Relative to this series, we could build a *sorites argument*: the first man is bald; if a man with n hairs is bald, another with n + 1 hairs is still bald; therefore, the last man is bald. Predicates such as "bald", which have borderline cases and allow for sorites paradoxes, are vague.

variable: A variable is an expression that has variable **semantic values**. Thus, in a standard Tarskian semantics for a formal language, variables are assigned semantic values only relative to an "assignment of values to variables". Variables therefore contrast with *constants*. Constant expressions have the same semantic value with respect to every assignment. In natural language, variables are often claimed to occur at the level of deep structure or LF, without being visible at the surface level. The evidence for their existence comes from phenomena such as binding. Pronouns are sometimes claimed to be surface expressions that function like variables.

verification: To verify something is to find evidence that it is true.

Select Bibliography

The following contains suggestions for further reading corresponding to each of the main chapters of this volume.

1. Editorial Introduction: History of the Philosophy of Language
(Manuel García-Carpintero)

Dever, Josh (2006), "Compositionality", in E. Lepore and B. Smith (eds), *The Oxford Handbook of Philosophy of Language*, Oxford: Oxford University Press, pp. 633–66. [An excellent introduction to contemporary discussions of compositionality (which can be completed with the two articles by Pagin and Westerståhl mentioned below for Chapter 4)]

García-Carpintero, Manuel and Josep Macià (eds) (2006), *Two-Dimensional Semantics*, Oxford: Oxford University Press. [Contains many influential papers on two-dimensional semantics, with an introductory exposition.]

Sainsbury, Mark (1993/2002), "Russell on Meaning and Communication", in *Departing from Frege*, London: Routledge, pp. 85–101. [A nuanced examination of Russell's actual views on proper names.]

Soames, Scott (2003), *Philosophical Analysis in the XXth Century, vol. 1: The Dawn of Analysis*, Princeton, NJ: Princeton University Press. [A very clear presentation of the Tractarian views, in the context of equally clear introductions to the views of Russell and Moore (needless to say, some of the interpretations suggested in the text differ from Soames's).]

Williamson, Timothy (2007), *The Philosophy of Philosophy*, Oxford: Blackwell. [A first-class provocative view on the methodology of philosophy.]

2. On the Nature of Language (James Higginbotham)

Baker, Mark C. (2002), *The Atoms of Language: The Mind's Hidden Rules of Grammar*, New York: Basic Books. [Contains a general view of parametric variation which does not require specialized knowledge.]

Chomsky, Noam (2000), *New Horizons in the Study of Language and Mind*, Cambridge: Cambridge University Press. [Recent material that links Chomsky's technical work with his views on general issues of scientific inquiry and its modern history.]

Guasti, Maria Teresa (2004), *Language Acquisition: The Growth of Grammar*, Cambridge, MA: MIT Press. [Excellent survey of contemporary developmental psycholinguistics.]

Guéron, Jacqueline and Liliane Haegeman (1998), *English Grammar: A Generative Perspective*, Oxford: Blackwell. [Excellent survey of contemporary comparative generative grammar.]

Heim, Irene and Angelika Kratzer (1998), *Semantics in Generative Grammar*, Oxford: Blackwell. [Standard volume on semantics and the interaction between semantics and syntax.]

Larson, Richard and Gabriel Segal (1995), *Knowledge of Language: An Introduction to Semantic Theory*, Cambridge, MA: MIT Press. [Standard volume on semantics and the interaction between semantics and syntax.]

3. Formal Semantics (Josh Dever)

Barker, C. and P. Jacobson (2007), *Direct Compositionality*, Oxford: Oxford University Press. [An anthology of papers developing an alternative framework to that given here, in which quantifier ambiguities are explained without syntactic movement rules.]

Cresswell, M. (2006), "Formal Semantics", in M. Devitt, M. and R. Hanley (eds), *The Blackwell Guide to the Philosophy of Language*, Oxford: Blackwell. [A recent overview of the nature of formal semantics.]

Heim, I. and A. Kratzer (1998), *Semantics in Generative Grammar*, Oxford: Blackwell. [A major textbook in formal semantics, developing in more detail some of the ideas presented here.]

Kamp, H. and U. Reyle (1993), *From Discourse to Logic: Introduction to Model-Theoretic Semantics of Natural Language, Formal Logic, and Discourse Representation Theory*, London: Springer. [A detailed overview of discourse representation theory, an alternative to the semantic approach developed here.]

Montague, R. (1974), *Formal Philosophy: Selected Papers*, New Haven: Yale University Press. [Contains several seminal works by one of the founding figures of formal semantics.]

Portner, P. and B. Partee (2002), *Formal Semantics: The Essential Readings*, Wiley-Blackwell. [A collection of a number of the most influential papers in formal semantics.]

Stanley, J. (2008), "Philosophy of Language in the Twentieth Century", in *The Routledge Companion to Twentieth Century Philosophy*, London: Routledge. [A survey of the historical development of the philosophy of language, which helps give a broader context for the projects of formal semantics.]

4. Theories of Meaning and Truth Conditions (Kathrin Glüer)

Davidson, D. (1967/1984), "Truth and meaning", in *Inquiries into Truth and Interpretation*, Oxford: Clarendon Press, 1984, pp. 17–36. [Davidson's seminal article arguing that a Tarskian theory of truth can be used as a formal semantic theory.]

Davidson, D. (1973/1984), "Radical interpretation", in *Inquiries into Truth and*

Interpretation, Oxford: Clarendon Press, 1984, pp. 125–39. [Davidson's classical meaning-theoretical article.]

Dummett, M. (1974/1993), "What is a theory of meaning (I)", in *The Seas of Language*, Oxford: Oxford University Press 1993, pp. 1–33. [The first of Dummett's classical meaning-theoretical articles.]

Dummett, M. (1976/1993), "What is a theory of meaning (II)", in *The Seas of Language*, Oxford: Oxford University Press, 1993, pp. 34–93. [The second of Dummett's classical meaning-theoretical articles.]

Grice, P. (1957/1987), "Meaning", in *Studies in the Ways of Words*, Cambridge, MA: Harvard University Press, 1987, pp. 213–23. [Grice's seminal paper providing the classical analysis of non-natural meaning in terms of intentions.]

Pagin, P. (2006), "Meaning holism", in E. Lepore and B. Smith (eds), *Handbook of Philosophy of Language*, Oxford: Oxford University Press, pp. 213–32. [Useful discussion, and the most complete overview, of different versions of semantic holism.]

Pagin, P. and Westerståhl, D. (2010a), "Compositionality I: Definitions and Variants", *Philosophy Compass* 5, 250–64. [Together with 2010b, a useful introduction to, overview over, and discussion of different versions of the idea that natural language has a compositional semantics.]

Pagin, P. and Westerståhl, D. (2010b), "Compositionality II: Definitions and Variants", *Philosophy Compass* 5, 265–82. [Together with 2010a, a useful introduction to, overview over, and discussion of different versions of the idea that natural language has a compositional semantics.]

Quine, W. V. O. (1960), *Word and Object*, Cambridge MA: MIT Press. [Chapter Two introduces radical translation and argues for the indeterminacy of translation.]

Stalnaker, R. (1997), "Reference and necessity", in B. Hale and C. Wright (eds), *A Companion to the Philosophy of Language*, Oxford: Blackwell, pp. 534–54. [Useful overview of the connections between reference and necessity. Coins the term "foundational semantics" for the theory of meaning determination.]

5. Reference (Genoveva Martí)

Braun, David (1993), "Empty Names", *Noûs* 27, 449–69. [Explores, from one perspective, the problem that empty names pose for new theories of reference.]

Devitt, Michael (2011), *Theoria*. [Also discusses the role of empirical evidence in the theory of reference.]

Devitt, Michael and Kim Sterelny (1987), *Language and Reality*, Oxford: Blackwell. [An exploration of fundamental issues in the theory of reference, from the perspective of a causal-historical and anti-descriptivist standpoint.]

Donnellan, Keith (1970), "Proper Names and Identifying Descriptions", *Synthese* 21, 335–8. [Another classic. Donnellan argues that the reference of a use of a name is not determined by an associated definite description.]

Evans, Gareth (1973), "The Causal Theory of Names", *Proceedings of the Aristotelian Society*, Supplementary Volume 47, 187–208. [An in-depth discussion of the causal-historical picture of reference.]

Kripke, Saul (1982), *Naming and Necessity*, Cambridge, MA: Harvard University

Press. [Kripke's classic 1970 lectures, in which he attacks descriptivism and argues that names are rigid designators.]

Machery, Edouard (2011), "Expertise and Intuitions about Reference", *Theoria*. [Discusses the role of empirical evidence in the theory of reference.]

Marti, Genoveva (forthcoming 2012), "Empirical Data and the Theory of Reference", in M. O'Rourke ed. *Topics in Contemporary Philosophy*. Vol 10. Cambridge, MA: MIT Press. [Also discusses the role of empirical evidence in the theory of reference.]

Reimer, Marga (2001), "The Problem of Empty Names", *Australasian Journal of Philosophy*, 79, 491–506. [Explores, from another perspective, the problem that empty names pose for new theories of reference.]

Soames, Scott (2002), *Beyond Rigidity*, New York: Oxford University Press. [An analysis of the lessons of *Naming and Necessity*. The book contains discussions of some of the descriptivist answers to Kripke's arguments, so it is also a good bibliographical source to follow the history of the development of the discussion after 1970.]

6. Intensional Contexts (Michael Nelson)

Braun, D. (1998), "Understanding belief reports", *Philosophical Review* 107, 555–95. [A defence of the substitution of co-referring names within propositional attitude contexts.]

Davidson, D. (1968), "On saying that", *Synthese* 19, 130–46. [A classic defence of sententialism, the thesis that propositional attitude verbs report relations to sentences.]

Frege, G. (1918/1956), "The thought: A logical inquiry", *Mind* 65, 289–311. [A classic discussion of indexical thoughts.]

Kaplan, D. (1986), "Opacity", in L. Hahn and P. Schilpp (eds), *The Philosophy of W. V. Quine*, La Salle: Open Court, pp. 229–89. [A discussion of intensional contexts, of both belief and alethic modality, and Quine's arguments against quantifying in.]

Kripke, S. (1979), "A puzzle about belief", in A. Margalit ed. *Meaning and Use*, Dordrecht: Reidel, 239–83. [A classic argument that Frege's puzzle is not driven by any theses concerning the semantics of proper names.]

Perry, J. (2000), *The Problem of the Essential Indexical*, expanded edition, Stanford: CSLI. [A collection of Perry's important contributions to propositional attitudes.]

Quine, W. (1956), "Quantifiers and propositional attitudes", *Journal of Philosophy* 53, 177–87. [A classic discussion of the problems of quantifying into intensional contexts.]

Quine, W. (1952/1980), "Reference and modality", 2nd revised version, in his *From a Logical Point of View*, 2nd edn, revised printing, New York: Harper and Row, pp. 139–59. [A classic argument against quantifying into modal contexts.]

Richard, M. (1990), *Propositional Attitudes: An Essay on Thoughts and How We Ascribe Them*, Cambridge: Cambridge University Press. [An accessible discussion of propositional attitude reports.]

Russell, B. (1910), "Knowledge by acquaintance and knowledge by description",

Proceedings of the Aristotelian Society 11, 108–28. [A classic discussion of the distinction between knowledge by acquaintance and knowledge by description.]

Salmon, N. (1989), "Illogical belief", *Philosophical Perspectives* 3, 243–85. [A discussion of rational belief in a proposition and its negation.]

7. Context Dependence (Kent Bach)

Bach, Kent (2005), "Context ex machina", in Z. Szabó ed. *Semantics vs. Pragmatics*, Oxford: Oxford University Press, pp. 15–44. [Debunks extravagant claims about the role of context.]

Braun, David (2007), "Indexicals", *Stanford Encyclopedia of Philosophy*, available online at http://plato.stanford.edu/entries/indexicals/ [Presents Kaplan's theory of indexicals and some alternative theories, and then discusses various issues raised by indexicals and demonstratives.]

Glanzberg, Michael (2007), "Context, content, and relativism", *Philosophical Studies* 136: 1–29. [Argues for a contextualist and against a relativist semantics for predicates of personal taste, and suggests that these are not importantly different from other gradable adjectives]

Kennedy, Christopher (2007), "Vagueness and grammar: The semantics of relative and absolute gradable adjectives", *Linguistics and Philosophy* 30: 1–45. [On the semantics of gradable adjectives and their apparent context sensitivity, contrasting the structure of scales associated with relative and absolute adjectives]

Neale, Stephen (2006), "Pronouns and anaphora", in M. Devitt and R. Hanley (eds.), *The Blackwell Guide to the Philosophy of Language*, Oxford: Blackwell, pp. 335–73. [A comprehensive discussion of various sorts of occurrences of pronouns that, because of having antecedents, seem sensitive to their linguist context]

Perry, John (2006), "Using indexicals", in M. Devitt and R. Hanley (eds.), *The Blackwell Guide to the Philosophy of Language*, Oxford: Blackwell, pp. 314–34. [Presents the distinction between automatic and discretionary indexicals and discusses their uses, including problem cases like the answering machine puzzle]

Soames, Scott (2010), "The limits of meaning", ch. 7 of *Philosophy of Language*, Princeton: Princeton University Press, pp. 145–73. [Discusses Kaplan's account of indexicals and demonstratives and applies the notion of semantic incompleteness to give an alternative account]

8. Pragmatics (François Recanati)

Austin, J. (1975), *How to Do Things with Words*, 2nd edn, Oxford: Clarendon Press. [Austin's pioneering lectures on speech act theory.]

Clark, H. (1996), *Using Language*, Cambridge: Cambridge University Press. [An investigation into the pragmatic dimension of language, by a leading psychologist.]

Davis, S. (ed.) (1991), *Pragmatics: A Reader*, New York: Oxford University Press. [An inclusive collection, where many papers mentioned in this entry can be found.]

Fillmore, C. (1997), *Lectures on Deixis*, Stanford : CSLI. [Indexicality in human languages.]

Grice, P. (1989), *Studies in the Way of Words*, Cambridge: Cambridge University Press. [Contains Grice's famous lectures "Logic and Conversation" and a collection of his papers on the philosophy of language, including the seminal "Meaning".]

Kadmon, N. (2001), *Formal Pragmatics*, Oxford: Blackwell. [A survey of the interface between pragmatics and formal semantics, with special attention to presupposition and focus.]

Recanati, F. (2004), *Literal Meaning*, Cambridge: Cambridge University Press. [A survey of the contextualism/literalism debate.]

Searle, J. (1969), *Speech Acts*, Cambridge: Cambridge University Press. [A classic of pragmatics.]

Sperber, D. and D. Wilson (1995), *Relevance: Communication and Cognition*, 2nd edn, Oxford: Basil Blackwell. [A cognitively oriented theory in the Gricean tradition.]

Stalnaker, R. (1999), *Context and Content*, New York: Oxford University Press. [Contains several of Stalnaker's influential papers on the foundations of pragmatics.]

9. Semantic Normativity and Naturalism (José L. Zalabardo)

Boghossian, P. (1989), "The Rule-Following Considerations", *Mind* 98, 507–49. [Defends the view that meaning is normative.]

Boghossian, P. (2003), "The Normativity of Content", *Philosophical Issues* 13, 31–45, [Rejects the author's earlier view that linguistic meaning is normative and argues that the normativity of mental content is defensible only if it can be derived from the normativity of belief.]

Brandom, R. (1994), *Making it Explicit*, Cambridge, MA: Harvard University Press. [An important defence of the view that meaning is normative from a point of view that hasn't been covered in this chapter.]

Glüer, K. and Å. Wikforss (2009a), "Against Content Normativity", *Mind* 118, 31–70. [Rejects semantic normativity.]

Glüer, K. and Å. Wikforss (2009b), "The Normativity of Meaning and Content", *The Stanford Encyclopedia of Philosophy (Summer 2009 Edition)*, Edward N. Zalta ed. available online at http://plato.stanford.edu/archives/sum2009/entries/meaning-normativity/ [Useful survey of the literature on semantic normativity.]

Kripke, S. (1982), *Wittgenstein on Rules and Private Language*, Oxford, Blackwell. [Widely seen as the contemporary source of the idea that the normativity of meaning poses a problem for semantic naturalism.]

10. Analyticity, Apriority, Modality (Albert Casullo)

Ayer, A. J. (1952), *Language, Truth and Logic*, New York: Dover Publications. [Ayer defends the view that some knowledge is *a priori* against Mill's contention that all knowledge is *a posteriori*, and offers a classical defence of the logical empiricist view that there is no synthetic *a priori* knowledge.]

BonJour, L. (1998), *In Defense of Pure Reason*, Cambridge: Cambridge University Press. [BonJour defends the traditional rationalist view that rational insight into the necessary truth of a proposition is the source of *a priori* knowledge. He argues against both logical empiricism, which limits *a priori* knowledge to analytic truths, and radical empiricism, which maintains that all knowledge is *a posteriori*.]

Casullo, A. (2003), *A Priori Justification*, New York: Oxford University Press. [Casullo offers an articulation of the concept of *a priori* knowledge and argues that the traditional arguments for and against the existence of *a priori* knowledge are inconclusive. He maintains that a resolution of the controversy over the existence of such knowledge requires empirical investigation.]

Kant, I. (1965), *Critique of Pure Reason*, translated by Norman Kemp Smith, New York: St. Martin's Press. [Kant introduces the four primary questions regarding *a priori* knowledge that frame the contemporary discussion of *a priori* knowledge. His answers to those questions remain controversial and continue to dominate the contemporary discussion.]

Kitcher, P. (1983), *The Nature of Mathematical Knowledge*, New York: Oxford University Press. [Kitcher offers a wide-ranging survey of traditional *a priori* accounts of mathematical knowledge. He rejects such accounts and articulates a version of mathematical empiricism.]

Kripke, S. (1980), *Naming and Necessity*, Cambridge: Harvard University Press. [Kripke sets the stage for the contemporary discussion of *a priori* knowledge by carefully distinguishing the concepts of *a priori* knowledge, necessary truth and analytic truth. He also challenges traditional assumptions about the relationship between *a priori* knowledge and necessary truth by offering examples of necessary *a posteriori* knowledge and contingent *a priori* knowledge.]

Peacocke, C. (2004), *The Realm of Reason*, Oxford: Oxford University Press. [Peacocke defends a version of moderate rationalism, which rejects the traditional rationalist account, according to which *a priori* knowledge is to be explained by a distinct psychological faculty. He offers in its place a metasemantic account, which explains such knowledge in terms of features of concept possession.]

Quine, W. V. (1963), "Two Dogmas of Empiricism", in *From a Logical Point of View*, 2nd edn, revised, New York: Harper and Row, pp. 20–46. [Quine rejects the logical empiricist tradition by arguing against the cogency of the distinction between analytic and synthetic truths. He also rejects Mill's inductive empiricist account of mathematical and logical knowledge, and articulates an holistic empiricist account of such knowledge.]

Index